*Praise for Marc Peyser and Timothy Dwyer's*

# HISSING COUSINS

"Moving.... Chronicl[es] the childhood losses each endured, and the rich web of family in which they were raised."     —*The Boston Globe*

"Ripping but poignant."     —*Time*

"Peyser and Dwyer tell the cousins' story with insight, humor, empathy and wisdom.... A welcome and absorbing addition to the ever-growing canon of Rooseveltiana."     —*Richmond Times-Dispatch*

"An insightful look at two remarkable Roosevelt women.... *Hissing Cousins* unravels the Machiavellian question that would haunt both women in their path to power: is it better to be clever, or is it better to be good?"     —*The Guardian* (London)

"A brilliant idea for a book, brilliantly executed.... A powerful and entertaining portrait of an important and overlooked American relationship."     —Jon Meacham, Pulitzer Prize–winning author of *Thomas Jefferson: The Art of Power*

"Just delicious—sharp, touching, funny, and wise. Marc Peyser and Timothy Dwyer have brought to life a pair of the great women of the twentieth century, in all their human flaws and glory."
—Evan Thomas, author of
*Ike's Bluff: President Eisenhower's Secret Battle to Save the World*

"This is the beautifully rendered and absorbing story of the seventy-year family rivalry between two of the most compelling women of the twentieth century—one Democrat, one Republican, both fascinating."
—Jonathan Alter, author of
*The Defining Moment: FDR's Hundred Days and the Triumph of Hope*

MARC PEYSER AND TIMOTHY DWYER

# HISSING COUSINS

Marc Peyser is a writer and former deputy editor at both *Newsweek* and *Budget Travel*. His work has appeared in *The New York Times*, *Life*, *Vogue*, *Time*, *Time Out New York*, *Condé Nast Traveler*, and *The Huffington Post*. He is currently the deputy editor of *All You* magazine.

Timothy Dwyer was raised on Long Island's Eaton's Neck, swimming distance from Theodore Roosevelt's homestead at Sagamore Hill. He studied history and politics at Georgetown University's School of Foreign Service and at the College of Europe in Bruges, Belgium. His work has appeared in *Time*, the *Washingtonian*, and online at *The Atlantic*. He is the chief executive officer of The School Choice Group, an education advisory company.

# HISSING COUSINS

*The Lifelong Rivalry of Eleanor Roosevelt*
*and Alice Roosevelt Longworth*

MARC PEYSER AND TIMOTHY DWYER

ANCHOR BOOKS
A Division of Penguin Random House LLC
New York

*For Caroline and Sophie,*

*the most wonderful girls in the world*

The Library of Congress has cataloged the Nan A. Talese / Doubleday edition as follows:
Peyser, Marc N.
Hissing cousins : the untold story of Eleanor Roosevelt and Alice Roosevelt Longworth / Marc Peyser and Timothy Dwyer. — First edition.
pages   cm
Includes bibliographical references and index.
1. Roosevelt family.   2. Roosevelt, Eleanor, 1884–1962—Family.   3. Longworth, Alice Roosevelt, 1884–1980—Family.   4. Presidents' spouses—United States—Biography.
5. Cousins—United States—Biography.   I. Dwyer, Timothy, 1965–   II. Title.
III. Title: Untold story of Eleanor Roosevelt and Alice Roosevelt Longworth.
E807.1.P39 2015   973.917092'2—dc23   [B]   2014026766

**Anchor Books Trade Paperback ISBN: 978-1-101-97162-8**
**eBook ISBN: 978-0-385-53602-8**

*Author photographs © Michael Lionstar*
*Family tree graphic by David Foster*

www.anchorbooks.com

Printed in the United States of America
10   9   8   7   6   5   4   3   2

# CONTENTS

# Roosevelt Family Tree

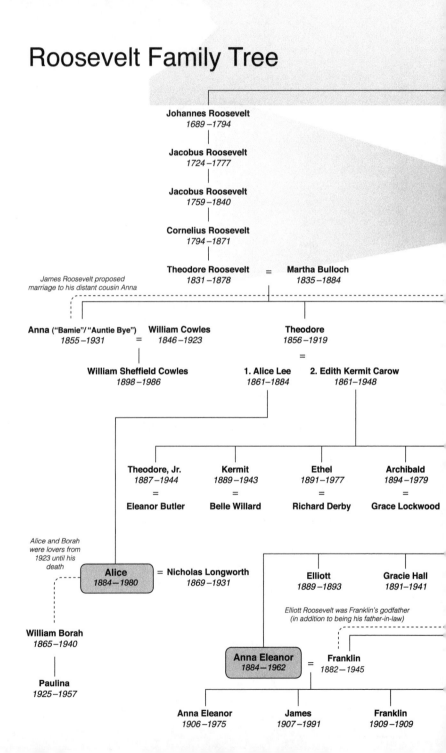

**Johannes Roosevelt**
*1689 –1794*

**Jacobus Roosevelt**
*1724 –1777*

**Jacobus Roosevelt**
*1759 –1840*

**Cornelius Roosevelt**
*1794 –1871*

*James Roosevelt proposed marriage to his distant cousin Anna*

**Theodore Roosevelt** = **Martha Bulloch**
*1831 –1878*           *1835 –1884*

**Anna ("Bamie"/"Auntie Bye")**   **William Cowles**           **Theodore**
*1855 –1931*           =           *1846 –1923*           *1856 –1919*
                                                            =

**William Sheffield Cowles**                   **1. Alice Lee**      **2. Edith Kermit Carow**
*1898 –1986*                                    *1861–1884*          *1861–1948*

**Theodore, Jr.**      **Kermit**      **Ethel**      **Archibald**
*1887 –1944*          *1889 –1943*    *1891 –1977*   *1894 –1979*
=                     =               =              =
**Eleanor Butler**     **Belle Willard**   **Richard Derby**   **Grace Lockwood**

*Alice and Borah were lovers from 1923 until his death*

**Alice** = **Nicholas Longworth**           **Elliott**      **Gracie Hall**
*1884 –1980*    *1869 –1931*                  *1889 –1893*    *1891 –1941*

*Elliott Roosevelt was Franklin's godfather (in addition to being his father-in-law)*

**William Borah**
*1865 –1940*

**Anna Eleanor** = **Franklin**
*1884 –1962*        *1882 –1945*

**Paulina**
*1925 –1957*

**Anna Eleanor**      **James**      **Franklin**
*1906 –1975*         *1907 –1991*   *1909 –1909*

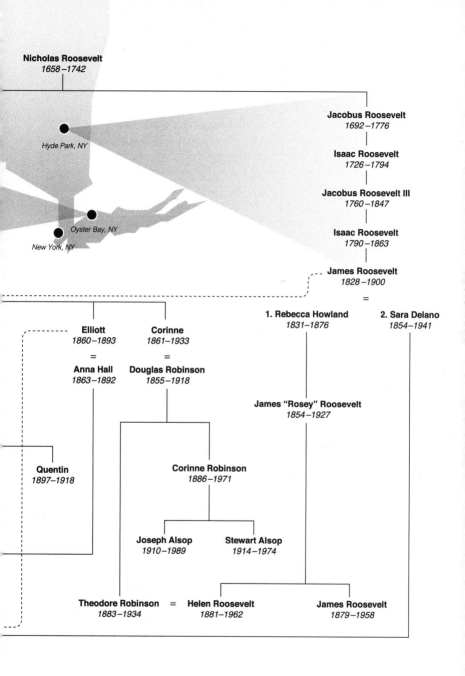

**Nicholas Roosevelt**
*1658–1742*

Hyde Park, NY

Oyster Bay, NY

New York, NY

**Jacobus Roosevelt**
*1692–1776*

**Isaac Roosevelt**
*1726–1794*

**Jacobus Roosevelt III**
*1760–1847*

**Isaac Roosevelt**
*1790–1863*

**James Roosevelt**
*1828–1900*

=

**1. Rebecca Howland**
*1831–1876*

**2. Sara Delano**
*1854–1941*

**Elliott**
*1860–1893*

=

**Anna Hall**
*1863–1892*

**Corinne**
*1861–1933*

=

**Douglas Robinson**
*1855–1918*

**James "Rosey" Roosevelt**
*1854–1927*

**Quentin**
*1897–1918*

**Corinne Robinson**
*1886–1971*

**Joseph Alsop**
*1910–1989*

**Stewart Alsop**
*1914–1974*

**Theodore Robinson**
*1883–1934*

=

**Helen Roosevelt**
*1881–1962*

**James Roosevelt**
*1879–1958*

**Elliott**
*1910–1990*

**Franklin**
*1914–1988*

**John**
*1916–1981*

# HISSING COUSINS

# Chapter 1

# ORPHANS

E leanor Roosevelt hoped no one would come to her funeral. What she really wanted was to scotch the whole affair and just have someone announce her death after she'd already been buried. "I'd like to be remembered happily if that is possible," she said. "If that can't be I'd rather be forgotten." Forgotten? "I had to tell her," said her friend William Turner Levy, "that she was being unrealistic."[1]

Unrealistic, but not surprising. After all, this was the famously unfussy First Lady who served hot dogs to the king and queen of England during their 1939 state visit, who dragged her own suitcase around the world on countless humanitarian missions, and who insisted, after her husband died, that she'd never do anything newsworthy again. Naturally, she wanted her afterlife to be just as unpretentious as what came before. "Just a plain pine coffin covered with pine boughs. Inside the coffin are to be plain pillows and sheet with cloth," she'd written in a letter to her doctor years earlier.

The service was held in Hyde Park's St. James' Church, which seated just 250 people. Among those who didn't make the guest list: Horace W. B. Donegan, the grandstanding Episcopal bishop of New York. The five Roosevelt children refused to invite him, dreading he would eulogize their mother at length. (He showed up anyway but otherwise kept quiet.) Even the weather seemed to cooperate with Eleanor's wishes. November 10, 1962, was a cold, damp day with the wind blowing off the Hudson River and pushing the chill through the streets of the town.

Yet the mourners, like the good bishop, weren't going to let a cold shoulder stop them from saying good-bye. Thousands lined the roads, some standing five-deep to watch the hearse carry Mrs. Roosevelt from St. James' to the Roosevelt mansion, Springwood, two miles away. For generations, the Roosevelts of Hyde Park had been buried in the quiet graveyard behind the little church, but President Roosevelt had requested that he and Eleanor be laid to rest in the large rose garden just to the side of the family home. It was, in its way, the perfect spot. After all, "Roosevelt" in Dutch means "field of roses." Perhaps just as important, FDR's overbearing mother, Sara, was tucked a safe distance away, resting in uncharacteristic silence back behind the church.

The president's arrangement, however, helped produce exactly the kind of funeral Eleanor wanted to avoid. It was as if someone had picked up the entire Macy's Thanksgiving Day Parade and dropped it into small-town America. The nightly news, including the BBC, delivered extensive coverage. Limousine-lock tied up the roads; amid all the excitement, two local keystone cops crashed their cruisers into each other right in front of the Hyde Park state police barracks. Most people were fans, but there were haters, too. One man standing along the funeral route waved a sign that read, "I'm glad you're dead, Eleanor."[2] Two other men were arrested for carrying "derogatory" signs.[3]

The roster of invited guests might have been small, but it was A-plus-list. President and Mrs. Kennedy arrived on Air Force One (which was taking its maiden voyage and would be used, almost exactly one year later, to transport JFK's body back from Dallas). Vice President and Mrs. Johnson came, as did the former presidents Truman and Eisenhower, making this the first time that three presidents attended the funeral of a First Lady. Chief Justice Warren, Secretary of State Rusk, Secretary of Defense McNamara, Attorney General Robert Kennedy, Governor Rockefeller of New York, the United Nations ambassador Stevenson, and a sizable contingent of the Washington establishment were there. One well-aimed Soviet missile would have decimated the U.S. government.

That was no idle concern. Mrs. Roosevelt's funeral came at the tail end of the Cuban missile crisis. Just days earlier, Nikita Khrushchev had agreed to dismantle the Soviet missiles he'd lined up in Cuba like cigars ready to be lit, and Castro was still threatening to shoot down anything bigger than a kite that wandered into his airspace. The U.S. military was so concerned, the Pentagon wanted to install a kind of hotline in the pew at St. James' where President Kennedy was to be seated. The Reverend Gordon Kidd said no. "If he had to talk on the phone during the service it would be terribly frustrating and confusing," Kidd reasoned.[4] The Feds settled for a phone placed unobtrusively on an outside wall of the church, though Eleanor would undoubtedly have scoffed at that, too. After all, Khrushchev didn't scare *her*. She had visited him on his home turf in 1957 for a magazine interview, a somewhat tense meeting that ended with Khrushchev's declaring his own sort of détente with one of the world's most formidable women. "At least," he said, "we didn't shoot each other."[5] When he popped in for a visit at her woodsy Val-Kill cottage two years later, Eleanor had only one real worry. She realized she had no vodka—even though Khrushchev was coming at 7:00 a.m. (Her son John dutifully ran down a bottle.)

Given all the world leaders Eleanor met and hosted over the years, it's hardly surprising that she received what was arguably the first power funeral of an American woman. What was notable was that one of Washington's most influential women was among the few who declined to attend. Her name was Alice Longworth. Mrs. L., as she was known, was a battle-ready Republican, a Capitol Hill institution with a biting wit, and a woman who, like Eleanor, tossed aside gender barriers as easily as she flicked the ashes off her long-stemmed cigarette holder. She was also Eleanor's first cousin.

Alice's father, Theodore Roosevelt, was the older brother of Eleanor's father, Elliott. To her cousin Eleanor, Alice was a childhood playmate, a teenage confidante, and, in adulthood, a relentless rival. Their relationship had taken a sharp turn for the worse thirty years earlier, when Franklin Roosevelt was elected president, a job Alice believed rightly belonged to her favorite brother, Theodore Roosevelt Jr.

Over the years, the press played Alice and Eleanor off each other like rivals in a blue-blooded version of Oz: the good witch and the bad witch. Eleanor was the saint, the woman who revolutionized the role of First Lady with her very public activism, obvious concern for the poor and oppressed, and outspoken passion for human rights. She did more to cement the role of the United Nations in American and world diplomacy than any other woman and almost any man. Alice played the troublemaker. She relished any opportunity to tweak the stodgy establishment, and no one was more establishment—or, in Alice's eyes, more sanctimonious—

than Anna Eleanor Roosevelt Roosevelt. Eleanor didn't just marry into the esteemed Roosevelt clan when she wed her fifth cousin Franklin. Roosevelt was also her *maiden name*.

Yet Alice was, in her own way, as much a pillar of power as Eleanor. As Theodore Roosevelt's beautiful and flamboyant daughter, she became arguably the century's first global celebrity when her father entered the White House in 1901. "Princess Alice," as she was known on the front page, made headlines for her clothes, her smoking, her parties, even her pets. Her straitlaced parents despised all that frivolous attention—except when they wanted to leverage her popularity for their political advantage. In 1905, when the president needed someone who could charm the Japanese as he tried to negotiate the end of the Russo-Japanese War, he sent twenty-one-year-old Alice as part of the delegation. When the trip was over and the treaty was signed, Theodore Roosevelt was awarded the Nobel Peace Prize. Alice had to settle for marrying one of the men who traveled to Asia with her, though Nick Longworth was an Ohio congressman and future Speaker of the House.

As administrations came and went, Alice's backroom influence ebbed and flowed, but like the Potomac she always cut a swath through Washington. She appeared on the cover of *Time* magazine in 1927, joined official American delegations overseas into the 1950s, and was still sitting in the front row at presidential races into the 1970s. Along the way, Mrs. L. acquired another nickname: Washington's Other Monument. She remained a force until she died, in 1980, at ninety-six. Such a force that every president from Truman to Ford made sure to pay homage at Longworth's Massachusetts Avenue home on February 12—her birthday. Nixon, one of Alice's personal favorites, came even at the height of the Watergate scandal.

And so Mrs. Democrat and Mrs. Republican, as they were called in a Press Club comedy sketch in 1933, spent half a century engaged in an epic political battle while locked in familial embrace. During the height of the New Deal, it was not unusual for Alice to attack her Democratic cousins' policies in the afternoon, via her syndicated newspaper column, then head over to the White House to join them for dinner. Their sparring could get painfully personal, given that both women staked a claim to the extraordinary, complicated, and sometimes contradictory legacy of Theodore Roosevelt. Before the Kennedys, the Bushes, or the Clintons, the Roosevelts showed just how close to a monarchy American democracy can veer. The name Roosevelt appeared on a national ticket an astonishing eight times in the twelve presidential elections from 1900 to 1944, and the extended Roosevelt family held dozens of elected and appointed positions at all levels of government throughout the twentieth century, right down to Franklin and Eleanor's son Elliott's term as mayor of Miami Beach in 1966.

But this was much more than a family feud. As the twentieth century became the American century, Alice and Eleanor became vocal symbols of the country's great debates. What was the right role for America on the world stage? The best way to prevent war? To address the gap between rich and poor? For that matter, what was the role of government—to shape society or get out of the way? Eleanor and Alice represented opposing sides on just about every one of those issues, and they fought for their beliefs—and against each other—as fiercely as any passionate partisan around. Typically, even their means of engagement were radically different. Eleanor was the dutiful but stubborn wife who used her First Lady status to fight for her beliefs in public, and even harder in private. Alice was more comfortable behind the scenes, wielding a whisper rather than a megaphone. But a few well-chosen, carefully placed words from Mrs. L. could torpedo a campaign or give new hope to an underdog. The Republican presidential candidate Thomas Dewey, belittled by Alice as looking like "the little man on the wedding cake," saw his political career gravely injured amid smirks and laughter. For all their differences, the cousins share part of at least one important legacy: they short-circuited the twentieth century's rules of gender. Their roles as power players are all the more impressive given that they didn't even have the right to vote until they were thirty-six.

Alice never explained why she didn't join the pilgrimage to Hyde Park to say good-bye to Eleanor; after all, she rarely missed an opportunity to rub elbows with influential people. Some wondered if it was a parting shot, a final snub in a relationship often interrupted by stubborn, stony silences. But by the time Eleanor died, the personal barbs and caustic exchanges between the two cousins were largely a thing of the past. Like the late-in-life reconciliation between Adams and Jefferson 140 years earlier, the perspective of the passing years changed them. Their political passions never exactly cooled, but they boiled over less frequently amid the baggage of flawed marriages, difficult children, and the premature loss of parents and siblings. In those more human respects, Mrs. Democrat and Mrs. Republican found their lives mirroring each other in ways that must have astonished even them.

————

For Alice and Eleanor, their oil-and-water bond was something of a birthright, bequeathed to them from their respective fathers and beyond. Even though he was almost two years younger than Theodore, Elliott had long been the Roosevelt family's prime hope. Handsome and athletic, he was the favorite of his sisters and his mother, the kind of bighearted boy who would literally give you the clothes off his back, as he did one December when he saw a "street urchin" shivering in the New York cold and handed the boy his new overcoat. Elliott was seven. The family called him Nell, after the saintly Dickens character in *The Old Curiosity Shop*. Charm became his calling card. When he was twenty, Elliott took off on an around-the-world hunting excursion. On the ship from New York to England, he bumped into his distant cousins James and Sara Roosevelt, who were on their honeymoon. They became so taken with handsome, dashing, life-of-the-party Elliott that they asked him to be the godfather to their first child, who was born a little more than a year later. They named him Franklin Delano Roosevelt, making Eleanor's father the godfather to her future husband.[*]

The Roosevelt boys were intrepid adventurers, but they were plagued by health problems. Theodore was an asthmatic child who spent much of his earliest years indoors, playing dolls with his sisters or reading in bed. Elliott developed debilitating headaches and unexplained seizures that forced him to drop out of St. Paul's boarding school after one year. What made the brothers different was how they responded to their frailties. Theodore was determined and disciplined; he essentially worked and willed himself to health and to the apex of public life.

Elliott slid in the other direction. Always the bon vivant, he acquired a

---

[*] Even the Roosevelts could get lost in their own family tree. "The Mrs. Roosevelt who thanked you for a wedding gift is the wife of Nicholas Bay Roosevelt—brother of Harry—and working in Philadelphia," Franklin once had to explain to Eleanor. "I am going to write a new Roosevelt genealogy in words of one syllable for beginners showing everybody's relationship to everybody else!" FDR to ER, n.d., FDRL.

self-destructive taste for liquor and women. The more his vices tarnished his status as the family golden boy, the more energy he poured into besting his big brother. If Teddy went to shoot big game out west, Elliott would go further—to hunt for tigers and elephants in India and the Himalayas. If Theodore married a great beauty, Elliott would snag a woman who was so breathtaking that the poet Robert Browning once asked to watch her portrait being painted, as a kind of inspiration. They could turn a garden-variety sibling rivalry into something practically Shakespearean. When Alice and Eleanor were about four, their fathers competed against each other in a polo match that almost became a medieval joust. It was Teddy's Oyster Bay club versus Elliott's "third-rate" Meadowbrook squad, as Theodore teasingly described them. With time running out, Teddy's side had the match locked up, leading 6–1, but that didn't stop him from taking off after Elliott when his little brother headed downfield at breakneck speed. Before anyone could see it coming, their horses collided. "There was a thump of horseflesh as brother tried to ride brother out. Suddenly—no one saw how—Theodore was thrown," their younger sister, Corinne, wrote in a letter to their older sister, Anna. For several minutes he "neither moved nor stirred, and looked like a dead man."[6] When Theodore finally pulled himself up, he staggered around for hours and was unsteady on his feet for days. A week later, his wife, Edith, suffered a miscarriage.

———

The Roosevelt family had long had something of a split personality, dating back to the eighteenth century, when the Dutch-American brothers Johannes and Jacobus made their mark in the United States. The brothers were merchants and investors, first with flaxseed mills and later via timely purchases of land in fast-developing New York City. They set the pattern for generations of Roosevelts: they were almost all businessmen (sugar refiners, hardware store owners, bankers), and they appreciated the value of real estate.

The brothers ultimately decamped to what became the family's twin forks: Johannes's offspring migrated to Long Island's Oyster Bay, and Jacobus's found their way to Hyde Park, along the Hudson River. The distance between the two was less than a hundred miles, but that was enough to foster distinct branches of the family tree.

The Oyster Bay clan became more civic-minded and philanthropic.

It was this flank that helped found the Bank of New York, the Children's Aid Society, the Metropolitan Museum of Art, the American Museum of Natural History, and Roosevelt Hospital, which was built on the family's land and financed with a large donation of the family silver. In 1882, it also produced the youngest New York state assemblyman in history: Theodore, age twenty-four.

The Hyde Park branch wasn't without notable ancestors, including a founder of Chemical Bank and a man known as Isaac the Patriot, FDR's great-great-grandfather, who earned his nickname by refusing to pay taxes to the British government. But over time the Hyde Park Roosevelts gravitated toward lives as landed gentry, aided and, more important, financed by wives who came from wealthier families: Astor, Aspinwall, Penn. James Roosevelt, FDR's father, brought far less money to his marriage than Sara Delano did. Her father made his fortune in Asia, much of it in the opium trade.

But by the end of the nineteenth century, the big difference between the branches was their politics: the Democrats in Hyde Park and the Republicans in Oyster Bay.* Politics was the wedge that would drive the two sides apart, one insult layered on top of the last, and spread over the twentieth century. The Roosevelts fired each other from high-profile jobs. They disowned each other. When they were playful, they would declare how their side of the family "got all the looks and the money." When they were being vicious, they'd compare a certain four-term president to the enemy. "Elected four times! Hitler disarmed, didn't he?" Alice once said.[7] The intra-family rivalry ultimately grew so intense the two sides could not even agree on how to pronounce their name: *Rose*-eh-velt (Oyster Bay) or *Rooze*-eh-velt (Hyde Park).

————

* The two parties at the beginning of the twentieth century differed in a few significant ways from their modern-day descendants. The Republicans were still seen as the party of Lincoln and thus the logical political home for black Americans. Popular in the North and the East of the country, and associated with establishment moneyed interests, the Republicans won eleven of the thirteen presidential elections from 1860 to 1908. The Democratic Party of this era was conservative and generally opposed to big business; its strength lay in farmers and southern white voters, who were still seething with resentment from the Civil War and its aftermath and actively seeking to disenfranchise black Americans. It was not until FDR's run for the White House that progressives and black voters moved in substantial numbers toward the Democrats.

When Alice and Eleanor were born, in 1884, the family was intact, even quasi-incestuous: Eleanor wouldn't be the only Roosevelt to marry within the bloodline. The cousins were close as children, born eight months and twelve blocks apart in New York City. Elliott and his wife, Anna Hall, were actually subletting his brother Theodore's old apartment on Forty-Fifth Street when Anna Eleanor Roosevelt was born on October 11. Elliott had also been tending to Theodore's wife, Alice, when she gave birth eight months earlier to Alice Lee Roosevelt on February 12, at the Fifty-Seventh Street home of Theodore and Elliott's mother, Martha. Theodore had left New York for Albany that very morning with the romantic notion that his wife wouldn't go into labor before Valentine's Day, which was also the fourth anniversary of the day they announced their engagement. When a telegram arrived at the capitol on February 13 with news of a healthy daughter, Theodore passed out cigars and went back to work in the assembly, confident that he would be home later that night. Then a second telegraph arrived. Baby Alice was fine, but her mother had taken a turn for the worse. What's more, Theodore's mother, who had been nursing what seemed like a bad cold while waiting for her first grandchild's birth in an upstairs bedroom, clearly had contracted something more serious.

Theodore left Albany immediately, but much of New York state had been swallowed by an epic fog—"suicide weather," the *New York Times* called it—and the five-hour train trip stretched on and on. His younger sister, Corinne, traveling from Washington, arrived before him at the Roosevelt family home. Elliott met her at the front door looking and sounding as grim as an undertaker. "There is a curse on this house!" he wailed. "Mother is dying, and Alice is dying too!"[8]

Theodore finally arrived an hour later, at about eleven o'clock. The prognosis was indeed grave: His wife had an undiagnosed case of Bright's disease, an inflammation of the kidneys. His mother had typhoid fever. He went to see his wife first. Baby Alice had already been removed to an aunt's house, so he sat and cradled his wife's nearly unconscious body for several hours. He only stopped when his siblings summoned him downstairs to join their vigil by their mother's deathbed. Martha died at 3:00 a.m., and Theodore ran back upstairs to Alice. About twelve hours later, she died, too, having held her daughter only once and with time to say little more than "I *love* a little girl."[9] It was February 14, the day Theodore had expected to be magical. Instead, he scrawled a large *X* in his diary on that date, and underneath it he wrote, "The light has gone out of my life."[10]

And Theodore soon went out of his daughter's. A week after the double funeral for his wife and mother, he returned to Albany to finish out his term. Everything associated with his old world now made him miserable, including his own daughter. In May, he gave up his assembly seat and escaped to the Badlands of North Dakota, leaving baby Alice with his sister Anna, whom the family called Bye. "Her aunt can take care of her a good deal better than I can," Theodore explained to one of his Dakota buddies. "She never would know anything about me anyway. She would be just as well off without me."[11] For the next three years, Alice saw her father only occasionally, in the summers and at holidays.

Bye was the oldest of the four siblings (Bye, Theodore, Elliott, Corinne) and the family rock, the one everyone relied on for guidance and support. "There is always someone in every family who keeps it together. In ours, it was Auntie Bye," Alice said. "I always believed that if she had been a man, she, rather than my father, would have been President."[12] "Teedie," as Theodore was called by his family, was especially dependent on Bye. She handpicked his freshman apartment at Harvard (nothing too drafty, on account of his asthma) and persuaded him to run for mayor of New York. Throughout Theodore's long political career, Bye would prove to be his most trusted and perceptive adviser. Whenever a new job necessitated a move, Bye turned over her own homes, in New York and Washington. It was a pattern that started when they were young: the big sister looking out for her sickly but irrepressible little brother. Once, when Teedie was beginning his lifelong obsession with animals and taxidermy, the budding naturist placed a newspaper ad for field mice: ten cents each, thirty-five cents for a family. But he had an asthma attack before he could receive any deliveries, and his mother took him to the mountains to recover. When their New York City neighbors began arriving with critters, it was Bye who collected them—and paid the finder's fees out of her own allowance.

So it was natural that Bye would collect little Alice, too. When the grieving Theodore ran off to the Badlands, Bye was twenty-nine, unmarried, and, frankly, homely. Though she had deep-blue eyes, richly dark hair, and a pert little nose, she had developed something of a hunchback. For all her adult life, she had to wear a specially made corset to help her stand up straight. She was also beginning to lose her hearing. Naturally, the family assumed she'd spend her days as a spinster, which made her the perfect repository for parentless children.

Bye clearly adored her firstborn niece. "She was the single most important influence on my childhood," recalled Alice. "She called me her 'blue-eyed darling,' can you believe, and she protected me from my father with his guilt fetish."[13] For the rest of his life, Theodore never mentioned his dead wife—not to his family, not in his autobiography, and not to his daughter. Before his wife died, he had begun to build a house in Oyster Bay on Long Island's North Shore that he was going to call Leeholm, after Alice's maiden name. When she died, he renamed the place Sagamore Hill.* "It was pathetic, yet very tough at the same time," Alice said. "I think my father tried to forget he had ever been married to my mother, to blot the whole episode out of his mind. The whole thing was really handled very badly. It was awfully bad psychologically."[14] Aunt Bye was the only person who dared break Theodore's perverse code of silence. "Finally, Auntie Bye did tell me something very revealing, such as that [my mother] had been very pretty and attractive. And she gave me some of her things, from my father I suppose, some of which (like the jewelry) were fun to have later on."[15]

Her father's almost cruel reticence made Alice defiant. She came to loathe being shielded from the past or pitied in any way. "Early on I became fairly hard-minded and learnt to shrug a shoulder with indifference," she said. "I certainly wasn't going to be part of everyone saying, 'the poor little thing.'"[16] She had an excellent role model in Auntie Bye. Recognizing his eldest daughter's ever-thirsty mind, Bye's father sent her to France when she was fourteen to study with the freethinking proto-feminist Marie Souvestre, who specialized in grooming awkward girls with untapped leadership potential. Mlle Souvestre helped turn Bye into a voracious reader and a vivacious conversationalist, the kind of person who somehow commands attention no matter how crowded the room. "She [Bye] was certainly not beautiful—she was a great big handsome man of a woman—but oh so attractive!" marveled Alice. "She was both crippled (they say she had been dropped as a child, but I think it more likely that she had had infantile paralysis) and deaf, but somehow she managed to overcome these handicaps and certainly never made one aware of them."[17]

---

* A sagamore was a type of chief among the Algonquian Indians of the North Atlantic coast.

Bye held the rest of the world to her same unforgiving standards. She might have employed a spoonful of sugar now and then, but she believed in strong verbal medicine. "Aunt Bye had a tongue that could take paint off a barn while sounding unusually syrupy and cooing," remembered the newspaper columnist Joseph Alsop, whose grandmother was Bye's younger sister, Corinne Roosevelt. "For example, when Auntie Bye would sum up a foolish woman, she would almost coo as she said commiseratingly, 'Poor little *irrelevant* Mary.'"[18]

Few nineteenth-century women dared to be that frank, even opinionated. Those who weren't shocked by her were often smitten, especially—against considerable odds—men. Senator Henry Cabot Lodge, the British ambassador Cecil Spring-Rice, and various other friends of Theodore's became enamored of Bye's sharp mind and tongue. Teddy called them her "potpourri of admirers," and they included a dashing eighteen-year-old Scot named Robert Munro Ferguson (Bye was thirty-two when they met), and fifty-year-old James Roosevelt, her fourth cousin, who asked her to marry him after his first wife died. Bye was twenty-three, and she said no. It was a decision which arguably changed the course of American history, given that James went on to marry Bye's good friend Sara Delano.

———

Aunt Bye, the family fixer, also came to the rescue of the other lost girl of the Roosevelt family. Eleanor's troubles didn't start as early as Alice's, but they were, if anything, more heartbreaking. Her father, Elliott, met Anna Hall when she was almost nineteen and already a legendary beauty, with milky skin, saucerlike eyes, and golden ringlets worthy of a Botticelli. The *New York Tribune* noted that Anna was already "celebrated for her pale loveliness," and she and Elliott quickly became one of New York's It couples, mainstays of the society pages and on Mrs. Astor's "400 list" of the city's most prominent families.[19] Their December 1883 wedding was, according to the *New York Evening Telegram*, "one of the most brilliant social events of the season."[20]

Unfortunately, Anna never considered plain and dour Eleanor worthy of her parents' place among the beautiful people. Eleanor certainly didn't win much of Anna's time, which was largely spent hobnobbing at charity balls and performing in amateur theater productions. When Eleanor was six, her great-aunt Elizabeth Ludlow was appalled to discover that no one had taught her how to read. In fact, Anna had sent her daughter away to a French convent school the year before with these words of encouragement: "You have no looks, so see to it that you have manners."[21] (Defiant and desperate for attention, Eleanor promptly got herself expelled, after the nuns accused her of fibbing about swallowing a penny.) Back home again, Anna's disparaging comments about Eleanor's appearance were the one consistent source of maternal attention she would offer. "My mother was always a little troubled by my lack of beauty, and I knew it as a child senses those things," she wrote. "I can remember standing in the door, often with a finger in my mouth, and I can see the look in her eyes and hear the tone of her voice as she said, 'Come in, Granny.'"[22]

Eleanor's relationship with her father was just the opposite—complete, mutual adoration. He took her on carriage rides, bought her a pony, and doted on her as only a father can, calling her "Little Nell," a chip off his old childhood nickname. On the day she returned home after that disastrous stay at the convent school, her father was "the only person who did not treat me as a criminal." He was her savior in every sense. On May 18, 1887, two-year-old Eleanor and her parents set sail for Europe aboard the *Britannic*. The seas were calm, but the second day out was extremely foggy, well into the afternoon. The ship had been clanging its fog bell for hours when, at about 5:25 p.m., the entire vessel seemed to jump in the water. The *Britannic* had been rammed by another steamship, the *Celtic*. (As it happened, both ships belonged to the White Star Line, whose *Titanic* sank almost exactly twenty-five years later.) There was pandemonium on board. At least six *Britannic* passengers were killed instantly when the prow of the *Celtic* sliced it like a knife through a cake, boring ten feet into the steerage cabins; all that was found of one victim was a severed leg. The *Britannic*'s captain had to brandish his gun and threaten to shoot the men who were pushing ahead of the women and children into the lifeboats. Eleanor remembered only one thing: her father, standing below her on a lifeboat, reaching up for her as a crew member dropped her safely into his arms. "With my father I was perfectly happy," Eleanor said. "He dominated my life as long as he lived and was the love of my life for many years after he died."[23]

Even under normal circumstances, however, Elliott was the most unreliable of parents. As much as he loved her, he couldn't possibly take care of her. He could hardly take care of himself. That ill-fated voyage on the

*Britannic* had actually been Anna's attempt to get her husband to dry out, away from his polo pals and assorted drinking buddies. She and Elliott still made the trip a few months later, but Eleanor now stayed behind with her great-aunt Gracie, Elliott's mother's sister, and Gracie's husband in Oyster Bay. She lived with them for six months, and initially it was a shock. "She asked two or three times in the train coming out here where her 'dear Mamma was & where her Papa was,'" Gracie wrote to Corinne. "I told her, 'They have gone to Europe.' She said, 'where is baby's home now?' I said, 'baby's home is Gracewood with Uncle Bunkle & Aunt Gracie,' which seemed to entirely satisfy the sweet little darling. But as we came near the Bay driving by Mrs. Swan's she said to her uncle in an anxious alarmed way 'Baby does not want to go into the water. Not in a boat.' It was really touching."[24]

Baby soon thrived, removed from the stresses of her unhappy parents and enveloped for the first time in a family who appreciated her for herself. "She has such a gentle, affectionate nature. It is impossible not to love her," Aunt Gracie wrote to Bye.[25] What's more, she acquired a steady playmate. Aunt Bye was overseeing the construction of Leeholm, just down the road in Oyster Bay, and in the spring and summer of 1887 Alice and Eleanor became fast friends. Aunt Gracie, who had taught their fathers how to read, made a point of reading every day to the young girls. They played on the lawn and on the porch and even, after a time, by the water. Oyster Bay became a kind of haven for Eleanor that year and beyond, and Alice was at its center. "Aunty and Uncle Bunkle took Alice and Eleanor sailing yesterday. They did enjoy it so much," Anna wrote to Elliott the next summer. "She won't hear of going home; as she says, she would not have Alice any more."[26] On another occasion, after Eleanor had spent several days with her, Aunt Gracie wrote to Corinne, "Sweet little Eleanor was sent for Friday and I felt very sad to give her up. I love her dearly. She has such a gentle, generous, affectionate nature. It is impossible not to love her. She talked incessantly and a great deal of it is about 'Baby Lee' [Alice]."[27]

Alice was adjusting to a new chapter in her life as well. On one of his periodic visits back east from his exile, Theodore ran into an old friend leaving Bye's house. Edith Carow grew up with the Roosevelts; there is a famous photograph, taken in 1865, of young Teedie and Elliott standing at their grandfather's window to watch Abraham Lincoln's funeral procession near New York's Union Square. What can't be seen is little Edith, age three, who was playing with them that day. She began to cry when the black-robed masses started to file by, so the boys had locked her in a back room. Edith later went to school with the Roosevelt clan, and she and Theodore became high school sweethearts with an eye toward marriage. But during his junior year at Harvard, Theodore met the stunning (and wealthy) Alice Lee, and plain, middle-class Edith was left behind (though as Corinne's oldest and dearest friend, she was the only non-Roosevelt invited to Theodore and Alice's wedding). Just over three years later, when Alice died in childbirth, Theodore made a point of telling Bye not to ask Edith to her house, where he stayed when he was in New York. According to his Victorian moral code, a man must remain faithful to his wife even after death, and he feared that if he saw his old flame again, he might weaken. And so he did. The "chance" meeting—Bye would never say if she'd arranged it, despite her brother's orders—happened in October 1886. On December 2 of that same year, they were married.

Having capitulated on the marriage issue, Theodore intended to stand firm on the rest of his solemn commitment to widowerhood. He planned to leave Alice with his sister in perpetuity. "As I have already told you, if you wish to you shall keep Baby [Alice] Lee, I of course, paying the expense," he told Bye just before his wedding.[28] "He obviously felt tremendously guilty about remarrying, because of the concept that you loved only once and you never loved again," Alice later said.[29] But Edith objected. Three months later, he wrote to Bye from his honeymoon in Europe: "I hardly know what to say about Baby Lee. Edith feels more strongly about her than I could have imagined possible. We can decide it all when we meet." When Theodore and Edith arrived back in New York, at the end of March 1887, it had been resolved. Alice appeared at the top of the stairs at Aunt Bye's house, wearing her best dress and clutching a bouquet of pink roses. She walked down slowly and handed them to "Mother," as Edith insisted on being called. "Alice was hardly four years old," Bye said, "and it almost broke my heart to give her up."[30]

It wasn't long before Bye found herself paddling the family lifeboat again. Elliott returned from Europe that November much improved—no longer drinking and now working at Uncle Gracie's brokerage firm. But the old demons crept back. By 1890, his alcohol-fueled mood swings became so debilitating that Anna insisted they go back to Europe for serious medical treatment. This time the children—Eleanor's brother, Elliott junior, was born in 1889—went along, traveling with their parents to Italy, France, Austria, Switzerland, and Germany. Some stops went better than others. In Berlin, they ran into Theodore's pal Buffalo Bill Cody, who promptly offered Elliott a shot of whiskey, which he managed to decline. But as time went on, Elliott weakened. Anna, who tailed her husband most everywhere and monitored his drinking like a seasoned AA sponsor, could no longer keep up. She was pregnant with their third child. So in January 1891, she wrote to New York and summoned Bye.

But the case was now beyond even Bye's ability to salvage. Elliott would wander off on a bender and not return for days. He had an affair with a married expatriate woman from Detroit, just as word came from the States of a lawsuit filed by one of Anna's former servants, alleging that he was the father of her soon-to-be-born child. (He denied fathering the child at first, then said he "couldn't remember" if he'd been intimate with her. Given his near-constant state of inebriation, that might well have been true.) Bye spent eight months with the family in Europe, even living for a time with Elliott at a detox facility in Graz, Austria. Nothing helped. In fact, the birth of his second son, Gracie Hall, on June 28, 1891, in Paris, seemed to push Elliott further down his black hole. Make that his third son. About three months earlier the servant had given birth to a boy. She called him Elliott Roosevelt Mann, which meant that the older Elliott now had *two* sons named Elliott.

By the end of July 1891, Theodore and Bye had had their brother committed to an asylum just outside Paris. In August, word of Elliott's situation reached the States: "Elliott Roosevelt Mad" was the headline in the *New York Herald*.[31] The story detailed the previous year's attacks of "mental derangement," including claims that Elliott had threatened suicide three times. It also cited court testimony from both Bye and Theodore, who said that Elliott "has been of unsound mind for some time and is now unable to take care of himself." Theodore was insisting that his brother relinquish any claim on his estate, which he valued at $175,000 in real estate, stock, and bonds. Elliott responded by firing a letter back to the *Herald*. "I wish emphatically to state that my brother Theodore is taking no steps to have a commission pass on my sanity with or without my wife's approval," he wrote—from the asylum. "I am in Paris taking the cure at an *establissement hydrotherapeutique*, which my nerves, shaken by several severe accidents in the hunting field, made necessary."[32] By then, Elliott's protest didn't matter much. The week before, Bye had taken Anna and the children back home.

———

The Elliott Roosevelts never lived together again after Anna's return to New York in late 1891. She and the children moved into a house on East Sixty-First Street, a block from Aunt Bye. Anna tried to make the most of her meager maternal instincts. She converted the top floor of their home to a school, where Eleanor and other well-bred girls were tutored. She also made a point of reading to and playing with her three children, particularly in the evenings from 6:00 to 7:00. "If anyone comes to see me during that hour, they must understand they are welcome, but the children are of the first importance then, and my attention must be given to them," she told Bye.[33] But Eleanor still felt like an interloper in her mother's world, the girl who didn't know where her home was. "My little brother Ellie adored her and was so good he never had to be reproved. The baby Hall was always called Josh and was too small to do anything but sit upon her lap contentedly. I felt a curious barrier between myself and these three," Eleanor said. "If a visitor was there she might turn and say, 'She is such a funny child, so old-fashioned that we always call her Granny.' I wanted to sink through the floor in shame."[34]

It didn't help that her mother was just as miserable, like a child whose friends frolicked outside her window while she was punished in her room. Beautiful Anna Hall hadn't been raised to be a homebody. Fashionable folks would come over for tea and dinners, but tea hardly satisfied a woman with champagne tastes. She longed to go out in the world—and she did take a trip with Eleanor to ritzy Newport, to visit some family— but in the real-life *Age of Innocence* a married woman didn't dare kick up her heels without her husband. "One feels desperately lonely and wildly furious with the world at large," she wrote to Bye.[35] Anna spent hours and hours in her room, frequently with Eleanor at her bedside to massage her throbbing head. "People have since told me that I have good hands for rubbing," Eleanor said.[36]

The rare moments when "Granny" was free to have fun were away from her needy mother. Eleanor spent as much time as she could at Aunt Bye's house, drinking tea and nibbling cookies in the maid's sewing room.

"You always had a sense of the closeness of family feeling," said Eleanor. "She went to a great deal of trouble to see that [we] had a good time, but actually you wanted to be with *her*."[37] Eleanor saw a lot of Alice there, and their bond began to strengthen. "Much of her shyness and sense of insecurity stemmed from her enforced separation from [Elliott] and the unhappiness it created," Alice said. "I understood that from a fairly early age. In a way, we both suffered from being deprived of a parent. She had an idealized image of her father and I had one of my mother."[38]

The girls also had something of a standing date on Saturdays with Aunt Gracie. She would take them on the rounds of doctor and dentist appointments in the morning, then they'd play tourist, sightseeing around the city at places of culture high and low. "Mrs. Jorley's wax works I first saw with her!" Eleanor remembered.[39] Rainy days, when the group hunkered down at Aunt Gracie's home, seemed to please Eleanor just as much. Grandmother Martha and her sister, Gracie, grew up in Roswell, Georgia. Their brothers actually fought for the South in the Civil War and afterward fled to England rather than capitulate. Gracie delighted in sharing her heritage with the children, who would eat southern food (pecan pie was a favorite) while playing games or listening to her nostalgic stories about life on a plantation. For Elliot's daughter, a vicariously happy childhood was better than no childhood at all.

Eleanor's other sanctuary was Sagamore Hill. Her summer trips there were, relatively speaking, blissful. Uncle Ted was the perfect antidote for a mother who loved her sparingly and a father who was out of reach. Theodore had come to adore children and childishness of any kind: he could never resist a good pillow fight, even when he was living in the White House. But he was especially taken with Eleanor. "Eleanor was always my brother Ted's favorite niece," Corinne recalled. "She is more like him than any of his children."[40] When she would arrive for a visit, her uncle would practically tackle her. "He was a bear," Edith said after the time her husband hugged Eleanor so tightly that he "tore all the gathers out of Eleanor's frock and both buttonholes out of her petticoat."[41]

Theodore was a lightning bolt with a mustache, someone who could send jolts of energy through everyone around him, even an unnaturally solemn little girl. Eleanor never considered herself athletic, but around Uncle Ted and his rambunctious brood she rose to the challenge, just as young Teedie used feats of stamina to push back against his asthma. One day might be spent on a lengthy hike and bird-watching jaunt. Another might feature relay races outside the barn or rowing to a picnic spot along the shore. Sometimes the kids would gather upstairs in the "gun room," where Theodore hung his rifles and the stuffed prizes he'd bagged with them, and listen to him recite reams of poetry.

Almost every summer day involved a quarter-mile hike (the youngest children got to ride in a donkey cart) to the Long Island Sound. "I can see my father at Sagamore shouting to me from the water, 'Dive, Alicy, dive,'" Alice recalled. "And there I was, trembling on the bank saying through tears, 'Yes, Father,' to this sea monster who was flailing away in the water, peering near-sightedly at me without glasses and with his mustache glistening wet in the sunlight. It was pathetic. My cousin Eleanor was always so fine about that sort of thing. She hated it as much as I did but was much more unprotesting. I was not. I cried. I snarled. I hated."[42]

The family used to say that after a diving lesson, Alice's copious tears caused a perceptible rise in the tide. But she was right about Eleanor, who not only made the best of it but turned the experience into yet another feat of goody-two-shoes stoicism. "Occasionally, he [Uncle Ted] would take us on a picnic or camping trip and taught us many valuable lessons [such as] that camping was a good way to find out people's characters," Eleanor recalled. "Those who were selfish showed it very soon, in that they wanted the best bed or the best food, and they did not want to do their share of the work."[43] No wonder Alice came to find her cousin's sanctimony about as appealing as diving practice. She made Alice look bad. Alice preferred to spend time in Sagamore's small apple orchard, which she "owned" by virtue of being the oldest. The other children paid "rent" by climbing one of the trees when Alice ordered them to.

———

It wasn't really the sporting life that Alice resisted. She might have lost her mother, but she blamed her father for abandoning her, too. After all, he had effectively tried to give her away to Bye, only to destroy that stability when Edith insisted on reclaiming her—over his objections. "I had a great affection for him but tended to worship from afar," she said. "I don't think he had any special affection for me."[44] He certainly had little time for her. He had campaigned throughout the West for the Republican Benjamin Harrison in the presidential election of 1888 and was rewarded with an appointment to the Civil Service Commission, requiring the family to move to Washington. When she was six, Alice got to meet the president, a feat she would repeat sixteen times over the next eight decades. "[Harrison] appeared to me to be a gnarled, bearded, gnome of a man gloomily ensconced in a corner of the red room at the White House," she said.[45] But Alice saw relatively little of her father. Theodore Roosevelt served with such distinction that he was reappointed to the same post when the Democrat Grover Cleveland won the election of 1892, despite Theodore's having supported Harrison's reelection. He returned to New York in 1895, becoming president of the board of New York City Police Commissioners, where he shook up the establishment and made a name for himself as an honest, energetic, and hardworking public servant. In his spare time, he wrote books on the War of 1812, the history of New York, the life of Thomas Hart Benton, hunting trips of a ranchman, and more.

As a result, Alice could be almost as unhappy in her family as Eleanor was in hers. Her stepmother, Edith, began having children almost immediately after she was married. Ted junior was born exactly nine months and eleven days after his parents' wedding, and he was followed by four more little Roosevelts over the next ten years.* Just as Eleanor felt left out of the relationship between her mother and her brothers, Alice could never get over being the only child in the family with a stepmother. She liked to claim that she shrugged off self-pity, but she carried a lifelong grudge over Ted junior's teasing her about having a wet nurse: "So this horrid little cross-eyed boy of about five would go around to all and sundry exclaiming: 'Sissy had a sweat nurse! Sissy had a sweat nurse!' It was frightfully wounding to the character."[46]

It didn't help that Edith was about as warm as February in the Badlands. Her own father's slide into alcoholism drove his family into the dreaded middle class, and like many children of alcoholics (including Eleanor) Edith clung to order and propriety as if her life depended on it. "Both Aunt Bye and my mother-in-law [Theodore and Bye's sister, Corinne Roosevelt] were a little bit afraid of her, which always amused me because they weren't afraid of anybody, ever," said Helen Roosevelt Robinson, Corinne's daughter-in-law. "They were watching their p's and q's a little bit when they were with her."[47] Stern and cool, she was unemotional almost to the point of

---

* Following Theodore Roosevelt III (Ted junior) in 1887 came Kermit in 1889, Ethel in 1891, Archibald (Archie) in 1894, and finally Quentin in 1897.

comedy. When the sixty-foot windmill at Sagamore Hill got stuck one summer, Theodore grabbed an oilcan and shimmied up the support pole to the jammed turbine. He reached the top easily enough, but as he did, the wind shifted and the blades started spinning on their own—one of them slicing off a good chunk of his scalp. With blood leaking into his eyes and onto his shoulders, he climbed down and staggered into the house, where he was met by Edith in the front hall. Most wives would have screamed or at least hurried to help. Not stoic, orderly Edith. "Theodore," she said, her exasperation dripping along with his head, "I wish you'd do your bleeding in the bathroom. You are spoiling every rug in the house."[48]

None of which made Edith a bad mother, or even an uncaring one. She worried about her stepdaughter's education, her friends, even her clothes. "I got Alice a beautiful dress at Stern's, dark large plaid with navy blue velour, but how much do you think it cost? Forty-two dollars," she wrote to her sister, Emily. "Mrs. Lee [Alice's maternal grandmother] wishes it, and I am glad as Alice is a child who needs good clothes, and would look quite forlorn as Eleanor in makeshifts."[49] But Alice only reluctantly gave her stepmother credit for her thoughtful upbringing. When Alice was eight, she had to get braces on her legs, to straighten them after what might have been a mild case of polio. Edith painstakingly stretched Alice's Achilles tendons to make sure they grew properly: five minutes on one leg, seven and a half on the other, every night. Alice's response? "My step-mother made an enormous effort with me as a child," she said, "but I think she was bored by doing so."[50]

———

Elliott, on the other hand, was desperate to return to his family, but it would come with conditions. Theodore wouldn't sign the release from the French asylum unless Elliott agreed to continue treatment in the States. He also demanded, with Anna's backing, that Elliott keep away from his family for a year, to prove that he could stay sober and employed. Arriving back in the United States in February 1892, Elliott spent five weeks taking the renowned Dr. Keeley's Bichloride of Gold Cure* in Dwight, Illinois, then went to work tending to his brother-in-law's real estate holdings in

---

* The "Gold Cure," a popular treatment for alcoholism through the mid-1960s, combined daily injections of a secret, gold-based solution along with talk therapy in residential settings around the country.

Virginia.[51] After only a few months there, Elliott began a sort of letter-writing campaign, begging Anna, Bye, even Anna's mother to allow him to return to the fold in New York. Elliott reached out to Eleanor, too. "Because father is not with you is not because he doesn't love you. For I love you tenderly and dearly. And maybe soon I'll come back all well and strong and we will have such good times together, like we used to have," he wrote two days before her eighth birthday.[52] He also sent her a pony. As her present to him, she learned to recite much of Longfellow's poem "The Song of Hiawatha" by heart—"because that happened to be a favorite poem of his," she said.[53]

Unfortunately for Eleanor, she was the only one who responded to her father's overtures: "Sometimes I woke up when my mother and her sisters were talking at bed time, and many a conversation which was not meant for my ears was listened to with great avidity. I acquired a strange and garbled idea of the troubles which were going on around me. Something was wrong with my father, and from my point of view nothing could be wrong with him."[54] When Anna became ill and needed to go to the hospital in November 1892, her mother sent Elliott a telegram that said plainly, "Do not come." "It is most *horrible* and full of *awe* to me that my wife not only does not want me near her in sickness or trouble but fears me," he telegraphed back to Mrs. Hall. "If Anna cares for it give her my love."[55] The note was dated December 7, 1892. Anna died, of diphtheria, that day. It's a measure of Eleanor's blind adoration of Elliott that even when she wrote about her mother's death years later, she still couldn't summon any sadness. "She was very sweet to me, and I must have known that something terrible had happened," she said. "Death meant nothing to me, and one fact wiped out everything else—my father was back and I would see him very soon."[56]

To no one's surprise except perhaps Eleanor's, her father failed to make her world better. Anna's will left the three children in custody of her mother, Mary Livingston Ludlow Hall, and Elliott was in no condition to fight back. He visited them infrequently when they were at their grandmother's Manhattan residence, drifting in and out of New York amid sporadic letters overflowing with unfulfilled promises. One time when he did collect Eleanor for a walk, he arrived with a large collection of hunting dogs, which had become his steadiest companions (besides his drinking partners at his men's club). "He took me and three of his fox terriers and left us with the doorman at the Knickerbocker Club," Eleanor said. "When he failed to return after six hours, the doorman took me home."[57]

From there, things actually got worse. In May 1893, just five months after their mother's death, both of Eleanor's little brothers came down with scarlet fever. Elliott was in Virginia working for his brother-in-law, and he rushed back to New York, but three-year-old Elliott junior died within days. Motherless Eleanor had already begun to assume the role of a parent, even to her own father. "We must remember Ellie is going to be safe in heaven and to be with Mother who is waiting there and our Lord wants Ellie boy with him now, we must be happy and do God's will and we must cheer others who feel it too," she wrote to Elliott. "You are alright I hope."[58]

Elliott was as far from "alright" as he could be. He continued to tell his family that he was receiving his mail at the Knickerbocker Club, but he had secretly moved into an apartment on New York's very unfashionable West 102nd Street, where he lived with a new mistress named Mrs. Evans. He also occasionally snuck away to visit the Detroit expatriate with whom he had cavorted in Europe. Theodore wrote to Bye that their brother was now "drinking whole bottles of anisette and green mint—besides whole bottles of raw brandy and of champagne, sometimes half a dozen a morning."[59] Elliott was thrown from his carriage after drunkenly driving it into a lamppost, and he burned himself badly after tipping over a reading lamp. He could only manage sporadic contact with Eleanor, writing her letters equally full of apology and self-pity: "What must you think of your father who has not written in so long." On August 13, 1894, he wrote and tried to explain himself: "I have after all been very busy, quite ill, at intervals not able to move from my bed for days," he said. "Kiss Baby Brudie for me and *never forget* I love you."[60]

On that August night, he began acting more strangely than usual. His valet said he collected his dogs and proceeded to introduce them all to Elliott, his dead son. At one point he ran up to the fourth floor of his apartment house and knocked on a neighbor's door and asked "if Miss Eleanor Roosevelt were at home." No, the neighbor said, she wasn't. "Tell her her father is so sorry not to see her," Elliott replied.[61] He then started running up and down the stairs like a rabid dog. When he tired of that, he jumped out the parlor-floor window. His valet got him into bed, but he started to have convulsions. He finally fell asleep some time before 10:00 p.m. By the morning he was dead.

———

Dead to the world—all the major New York papers wrote news stories about him—but of course not dead to his daughter. It was as if she lived in some kind of shiny, happy fantasyland. She would later admit that she survived those bleak and bereft years by retreating to "my dream world." "My grandmother decided that we children should not go to the funeral, and so I had no tangible thing to make death real to me," Eleanor said. "From that time on I knew in my mind that my father was dead, and yet I lived with him more closely, probably, than I had when he was alive."[62]

In less than two years, Eleanor had lost her mother, her brother, and her father. Nonetheless, Grandmother Hall now decided to keep ten-year-old Eleanor and three-year-old Hall away from their paternal relatives as much as possible. Though her grandmother's New York house, on West Thirty-Seventh Street, was only about a mile from her devoted aunts Corinne and Bye, Eleanor rarely saw them in the wake of Elliott's death. "Perhaps she feared we might slip away from her control if we were too much with our dynamic Roosevelt relatives," she reasoned.[63] She was probably right, given the bleak condition of Eleanor's latest temporary home. "I was sent by my mother for supper with Eleanor," said her cousin Corinne Robinson Alsop. "I say advisedly that I was sent, because I never wanted to go. In her own words Eleanor has pictured her distressingly grim childhood, and I can only reinforce her statements by confessing my own horror at the atmosphere of the brownstone house with the narrow dark hall lit by a gas jet, the formal, uninviting drawing room, the room back of the drawing room that was even darker than the hall, and the frigid looking dining room where we had our supper in solemn silence as we were all affected by the unbroken gloom."[64]

Eleanor's time at the family's country house north of the city was even worse. Mrs. Hall's five surviving children still lived with her at Tivoli, the family's baroque estate on the Hudson, and they were already more than she could manage. Eleanor's uncle Vallie was a particular nightmare. Another in the long line of alcoholic men in Eleanor's family tree, he liked to sit in his second-floor window and shoot his rifle at unsuspecting passersby (though he invariably missed them because he was invariably too drunk to shoot straight).[*][65] Mrs. Hall felt compelled to put a lock on Eleanor's bedroom door to keep Vallie out. Or was it to keep Eleanor in?

Alice's experience with her maternal grandparents, the Lees, could hardly have been more different: "There never were such kind, indulgent, affectionate grandparents—four aunts and an uncle as well—who let me have my way until I ought to have been spanked."[66] Alice escaped to their home in Massachusetts for several weeks each spring and fall. Unlike dour and overwhelmed Mrs. Hall, the Lees were delighted to indulge their firstborn grandchild. Mr. Lee, a successful banker, had already set up a trust fund for Alice upon her mother's death, and the grandparents yielded to her every whim. "Everything belonged to me," Alice remembered. "I would come in and jump up and down on the sofa, hoping the springs would break, and they would merely smile indulgently."[67]

Edith was just as wary of Elliott's children as Mrs. Hall was of Theodore's, especially considering the blotch Elliott had attached to the Roosevelt name. "As you know I never wished Alice to associate with Eleanor so shall not try to keep up any friendship between them," Edith wrote to her own mother.[68] With Elliott's death she closed the door further, allowing only a brief visit or two in the summer. She wasn't all that gracious then, either. "Eleanor has been here too—poor little soul; she is very plain," Edith wrote to Bye. "Her mouth and teeth seem to have no future but as mother (always said) . . . the ugly duckling may turn into a swan."[69]

To top it off, Alice and Eleanor then lost their mutual anchor: Aunt Bye. James "Rosy" Roosevelt, Franklin's older half brother, was serving as the first secretary at the American embassy in London when his wife, the former Helen Astor, died unexpectedly. Rosy, a somewhat aimless and decidedly foppish playboy who made liberal use of the Astor money, found himself stranded abroad with no one to care for his family, fifteen-year-old James and thirteen-year-old Helen. Rosy cared deeply for his chil-

---

[*] Ironically, Vallie had once been an excellent shot—on the tennis court. Before being swallowed up by his drinking, Uncle Vallie, a.k.a. Valentine Gill Hall III (1867–1934), was a tennis champion. He was the U.S. national champion in men's doubles in 1888 and 1890 and runner-up in 1891 and 1892. His doubles partner in 1892 was his brother Edward Ludlow Hall (1872–1932). Vallie retired in 1894, shortly after Eleanor and her brother Hall moved to Tivoli. In an astonishing coincidence, Franklin Roosevelt's first cousin, Ellen Crosby Roosevelt (1868–1954), was the women's champion in 1890, and that same year won the doubles championship with her sister Grace (1867–1945). They were the only pair of sisters to win the U.S. doubles championship until Venus and Serena Williams more than a century later.

dren; he just had no idea how to care *for* them.* So despite the awkward fact that Bye had rejected Rosy's father's marriage proposal two decades earlier, she moved to London to care for yet more neglected Roosevelt children. She lived off and on with Rosy and the children for the next two years. Nannie Lodge, wife of Henry Cabot Lodge and an old family friend, wrote, "You are an angel, as usual, to go and take care of the poor forlorn things of the world."[70]

Bye did her best to keep Alice and Eleanor connected from afar, writing to each about the other, even sending them identical sets of Shakespeare for Christmas. But the girls no longer had any neutral territory in the city where they could sip tea and find sympathy. "I am so glad Alice is going to be in town this winter," Eleanor wrote to Bye. "I wish she went to school with me then I would see her every morning."[71] It was left to Aunt Corinne to pick up the slack. A somewhat softer touch than Bye—she was the family poet and resident Sunday school teacher, and she could still turn a dandy cartwheel—Corinne had her own bond with her nieces. She was in the house on Fifty-Seventh Street when Alice was born, and Elliott had introduced her to his business partner, Douglas Robinson, whom she later married. The Robinsons lived on a seventy-acre estate in Orange, New Jersey, called Overlook, which was where Corinne gathered the family each year just after Christmas for skating on Mitchell's Pond, riding one of their fourteen horses, and other feats of Rooseveltian exertion.

The highlight of the annual family reunion in Orange was a grand dance, held at the Essex County Country Club. Corinne was perhaps the most popular and easygoing of the Roosevelts—she even got along with stony Edith—and the cousins came from far and wide. It was one of the few times that Mrs. Hall allowed Eleanor free rein with her father's family. It was also the only social occasion where the budding teen could mingle with kids her own age—and she hated it. Trapped in gothic seclusion by her grandmother, Eleanor knew more about the love life of the Romantic poets than she did about acting like a teenager. The clothes, the jargon, the latest dances—it was all lost on her. One year she showed up wearing the

---

* Though he did go to court to try to force the Astor trust to raise his children's allowance, which stood at a mere $30,000 a year, or more than $825,000 in 2015 dollars. The judge not only said no; he cut the allowance down to $15,000 and chastised Rosy for indulging the kids.

same blue dress as the year before, now several inches too short. Another time she wore long black stockings and a white organdy dress that stopped above the knee, giving her a pre–*What Ever Happened to Baby Jane?* look. "No one, young or old, wore very short skirts in those days, even for sports, but her grandmother bought her a dress that could have been for a five-year-old," said Corinne Alsop.[72] "She was," said Augusta Tilney, a friend of Corinne's, "a living freak."[73]

Alice attended these gatherings, too, and the differences between her and Eleanor were becoming as glaring as those black stockings. Dressed in elegant clothes purchased with her grandparents' limitless funds, Alice was the center of attention, surrounded by young men who wanted to dance with her or just watch her hold court. "[She was] so much more sophisticated and grown up that I was in great awe of her," Eleanor said. "She was better at sports, and my having so few companions my own age put me at great disadvantage with other young people."[74] In later years, Alice would scoff at Eleanor's feelings of inadequacy. "She was always making herself out to be an ugly duckling but she was really rather attractive. Tall, rather coltish-looking, with masses of pale, gold hair rippling to below her waist, and really lovely blue eyes," Alice said. "It's true that her chin went in a bit, which wouldn't have been so noticeable if only her hateful grandmother had fixed her teeth. I think Eleanor today would have been considered a beauty."[75]

It's easy to chalk up Alice's backhanded compliment to her growing determination to be contrary at all costs, a desire to be kind, only to be cruel. But Alice truly cared for her cousin. One fateful evening in Orange, she not only confirmed her warmest feelings for Eleanor; she also—to borrow Edith's callous phrase—helped turn the duckling into a swan. The orchestra was playing a polka, and as usual Eleanor was on the sidelines, staring at the ceiling, fidgeting with her dress, and generally trying to disappear into the wallpaper, while Alice and the others were kicking up their heels. When the music stopped, Alice and her handsome partner stood together laughing. She whispered something in his ear, and he suddenly looked over in Eleanor's direction. Alice had suggested that he walk across the room to talk to her cousin, and so he did. "Eleanor, may I have the next dance with you?" asked the tall young man with a radiant smile. "Oh, Franklin," she replied. "I'd love to."[76]

Oh, Franklin indeed. For the rest of their lives, he would form a sort of dividing line between the cousins. It wasn't that they fought over him.

Alice vehemently denied ever having romantic designs on Franklin; in fact, she said her family always thought he was an intellectual lightweight: they joked that the initials "FD" stood for "Feather Duster." But he stood between them, less like a net on a Ping-Pong table than the ball itself, bouncing from Alice's side to Eleanor's, and often in ways that underscored how far apart the cousins stood politically, socially, even morally.

The Orange dance revealed just how differently the two young women had matured. Eleanor and Franklin had been occasional playmates through the years. He gave her a piggyback ride on her first visit to Hyde Park—she was two, and he was four—and they would later spend a few days in the summer among the extended family at Sagamore Hill. But their meeting in 1898, when they were now fourteen and sixteen, was the first where hormones played a part. Alice, however, had been flirting with Franklin for months. The year before, when she and Franklin's half-niece, Helen, were staying at Aunt Bye's, they co-wrote Franklin a note in which Alice asked teasingly, "I want to know the name of the girl James told me you were stuck on instead of me," she said. "Please write and tell us her name as we are very anxious to know." A few months later, Helen wrote to Franklin alone, "Alice Lee Roosevelt is certainly a very silly and decidedly vain young lady, and I agree with James, the less we have to do with her the better. 'Flirtatious girls' may be attractive at first sight but I think one soon discovers their true qualities, don't you?"[77]

Certainly Edith and Theodore had long had their hands full with Alice. She had always been willful, as Alice herself was the first to admit, and needed a strong hand more than ever as she became a teenager. Unfortunately for the cause of discipline, the Republicans returned to the White House with the election of 1896, and President McKinley appointed Roosevelt assistant secretary of the navy. He moved his family back to Washington (though they still summered at Sagamore Hill) and became absorbed in his new job. Before his political career, Theodore had won acclaim for his first book, *The Naval War of 1812*. Now he delighted in occasionally borrowing a torpedo boat to visit the family on vacation in Newport. Edith was busy with the ever-growing family; she gave birth to her fifth child, Quentin, in November 1897. And so thirteen-year-old Alice became, in her father's words, a "guttersnipe." She soon teamed up with a group of eight neighborhood boys who liked to "run riot" around the city, racing their bikes down Connecticut Avenue from Dupont Circle and sneaking out of the house whenever they could. "We met in a stable loft and the boys would come dressed in their sisters' clothes in order to deceive their parents," she said. "My father opened the door once on a petrified boy struggling to adjust one of his sister's dresses. They must have looked at each other with mutual consternation."[78]

Fortunately for all concerned, Aunt Bye had recently returned from London to live in New York. Much to everyone's shock, she arrived with a husband, a naval officer named William Cowles, though with his sea-dog mustache and ample belly Bye liked to call him "Mr. Bearo." At the time of her wedding, she was forty; Cowles was forty-nine. "We were," said Alice, "absolutely flabbergasted."[79]

But at least she was home, and she was more than ready to resume her role as family fixer. When Edith became ill after giving birth to Quentin, Theodore sent Alice and Ted junior to live with Bye. Alice said, somewhat bitterly, that she had been "expelled." It didn't help that her parents informed her of her impending banishment on her fourteenth birthday, then shipped her off the very next day. Nor was Alice thrilled by Bye's house strictures: "Now darling, I am too happy you are coming, but, there will be a few rules and regulations," she wrote to her niece, having heard about Alice's guttersnipe tendencies.[80]

Yet Alice was obviously a girl who needed to be watched, in the sense of both oversight and plain old parental attention. Even though she was a newlywed, ever-adoring Aunt Bye provided just the kind of audience Alice required. Theodore himself noticed the change in the "interesting and amusing" letters that Alice wrote to her parents. "You are doing her a world of good and giving her exactly what she needed," he wrote to Bye from Washington. "I am sure she really does love Edith and the children and me; it was only that running riot with the boys and girls here for the moment drives everything else out of her head."[81]

New York also provided a far tamer circle of peers—her extended family of patrician cousins. Once again, Bye's Madison Avenue home became a central meeting place for the younger generation, and once again Eleanor became a somewhat regular companion, at least when Mrs. Hall would let her get away. If the dances at Aunt Corinne's began to show how quickly the cousins were growing apart, their time at Bye's added an exclamation point. Nowhere were their differences more pronounced than when they began to gossip, as teenage girls do, about sex.

Alice remembered a particularly fraught afternoon holed up with Eleanor in a bedroom at Bye's house:

> By the age of fifteen I knew quite a bit from the Bible and from my rabbits and guinea pigs. Living in the country as I did, you take those things for granted. [My parents] wouldn't admit that the Bible was a good place to learn the facts of life but I did just that. However, when I tried to pass some of the information on to my cousin Eleanor, I almost came to grief. She suddenly leapt on me and tried to sit on my head and smother me with a pillow, saying I was being blasphemous. So I shut up and I think she probably went to her wedding not knowing anything about the subject at all. It was that kind of difference between us from the start.[82]

———

Those differences were becoming more pronounced by the minute, though they were triggered by events far from their gilded corner of the world. Only two days after Alice arrived in New York, in February 1898, the Spanish navy sank the American battleship *Maine* in Havana harbor (or so William Randolph Hearst and Joseph Pulitzer, the grandfathers of yellow journalism, reported in their sensationally pugnacious newspapers).* Assistant Secretary Roosevelt had long been an advocate—head cheerleader, really—for war against Spain. Now he got his wish. In April, he resigned from his job and gathered an unlikely collection of Ivy-educated blue bloods and Wild West sharpshooters into Roosevelt's

---

* In the late nineteenth century, the United States began eyeing the remnants of Spain's decaying and restive colonial empire, especially Cuba, the Philippines, Puerto Rico, and Guam, for a host of economic and geopolitical reasons. With regard to Cuba especially, prowar Americans veiled their interest in idealistic terms, such as likening the Cuba Libre independence movement to the patriots of 1776. When the *Maine* exploded in Havana harbor on February 15, 1898, killing 266 American sailors, it didn't take long for the United States to act, despite uncertainty that lingers to this day as to whether the Spaniards had blown up the American ship or if spontaneous combustion in its coal bunker ignited the adjacent munitions stores. War was declared on April 25. By August 12, the Spanish called a truce. The peace treaty signed the following December required Spain to cede all of its colonies outside Africa to U.S. control. Soon to be appointed secretary of state, John Hay wrote to Theodore Roosevelt that the ten weeks of hostilities amounted to a "splendid little war," in large part because it had propelled the United States to the forefront of world affairs and Theodore Roosevelt to national prominence.

Rough Riders and headed for Cuba. In July, Colonel Roosevelt rode his chestnut-colored quarter horse, Little Texas, into the Battle of San Juan Hill and emerged as a bona fide war hero. In November, he was elected governor of New York. Within two years, he would become vice president of the United States.

Alice did not wear her father's ballooning fame well. It played to her worst impulses: her lifelong need for attention and her adolescent desire to defy her parents. "Being the offspring of a very conspicuous parent, I wasn't going to let him get the better of me," she said.

> I valued my independence from an early age and was always something of an individualist. Well, a show-off anyway. One of the only things I remember about the Forsyte Saga [a series of satiric novels about a nouveau riche British family] was when the little dog comes in and wanders around. Nobody pays any attention to it. It goes to the middle of the floor and throws up, so the lady calls the butler to take it away and to wipe up the mess. As he leaves the room the butler says, "The little animal likes to make itself felt, madam."[83]

Though Alice supported her father's war exploits like the proudest of daughters, it's no coincidence that she picked the summer of his great war victory to make her biggest stink to date. Like most of the Roosevelt children, Alice had been primarily schooled at home by tutors. Edith, always mindful of propriety, decided that it was time for her to receive a formal education. Clara Spence had founded a boarding school for girls only six years earlier in New York. Miss Spence's School had already become the place for the daughters of the rich and powerful to be groomed; Andrew Carnegie and Henry Frick both sent their daughters. And so Edith enrolled Alice, the daughter of one of the most famous men in America.

Alice Roosevelt wanted nothing to do with it. She threw a tantrum almost every day and went running up to her room in tears. "I had seen Miss Spence's scholars marching two by two in their daily walks and the thought of becoming one of them shriveled me," she said.[84] Edith resisted. As the school linens and uniforms arrived and were readied for packing, Alice turned up the drama. "I said that if the family insisted and sent me, I would do something disgraceful. I will humiliate you. I'll shame you.

You will see."[85] And then, at the last minute, Edith gave in. She sent back the uniforms and hired a governess. Alice did not attend Spence. No one wanted to call her bluff. Not surprisingly, in later years Alice also became an excellent poker player.

---

Not long after school provided a turning point in Eleanor's life as well, though as usual she turned in the opposite direction. Like her cousin, Eleanor was a voracious reader who was largely self-taught or tutored. All the Roosevelt women loved reading and learning; Aunt Bye used to keep a pile of books by her bedside that she called "mental manure," because they primed her for her regular morning chats with her brother and the various politicians who came to talk shop.[86] As a result of her time as a young woman in France studying with Marie Souvestre, Bye was the rare woman of her generation to receive a formal education. She was convinced that Eleanor would benefit from Souvestre's tutelage. Mademoiselle had since moved to England, where she opened a school called the Allenswood Academy just outside London. Bye had been lobbying Grandmother Hall, to no avail. But by 1899, life at Tivoli—with the gun-toting uncle and an aunt who was becoming more morose and suicidal with every lost boyfriend—was becoming unlivable. One day, Grandma Hall called Eleanor into her bedroom. "Your mother wanted you to go to boarding school in Europe," she told a stunned Eleanor. "And I have decided to send you, child."[87]

# Chapter 2

# HOME ABROAD

B y the time he was serving only his second term in the New York State Assembly, Theodore Roosevelt had collected enough political enemies to field a small army. In fact, he called his opponents the "black-horse cavalry," because in his black-and-white worldview they rode with the forces of evil.[1] Even at this early point in his career, Roosevelt fashioned himself as a take-no-prisoners reformer, a man who would sink his impressive teeth into any worthy cause. Among his rookie-term targets: railroad monopolies, police corruption, civil-service patronage, undertaxed saloon owners, cigar sweatshops, water pollution, and one particularly venal state supreme court justice, who only escaped Roosevelt's impeachment campaign after three key Democratic politicians received $2,500 to vote for the judge. In one of his most celebrated campaigns, Roosevelt went after the robber baron Jay Gould's Manhattan Elevated Railroad Company, which had a monopoly on building New York City train stations. Gould had enough politicians in his pocket that Assemblyman Roosevelt felt compelled to bring reinforcements to a potentially hostile hearing in 1882. "There was a broken chair in the room, and I got a leg of it loose and put it down beside me where it was not visible, but where I might get at it in a hurry if necessary," he said. "The riot did not come off; partly, I think, because the opportune production of the chair-leg had a sedative effect, and partly owing to wise counsels from one or two of my opponents."[2] TR wasn't being metaphorical when he advocated speaking softly and carrying a big stick.

Roosevelt lost the battle against Manhattan Elevated Railroad, but he won something far more enduring: a reputation as a principled public servant willing to stand up to corruption. "Rarely in the history of legislation here has the moral force of individual honor and political honesty been more forcibly displayed," the *New York Herald* wrote after he beat back one of his own party's power grabs.[3] Theodore Roosevelt rode his white horse in every political job that followed. In Washington, he spent six years, from 1889 to 1895, trying to eliminate patronage on a national scale as a member of the new Civil Service Commission. From there he became commissioner of the New York City Police, then went back to Washington to serve as assistant secretary of the navy under President McKinley. In January 1899, less than six months after his triumph on San Juan Hill, he returned to Albany as governor of New York. By then, his reputation was so enormous he had become a bull moose in the political china shop, determined to smash every shard of corruption in sight.

————

The brash young governor—he was still only forty at the beginning of his term—succeeded almost too well. The Democrats' infamous Tammany Hall political machine* and Republican Thomas "Easy Boss" Platt's organization were formidable adversaries, but Governor Roosevelt leveraged his reputation for reform, his standing as a war hero, and his genius for courting the press to level the field. In his first year, he took on New York's powerful insurance industry and business franchises, which at the time paid no corporate tax. For an encore, he planned to go after the state's "defective" laws on the environment and the public utilities. Platt and his various industry cronies realized they weren't likely to stop the governor's stampede, so they looked to sidetrack him. The day after Theodore succeeded in ousting the state's corrupt superintendent of insurance, two stories appeared in the New York *Sun* claiming that President McKinley, whose vice president had died in office two months earlier, was considering Governor Roosevelt as his running mate that November.

---

* Tammany Hall was founded in New York as a political club in 1789, and developed quickly into a machine that delivered votes (especially of immigrant communities) in exchange for patronage and other favors. It reached its apex in the decades between the Civil War and World War II, dominating New York City and State politics, and tangling frequently with the Roosevelts.

The stories, planted by Platt, were in fact true; Theodore had traveled to Washington to talk to McKinley's people. But that didn't mean Roosevelt wanted the job. He was much happier riding roughshod over Tammany Hall and answering to no one. In 1900, the vice presidency was about as coveted as first runner-up in a beauty pageant. "That he should be in the second place on the ticket offended my family sense of fitness," said Alice, who, like the rest of the family, wanted him to stay in Albany.[4] Besides, the governor of New York actually earned $2,000 more a year than the vice president of the United States, no small consideration for a man with a large family—or for his penny-pinching wife.

On the other hand, he chafed at suggestions that he *not* run. "Don't any of you realize," Mark Hanna, the national Republican boss, told Platt and his New York scheming henchmen, "that there's only one life between this madman and the Presidency?"[5] Ultimately, Theodore couldn't resist accepting McKinley's offer—"to my deep disgust, as I well remember," Alice said.[6] It was a sign of his humility but also his ambivalence that 925 out of the 926 delegates to the Republican National Convention voted for him—the only nay was cast by Roosevelt himself.[7] Alice remained indifferent, too, even though the move back to Washington meant that the family got to pile in with Aunt Bye again. (The vice president didn't get his own official residence until 1974.) Alice remained ambivalent for a good six months, until September 6, 1901. It was on that day that President McKinley, on a tour of the Pan-American Exposition in Buffalo, was shot by an anarchist named Leon Czolgosz. "We put on long faces," Alice said, "and then my brother and I went outside and did a little jig."[8] McKinley died eight days later. The madman was now president.

———

Eleanor didn't see President Roosevelt until more than a year later, but not because she didn't support him. She was enormously proud of her uncle, despite ultimately finding herself in the opposing political party. In fact, much of her later activism—and FDR's—came directly from Theodore's own tireless, reform-minded political program. But while Uncle Ted, Alice, and the rest of the family were busy moving into the White House, Eleanor's life was being transformed too. She was fifteen in 1899, when she sailed for the forty-student Allenswood Academy. She was thrilled to be going, despite her mixed emotions about leaving her family. "Thanks ever so much for your letter, there was no danger of my forgetting you but I was awfully glad to hear from you," she wrote to Alice. "I really *must* see you for I am to stay abroad two or three years."[9]

No one ever accused British boarding schools of coddling their charges, and Allenswood was strict enough to satisfy even crusty Grandmother Hall. Classes were taught exclusively in French; any student who uttered a single word in English during the day was required to report her own linguistic transgression at dinnertime. If a girl was found to have messy drawers, she might come back to her room to find her entire bureau dumped on the floor, sometimes along with her bed. Baths were limited to three a week, each no longer than ten minutes, "unless we happened to have the last period, and then perhaps we could sneak another five minutes before 'lights out' was sounded," said Eleanor, adding that she was "a little appalled" by the sanitary strictures.[10]

And yet Eleanor had never been more content. Of course, her happiness bar was set exceedingly low. After she had been out in the cold for so long—and the cloistered, semi-crazy life at Tivoli was about as far from warm and fuzzy as any home could be—even a tepid breeze felt good. But Allenswood suited her. She excelled at following the rules. They encouraged her, gave her strength and direction, like a trellis supporting a fast-growing rosebush. "This was the first time in all my life that all my fears left me. If I lived up to the rules and told the truth, there was nothing to fear," she said.[11] It's no coincidence that she stopped slouching and proudly stood to her full five-foot-eleven height at Allenswood. She even felt better, free from the headaches and assorted ailments she'd suffered with for much of her early life. "I never spent healthier years," she said.[12]

Allenswood's rigid yet supportive atmosphere came directly from its headmistress, Marie Souvestre. Souvestre was sixty-nine when Eleanor arrived at Allenswood, but with her stout body, leonine head, deep voice, and deeper convictions Souvestre was just as imposing as she had been when Auntie Bye had been her student thirty-two years earlier. She was a fearless social progressive; she led class discussions on the Boer War that clearly favored the Boers, not exactly a popular view among the British boarding-school set.* On the other hand, she never expected her girls

---

* The Dutch-speaking white settlers of South Africa, known as Boers, had been living in uneasy proximity to the expanding British colonial administration of the region throughout the nineteenth century. To escape British domination of the coastal areas, the Boers

to just ape her opinions. In fact, she discouraged it. "You are giving me back what I gave you and it does not interest me," Eleanor remembered Souvestre telling one stunned girl as she ripped up the student's paper in front of the class. "Why was your mind given you but to think things out for yourself?"[13]

For the bright but long-constricted Eleanor, permission to think freely and independently was a revelation. Souvestre recognized Eleanor's potential and responded by turning her into a combination of a pet and a project. Souvestre sat "Tottie," as she called ER, across from her at dinner, the better to share her special food, spicy conversation, and occasional guests. In the evenings Eleanor was invariably one of the select few to repair to little chairs around the fireplace in Souvestre's cozy library for more discussions on literature and current events. School was just the beginning of their unconventional, Pygmalion-like relationship. During vacations, Souvestre and Eleanor traveled together around Europe. Eleanor was charged with making all the arrangements, from the tickets to the packing. Souvestre selected the locations—Paris, Florence, the Mediterranean—the restaurants, and even, sometimes, the wardrobe, encouraging Eleanor to spend some of her limited allowance on clothes fit for a young woman, rather than her grandmother's infantilizing choices. "I still remember my joy in that dark red dress made for me by a small dress maker in Paris," Eleanor said. "I wore it on Sundays and as an everyday evening dress at school and probably got more satisfaction out of it than from any dress I have had since!"[14]

Eager to foster Eleanor's budding independence, Souvestre frequently sent her pupil out to explore a select city alone, a decided breach of propriety and maybe even common sense. "Perhaps she realized that I had not the beauty which appeals to foreign men and that I would be safe from their advance," said Eleanor. "I really marvel now at myself—confidence and independence, for I was totally without fear in this new phase of my life."[15] Not everyone supported Mlle Souvestre's empowerment methods. One spring day in Paris in 1901, Eleanor was out exploring by herself when she decided to stroll in the Luxembourg Gardens. As luck would have it,

fled inland in the mid-nineteenth century. Continued tensions between the British and the Boers led to two wars, the first in 1880–1881 and a larger, more brutal war of 1899–1902. High casualties and accounts of atrocities made the second war increasingly controversial and unpopular.

she walked straight into the family of Thomas Newbold, neighbors from Hyde Park (and relatives of the novelist Edith Wharton). Mrs. Newbold, a charter member of Mrs. Astor's four hundred most prominent New York families, promptly fired off a letter to Grandmother Hall, reporting how shocked she was to encounter Hall's unchaperoned granddaughter. When Eleanor returned home for the summer, a scandalized Grandmother Hall threatened to yank Eleanor out of Allenswood after only two years.

———

Ever the guttersnipe, Alice scoffed at what passed for brazenness on her cousin's side of the family. She and Eleanor spent a good amount of time with each other during those summer breaks—brought together, naturally, by Auntie Bye. When she wasn't in Washington, Bye now lived at her husband's ancestral home in Farmington, Connecticut, on a Connecticut River estate called Oldgate. Oldgate became, like Sagamore Hill and Aunt Corinne's house in Orange, New Jersey, one of the poles in the Roosevelt universe, a place large enough for the family to reconnect and exchange news and confidences. It was during one of those outings when Alice was reminded of her cousin's Victorian sense of propriety. "I remember one afternoon rowing on the river at Farmington with Eleanor," said Alice. "For some reason or other she started lecturing me on the sort of presents one could receive from gentlemen—flowers, books, cards were all possible, I was assured, but jewelry of any kind, absolutely not. I listened to her earnest discourse, fingering all the while a modest string of pearls that an admirer had given me the week before."[16]

Admittedly, Alice, the daughter of a war-hero governor, had more admirers than your average teenage girl. But that was nothing compared with the following she amassed shortly after the family moved to 1600 Pennsylvania Avenue in September 1901. For the first few months, the First Family kept a low profile; out of respect for the late President McKinley, the White House didn't host any social events until New Year's Day 1902. Then, on January 3, seventeen-year-old Alice had her "coming out" party, the social rite of passage for every proper young lady of means. Within weeks, she was a bona fide celebrity. "Two years ago she was of no more prominence than hundreds of American girls who, like her, are the daughters of well-to-do men of more or less note," said the *Baltimore Sun*. "Now her name is known throughout the world. Such transformation comes to the lives of few."[17]

The coming-out party itself was relatively modest. Edith and Theodore were always strapped for money—he made notoriously bad invest-
ments, especially in livestock—and the family couldn't afford a proper,
debutante-laden cotillion. Alice did wear a perfectly lovely white taffeta
and chiffon gown edged with white roses to greet her five hundred or
so guests, who included "a generous contingent of gentlemen from Harvard, Yale, and Princeton universities."[18] In the Blue, Red, Green, and East
Rooms, the mantels, columns, windows, and chandeliers were stuffed with
flowers: six hundred roses, eight hundred hyacinths, and twelve hundred
ferns, supplied by the Department of Agriculture (and distributed the next
day to hospitals around Washington "to gladden the eyes of the less for-
tunate").[19] The music was courtesy of the Marine Band *and* the Artillery
Corps Band, which played during the Marine Band's breaks.

But compared with coming-out parties in New York and Boston for
other girls in the "400," the affair came off, in the discriminating eyes of
the *New York Times*, as "extremely simple," much to the displeasure of the
evening's honoree. The fact that punch was served in lieu of champagne
was a "horrid blow to my pride," Alice said.[20] She also complained that
the East Room lacked a proper wooden dance floor. Edith had told her
if she wanted one, she'd have to charm Representative Joseph Cannon,
the Speaker of the House, into appropriating the money for it. "I worked
every ploy I knew on him," Alice said, "but to no avail. The floor was
still unwooded when the dance took place."[21] When it was all over, Alice
issued this verdict: "I myself enjoyed it moderately." On the other hand,
her cousin Franklin, one of the Harvard "gentlemen" who took the train
to Washington to attend the event, reported to his mother that "from start
to finish it was glorious."[22]

Fortunately for Alice, the party turned out to be only the appetizer.
The main course, the meal that nourished her then and for the rest of her
life, was the post-party publicity. The next day, Alice Roosevelt was front-
page news across the country. In part, that was because Americans were
ready to stop mourning President McKinley. In part, it was because Alice
was a rarity, the first glamorous young woman to live in the White House
since Ulysses S. Grant's daughter, Nellie, took up residence in 1869. Whatever the reason, most reporters—either less discriminating than the *New
York Times* or more eager to curry favor with the White House—gushed
over her evening as if they'd just seen the first production of *La bohème*.
Her dress was "rarely beautiful" and her hair "a profusion of very pretty

blond." The menu was "one of the finest ever furnished even by a president." "To the long and varied record of a century of social events at the White House, the very beautiful ball given last evening must be added and given a place all its own in the annals of the historic old mansion," wrote the *Washington Post*, under the headline "A Brilliant Gathering Greets Miss Alice Roosevelt."[23] For a girl who long felt overlooked by her ambitious father and chilly stepmother, here was a miracle drug: fame.

It didn't take long for the press-savvy president to recognize the advantages of having another, prettier media darling in the family, someone to play the carrot to his sticklike personality. He sent her on a charm offensive: lunch with the congressmen's wives, meet and greets with foreign athletes, and more. Her first really big assignment was to christen a yacht being built for Germany's kaiser, Wilhelm, on Staten Island. Like many of her First Daughter assignments to come, the christening was less ceremonial than it seemed. The president wanted to cozy up to the Germans as a sort of attention-getting move, a way to snap his towel at the British—Germany's chief military rival—and show them they shouldn't take American support for granted.

Alice certainly got the Brits' attention, along with everyone else's. The papers produced yet more bushels of stories on her. One asserted that the kaiser planned to pay Alice the "pretty compliment" of naming the ship *Alice* (in fact, Wilhelm named it *Meteor*, as he had with two previous boats). Another touted "the first up-to-date photographs" of Alice "as she really looks," along with three carefully posed pictures and a small text block that described her as "about 5 feet 5 inches tall, is straight and slender in build, but supple and graceful."[24] The Germans themselves were reportedly delighted by the "splendid effect" her reflected glamour had on their international standing.[25] In fact, a few weeks before the christening the news broke that the British, eager to keep up with the Germans, had invited Alice to Edward VII's coronation in London planned for that June. President Roosevelt, fearing that his daughter's presence would give the rough-riding First Family an inappropriate air of royal remove, vetoed the plan. He was right to be concerned. Papers across the country were starting to call her Princess Alice. She hated the name almost as much as she hated her father at the time for canceling her trip to Westminster Abbey.[*]

---

[*] Arguably, he did Alice a favor. Just two days before the coronation, the king was felled by

The kaiser, however, could not have been more pleased. He had sent his brother Prince Henry of Prussia to collect the *Meteor* from its shipyard. Henry seemed nervous, and perhaps a little cold, on that rainy February morning. On the other hand, Alice—"radiant in blue velvet"—seemed entirely in her element. She chatted with the prince in German, smiled at some of her girlfriends in the crowd, and enlisted Edith as her hand-maiden. "Here, Mamma, take my muff," she announced before grabbing the bottle of champagne and smashing it into the *Meteor*'s gleaming white hull with all the confidence of Cy Young on opening day. "Miss Roose-velt," said the *New York Times*, "was the most self-possessed person on the stand."[26] When the deed was done and the Roosevelt party was whisked away to a private lunch with the Germans, Prince Henry handed her a token of his brother's appreciation: a gold bracelet embossed with the kai-ser's portrait—made out of diamonds. Cousin Eleanor would surely not have approved.

Fortunately, Eleanor missed the coronation of Alice. With a little help from a beseeching letter to Grandmother Hall from Mlle Souvestre ("Eleanor has had the most admirable influence on the school," she wrote. "To me personally I feel I lose a dear friend in her"), Eleanor had been allowed to return to Allenswood for a third triumphant year.[27] She was treated a little like royalty herself. "When I arrived she was everything at the school, she was beloved by everybody," said Corinne Robinson, who overlapped with Eleanor during her cousin's last semester in England. "Saturdays we were allowed a *sortie* when we went to Putney, which had stores with flowers, books, etc. Girls had crushes and you bought violets or a book and you left them in the room of the girl you adored. Eleanor's room every Saturday would be decorated with flowers."[28]

She had to give all that up in the spring of 1902. With her eighteenth birthday approaching in October, her grandmother insisted that Eleanor return to New York and prepare for her own coming out. Alice had engi-neered her debut to fall in January, when she had the stage to herself; Elea-

---

appendicitis and forced to undergo emergency (and very risky) surgery. He initially resisted his doctors' advice, announcing that he was determined to go to Westminster Abbey in two days' time. They agreed that he would get there—as a corpse—if he didn't have the surgery. Edward gave in, and knighted his doctors in advance. The coronation was delayed until August 9, by which time the hordes of royalty and other notables who had come to London for the event had long-since packed up and returned home.

nor's would come in December, when she would be part of a traditional grouping of young women who were presented together and attended each other's functions. In fact, the cotillion class of 1902 included no fewer than five Roosevelt cousins: Eleanor, Christine (daughter of Theodore's first cousin Emlen), Elfrida (from Alfred, another first cousin), Dorothy (Hilborne, first cousin once removed), and Alice, who was technically still a deb and therefore attended many of the biggest balls, where she was sometimes billed as a "special guest." Some newspapers called the Roosevelt ladies "The Magic Five," perhaps because they couldn't always tell one from the other. "One of the Miss Roosevelts wore a fillet in her hair, and another, Miss Dorothy, had yellow orchids," was the reporting from the prestigious Assembly Ball, which was thrown at the Waldorf-Astoria by none other than Mrs. Astor.[29]

In fact, Eleanor left the Assembly Ball early, declaring the evening "utter agony." Like Alice's lukewarm verdict on her own triumphant affair, Eleanor was clearly overreacting. In later years, she would claim that she didn't know any of the girls at the ball and had felt like a stranger, which couldn't have been true given the sheer number of Roosevelt cousins alongside her. She might not have been the most popular deb at the ball, but she had her share of dancing partners, led by Auntie Bye's old Scottish friend Bob Ferguson and his circle of buddies in attendance. The truth was, she had never felt comfortable in social situations. Whatever confidence she stockpiled at her all-girls school evaporated in the face of coed interaction and expectation. "I imagine that I was well dressed, but there was absolutely nothing about me to attract anybody's attention," said Eleanor, who had her dresses for the season made in Paris. "I was homely. I was taller than a good many of the boys. And I still did not dance well."[30] Coming out, when a young woman was supposed to glitter and be gay in the harsh light of formal society, was hard enough for most girls. Eleanor was forced to shine in two considerable shadows: the one cast by her mother, who had been a legendary 1881 debutante; and the other by Alice, who was already the most famous deb in the country, if not in history.

And yet, the glamour gap didn't seem to affect the cousins' relationship with each other. Just after the frenzy created by her own coming out, Alice made a coed list of about two dozen names in her diary that she labeled "Those with whom I would like to go into seclusion with at a convent or a ranch." The first name on the list: Eleanor. During the full-blown cotillion season in December, the cousins were together almost every day. Alice sometimes stayed with Eleanor at the Halls' home on West Thirty-Seventh Street when she was in New York, and they were often together at meals, having tea with Aunt Bye, going to the theater, visiting friends, and embarking on various teenage-girl adventures. "Lunch at Eleanor's," Alice wrote in her diary on December 17, 1902. "She and I hunted around for a fortune teller this afternoon."[31]

There was one confidence, however, that the cousins did not share. Earlier that summer, Eleanor had been sitting quietly with a history book on the train from New York to Tivoli when a familiar voice interrupted her. "Hello, Eleanor," said her cousin Franklin. He was on his way home to Hyde Park, just twenty miles south of Grandmother Hall's house at Tivoli. "Hello, Franklin," she replied. "So you remember me," he said.[32] They hadn't seen each other since Alice pushed them together at Aunt Corinne's Christmas dance in 1898, when Eleanor was fourteen. But like two long-lost school pals who had run into each other on vacation, they fell into a warm conversation—other than the awkward moment when Eleanor asked after his parents, only to have Franklin report that his father died almost two years earlier. They spent more than an hour catching up before Franklin remembered that he'd left his mother sitting alone in the dining car.[33] "Won't you come and meet her?" he asked.[34]

Sara Roosevelt looked even more imperial, and intimidating, than usual, dressed in black from the top of her hat to the floor-length veils that signaled she was still in mourning for her husband. But she was delighted to see Eleanor. After all, she had been very fond of Eleanor's father—FDR's godfather—Elliott. They chatted amiably. Sara even remembered watching young Eleanor learn to waltz and polka in Mr. Dodsworth's dance class when she was fourteen. When the train stopped at Hyde Park, Franklin and his mother got up to leave. "You must come and visit us," said Sara, more brightly than you'd expect from a woman dressed in full mourning attire.

Eleanor did drop by Springwood, about a year later in the summer of 1903, but by then her visit carried more emotional freight than Franklin's protective mother could have imagined. Eleanor and Franklin saw each other off and on during her debutante season in the winter of 1902–1903: at the coming-out affairs of their cousins Christine and Dorothy; at Franklin's twenty-first birthday party, thrown by his half brother, Rosy;

and at the big horse show at Madison Square Garden, where he was Rosy's guest and Eleanor was with Rosy's daughter, Helen. They were also both invited to spend New Year's with the president and the extended Roosevelt family at the newly renovated White House. Eleanor took the train from New York to Washington with Alice and a group of friends and stayed at the White House, while Franklin bunked at Aunt Bye's. On New Year's Day, they watched the president greet his guests in the Blue Room, had tea with him and the family, and then lunch in the State Dining Room. That evening, the younger set went to the theater. "Sat near Eleanor," FDR wrote in his diary. "Very interesting day."[35]

Many of these were casual, unromantic encounters; the Roosevelt cousins were, after all, spokes in the same gleaming social wheel. But Franklin and Eleanor were clearly smitten with each other, even if she didn't entirely realize it at first. Two years older and a sophomore in college, Franklin already had a few romances under his belt, including an almost engagement earlier that year to a Boston beauty named Alice Sohier. Eleanor had no hormone-charged experience to draw from. In the spring of 1903, Franklin dropped by a children's dance and movement class that she was teaching in the housing projects of the Lower East Side, part of the social outreach program spearheaded by a new group of debutantes calling themselves the Junior League for the Promotion of the Settlement Movement. After meeting the tall, dapper man with the easy smile, Eleanor's schoolgirls began "demanding to know if he was my 'feller,' an expression that, believe it or not, had to be explained to me!" she said. "When I understood what it meant, I was amused, for I had not yet begun to think of Franklin that way."[36]

Still, she and her "feller" knew enough to tread lightly when it came to their uniquely blended families. If Grandmother Hall was overly protective of Eleanor, Sara was downright possessive of Franklin, and always had been. When he turned twelve, Sara refused to let him leave for Groton preparatory school, and as a result he always felt like a bit of an outsider among his classmates. When Franklin was sixteen and came down with a case of scarlet fever, his doctors told Sara she had to leave him alone to rest. Instead, she walked outside and climbed a ladder to his second-floor infirmary window, where she perched for hours reading, chatting, and fussing over him like a mother bird tending to her nesting chick.[37] She never liked being kept away from her boy. The pattern repeated itself when he left for college. Sara couldn't rightly refuse to let Franklin attend Harvard, so she went with him, renting an apartment in Boston for a few months in the winters. They ate dinner together often, and he occasionally spent the night with her in town.[38] She insisted later that she merely wanted to be "near enough to the University to be on hand should he want me and far enough removed not to interfere with his college life," though that apparently didn't preclude her from helping Franklin with his homework. (Franklin didn't seem to mind.)[39] Nor did it stop her from strongly advising him to break up with a young woman named Frances Dana, the granddaughter of Henry Wadsworth Longfellow. She was unsuitable, Mama informed him. After all, she was Catholic.

So it's not surprising that Franklin and Eleanor kept their growing relationship a secret for almost a year. Once, when he was out shopping in New York before Christmas, he hastily delivered his mother to her apartment in the Renaissance Hotel so that he could duck out for tea with Eleanor at 3:30.[40] He rarely even mentioned her by name in his diary. "E is an angel," he wrote after a cozy dinner cruise—with his mother and her nurse-chaperone in attendance, of course—on his sailboat, the *Half-Moon*.[41] Later still, FDR resorted to writing in full-blown code, with the numbers 1 to 6 in place of the vowels *A* to *Y* and bits of each consonant snipped off, so that a snoop would, in a sense, have to read between the missing lines to decipher the entry. On November 22, 1903, the translated code read, AFTER LUNCH I HAVE A NEVER TO BE FOR- GOTTEN WALK WITH MY DARLING.

It was on that walk, during a visit to Groton to check on her kid brother Hall, that Franklin proposed. One week later, right after Thanksgiving dinner with the Delano family, he broke the news to Mama. She was clearly not pleased. "Franklin gave me quite a startling announcement," she wrote in her journal.[42] They were too young, she told him. He still had to finish college, then law school. He listened but wouldn't bend. Five days later, Sara had Franklin deliver Eleanor to her in New York. "I had a long talk with the dear child," Sara wrote, which really meant that she laid down ground rules limiting Eleanor's trips to Boston.[43] She also threw a Hail Mary pass: she insisted that the love birds keep their engagement a secret for a year. Franklin, keenly aware that his mother controlled his inheritance, could not object. Eleanor, ever allergic to confrontation, wrote Sara a limp note the next day that sounded as if she were apologizing for breaking a piece of expensive china, which in a sense she had. She had shattered Sara's fantasy of keeping Franklin to herself. "I must write you and thank you for being so good to me yesterday. I know just how you feel & how hard it must be, but I do so want you to learn to love me a little," she said. "You must know that I will always try to do what you wish for I have grown to love you very dearly during the past summer."[44]

———

By the end of 1903, Alice had been engaged three or four times, at least according to the newspapers. Princess Alice was now the object of national, even international, fascination, ogled, emulated, and gossiped about unlike any young woman alive. Presidential children occasionally attracted attention, but Alice's moment in the spotlight was evolving into something larger. "The Horse Show in Chicago, which closed last Saturday night, came nearer being an Alice Roosevelt Show than anything else," a gossip rag called *Town Topics* reported more than a year after her grand White House debut. "Never did Chicago rudeness manifest itself more forcefully than in the gawking throng that paraded around the tanbark inclosure and, open-mouthed, paused and gazed out of countenance Exhibit A (Miss Roosevelt) in the Preston Gibson box. The increased financial success of this year's Show can be credited to the presence of the President's daughter."[45]

It helped that she was beautiful and poised, with high cheekbones, perfect posture, and angular eyes that looked as if they had been carved from a shiny, cool piece of Wedgwood china. The Alice-hungry press soon transformed that particular shade of blue-gray into "Alice Blue," which in turn became a favorite color for women's dresses. It was still popular more than a decade later, when the 1919 Broadway musical *Irene* featured a hit song called "Alice Blue Gown," in which a working-class girl sings about how she suddenly catches everyone's eye on the street when she wears her Alice Blue dress.

Though *Irene* had nothing to do with the real-life Alice, that song captured something of her situation. From the moment she moved into the White House, Alice recognized that people were interested not in her but in something far more superficial. "Lunch at Mrs. Congressman Jays, given in my honor," she wrote in her diary in January 1902, "or rather to give the wives and daughters of the congressmen the keen pleasure of meeting (not me, but) the 'President's daughter.'"[46]

And yet, she was more than happy to play the part, as long as she could do it on her own terms. Alice wasn't only the First Daughter; she was the First Teenager, hell-bent on raising adolescent defiance to a new level. She knew how much the press attention irked her parents—only semi-disreputable young women, such as actresses, got their names in the papers—so Alice hoarded publicity as if it were water in the desert. "Do not like the advertisements of your appearing at portrait show," her father telegrammed from Washington in November 1903, when he opened the morning paper and saw that she planned to appear at a charity event to benefit the New York Orthopaedic Hospital. "They distinctly convey the impression that any person who wishes to pay five dollars may be served with tea by you and Ethel Barrymore. I cannot consent to such use of your name and must ask you not to serve tea."[47] That was Ethel Barry-more, the *actress*, and Alice's fast friend. They served the tea as scheduled. "The family were always telling me, 'Beware of publicity!' And there was publicity hitting me in the face every day," she said. "And once the stories got out, or were invented, I was accused of *courting* publicity. I destroyed a savage letter on the subject from my father because I was so furious with him. There he was, one of the greatest experts in publicity there ever was, accusing me of trying to steal his limelight."[48]

Which was, of course, exactly what she was trying to do. Alice was right about one thing: the papers had a field day inventing stories about her, especially about her love life. At eighteen, finding a suitable husband was Job One of every proper young lady, and the nation followed the First Daughter with red-blooded gusto worthy of a Roosevelt big-game hunt. Never mind that her alleged fiancés were usually men she never even dated. The press got her hitched to a prominent army lieutenant in July 1902, one former Rough Rider in October, and another in February 1903.[49] They also reported at length on a fight with a childhood friend over the attention of the Earl of Yarmouth and the rivalry of two men (a Belgian versus a Bostonian) for her attention.[50] "Had a foolish temper fight with mother this morning," she wrote in her diary. "A newspaper saying [two men] in love with me."[51] Not long after, when the gossip had turned to talk of her making a trip across the Atlantic, a French magazine put her on its cover surrounded by the crown prince of Sweden, the prince of Greece, and two of the sons of the German emperor—the continent's most eligible bachelors.[52]

Alice never commented on any of these alleged liaisons (though at one point the president felt compelled to deny "in somewhat strenuous terms" that she was engaged to a Lieutenant Peter Sterling Clark).[53] They were really nothing more than the low-hanging fruit in her personal PR offensive, almost too easily dangled in front of gossipmongers. In order for Alice to establish her own identity in her father's shadow—for people to see beyond her Alice Blue gown—she needed to pioneer new rebel territory. Cigarettes gave her one outlet. At the turn of the century, proper women didn't smoke, so Alice did. "Father had said I was to never smoke under his roof, but I remember circumventing that rule by kneeling by the fireplace and puffing up the chimney," she said. "I also sat on the roof of the White House, smoking."[54] The *Washington Mirror* not only wrote an editorial taking Alice to task for lighting up in public but also blamed her personally for a spike in cigarette sales in the city.[55]

Young, independent women didn't have many role models at the turn of the twentieth century, but Alice was becoming one. After she took to carrying a walking stick—bamboo, with a silver handle, and mono-grammed with her initials—the papers predicted that the new style "can hardly fail to be widely copied."[56] To a country with one foot in the Victorian era and the other on the cusp of a new century, Alice deftly bridged the gap. She could, when she chose, perfume herself with poise, as she did at the *Meteor* launching. But she never failed to punctuate her presence with a knowing, devil-may-care smirk. "Miss Alice Roosevelt, the charming daughter of the president, called by some dyspeptic scribblers 'Princess Alice,' is unquestionably one of the most lovable girls of her age in the capital," wrote the *Washington Bee* in an editorial titled "Public Likes Miss Alice." "If the women who criticize her would just think for a moment of their own young womanhood, with its illusions and self-consciousness, they would be more charitable and quite ready to admit that Miss Alice, everything considered, is displaying a remarkable amount of tact."[57]

As that editorial implied, Alice's exploits did earn her a good number of detractors. When she and her friend Ellen Drexel Paul drove unchaperoned from Newport to Boston at breakneck speeds approaching twenty-five miles per hour, the country was scandalized by the fast young women—in both senses of the word. "Miss Roosevelt Loses Her Way," the *New York Herald* snarled.[58] Alice was delighted. For her next trick, she drove alone from Newport to Washington, then attempted to buy her own car, with $2,500 from her mother's inheritance money (roughly

$63,000 in 2015). "Hopes have been entertained by Miss Roosevelt's family that her infatuation for the auto was only a passing fancy," said the *Los Angeles Times*. "Even now it is doubtful if they know that she allowed a machine to be built especially for her with the belief she would buy it, and even selected the trimmings and upholstery for it."[59] Thanks to the *Los Angeles Times*, they knew now. Her father demanded that Alice cancel her car.

The *Times* reported that the president's dislike for Alice's auto fixation stemmed from his passion for horses, which was true. He also had a love-hate relationship with technology.* What angered him about cars, however, was their association with the nouveau riche, the only people who could afford to drive, not to mention to hire the de rigueur chauffeur. If Alice was spending her time motoring around the country, then she'd have to be rubbing elbows with a very unsavory crowd. "Alice has been at home very little—spending most of her time in Newport and elsewhere, associating with the Four Hundred—individuals with whom the other members of her family have exceedingly few affiliations," he wrote to his sister Corinne.[60] "He minded the idle rich. He considered them vulgar," Alice said. "But they were tribal friends, and they were the only people with big houses and big dances."[61]

Alice's introduction to the car culture came via Countess Marguerite Cassini, the glamorously reckless daughter of the czar's ambassador and, according to *Motor Age* magazine, "one of the most noted automobilists in Washington."[62] Cassini drove a four-cylinder, bright red convertible; when she wasn't joyriding with eligible young men, she lent it to Alice.[63] Maggie did everything fast, and with the First Daughter as her wing woman, they became the toast of Washington and beyond. One admirer, the inventor George Westinghouse, told the pair he'd throw a ball for as many invitees as they wished. Their list was so long he had to build an extension on his ballroom. But when the hundreds of orchids attached to the walls as decorations began to wilt forlornly, the ungrateful honorees skipped out early. "Our friendship had the violence of a bomb," Cassini wrote

---

* When a telephone was installed at Sagamore Hill, in 1902, he hated it so much he refused to answer it. But in August 1905, when the U.S. Navy brought one of its submarines to Oyster Bay for a presidential inspection, the president ordered the hatches closed, climbed aboard, and piloted the largely unproven vessel under the water for almost an hour. Not long after leaving office, in 1910, he became the first president to ride in an airplane.

in her memoirs. "We were two badly spoiled girls set only on their own pleasure."[64] James Hazen Hyde, whom the *Chicago Tribune* called one of "the seven most eligible bachelors in the United States," spent $100,000 on a Versailles-themed soiree in New York for the girls, complete with the corps de ballet from the Metropolitan Opera. On the morning before the party, however, Maggie and Alice received an invitation to dine at the private club of another stud in the *Tribune*'s Top 7: a dashing young congressman from Ohio named Nicholas Longworth. The girls sent Hyde a short telegram with their last-minute regrets and stayed in Washington with Longworth. (Franklin, however, did attend, though without Eleanor.)[65]

Cassini might have been her prime partner in crime, but Alice had another potent role model—or, rather, anti-model. While Alice was busy joyriding her way through the East Coast establishment, Eleanor was back in New York, devoting herself to a growing list of social causes. She volunteered with the National Consumers League, inspecting the working conditions—even the bathrooms—in garment sweatshops and department stores. She also took a "practical sociology" class because she thought it would help her understand the impoverished people she worked with at the Rivington Street settlement on the Lower East Side.[66] Eleanor was enormously proud of her work there. She brought Franklin along a few times, including once when they visited a student's tenement apartment. "When we got out on the street afterward he drew a long breath of air," Eleanor remembered. "'My God,' he said, aghast. 'I didn't know people lived like that!'"[67] Her friend Jean Reid worked with her, playing the piano while Eleanor taught the girls to dance, but they almost always arrived and left separately. Jean traveled by private carriage; Eleanor insisted on taking the elevated train or the Fourth Avenue streetcar, followed by a walk across the Bowery, one of the most unsavory streets in New York. "Needless to say, the streets filled me with a certain amount of terror and I often waited on a corner for a car, watching, with a great deal of trepidation, men come out of the saloons or shabby hotels nearby," she said. "But the children interested me enormously."[68]

Not everyone in her family approved of Eleanor's good works. Her cousin Susie Parish, with whom she lived now when she was in the city, was deathly afraid that Eleanor would contract some kind of disease from the children or from the teeming masses who used public transportation.

Franklin's mother, Sara, had similar fears, and before long she persuaded Eleanor to give up her work at the Rivington settlement.[*]

But no one disapproved of Eleanor's charity work as much as Alice. She'd long ago vowed to shrug off sympathy—or any tender emotion, really—associated with losing a mother. Eleanor veered in the opposite direction, spreading self-righteousness on top of a good deed as if it were icing on a cake. Hence her insistence on taking the streetcar. "Poor Eleanor! She took everything—most of all herself—so tremendously seriously. If only she had allowed a little levity into her life," Alice said. "Whereas she responded to her insecurity by being do-goody and virtuous I did by being boisterous and showing off."[69]

Her cousin's saintliness was only half her issue with Eleanor. The bigger problem was that Alice had hardened herself because that's what she believed her tough-minded father wanted; after all, he never even mentioned Alice's mother's name after she died. But Theodore not only accepted Eleanor's bleeding heart; he threw it back at Alice as evidence of his daughter's faults. "My father was always taking me to task for gallivanting with 'society,'" she said, "and for not knowing more people like my cousin Eleanor." Alice was becoming her own worst enemy. She acted out to get her father's attention, not to reinforce her feelings of being an outsider in the family. Yet it was Eleanor who was the do-gooder chip off her uncle's block, a fact that clearly pained Alice. "The same sort of thing was said about my cousin Eleanor being more like my father's daughter than I was," Alice said. "Odious comparisons that added nothing to family solidarity!"[70] Eleanor wasn't above laying it on thick either, such as the time she wrote to Franklin about running across Alice in New York "looking well but crazier than ever. I saw her this morning in Bobbie Goelet's auto quite alone with three other men! I wonder how you would like my tearing around like that."[71] Theodore couldn't have said it better himself. As a matter of fact, Gore Vidal, a friend of both Alice's and Eleanor's, later wrote that Eleanor and her uncle sounded alike: "His high-pitched voice and upper-class accent proved to be a joy for imitators, just as his niece Eleanor's voice—so very like his—was a staple of mimics for fifty years." And so the seeds of a rivalry were planted, plucked from not one but two

---

[*] In a neat little piece of irony, in 1934 the City of New York created the Sara D. Roosevelt Park, which to this day bisects Rivington Street, stopping traffic cold.

classic story lines: daughters competing for the patriarch's love, and the good girl versus the bad girl.

———

Needless to say, saintly Eleanor (and Franklin) followed Sara's orders to keep their relationship a secret, despite socializing together at family weddings, in Hyde Park, and on Campobello, the small Canadian island just off the northern coast of Maine that served as the family's summer retreat. "Eleanor and I went to Caroline Drayton's for lunch," Aunt Corinne's daughter, Corinne Robinson, wrote in her diary on July 18, 1904, seven months into the engagement that dared not speak its name. "Franklin Roosevelt arrived in the morning and it was very nice to see him again. I cannot decide whether it filled Eleanor with joy or not. I think he is very crazy about her, but she not about him. It is truly pathetic."[72] (Eleanor's faux cold shoulder might not have been the only cause of Corinne's confusion. Two months earlier, Corinne had recorded a "very warm day at Groton and what fun it all was. After tea, I went into Warren Robbins study with Franklin Roosevelt. Very naughty.")[73]

When the happy couple did finally reveal themselves to the world in November 1904, the Oyster Bay faction seemed genuinely delighted to reunite the two branches of the family in holy matrimony. (Make that *re*-reunite. That June, Franklin's half niece, Rosy's daughter Helen Roosevelt, had married Aunt Corinne's son Theodore Robinson at St. James' Church in Hyde Park. Alice and Eleanor were both bridesmaids.)[74] Franklin and Eleanor received gushing letters from the president, Edith, Auntie Bye, Aunt Corinne, and Alice, who wrote on White House stationery, "Oh! dearest Eleanor—it is simply too nice to be true you old fox not to tell me before. I can't begin to say how much I wish you the very very best of everything."[75]

Eleanor and Franklin had planned to marry in New York at her cousin Susie's house, and she asked if Uncle Ted would give her away. He had a better idea: Why not get married at the White House? "He feels that on that day he stands in your father's place and would like to have your marriage under his roof," Edith wrote to Eleanor. "We wish you to know how very glad we should be to do for you as we should do for Alice."[76] Eleanor declined the offer but agreed to schedule the ceremony for March 17, when the president would be in town to lead New York's big St. Patrick's

Day Parade. (It was also, as luck would have it, her mother's birthday.) Eleanor asked Alice to stand with her at the ceremony. "You angel to ask me to be your bridesmaid. I should love to above anything. It will be too wonderful."[77]

But first the family had an even bigger party to attend: President Roosevelt's inauguration, on March 4, 1905. Theodore Roosevelt had won reelection by a margin of 2.5 million votes, the landslide erasing his fear of going down in history as the "accidental president" who succeeded only because McKinley died in office. Even Franklin, the lifelong Democrat, crossed party lines to vote for Uncle Ted. The soon-to-be-married couple stayed at Auntie Bye's, arriving at the White House at 9:00 a.m. to wish the president good luck on his big day. They rode in the Roosevelt family procession to the Capitol, sitting just a few rows behind the president on the steps to watch the swearing-in ceremony, though the speech (most famous for the line "Much has been given us, and much will rightfully be expected from us") made very little impression on either Eleanor or Alice. Eleanor was overwhelmed by the events of the day. "I was very excited, but politics still meant little to me," she said. "So although I can remember the forceful manner in which Uncle Ted delivered his speech, I have no recollection of what he said."[78] Alice was, as usual, just interested in Alice. She wore a white toile dress and a white hat edged in black satin that looked, thanks to its army of decorative ostrich feathers saluting in the breeze, "the size of a not-so-small wheel," she said.[79] She sat—or stood, mostly—right behind her father on the viewing stand. "I was chided by him because I was waving to my friends and I said, 'Well, you do it. Why shouldn't I?'" she remembered. "And he said something to the effect of, 'But this is *my* inauguration.'"[80]

Upstaging one another was fast becoming a Roosevelt family sport. Two weeks later, the family made the trip north for Eleanor and Franklin's wedding in New York. The bride, by all accounts, looked truly lovely in a heavy white silk dress with a long train and capped sleeves, her grandmother Hall's rose-point Belgium lace veil, and a pearl collar necklace from her mother-in-law, Sara (by way of Tiffany, where it cost $4,000, or about $100,000 in 2015 dollars).[81] Even Alice approved. "I saw a picture of Eleanor at her wedding the other day and thought it was a picture of me at mine," she later recalled. "We looked so much alike."[82] Alice and the five other taffeta-wrapped bridesmaids led the wedding procession through the hundred guests lining the aisle in cousin Susie's town house; Franklin stood waiting at the altar in the drawing room with the officiant, his Groton mentor, Endicott Peabody. When Eleanor arrived at his side, she handed her wedding bouquet of lilies to Alice, standing beside her.[83] But it was the surrogate father of the bride who stole the show. Having made the 3:30 p.m. wedding a pit stop in the middle of the St. Patrick's Day Parade, the president had left the Ancient Hibernians wanting more. The crowd loitered outside on East Seventy-Sixth Street shouting, "We want Teddy!" occasionally drowning out Peabody.[84] When the bride had been kissed, Theodore turned to the groom and said, "Well, Franklin, there's nothing like keeping the name in the family!" Then he beat a path to the reception in the library—followed closely by every single guest. Franklin and Eleanor were left standing alone, like the proverbial bridesmaids at their own wedding.[85] "My father," Alice said with a sneer, "lived up to his reputation of being the bride at every wedding and the corpse at every funeral."[86]

By that time, Alice had just turned twenty-one and had begun zeroing in on a groom of her own. Her taste veered toward men with big personalities and bigger bank accounts. After all, she repeatedly overspent her annual $2,000 inheritance from her mother (about $50,000 in 2015 dollars); at eighteen, she wrote in her diary, "I swear to literally angle for an enormously rich man ... I cannot live without money."[87] She'd had a few serious crushes, including Robert "Bobby" Goelet (a New York land baron), J. Van Ness Philip (lawyer), Charles de Chambrun (French diplomat), and Arthur Iselin (from a banking family so wealthy there's an entire town in New Jersey named for it). But her most ardent admiration was saved for Nick Longworth, the same man for whom she and Maggie Cassini ditched James Hazen Hyde's mock Versailles ball.

The congressman met Alice's monetary requirements. The Longworths had been one of the richest families in Ohio, having made their fortune buying up land in and around Cincinnati and later turning some of it into Catawba grape vineyards. (A Longfellow poem called "Catawba Wine" was actually dedicated to Nick's great-grandfather.)[88] Nick was a first-rate violinist, a cracking raconteur, and, at thirty-five, a good fourteen years older than Alice. "I didn't particularly like boys. They were all over the place when I came out but there was I, one of those dear little virgins giving the older ones a good time," Alice said. "I always liked older men. A father complex coming out, presumably."[89] Nick fed her daddy issues in other ways: like Theodore, he was a short, mustached Harvard man (he even belonged to Roosevelt's beloved Porcellian Club) and a die-hard Republican. His political patron, the Ohioan William Howard Taft, later became Theodore Roosevelt's handpicked successor.

But Nick differed from Theodore in one telling way. He was a wild man: a gambler, a lothario, and a boozer, with morals as loose as TR's were ossified. It was one thing when a scandal sheet such as *Town Topics* identified Nick as "the gay young representative, who is as familiar with the role of Romeo in everyday life as he is with politics on the floor of the House."[90] It was another when Alice's own stepmother noticed his waywardness. "Your friend from Ohio," Edith told Alice, "drinks too much."[91] Of course, that was a big part of his appeal. He was a bad boy, but with credentials so impeccable her father couldn't possibly object. In fact, it was her father who had introduced them.

Alice was hardly the only Washington woman in Representative Romeo's sights. For a time he wooed her friend Eleanor "Cissy" Patterson, though the fact that Cissy was engaged to another man posed a slight problem. (Nick and Cissy still managed to carry on an affair years later after they were both married to other people.)[92] Before Alice had shown the slightest interest in him, Nick began pursuing her friend Maggie Cassini, who was introduced to him by the hostess at a lavish Massachusetts Avenue party. "Here is someone who wants to meet you," the hostess said as she presented Nick to Maggie. "Be careful; he's dangerous." Then she turned to Nick: "And you be careful because she is *very* dangerous."[93]

Together they became a toxic triangle. Alice, Maggie, and Nick romped around Washington just as you'd expect from Capitol Hill royalty, holding court at embassy parties and yacht outings, gossiping at House lunches, private teas, and dinners at the Alibi, Nick's bachelors' club where the members sometimes cooked for their guests. (Nick's specialty was Welsh rarebit and other haute chafing-dish cuisine.) They even hit the occasional taffy pull. "Everyone was sure Nick was going to marry either Alice or me—but which one was the question that so agitated them," Cassini said. "The reporters were in a spin trying to keep up with the latest development."[94]

To Maggie, this was all good, dirty fun. Not to Alice. Despite their friendship, she had always been wary of Maggie's reputation as a temptress. Alice had already lost Charles de Chambrun to Maggie the year before, only to have Maggie dump him after he fell for her.[95] (To complicate matters in this six-degrees-of-separation world, Nick's sister Clara was already married to de Chambrun's brother Adelbert.) But Nick was different. Alice was in love with him. Dozens and dozens of her diary entries, including the one written on the day of Eleanor's wedding, end with the words "Nick oh dear Nick." "I am sure she has him. N.B. Revenge on her," Alice wrote after Maggie skipped out on a horseback-riding date with her and lunched instead at Congressional Country Club alone with Nick. "Old nasty Maggie. I'll get even yet. See if I don't."[96] It was almost enough to turn her Alice Blue eyes a monstrous shade of green.

She had good reason to be jealous, for Nick was very much in love with Maggie. He proposed to her more than once, the last time at a sleighing party on a frosty night in Washington. At one point, en route near Lafayette Square, he stopped the carriage to fix the horse's harness, then took the opportunity to propose to her again. Her reply: "'All right,' I said, suddenly gathering up the reins. 'Here's my answer!' I flicked the horse with the whip, the sleigh bounded forward and Nick was left standing in the snow. How he got home I never found out."[97] Maggie promptly informed Alice, while they were perched together on the White House roof, carefully avoiding her father's no-smoking rule.[98] "It became more and more fun," Maggie said, "to tease my friends by trying to take their beaux away from them."[99] She didn't love Nick or Alice. She loved toying with them.

Alice and Nick's relationship ran hot and cold that winter and into the first half of 1905. It was saved by the Russians—or, rather, by President Roosevelt's determination to end the Russo-Japanese War before it threatened America's "open door" trade interests in Asia. Theodore Roosevelt had no love for the Russians; he considered them to be "colossal in their mendacity and trickery"[100] and the czar a "preposterous little creature."[101] And while he favored the Japanese and respected their superior military, he worried that if the war left them with too much unchecked power, they might start to eye the United States' newest Pacific outpost: the Philippines. So the president began to formulate a working cease-fire treaty: Japan would get to keep and colonize Korea, while Russia would cede what it had taken of Manchuria back to China but keep territory it needed to run the Trans-Siberian Railway. The problem was how to sell it. Both sides wanted to stop fighting—by the middle of 1905 the Japanese were winning, but they were also broke—yet neither wanted to lose face by seeming to capitulate. So the most grandstanding, media loving of presidents had to negotiate largely in secret, holding a series of meetings in Washington and at Sagamore Hill with diplomats from each country to hammer out all the details.

There was one element that required top secret treatment. In order to extract a promise from Japan to stay away from the Philippines, the president had to promise in turn that the rest of Asia would be free for Japanese expansion. There were two problems with this quid pro quo. First, while he could guide American foreign policy as president, Roosevelt couldn't effectively control it unilaterally. He had the constitutional power to negotiate treaties with foreign governments, but the Senate would still have to consent. In other words, while the deal between Russia and Japan could be hammered out privately, a broader regional solution involving the United States and committed to writing would open the door to rejection by other American politicians. In order to tap-dance around this problem, the president needed to make the strongest hand-shake agreement possible—by making a personal connection with the Japanese emperor himself.

Of course the president couldn't do the deed; that would blow his cover. So he decided to dispatch Secretary of War William Howard Taft on a trip to Asia. Taft had been America's first governor-general of the Philippines, so sending him to check on the colony's progress seemed credible enough. And because he was going to be in the Pacific region, Taft might as well drop in on the neighbors: Hawaii, China—and Japan. Amid all the fanfare of this Grand Asian Tour, Taft could sneak away for a one-on-one meeting with the emperor without raising much suspicion. Unfortunately, at 320 pounds Taft would require a whale of a distraction to escape the media unnoticed. Fortunately, the most distracting person in the world in 1905 was Alice Roosevelt.

Alice had already proven herself useful on international junkets. In 1902, as a consolation prize for reneging on his promise to send her to King Edward's coronation, her father posted her to Cuba for a month, where his buddy Leonard Wood, one of the Rough Riders, was the American-appointed military governor. The next year, she went to Puerto Rico on a three-week goodwill tour: "Welcome to Miss Alice Roosevelt" said the sign that greeted her in San Juan—written in fireworks. Whatever agita she caused her father at home, Alice made a point of behaving herself overseas. She never wanted to embarrass her father; she merely wanted his attention, and when he dispatched her as his ambassador, she was more than happy to serve him. "I had been very much pleased with all I had heard of how you acted in Porto Rico," he wrote her. "You were of real service down there because you made those people feel that you liked them and you took an interest in them."[102]

Alice's dive into Asian diplomacy carried a much higher degree of difficulty, however, not least because she was exponentially more famous in 1905 than she had been in Puerto Rico two years earlier. Her free-spirited exploits made headlines from the minute she boarded her private railcar on July 1, 1905, en route from Washington's Union Station to San Francisco, where the steamship *Manchuria* awaited her and the rest of Taft's forty-person entourage. In Nevada, she fired a revolver off the rear of the train at some telephone poles to celebrate July 4. In San Francisco, she ditched her chaperones (a senator's wife, her nurse, two friends from home, and Taft) and journeyed to the fringes of seedy Chinatown. And somewhere between Honolulu and Tokyo, she jumped, fully clothed, into the small swimming pool set up for her amusement on the deck of the *Manchuria*. The press's quippy headline for her pending Asian adventure: "Alice in Wonderland."

It was meant, mostly, as a compliment. Sure, there was the occasional sarcastic comment about Princess Alice and a serving or two of sour grapes.* But the truth is that Alice acquitted herself well on her four-month trip. She dined at the Japanese imperial palace and toured the royal gardens with the emperor himself, one of the few Westerners to ever see the grounds.[103] In the Philippines she was feted at Malacañang Palace and, wearing a traditional Filipina dress, shook hands with more than twenty-four hundred people at a party in her honor. "Even possessing eight trunks and a maid, with the necessity of a fresh frock for every occasion, with the knowledge of being the cynosure of all eyes every moment of the day

---

* A bit of it coming from Mrs. Taft, who didn't make the trip but fumed about it from afar. She was especially peeved, on vacation with her sons in Great Britain, when a British train conductor ignored what should have been a foolproof command for assistance: "I am Mrs. William Howard Taft of Washington ... My husband is the Secretary of War of the United States." Even worse, the conductor only snapped to attention when she added, "You must have heard of him. He's traveling now with Miss Alice Roosevelt." Cordery, *Alice*, 117.

and night most women would find the situation difficult, yet this young woman is as self-possessed as a princess and uses her tiny hand glass and powder puff with an unconcern which is the marvel of all observers," the *Manila Times* wrote.[104]

Most daunting of all was her stop in Beijing, where the Chinese were far less enamored of Americans, whom they viewed as pro-Japanese. Alice stayed at the summer palace of the dreaded dowager empress Cixi, who was said to have had her own son assassinated to preserve her hold on power and would soon do the same with her nephew the emperor Guangxu. Alice's lunch with the dowager empress was mediated by an interpreter, Dr. Wu Ting-fang, who had served two stints as minister to the United States. Dr. Wu initially stood between the two women as he translated, but after some sharp (and untranslated) words from the dowager empress, "the poor man turned quite gray, and got down on all fours, his forehead touching the ground," Alice said, and he continued to translate while prostrating himself.[105] The dowager had wanted to make it clear, Alice later realized, "that a man whom we accepted as an equal was no more than a lackey she could put her foot on."[106] Alice was fascinated— and well rewarded by the apparently charmed empress. She received gifts throughout her trip, but the dowager's were the most lavish, even if Alice found fault with a few of them: "Gold bracelets (set with rather inferior rubies), rings (lost those), jade and pearl earrings (still have those), some of those extraordinary long nail sheaths which they used to wear (I later made them into a brooch) and of course bolts and bolts of brocade."[107] It wasn't long before the newspapers amended their snappy description of her trip with an even snappier one: "Alice in Plunderland."

But the world wasn't just watching Alice. Not long after President Roosevelt asked her to join the Taft trip, one of the members of the House Foreign Affairs Committee signed on to the mission—Nicholas Longworth. The purported reason for his accompanying Taft was Nick's long-standing interest in Hawaii and the Philippines, but no one believed that. When Alice had visited Nick's family in Cincinnati the previous April, it made front-page news. The prospect of the two of them sailing the Pacific on a "floating palace" could only portend one thing, at least to the readers of the *Herald*: "Tropical Romance Anticipated."[108]

Alice and Nick did little to camouflage their deepening relationship; after all, part of her assignment was to be conspicuous, to deflect attention from Taft's cloak-and-dagger diplomacy. On Waikiki Beach, she and Nick and a few others frolicked in the waves for so long their floating palace sailed without them, and they had to be ferried out to catch the *Manchuria*.[109] Though their shipboard table included Taft and about a dozen other congressmen and their wives, the couple often acted as if they were the only people aboard the ship. "She and Nick indulge in conversations on subjects that are ordinarily tabooed between men and women much older than they are and indeed are usually confined to husband and wife," Taft wrote to his wife.[110]

It wasn't always the love boat. Alice had witnessed Nick's wandering eye before, and she still wasn't sure she could trust him. "Oh my heart, my heart, I can't bear it. I don't know what is the matter with me. Nick . . . looked at me . . . as if he didn't like me, and said he wouldn't play with me tomorrow morning and I feel as if I might die. He will go off and do something with some horrible woman, and it will kill me," she wrote in her diary in July.[111] They would eventually patch things up, as they did repeatedly during the years of their bipolar relationship. A few days later at dinner, she found herself standing next to Lloyd Griscom, an American foreign minister posted to Japan. "Do you see that old, bald-headed man scratching his ear over there?" Alice asked. "Do you mean Nick Long-worth?" Griscom replied. "Yes," said Alice. "Can you imagine any young girl marrying a fellow like that?" she asked. "Why, Alice," Griscom replied. "You couldn't find anybody nicer."[112]

Alice must have known that would be a minority view. When she returned home from Asia in mid-October, she broke the news with unusual care. While Nick was dispatched to the White House study to formally ask the president for his daughter's hand in marriage, Alice pinned down Edith—in the bathroom. She had contrived to break the news while her stepmother was brushing her teeth "so that she should have a moment to think before she said anything."[113] The news couldn't have been that much of a surprise. The papers had been buzzing about an engagement since the couple returned to American soil, some even speculating on the exact moment when Nick had popped the question. "Rumor says," reported one paper, "that the fateful question was put as they were entering the door of the Empress Dowager's palace in Peking, and that the affirmative came at the same spot as they emerged!"[114]

The only person who might have been left out of the matrimonial loop would have been Eleanor. While Alice had been working her magic throughout Asia, she and Franklin had been on a four-month honeymoon in Europe. Though regular letters from Sara kept them abreast of family news, the happy couple seemed blissfully ignorant of Alice's exploits, lost in their own fog of sightseeing, shopping, and connecting with relatives and friends, including lunch with the American ambassador in London, Theodore's old friend Whitelaw Reid. The Roosevelt connection didn't always suit them. When they checked into the legendary Brown's Hotel, they found themselves escorted to the Royal Suite, a $1,000-a-night palace within a palace that the hotel thought to be the only fitting place for the president's family. They moved out only a few days later. While they could certainly afford the hotel bill, Franklin and Eleanor—unlike Alice— weren't interested in traveling like royalty. "I am getting Eleanor a long sable cloak and a silver fox coat for myself," Franklin wrote to his mother, one of a series of jokes poking fun at his mother's old-money disdain for extravagance. "Don't believe *all* this letter please," wrote Eleanor as a sort of postscript. "I may be extravagant but—!!!" [115] (In the end, the joke was on FDR. When Sara went on a trip to Europe two years later, she discovered that Franklin had still not paid for some of his honeymoon purchases and fired off an angry letter to him in New York. "I am not accustomed to this way of doing business," she barked.) [116]

Eleanor was one of the few to receive word of Alice's nuptials directly from the bride-to-be. "Dearest Eleanor," she wrote on December 5, 1905, "I want to tell you of my engagement to Nick Longworth. I am trying not to announce it until the 17th so don't say anything about it until then. I hope you are surprised but I am much afraid you are not! Love to Franklin. It was too nice seeing you even for that brief moment the other day. A best love for yourself from Alice." [117] Alice didn't make it to her deadline; the papers printed the official announcement on December 14. It came complete with details on the wedding and the honeymoon, such as the line in the *New York Times* that read, "Miss Roosevelt has not yet decided on her bridesmaids, who probably will be chosen from her cousins in New York." [118] That, like so much of the news about Alice, would prove to be wrong.

# Chapter 3

# DOMESTIC AFFAIRS

⚜

Even a U.S. congressman has to apply for his own wedding license, and on February 15, 1906, two days before his scheduled nuptials, Nick headed to the District Supreme Court in Washington to complete the paperwork. He arrived late, fifteen minutes after the 4:00 p.m. closing time, and with four wisecracking groomsmen in tow. The court clerk overlooked the buddies' ribbing of Longworth: Are you sure you've got the $1 license fee? the best man asked him. Are you really thirty-six years old? But the clerk wasn't going to tolerate any funny business when it came to the official procedures. Any previous marriages? he asked, checking off the items on his lengthy list. No, said Nick. Born in this country? Yes, Nick said. "This begins to look like a case of hazing," said one of the smirking groomsmen. How about the future bride? the clerk asked. How old is she? What is her father's full name? Where does the family live? Nick tried to keep smiling along with his pals, yet he couldn't help but sigh and mop his forehead anxiously. And no wonder: he was facing perhaps the only person in the free world who could ask for Alice Roosevelt's address with a straight face.[1]

Nick and Alice only gave themselves two months between announcing their engagement and their February 17, 1906, wedding day. It was a relatively short window that only served to magnify the frenzy of attention, like a big football game with the clock winding down. The press tailed Alice nearly everywhere: to dinners and doctor's appointments, on trains and ferries, and most of all to destinations that might unearth any detail of the wedding day itself. When she and Nick spent an early February afternoon shopping in New York at Fifth Avenue dress shops, they literally stopped traffic. It took half a dozen mounted Gotham policemen to clear the crowds that gathered to ogle the happy couple.[2]

The hoi polloi weren't the only ones jockeying for position. Official Washington and establishment New York were both desperate to get ringside seats for the ceremony, a problem considering that the White House East Room would only hold about eight hundred guests. Some folks with middling connections sent gifts before the invitations were mailed, in hopes of improving their chances. Others made conspicuous plans to be out of town, to avoid any embarrassment at being snubbed. "Everybody who has the slightest reason for expecting one of these priceless pasteboards is on the *qui vivre*, hoping, fearing, and planning," said the *Baltimore Sun* the week before the family mailed out the invitations.[3]

The first gift to arrive was actually charmingly humble: a bunch of turnips, sent by a Kansas farmer "who says the tillers of the soil shall not be outdone by the jewelers," reported the *New York Times*.[4] It was a short-lived victory for the tillers. The press positively salivated over the most lavish gifts: a $25,000 pearl necklace from the Cuban government; a $40,000 Gobelin tapestry from France; a diamond bracelet from the kaiser to match the one he gave her at the *Meteor* christening; and a whole treasure chest from her friend the dowager empress of China, which included jewelry, bolts and bolts of fabric laced with gold thread, and two fur coats— one ermine, one white fox.[5] The bride salivated, too. "There was fantastic exaggeration about my wedding presents, so far as the number and grandeur was concerned," Alice said later. "I had about the sort of presents that any girl gets from her relatives and friends and friends of the family, with the exception of a few from foreign potentates."[6] She was right to be defensive; not everyone was so enchanted by the 24-karat wedding news. When the Ohio House passed a bipartisan resolution congratulating its native son on his wedding, Senator P. W. Ward bashed it as "undignified"[7] and "a joke."[8] "While it might do in a monarchy for the representatives of the people to congratulate the ruling powers on such an event, it was in bad taste for this nation," Ward said, and he squashed the resolution like a cockroach.[9]

Remarkably, Ward's wrath was by far the minority view. In fact, working-class Americans went out of their way to congratulate and celebrate Princess Alice. Some sent homespun presents: baked goods, stuffed animals, even a railcar full of coal, courtesy of the United Mine Workers of America.[10] In New York, the Deaf-Mutes' Union League stopped its annual dinner to deliver a special toast to Alice, which the *New York Times* said "was received with wild (but mute) enthusiasm."[11] In Boston, the bells on every public building and many of the churches pealed for fifteen minutes, as ordered by Mayor John "Honey Fitz" Fitzgerald.* And in Pittsburgh on the day of the wedding, roughly two thousand young women working at downtown department stores left their counters and walked to a nearby newspaper office so they could watch the official press bulletins about the wedding come over the wire. "They all seemed as thoroughly happy as though they had been personally concerned," the *New York Times* said.[12]

No one would be happier to hear that than the father of the bride. TR owed much of his political success to his everyman image, which he cultivated amid the tumbleweeds of his Harvard degree, his Long Island estate, and his polo ponies. The Roosevelt children played a supporting role in that just-folks portrait. It was why he'd fumed when Alice frolicked in Newport and among the snobs of Mrs. Astor's 400, why he pointedly enrolled his sons at the local Oyster Bay primary school along with the sons of the village's servants (and made far less notice of shipping them off to Groton in their later years). He was (and still is) the youngest man to become president, and his irrepressible family underscored his vitality. "One of the great political assets for Theodore Roosevelt was the perception of him as a special father with a harmonious and engaging set of children," one scholar noted.[13]

They were not the first conspicuously precocious offspring to invade the executive mansion. Forty years before, young Tad Lincoln set up a stand on the front lawn to charge admission to visitors; he once hitched the White House goats to a chair and drove his improvised sleigh through one of his mother's receptions. But the Roosevelts had *six* rambunctious kids (well, five plus demure Ethel), and the evidence of their spirited lives practically perfumed the place, as did their pet guinea pigs, roosters, lizard, bear, rabbits, and blue macaw. When nine-year-old Archie was sick in bed with the measles, Quentin and Kermit loaded their pony, Algonquin, into the White House elevator so he could pay a get-well visit to their brother

---

* Maternal grandfather of President John Fitzgerald Kennedy.

in his second-floor bedroom. Alice herself frequently strolled into official social functions with a green garter snake called Emily Spinach, named for its color and for her stepmother's rail-thin, old-maid sister, Emily Carow.

It's no accident that perhaps the most famous quotation about Alice grew out of her frolicking around the White House as if it were her private playground. One day during Theodore's first term, his old college buddy Owen Wister, who wrote *The Virginian* and other best-selling novels, dropped by for a visit. As the two men were chatting in the president's private office about preserving a national forest in Wyoming, Alice (with Emily Spinach) bounded in to say hello, then bounded out just as quickly. After the men resumed their talk, she barged in again to ask her father a question and left again. Just as Wister was regaining his train of thought, Alice arrived for the third time. "Alice," said her father, "the next time you come I'll throw you out the window!"[14] When Wister turned to the president to ask why he couldn't do anything about Alice's manners, Theodore replied, "I can run the country or I could control Alice. I can't possibly do both."[15]

At least that's the way Alice told the story, and the way it's recorded in all her biographies. Except that's not exactly what Wister said. In Wister's own telling, he and the president merely concluded their chat with Theodore's writing him a note intended to help with the Wyoming forest. It was Wister who inserted the "I could control Alice" quip into his memoir, explaining that "a friend once asked" the president what he could do about Alice. (Wister never mentions the snake, either.) Does this mean the story is apocryphal? Not necessarily. But the Oyster Bay Roosevelts were certainly eager to co-opt the homespun narrative: spirited child, befuddled parent—just like *Leave It to Beaver*.

As PR campaigns go, Alice's wedding was a case study in media manipulation. The details of the dress (white silk trimmed in satin and lace and embroidered with the Roosevelt family coat of arms, a twelve-foot train, and, most important of all, "not a particle of Oriental material")[16] were spoon-fed to the papers, much to their dismay. "For some reason best known to the president, but not understood by friends of the family— especially the feminine friends—extraordinary measures have been taken by Mr. Roosevelt to prevent publicity being given to any details of the trousseau," whined the *New York Times*.[17] There were no photographs taken of the event itself; no reporters allowed inside. There weren't any bridesmaids, either. Alice had been expected to select her sister, Ethel, or

Corinne Robinson, her last unmarried first cousin. She chose not to share her limelight.

Instead, she commandeered it. After the brief, fifteen-minute ceremony, the family and some close friends headed to a private dining room in the White House for a reception brunch. (The little people—a.k.a. the Supreme Court justices, the congressmen, the various foreign dignitaries—were shunted off to their own reception in the State Dining Room.) When it came time to slice the three-tiered wedding cake (romantically dappled with orange blossoms and doves), the knife provided proved too feeble for the job. Alice promptly turned to one of the White House military aides, grabbed his sword, and hacked away. Her father might have stolen the show at Eleanor's wedding, where the guests, mesmerized by Uncle Ted's war stories, didn't even bother to watch her cut her cake. But no one was going to upstage Alice.

———

Eleanor herself didn't attend the Longworth wedding. She was six months pregnant with her first child and therefore deemed unfit to be seen in polite society. So Franklin took Mama. "Alice looked remarkably pretty and her manner was very charming," Sara reported to Eleanor.[18] She didn't mention Franklin's cameo in the proceedings, but it was one of Alice's favorite moments. "The only funny incident I recall was when we—Nick, myself, and my father—were just about to be photographed in the Oval Room, and my veil had become disarranged and someone said, 'Who is tall enough to adjust the bride's veil?' And up popped Franklin to do the job. I wish I had a picture of *that*."[19]

Less than three months later, Eleanor gave birth to Anna Eleanor (the Roosevelts were fond of recycling girls names, too) on May 3, 1906. Eleanor would later admit that she struggled mightily, and often unsuccessfully, with the demands of motherhood. Her own mother, more interested in high society than in the rich but ordinary thrills of parenthood, wasn't much of a role model. Neither was her grandmother. As a child, her most nurturing relationships had been with Aunt Bye and with her father, when he wasn't propped up at the local bar or locked up in a sanitorium. As a result Eleanor was a deeply insecure parent. She hired strict French or English nurses, nannies, and governesses and allowed them, not her, to be the boss. "If I had it to do over again, I now know that what we should have done was to have no servants those first few years," she said. "My children would have had far happier childhoods."[20] She would listen to almost anything but her own instincts. One winter morning a neighbor called the family's New York City home and threatened to alert the Society for the Prevention of Cruelty to Children because one-year-old Anna was crying her head off—again. Eleanor liked to put Anna in a makeshift metal cage on the windowsill to get fresh air during her nap, but she refused to comfort the baby when she started to wail. "I thought I was being a most modern mother," Eleanor confessed. "I knew you should not pick up a baby when it cried, that fresh air was very necessary, but I learned later that the sun is more important than the air, and I had her on the shady side of the house!"[21]

It didn't help that she spent the first decade of her married life, as Eleanor noted, "just getting over having a baby or getting ready to have one"—six children in ten years.[22] Nor did it help that the third born, Franklin junior, died when he was less than eight months old of influenza, pneumonia, and a weakened heart. "To this day," she wrote twenty-eight years later, "I can stand by his tiny little stone in the churchyard and see the little group of people gathered around his tiny coffin and remember how cruel it seemed to leave him out there alone in the cold."[23]

But the biggest blockade between Eleanor and her children was erected by her mother-in-law. Sara Roosevelt was used to being the boss; she had been overseeing the family's sizable estate and finances since her husband died in 1900, and she had run much of Franklin's life since, well, forever. It was only natural—at least to Sara—that she should raise the next generation, too. She would hire the domestic staff for Franklin and Eleanor, inform them when to call the pediatrician, babysit when the parents were away, and rule (or sometimes overrule) on any and all child-rearing techniques. Her explanation to her grandchildren for usurping Eleanor's authority was simple: "Your mother only bore you. I am more your mother than your mother is."[24] Fiat by Sara lasted well into the children's adulthood. When James was in college, he bought a convertible that he ruined one winter night when he left the top down just before a blizzard. He asked his parents to buy him a new car, and when they refused, he went straight to Granny. She promptly replaced the old car with a new—and better—one. A few years later, when Franklin junior[*]

---

[*] Having lost baby Franklin in 1909, the Roosevelts would also name this child Franklin junior, when he was born on August 17, 1914.

was in an auto accident and his parents were unsympathetic, she did the same thing.

There was no better symbol of Sara's hegemony than the home she had built on New York's East Sixty-Fifth Street. She had long insisted that Franklin and Eleanor would need space for a growing family. As a Christmas present to them in 1905, she bought the lot at 49 East Sixty-Fifth Street. As a present to herself, she bought the adjoining lot, at 47 East Sixty-Fifth—and enlisted an architect to design the two houses as twins. The six-story brownstones shared their entryway and featured sliding doors that connected the two buildings on three floors, at their dining rooms, drawing rooms, and a space on the fourth floor where the children slept. A few weeks after the families moved in, FDR walked into the master bedroom and found Eleanor sitting at her dressing table in tears. "I said I did not like to live in a house which was not in any way mine, one that I had done nothing about and which did not represent the way I wanted to live," she said later.[25] That wasn't entirely true; FDR and ER had reviewed and even amended the architect's plans and shopped for at least some of the contents. The problem was Mama. She already controlled big swaths of ER's daily life (mandatory walks together every morning at 10:00, joint embroidery classes, regular lunches, weekly trips to the theater with Franklin, not to mention the children). The conjoined houses meant that ER could never escape her mother-in-law. "You were never quite sure when she would appear," Eleanor said, "day or night."[26]

———

Alice might have avoided the kind of wedding Eleanor endured, but she stepped into an astonishingly similar marriage. Nick was a hard-driving, hard-partying, Harvard-educated lawyer with an eye for the ladies, a trait Eleanor had yet to discover in her husband. Also like Franklin, Nick brought to the marriage a widowed, overbearing mother-in-law. He wasn't an only child, but Nick was Susan Longworth's only son, which meant she treated her quick-witted, violin-virtuoso baby boy (nicknamed Colie) like a demigod just the same. "They were devoted to one another and she was completely absorbed in everything that concerned him," Alice said.[27] When he was first elected to Congress, in 1902, Susan moved to Washington with him, "so as to keep in touch with the details of her adored Colie's public life," said his sister Clara.[28] When every newspaper in the country was reporting that Nick and Alice were going to get engaged, Susan refused to believe it, even after Taft himself gave her the news. "He is a thoroughly confirmed bachelor," Mrs. Longworth informed Taft.[29] (Nick and Alice were engaged two months later.) She was determined to remain the most important woman in his life. In fact, she was determined about everything. "She was a rather formidable lady who was better dressed and straighter backed than anyone in Cincinnati," Alice said. "I see her now leaving the house in a carriage with a stream of little furs indecently assaulting each other round her neck and down her front."[30]

By "the house," Alice meant the family estate in Cincinnati, an ivy-covered brick manse called Rookwood (not to be confused with FDR's family home, Springwood). At the time of their wedding, the *Chicago Daily Tribune* called it "one of the most interesting as well as one of the most beautiful houses in the country."[31] Alice begged to differ. "Rookwood," she said, "was *enchanting*, it was so awful. It was Hudson River Bracketed. The sort of thing Franklin's family had before they turned it into Long Island Georgian."[32] It didn't help that she had to share the place with Mummy. Susan vacated Nick's house in Washington when he got married, but she wasn't going to cede Rookwood to an unwelcome daughter-in-law. "So there she and I were, in the absurd, yet none the less trying, mother-in-law and daughter-in-law situation of the comic papers," Alice said. "I know how hard it was for her to have him marry at all, and I was not some one who 'merged' with the family she married into; not by a long shot."[33] Behind her back, she called Susan "bromide," either because Alice found the straight-backed midwesterner a tad boring or because spending time with her was like being forced to take medicine. She felt that way about much of her time at the Longworth family home. "There were a good many musical evenings at Rookwood—as often as three times a week," Alice grumbled. "Anyone caught starting a conversation during the music was shut up in the dining room. Once in a state of boredom bordering on stupefaction I said to the ardent music lover sitting next to me, 'Isn't it extraordinary to think that Mozart never composed anything exclusively for the viola?' He looked at me perplexed for the rest of the evening."[34]

Moving into Rookwood didn't bother her nearly as much as moving out of her previous home. "Everyone knew that Alice wanted a 99-year lease on the White House," said one Ohioan.[35] She spent as much time as she could in Washington, even when Congress wasn't in session and Nick was in Cincinnati. "With the perversity of human nature, having become removed from them by marriage, I became aware of how delightful families are," Alice said. "I think I saw more of the family during the three winters after I married—the last three winters that they were in the White House—than I did during the entire five that went before."[36] Alice's relationship with her stepmother magically improved; her favorite hideaway became Edith's bedroom overlooking the Ellipse and the Washington Monument, where she would repair in the afternoons to gossip with her stepmother, her siblings, and her father, when he could break away. In 1907, Alice had to have her appendix removed. Rather than have the surgery back in Ohio, or even in a hospital, she opted for a make-shift operating room created in the Rose Bedroom at 1600 Pennsylvania Avenue, where she also spent her recovery.[37]

The one magnet that could pull Alice back to Ohio was politics. Of course, she'd been in and around the political arena from the day she was born: her father missed getting home for her birth because he couldn't tear himself away from his desk in the New York State Assembly. But she never filled her dance card with the grind of campaigning, legislation, and the like unless there was a big party or high-profile ribbon cutting in the offing. That changed when she got married. For one thing, she genuinely loved Nick. She also loved being useful—being needed—and as a rising politician Nick needed his famous young wife on the trail with him. She signed up for a full helping of campaign whistle-stops and small-town shindigs, smiling and shaking hands as if she really wanted to be there. In a way, she did. Alice also loved being the center of attention, and there was no question that the large crowds that came to greet Representative Longworth in Cincinnati and elsewhere were there primarily to catch a glimpse of Mrs. Longworth, "the Daughter of the Nation and the dearly beloved stepdaughter of the Queen City," as one paper called her.[38] So beloved, in fact, that when the Cincinnati Zoo acquired a baby elephant in the fall of 1906, it was promptly named Alice.

Fun as it was—and Alice always loved a good laugh—the adulation had its serious ramifications. One newspaper declared that if her name were on the ballot instead of Nick's, "what a landslide there would be!"[39] It was the kind of emasculating remark that would, over the years, take its toll on the Longworth marriage. On September 14, 1906, more than fifty thousand people turned out in Columbus to watch the Longworths unveil a statue of Ohio's own dearly departed president McKinley. The event was supposed to start with an invocation by the Reverend Dr. Washington Gladden, but he only got out a few sentences before the audience shouted him off the stage, demanding to see Alice. With the crowd getting rowdier by the minute, she quickly stood up from her seat on the dais, walked to the podium, and tugged on a string that pulled back a curtain of flags, revealing the statue. That only made the crowd crazier. They surged toward the stage, grabbing at the flags and trampling at least two women. Alice and Nick were forced to climb through a window in the Ohio state capitol, which overlooked the plaza, only to be chased into the governor's office, then out of the building entirely. They finally took refuge in another building across the street until a carriage arrived to rescue them. "It was the worst crush I ever witnessed," Alice said. "I have seen nothing like it in my trip around the world."[40]

But that didn't dampen Alice's enthusiasm for politics—far from it. She became increasingly fascinated by the battle, much to the surprise of her worldwide audience. "'Princess Alice,' social butterfly, whose erratic traveling flights kept society guessing over her movements has disappeared completely," wrote one newspaper. "In her place the people of Ohio have discovered Mrs. Nicholas Longworth, woman politician."[41] As the 1908 election approached, she became positively obsessed with the campaign. Theodore, having impetuously announced during the 1904 race that he would not seek a third term,* took it upon himself to anoint his successor—such was his popularity and power within the Republican Party. When he picked Alice's old Asia cruising buddy Taft, she became a quasi adviser to her father. The fact that the Tafts and the Longworths were longtime Ohio compatriots only made Alice's involvement more valuable—and her stake in the outcome all the more personal.

The problem was that she didn't like the idea of Taft, or anybody else, stepping into her father's presidential shoes, even if he'd kicked them off himself. "No one will ever know how much I wished, in the black depths of my heart, that 'something would happen' and that Father would be renominated," she said. "It was against human nature, against mine anyway,

---

* The Twenty-Second Amendment, limiting presidents to two terms, wasn't ratified until 1951, after a *different* Roosevelt won four elections to the White House.

not to feel the prospect of all those great times coming to an end was something to be regretted, though most secretly."[42] Still, she did her part. When Taft returned from another trip to the Philippines in the summer of 1907, Theodore escorted him to Alice's recovery room in the White House so the two Roosevelts could coach him on an important pre-campaign speech in Boston. What red-blooded issues did he plan to discuss? they asked him. The Philippines, Taft said. Theodore and Alice were apoplectic to the point of laughter. "Indeed, I was so emphatic that one of the stitches in my scar broke," she said.[43]

The next year, she went to the Republican National Convention in Chicago, beginning an unbroken streak of convention attendance that would continue through the next six decades. "It was my first convention," she said, "and it gave me a taste for that form of entertainment that I do not think I shall ever get over."[44] As usual, she attracted almost as much attention as the main event, with women giving up their seats—or sometimes just standing on them—to get a look at her.[45] She created an especially big commotion when, ensconced in the front row, she refused to take off her towering Merry Widow hat despite requests from two election officials who explained she was blocking others' view. "I shan't and you shan't make me," she barked at Nick when he told her she was making a scene. "Alice, I want you to take off your hat," he replied. She finally, reluctantly, relented, earning Nick a sarcastic little newspaper headline: "Longworth Boss of the Family."[46]

With Roosevelt's backing, Taft walked away with the nomination and the general election, handing the Democratic flamethrower William Jennings Bryan his third straight loss. The family slowly made peace with its impending return to civilian life. Theodore, like Santa Claus without the red suit, proceeded to parcel out countless White House artifacts to the steady stream of friends and family who dropped by for a final White House visit. "Why mother, he has given away nearly everything in the study, and Aunty Corinne and nearly every other guest in the White House have their arms full of pictures, books, and souvenirs," Ethel reported to Edith one evening.[47] The Roosevelts invited the Tafts to dinner on the night before the inauguration. Alice was not pleased. "No one likes to leave the White House, whatever they say," she said. "There is a photograph of the whole family about to leave and I must say, we look as if we are being expelled from the Garden of Eden."[48] Just for good measure, Alice left behind her own snake in the grass: she planted a voodoo doll in a White House garden as a sort of ill-will gesture to her father's successor. "Perhaps someone will find it some day and say, 'How strange!'" she said.[49]

———

Despite being seven months pregnant with ill-fated Franklin junior, Eleanor accompanied Franklin on their own final visit to her uncle's White House, on January 7, 1909, joining twelve hundred guests at the president's farewell reception to the diplomatic corps. Alice left early that evening with a cold, but Eleanor noticed that her usual effervescence had gone a little flat. "She looks lovely & very well & so quiet!" she wrote to a friend.[50] As they both approached twenty-five, the cousins didn't see much of each other, except when Eleanor could steal away to Washington or Alice to New York. They mostly kept in touch via chipper cards and the occasional news of yet another of Eleanor's pregnancies, followed by a new-baby gift.[51]

Yet their lives continued to mirror each other in remarkable ways—this time as political wives. FDR had idolized Theodore since his swashbuckling cousin dropped in for a visit to the Groton School when Franklin was a student there, and the regular stays at the White House only solidified the connection. As Theodore Roosevelt's second term was winding down, Franklin boasted to his co-workers at the New York City law firm where he worked that he intended to follow his cousin Ted to the White House someday. He even planned to march the same route: state assembly, assistant secretary of the navy, governor, president.[52] It was a somewhat surprising assertion, given that FDR had shown far more interest in journalism than in politics; he never even graduated from Columbia Law School (though he did pass the New York bar).

But about a year after their farewell visit to the Roosevelt White House, the acorn of FDR's plan began to root. A group of Democrats in the district that included Hyde Park needed someone to run for an open seat in the New York State Assembly. They approached Franklin one spring day in 1910 at a local cattle auction. He dithered. It wasn't because of his uncertain party affiliation (even if the first man he ever voted for was a Republican—his cousin Theodore) but because he needed to get Sara's approval first. That wasn't just the usual mama's boy dynamic at work. FDR was expected to finance his own campaign, and Sara controlled the cash. "Frank, the men who are looking out that window are waiting for your answer," said Ed Perkins, the Dutchess County Democratic Party chairman, who turned up the heat by driving FDR to meet a group of potential backers he'd assembled at a bank in Poughkeepsie. "They won't like to hear that you had to ask your mother."[53] FDR took the plunge, and he kept going even after the Democrats asked him to step up in class and run instead for the local seat in the state senate, which the Republicans had only lost once in history.

Eleanor strongly supported Franklin's new zeal. She couldn't campaign with him, on account of the children. But she wrote him encouraging letters while he barnstormed the district in a red convertible (like Alice's) and fretted over him at the one speech she was able to attend. "He looked thin, then, tall, high-strung, and at times nervous," she remembered. "He spoke slowly, and every now and then there would be a long pause, and I would be worried for fear he would never go on." But he won, and in January 1911, the entire family (Franklin, Eleanor, three children, their respective nurses, and three servants) moved full-time to the state capital of Albany.

Eleanor was delighted. She and Franklin hosted a New Year's reception for constituents at their rented house, the first of many political gatherings at the Roosevelts'. True to cousin Theodore's form, Franklin quickly took over the insurgent wing of his party, a group of about thirty men opposed to the Tammany Hall political bosses who controlled the Democrats, especially a candidate for the U.S. Senate named William "Blue-Eyed Billy" Sheehan.[54] FDR and his compatriots would sometimes spend the entire day plotting strategy in the family's living room. Before long, their house became saturated with smoke, and Eleanor had to move the children's bedroom up to the third floor so they could breathe fresh air at night. It was her first peek behind the political curtain, and while it took years for her to become active in her own right, she welcomed the chance to be involved, even if that meant mostly serving the snacks, charming the wives, and humoring the pols. "I still remember the poems which Assemblyman Ed Terry from Brooklyn used to bring and read me," she said. "I was learning that the first requisite of a politician's wife is always to be able to manage everything."[55] Like Alice, she longed to be useful, needed. It didn't hurt that her mother-in-law was seventy miles away in Hyde Park. "For the first time in my life," she said, "I was going to live on my own."[56]

After only one term in Albany, twenty-nine-year-old Franklin had made enough of a name for himself—not to mention made the most of his family name—that the national party took notice. In the fall of 1911, he traveled to Trenton to meet with New Jersey's governor, Woodrow Wilson, a progressive who was viewed as a likely Democratic candidate for president. Franklin warned Wilson that his chances in New York were slim, given how much power the Tammany troops still wielded. But Franklin was charming and eager and, despite his youth, an extraordinarily nimble politician. That was never more true than in his own 1912 reelection campaign for New York State Senate. One September night when he and Eleanor were in Manhattan for dinner, Franklin became violently ill with a high fever and severe stomach cramps. After feeling terrible for almost two weeks, he was finally diagnosed with typhoid and ordered by the doctor to stay in bed indefinitely. The election was less than two months away. Even more perilous, Franklin's constituents lived at least seventy-five miles north of his New York City sickbed.

Desperate to keep his campaign alive, Eleanor suggested that he contact the "rather gnome-like looking little newspaper man from Albany" who had been so supportive of FDR's early career and moonlighted as a political operative.[57] Louis Howe did come across like someone who spent most of his time foraging underground. He was scrawny, pockmarked, and gruff, with wrinkled suits and the stench of cigarettes that followed him like industrial smog. He himself maintained he was "one of the four ugliest men in New York."[58] But he was also a veritable oracle of politics. He once began a letter to FDR with the salutation "Beloved and Revered Future President."[59] Howe wrote that letter in 1912—twenty years before FDR's first White House victory.

When Eleanor reached Howe, an unemployed father of two at the time, he accepted the job on the spot, both for the money and for the unusual challenge. He took FDR's blank checkbook and used it to fund his own brand of political black magic, a potion that was equal parts flooding the district with the Roosevelt name and drowning his opponents in the muck of dirty campaign tricks. On the positive side, he bought full-page newspaper ads announcing FDR's support for the workingman and for women's suffrage. He also mailed off thousands of "personal" letters (on which he forged FDR's signature) to apple farmers and Hudson River fishermen promising industry-friendly legislation.[60] Among his shadier ploys: planting an obviously false story in a local paper claiming that FDR (who was still sick in bed) had rescued a family in Pawling, New York, when their house caught on fire. He also chauffeured a monsignor from Fishkill around the district in FDR's red touring car to undercut claims that Roosevelt was anti-Catholic.[61] Toward the end of the campaign, Howe created the "Franklin D. Roosevelt Club," whose chief task was handing out $5 checks on Election Day.[62] It was money well spent. The final vote: Roosevelt 15,590 and the Republican Jacob Southard 13,889. The total number of days that FDR campaigned in person: zero.

————

Franklin wasn't the only member of the family balancing on a political tightrope in 1912. The Oyster Bay side spent the year fighting an unprecedented Republican civil war, between the party's progressives and its conservatives. President Taft, Theodore Roosevelt's handpicked successor, had pledged to continue his progressive policies, even tacitly agreeing to consult his former boss on cabinet selections—an impossible vow for any president to keep, not to mention any protégé looking to make his own mark in the master's shadow. Roosevelt departed the White House in March 1909 and immediately left on an extended African safari, in part to keep out of his successor's hair. Conservatives lost little time in manipulating the affable and malleable Taft. Before long Roosevelt became deeply disappointed. "It is hard, very hard," said Taft, "to see a devoted friendship going to pieces like a rope of sand."[63] The men never did agree on what transgression finally toppled their relationship. There were certainly plenty of body blows: Taft firing Roosevelt's friend the U.S. Forest Service chief, Gifford Pinchot; his waffling stances on tariffs and antitrust issues; and many petty snipes. "For instance," one Roosevelt insider said, "the Colonel* has had it reported to him that President Taft frequently refers to him as 'my Democratic predecessor.' He does not like this."[64] Whatever the reason, the feud broke into the open at the end of February 1912, when Roosevelt formally declared that he would challenge Taft for the Republican nomination, despite having vowed repeatedly that he would never run for a third term. "My hat is in the ring," he said. And another Rooseveltism was coined.[65]

The political implications—a former president challenging a sitting president from his own party—were obviously huge. For the extended

---

* The ex-president preferred to be called Colonel Roosevelt, a reminder of his glory days as a Rough Rider.

Roosevelt family, the personal consequences were downright monumental. As a man effectively straddling two bobbing ships, Nick was in the most tenuous position. One foot was firmly planted with Taft, his patron, his constituent, his party's standard-bearer, and his close friend. (In 1911, Taft had one White House lunch guest on his birthday—Nick.) At the same time, he desperately wanted to stay loyal to his father-in-law, whom he liked and respected. In the days before his father-in-law announced his candidacy, Nick was vowing to give up his seat rather than be forced to publicly take sides. "Nick feels it is a tragedy," Alice wrote in her diary.[66] "I have never been so sorry for anyone."[67] He could take some consolation in that neither of the presidents tried to strong-arm him. Taft told Nick the choice was his. Theodore, ever the political realist, told Nick to back Taft, knowing that the GOP would ditch a congressman who dumped the party's own president. If Roosevelt did defeat Taft, his father-in-law vowed to protect him. "He had a dear letter from F. [Father] today saying he was coming out and then with words to the effect that he would soak it to 'any Roosevelt creature' who dared to worry us in Cincinnati," Alice wrote in her diary.[68]

For Alice, the role of political wife had suddenly taken a hairpin turn. Campaigning at Nick's side had fed her vanity and her sense of self-worth. Now she stood next to him powerless to help and a major cause of his pain. Still, she decided to back her father completely. Partly, that was out of loyalty; she had never wanted him to pass the baton to Taft in the first place. Part of that was selfish, too. While she enjoyed being married to a congressman on the rise, he was still only a congressman. Too much of her identity was tied to being the daughter of the president to not want to reclaim that.

Her choice might have been clear, but that didn't mean it wasn't agonizing. She knew that if Nick went along with her, he would put his career at serious risk. "I've begun to have a desperate feeling again. That lost feeling of being absolutely alone. Darling Nick. I love him so much," she wrote in her diary. "If I can only keep him cheerful, sober and moderately contented."[69] She shuttled back and forth between the two most important men in her life, listening and advising them on potential solutions. You could measure her anxiety by the number of ways in which she stopped behaving like Princess Alice of old. First, she now often woke up before noon—before 9:00 a.m., even—because breakfast was the best time to consult with her father. Second, she lost her always-healthy appetite.

"Food choked me and I existed principally on fruit and eggs and Vichy," she said. "I had a chronic cold and cough, indigestion, colitis, anemia and low blood pressure—and quite marked schizophrenia."[70] And third, she occasionally cried, even in front of other people. "Had a talk with Nick and been a fool and wept," she wrote.[71] "That poor fat man [a.k.a. President Taft] has come courting for him. Why must he [Nick] sacrifice *us* for that lump of flesh?"[72]

The irony was that while she was miserable in her inability to rescue Nick, in a way Alice had become more important to him than ever. She had presented detailed plans on how to navigate the Taft-Roosevelt predicament, just as she did for her father. She became a sounding board for their ideas as well as for their speeches. Rather than serving as a mere ribbon cutter and all-purpose curio, she had graduated to trusted adviser to both men. Alice had stepped into the inner circle. She would stay there—with politicians from various backgrounds, and not just her relatives—for decades.

If that transition went largely undetected at the time (even by Alice), it was because the election of 1912 grew stranger and noisier by the day. Once he entered the race, Theodore took charge of it like—well, he said it himself when he arrived in Chicago on June 15 for the Republican convention: "I'm feeling like a bull moose!"[73] He had won 235 of the 254 contested delegates in the primaries, leaving Taft with only 19. But the sitting president controlled the convention and with it the delegates. Taft's henchmen proceeded to invalidate one Roosevelt backer after the next, as if they were tin cans lined up in a shooting gallery. Taft also pocketed the majority of heretofore uncommitted delegates. When it was over, Taft claimed 561 votes to 107 for Roosevelt, with the Wisconsin senator Robert "Fighting Bob" La Follette getting 41. Three hundred and forty-four disgruntled Roosevelt supporters refused to back anyone. They had been steamrolled, they shouted in the convention hall, loudly rubbing pieces of sandpaper together to simulate the sound of a steam engine. Before the votes were even counted, Roosevelt and his followers had decamped to Orchestra Hall down the street and convened a "rump" convention to form a third party. They called themselves the Progressive Party. Most of the time, though, they were known as Bull Moosers.

Alice promptly elected herself president of the Bull Moose Booster Club. "Mr. Roosevelt will be elected because the people believe in fair play," she announced to a group of reporters. "And he'll win too; don't forget that for a minute. He's full of life, and just now he thinks he's been unjustly treated and will fight with every ounce of strength that is in him."[74] She said this as she and Nick were boarding the train from Chicago back to Washington, and the reporters couldn't help but notice that Nick "wore a dejected look."[75] When they asked him if he would be supporting his father-in-law, he barked, "I have nothing to say." And he wanted to make damn sure to keep it that way. No one had seen Nick in Chicago the prior day, including Alice.[76] He had been avoiding everyone, in no small part because the Taft-Roosevelt rift was tearing his own marriage apart. Alice, fed up with their fighting and Nick's growing problems with drinking, had just asked him for a divorce. Her family quickly intervened. "They exercised considerable pressure to get me to reconsider," she said. "The whole thing would have caused too much of a hullaba-loo apparently. In those days people just didn't go around divorcing one another. Not done, they said. Emphatically."[77]

———

They were apparently able to patch things up in time to travel together to the following whistle-stop—the Democratic National Convention, which began the next day in Baltimore. It might have been enemy territory, but the Longworths found at least one pair of friendly faces: Franklin and Eleanor. "Alice & Nick sat near us in Baltimore & she told me that Uncle Ted's meeting in Chicago was wonderful," Eleanor wrote to her friend Isabella Greenway.* "Alice looks much better & she asked much about you & Bob."[78] Franklin had hoped to use the convention both to support Wilson and, in the event that he won the nomination, to secure a job in the new administration. The problem was that he garnered more notice for being "the Democratic Roosevelt," as a pro-Wilson newspaperman named Josephus Daniels referred to him, than he did on his own merits. Franklin wasn't a delegate or an alternate. He wasn't even allowed on the

---

* Isabella Selmes Ferguson Greenway's (1886–1953) life was intertwined with the Roose-velts from the moment of her birth. Her father was the co-owner with Theodore Roosevelt of a ranch in North Dakota, where she spent the first part of her childhood. As a schoolgirl in New York City, Isabella met Eleanor and they formed a lifelong friendship. She served as a bridesmaid at Eleanor's wedding, and would eventually marry two of TR's Rough Riders: Robert Ferguson in 1905 (with whom she was godparent to Eleanor's daughter Anna) and, after his death in 1922, Colonel John Greenway. She seconded FDR's nomination at the 1932 Democratic convention, and served two terms in the House of Representatives as Arizona's first female member of Congress before retiring in 1936.

convention floor. "Much attention is being given to the expected arrival to-morrow of the Roosevelts," reported the *New York Times*. "Someone started a story to the effect that 'Roosevelt had arrived.' This was true, but the Roosevelt referred to was not the former President, but State Senator James Roosevelt of New York, a cousin of the Oyster Bay man."[79] They didn't even get his first name right.

Like their husbands, the cousins inhabited vastly different rungs on the political pecking order. Alice was now both a superstar and an insider, notable as much for what she thought as what she wore. Eleanor was barely a face in the crowd. She later professed to having enjoyed her first convention, but she didn't stay all that long. It was hot and smoky and loud in Baltimore. She didn't always understand what was going on. "Finally, I decided my husband would hardly miss my company, as I rarely laid eyes on him, and the children should go to Campobello, so I went home," she wrote.[80] It was hard to blame her. It took the Democrats forty-six ballots and one impassioned speech from William Jennings Bryan to nominate Wilson. He was the worst possible opponent from Roosevelt's vantage, given that they were both progressives who supported an eight-hour workday, a federal income tax, and national health and unemployment insurance.* "My hopes were far from robust," said Alice, though the budding political operative in her couldn't help but be excited by the intraparty warfare. "It was comforting to see that there was no more sweet harmony in the Democratic ranks than in those of the erstwhile Republican Party."[81]

Eleanor, off in Campobello with the children, got the word from Franklin in a telegraph: "Wilson nominated this afternoon. All my plans vague. Splendid triumph."[82] Receiving the news long-distance was something of a blessing and perhaps part of the plan in skipping out of Baltimore early. It meant that Eleanor didn't have to react to Franklin's enthusiasm in kind. The truth was, she hadn't really wanted Wilson to get the nomination. After all, the Democratic candidate would be running against not just Taft but the Progressive Party nominee. "I wish Franklin could be fighting now for Uncle Ted, for I feel he is in the Party of the Future," she wrote to Isabella.[83]

---

* Theodore Roosevelt's 1912 Progressive Party platform called for many policies that would later be introduced during FDR's presidency.

The future was nearly over before it began. On October 14, Theodore Roosevelt was stumping in Milwaukee, where he drew yet another large and adoring crowd. A sizable group had collected in the lobby of the Gilpatrick Hotel just to wait for him to finish dinner before making that evening's speech. When Theodore finally emerged at about 8:00 p.m., the throng followed him into the street and toward the car that would take him to the Milwaukee Auditorium, three blocks away.[84] Just as Roosevelt stepped on the floorboard of his car and turned to wave, a stocky barkeep from New York named John Schrank pushed through the throng, aimed his shiny revolver at the former president, and shot him once in the chest from about six feet away.[85] At first, Theodore didn't realize he had been hit. When the crowd toppled Schrank and started yelling, "Lynch him!" Roosevelt announced that he was unhurt and begged, "Don't hurt the poor creature. I want to see him."[86] Later, Schrank told police that he feared Roosevelt's dictatorial ambitions. "Any man looking for a third term ought to be shot," he said.[87]

It wasn't until Roosevelt was driven away in the car that an aide noticed the hole in Roosevelt's shirt. Theodore found some blood there, but there wasn't any when he coughed into his hand, so he assumed that the bullet hadn't traveled to his lungs. In fact, it had been slowed by two objects in Roosevelt's left jacket pocket: his steel eyeglass case and his folded fifty-page speech, which he proceeded to deliver over the next hour as if nothing had happened. "It takes more than that," he told the hushed crowd, "to stop a Bull Moose." But over the course of the speech, as blood slowly soaked his shirt, his voice grew fainter and his face paler. His insistence on pushing through to the end only cemented his indomitable reputation. When Roosevelt finally did finish, he was rushed to a Milwaukee hospital. The reports were conflicting and confusing. Edith got word from a cousin while sitting in a Broadway theater. Alice, in Cincinnati, tried to follow the news by phone. Franklin, who was in the midst of recovering from typhoid, resorted to calling the *New York Times* office to get the latest updates.[88] The next day Theodore was transferred to a hospital in Chicago, where doctors decided that the wound wasn't life threatening and opted to leave the bullet in his chest.

The Roosevelts endured another kind of near-death experience in the election season. Nick and Theodore told Alice that she must not stump for the Progressive Party or attend any high-profile events, such as the official Progressive Party convention in early August back in Chicago. The men reasoned that any divided Longworth-family loyalty would confuse and maybe anger the staunch Taft supporters in Nick's district. Just as Nick didn't publicly back either Taft or Roosevelt, Alice needed to keep a low profile. "It was torture," she said, "not to be doing something."[89]

Of course, telling Alice Roosevelt *not* to do something was just like waving a red flag in front of a bull moose. Try as she might, she couldn't help herself from going to hear California's governor, Hiram Johnson, her father's running mate, when he came to speak in Cincinnati on September 20. "It was simply splendid," she told Johnson backstage after the speech. "I am so glad to meet you."[90] (This was said, somewhat obtusely, right in front of Nick, who went to the speech with her rather than give voters reason to believe the election was impacting his marriage.) Alice went alone when her father spoke in Chicago the following month and again when he stormed New York's Madison Square Garden on October 30, his first appearance after the shooting. After all, she'd helped to edit her father's speech, and it proved to be the high point of the entire campaign. "It was one of those resounding, enthusiastic crowds, the streets jammed for blocks around the hall, three-quarters of an hour of ear-splitting racket when Father came to the platform," she said.[91]

Unfortunately, the election itself proved far less exciting than the campaigns. Alice was correct: Roosevelt essentially split the vote twice, fighting for Republican voters with Taft and progressive voters with Wilson. In the end, Wilson took forty states and 435 electoral votes. Roosevelt won six states and 88 electoral votes. Taft only won two states (Utah and Vermont) and 8 electoral votes, still the worst showing ever by an incumbent president. Despite the loss, Roosevelt only solidified his standing as America's most intrepid and beloved warrior. He became not only the most successful third-party candidate (and still is); he was only the second, after Andrew Jackson, to campaign with a bullet in his chest.

Nick's career, however, went on life support. He lost his seat by a mere ninety-seven votes. It seemed likely that Alice's full-throated support for her father boomeranged and whacked her husband in the back. There was a real possibility that he was finished politically, and for the rest of her life Alice blamed herself for his defeat. It's fair to say that Nick blamed her, too, even before the votes had been counted. "Nick and I had a tremendous row after lunch—he accuses me of not being for him, not 'standing by' him and I am so hurt and angry," Alice wrote in her diary two days before the election. "We are surely drifting decidedly apart. It is so sad."[92] When the congressional session ended that March, they drifted back together— back to Cincinnati, where Nick plotted his return to office and Alice attempted to live under the same roof again with her mother-in-law. That might have been a sentence worse than death.

—————

Despite his candidate's crushing victory over Taft and Uncle Ted, Franklin's future was somewhat less clear than Nick's. He was reelected to the New York State Senate, thanks to Louis Howe's skill as a political magician. But FDR had hoped for something in the Wilson administration. For the upcoming 1913 term, Franklin and Eleanor rented a few rooms in an Albany hotel and left the children with Mama. He took his seat in the senate, but his real job was working his connections in Washington. In the middle of January, a telegram summoned him to New Jersey to meet with Wilson, but nothing concrete came of it. Then, three days before Wilson's March 4 inauguration, Franklin and Eleanor booked into Washington's Willard hotel, long the prime deal-making spot in town. Sure enough, FDR happened across William Gibbs McAdoo, the incoming Treasury secretary, and he offered Franklin his choice of two jobs: assistant Treasury secretary or collector of customs at the Port of New York. Franklin smiled, expressed his gratitude—and took neither. On the morning of the inauguration, he encountered Josephus Daniels, the North Carolina newspaper editor who had labeled him "the Democratic Roosevelt" at the Democratic convention in Baltimore. Wilson had recently asked Daniels to be secretary of the navy, and Franklin duly congratulated him. "How would you like to come to Washington as assistant secretary?" Daniels replied. Uncle Ted's old job? Franklin was delighted. "How would I like it?" said Franklin, breaking into his incandescent smile. "I'd like it bully well!" Right on schedule, Franklin had climbed up another rung of Uncle Ted's ladder to the White House.

# Chapter 4

# OTHER WOMEN

O ver the years, Eleanor would land in countless nerve-racking
situations courtesy of Franklin's career: speaking in front of
large crowds, staring down threats to drop her civil rights activism, even shimmying through the occasional coal shaft to chat with miners. But few assignments made her as physically ill as the time she found
herself perched atop the hundred-foot-high skeleton mast of the battleship *Rhode Island*. It was a crisp fall day in 1913, only a few months into
Franklin's new job as assistant secretary of the navy. The Roosevelts were
tagging along with his boss, Josephus Daniels, who had invited the cabinet secretaries and their wives to observe target practice off the coast of
the naval base in Hampton Roads, Virginia. The men boarded one of four
dreadnoughts doing the firing; the wives were all left on the *Rhode Island*,
which would sail about a mile behind the target ships. "My husband,"
Eleanor said, "was delighted." And she was almost instantly miserable. "To
the others I imagine the day seemed calm; to me it seemed extremely
rough. As the morning advanced I grew greener," she said. "I dreaded disgracing my husband by being ill."[1]

FDR was born with sea legs. He drew a sailboat on the first letter he
wrote (at age five) and got his own boat, the *New Moon*, when he was
sixteen. By the time he was named assistant secretary, Franklin had collected nearly ten thousand books and pamphlets on naval matters and
claimed to have read every volume except one (which, fortunately for its
author, he never named).[2] He adored being assistant secretary, and scam-

pering around ships was one of his favorite parts of the job. The fact that
his cousin Theodore Roosevelt held the office sixteen years before only
made the job sweeter.

To Eleanor the sea might just as well have been one giant shark tank.
She'd been terrified of the water in general and ships in particular since
she was two, when she and her parents had to be rescued from the ocean
liner *Britannic* after it collided with another ship off the coast of New Jersey. Add to that the death-defying dives and assorted leaps into the Long
Island Sound that she endured each summer with Uncle Ted's fearless
family and you get the makings of a white-knuckled landlubber.

There was, however, one thing Eleanor hated more than being on
the water: not completing a task, "disgracing" someone because of her
own fears or perceived failures. She climbed aboard the *Rhode Island*
because she felt she had to; a navy wife couldn't succumb to seasickness,
least of all in front of the wives of the most powerful men in the Wilson
administration. But Eleanor was never content to just slide by doing the
minimum.

Shortly after the *Rhode Island* set out to sea, Mary Bryan, the wife of
Secretary of State William Jennings Bryan, announced she wasn't interested in naval maneuvers—a reasonable assertion given that she was married to the country's foremost pacifist. So she deposited herself in a chair
and stayed there for the duration of the trip. Queasy ER could have easily followed Mrs. Bryan's lead. Instead, she said she wanted to see every
nook and cranny of the fifteen-thousand-ton *Rhode Island*. And when the
navy chaperones asked if anyone would like to venture up the mast—
which was the best place to observe the target practice—she was the only
woman to raise her hand. She gamely changed into navy dungarees (blue
work shirt, white T-shirt, and jeans), gritted her teeth, and ascended the
scaffold. "None of the other women seemed willing to risk climbing the
mast," said Yates Stirling, the executive officer of the *Rhode Island*. "I saw
Mrs. Roosevelt after the practice, covered with soot but radiantly enthusiastic over the experience."[3]

That grin-and-bear-it tour of the *Rhode Island* proved to be an apt
introduction to her life in Washington. Still painfully shy and socially awkward, Eleanor was forced to quietly confront her demons nearly every day
as the wife of an ambitious, high-profile official with a high-profile name.
Her time in Albany had helped her grow more comfortable as a hostess,

a good thing given that Franklin often came home for lunch with various Navy Department cohorts in tow. (Home being the four-story town house on N Street that belonged to Aunt Bye and happened to be Uncle Ted's residence when he first landed in Washington.) Yet making small talk over sandwiches was nothing compared with surviving the genteel Washington torture known as calling.

Calling was a decades-old ritual where women of a certain station made the rounds of the homes of women of similar standing, to introduce themselves via their calling cards. For a politician on the rise, there was no limit to the number of powerful men who might come in handy in his career, so there was no limit to the number of women his wife would attempt to meet and greet. Right after Franklin was appointed assistant secretary, Auntie Bye, an expert in Capitol comportment and the wife of an admiral to boot, told Eleanor that she must start calling as soon as possible. "I think my heart sank somewhat as she gave me careful instructions on my calls," Eleanor wrote in 1937, "but I doubt if I registered as much dismay as did my little daughter-in-law Betsey the other day when I gave her the list of people she was supposed to call on. Her face dropped and she said, 'I'm feeling very ill, Mama. I know I shall have to go to bed.'"[4]

Eleanor herself had a good excuse to lie down; she was newly pregnant when she began her calls toward the end of 1913. But Eleanor Roosevelt never made excuses. Instead, she dutifully made her rounds, paying as many as thirty calls a day on the spouses of Washington's elite and on a schedule as precise as a Swiss watch: Tuesdays were for members of the House, Thursdays for senators, and Fridays for the diplomatic corps. Women who didn't fit into any category were simply squeezed in wherever there was room on the calendar.

None of this guaranteed a meeting with the intended recipient, however. The caller sometimes sat in her car while her driver delivered his mistress's card. The lady of the house might agree to a ten-minute chat, or she could arrange to meet in the future, via her own card returned at a later date. On the other hand, if she wanted to acknowledge the visitor but wouldn't deign to meet her, she sent her own card back sealed in an envelope, the epistolary version of a corpse in a coffin. That was the sign to stay away, and it was one of many semaphore-like ways a card could convey an unspoken message. (For instance, folding down the upper right-hand corner meant that the eager caller had delivered the card to the door herself; folding down the lower left-hand corner meant she was paying a condolence call.)[5] The system was as byzantine as it was unforgiving. "Nearly all the women at that time were the slaves of the Washington social system," Eleanor said. "There were only two who broke loose."[6] One was the wife of a Massachusetts congressman. "The other woman," Eleanor said, "was Alice Roosevelt."[7]

Alice did go calling—twice, at least. The first time came when the Tafts handed over the White House to the Wilsons in March 1913. Curiosity got the better of Alice, and she drove to her dearly departed former home to leave cards for Mrs. Wilson and her three daughters. "It was almost impossible to believe that those odd beings called Democrats were actually there in the offing about to take things over," she said.[8] A few days later, Mrs. Wilson cordially invited Alice over, though Alice was peeved by the First Lady's "perfunctory and formal tea."[9]

The second documented call came a decade later, when Alice decided it was time to pay off some "social debts" and teamed up with Mary Borah, the wife of the Idaho senator William Borah. They drove around for the better part of an afternoon, calling on some thirty wives. But every time they stopped and Mrs. Borah readied one of her cards, Alice froze, telling her intrepid companion, "Oh I don't think I'll go in here. I'll wait for you." Though officially only the wife of an Ohio congressman, Alice knew that all of the thirty wives she avoided that day would have fallen all over themselves to get her into their parlors. By the end of the day, she hadn't delivered a single card. "I hate calling," Alice explained. "I just can't do it."[10]

She didn't need to. A woman made calls to blow hot air into her ballooning social circle, but Alice was already the most famous and sought-after woman in the city, if not the country. "Her house was the center of gaiety and of interesting gatherings," Eleanor wrote. "Everyone who came to Washington coveted an introduction to her."[11] Eleanor knew she could never compete, either with Alice's star power or with her willingness to smash social convention like a bottle of champagne against the kaiser's ship. "I was appalled by the independence and courage" of Alice, Eleanor said. "I was perfectly certain that I had nothing to offer of an individual nature and that my only chance of doing my duty as the wife of a public official was to do exactly as the majority of women were doing, perhaps to be a little more meticulous about it than some of the others were. Whatever I was asked to do must be done."[12]

————

Fortunately for Eleanor, she didn't have to worry much about Alice, at least right away. Her cousin was relegated to Cincinnati after Nick's narrow loss in the 1912 election, plotting his comeback and dueling with her mother-in-law. Neither proved to be much of a challenge. Alice had learned to deal with Susan Longworth by now, and when she couldn't, she simply left town, for either Sagamore Hill or somewhere farther afield. She and Nick went to the Panama Canal in 1913 (where Alice managed to scandalize the locals by smoking in public) and California in 1914. She also accompanied her father to Madrid in 1914 for her brother Kermit's wedding to Belle Willard, the daughter of the American ambassador in Spain. Father and daughter then toured Paris and London together, but Alice stayed and traveled by herself for a few more weeks. She wanted to pal around with the kinds of people Theodore detested: rich ones. On June 28, 1914, she was visiting the Rothschilds as part of a "weekend jaunt to Paris, to take in the Grand Prix," when news broke that Archduke Ferdinand had been assassinated in Sarajevo. "None of the people there who talked about it gave any sign of realizing that it was the match that touched off the fuse," Alice said.[13]

The war was still a distant European dustup come November, when Nick got his rematch against Representative Stanley Bowdle, the Democrat who had defeated him in the Wilson landslide of 1912. Ohioans were much more concerned about the threat of Prohibition and the economy, and Nick was swept into office, along with a wave of Republicans nationwide. "We were back once more in Washington, and great fun it was to be there again, to have our exile behind us," Alice said.[14]

Only this time, the Longworths carried some extra baggage. Alice might have ducked out from mother-in-law-plagued Cincinnati at every opportunity, but her absences were like termites gnawing at the foundation of her marriage. She and Nick papered over the holes with sweet letters filled with pet names and un-Alice-like sentimental goo. "Darling Bubby. I love you so very much. You are so much nicer and more attractive and more everything than anyone else in the world," Alice wrote to him in September 1913 from Sagamore Hill, where she spent a week celebrating her brother Ted's birthday.[15] "I want my Bubbie back badly," Nick replied.

Maybe he did; he wrote that same line in two different letters. But one reason Nick stayed in Ohio that fall was because he was on crutches. He'd broken his foot while doing the turkey trot—with another woman. Nick didn't exactly work hard to dispel his lover-boy image. Folks in Cincinnati were also dishing about the time Alice went for a walk in a local park and stumbled on Nick canoodling in the grass with yet another woman. "Hello, Mrs. Longworth," the woman was rumored to have looked up and said, as if she'd just bumped into her next-door neighbor at the grocery store.[16] Alice had always feared Nick's wandering eye. On their return to Washington, she had to worry about his wandering hands, too.

But by and large, Capitol Hill was as delighted to have the Longworths back as they were to be there. Even Nellie Taft's sister, Lucy Laughlin, threw a formal tea for Alice. "Washington society gave a royal welcome to Mrs. Nicholas Longworth, formerly the popular Alice Roosevelt of the former regime. Mrs. Longworth arrived here with her husband, Representative-elect Longworth of Ohio," reported the *Washington Post*. Almost always, Alice got top billing. At least the *Post* mentioned Nick before noting the return of Alice's other companion, "her famous chow dog Manchu."[17]

Among the Washingtonians on hand to greet Alice was a new neighbor: her cousin Eleanor. For the first time since they were children, the cousins found themselves living in the same city—only one block apart, in fact (1733 N Street versus 1736 M Street). They ran in different social circles, separated by their party affiliations and family obligations, so they mostly saw each other at home. Dinner at the Longworths' invariably featured fine wine, lively conversation, and the occasional violin recital from the host. "I wish I could tell you about Alice & Nick—having them here is so funny!" Eleanor wrote to Isabella Greenway. "I went to dine when F. was away the other night & one of the lady guests had a cocktail, 2 glasses of whiskey & soda & liqueurs & 15 cigarettes before I left at 10:15! It was a funny party but I'm glad I'm not quite so fashionable! Alice looks fairly well though & is very nice."[18] By comparison, the food and entertainment served up by Franklin and Eleanor seemed fairly wilted. "They would have rather fine and solemn little Sunday evenings where one was usually regaled with crown roast, very indifferent wine, and a good deal of knitting," Alice remembered.[19] Alice turned out to be far nicer in her own home than she was at Eleanor's. "I remember going there once with my stepmother, who maintained that she could always tell when I was bored because I appeared to swell up. My eyes recede and my face becomes fat,"

Alice said. "My stepmother said she thought I was going to lose my eyes that evening."[20]

Yet the women continued to see each other, if not daily, then at least far more than they had in years, at family get-togethers and the occasional society soiree. Despite their different temperaments, politics, and dinner menus, the cousins were knit together by a bond that wasn't easily broken. A good deal of that came from Theodore, who managed to smother the family's differences in an everlasting bear hug. "I am very anxious to see you and Franklin, whenever the chance offers, but I do not want to compromise Franklin by being with him just at this time," Uncle Ted wrote to Eleanor in 1915, as debate about the war, and the partisan passions it fed, grew more intense. "I wish you would tell him that from all quarters I hear praise of the admirable work he has done for the Navy, under very difficult conditions. With love, Your affectionate Uncle."[21]

That affection played a role in quieting one of the family's biggest, and strangest, crises to date. Though he'd apparently sworn off running for office, Teddy couldn't help but throw his weight around when he saw an opportunity. On July 24, 1914, he published a long and angry op-ed piece endorsing the Republican Harvey Hinman for governor of New York. Roosevelt argued that, as a progressive, Hinman wouldn't be under the thumb of political bosses "of the most obnoxious type." Then he named the bosses: the Democrat Charles Murphy and the Republican William Barnes. The next day, Barnes sued Roosevelt for libel. (Murphy did not; he was apparently just happy to sit on the sidelines and watch the Republicans duke it out.)

When the case finally came to trial in mid-1915, the ex-president's supporters weren't at all confident he would win. After all, he had to prove that Barnes controlled enough of the state's political machinery to be considered a "boss" (the "obnoxious" part would presumably then go without saying). At first the former president appeared unsteady and occasionally confused on the stand, his once famously prodigious memory frequently failing him. He found his footing over time, but he knew he needed to pull out every stop. So two weeks into the trial he telegrammed for help from a friend who'd crossed swords with Barnes himself: FDR. Franklin had made his name in New York as an insurgent politician squabbling with the party machines, including Republicans such as Barnes. Perhaps even more important, FDR was a Democrat. It was one thing for a pugilistic Progressive Republican such as the former president to go after Barnes.

Testimony from both sides of the aisle helped make Theodore's comments seem less motivated by intra-party politics. "Just to prove that blood is thicker than politics," reported the *Baltimore Sun*, "Franklin D. Roosevelt, Democratic Assistant Secretary of the Navy and ex-Democratic State Senator, came all the way from Washington this morning to help Theodore Roosevelt, ex-President of the United States, in the $50,000 libel suit brought by William Barnes Jr."[22] A little more than two weeks after the testimony of TR's "fifth cousin by blood, nephew by law" (as FDR proudly called himself on the stand), the Colonel won his case. Franklin cabled his congratulations, and Uncle Ted was quick to reply: "You have a right to congratulate me on the verdict, because you were a part of it. I shall never forget the capital way in which you gave your testimony and the impression upon the jury." And then he scrawled a handwritten note: "Love to dearest Eleanor."[23]

————

As happy as FDR was to connect himself to his cousin's triumph, the world at large didn't pay much attention. On May 7, 1915, two days after Franklin testified, a German U-boat trolling off the coast of Ireland torpedoed the British ocean liner *Lusitania*, killing 1,198 passengers, among them 123 Americans. It would take two more years before the United States joined the war and sent troops to Europe, but for FDR the changes came quickly. He had long championed the need to modernize the navy, and the *Lusitania* gave him the political muscle to gun the engines. Along with Louis Howe, the faithful consigliere he imported with him from Albany, Franklin scoured the world for battleship supplies, from tin, teak, and shellac to high-grade Chilean nitrate, for use in explosives.[24] He also lobbied tirelessly to boost the navy's budget to prepare for what he was sure was the gathering storm. It was a somewhat unorthodox, even presumptuous, mission for a mere assistant secretary—and exactly what cousin Theodore did anticipating the Spanish-American War some two decades earlier. After all, in 1916 Wilson campaigned on the slogan "He kept us out of war." Secretary Josephus Daniels, who generally supported rebuilding the navy, was an avowed pacifist.* More than once, FDR tried to rattle the

———

* He was also an avowed teetotaler. Josephus Daniels had recently banned alcohol from all navy ships, yards, and stations, suggesting instead that the men drink coffee. Thus the mocking phrase "a cup of Joe" was born.

cages behind his bosses' backs in hopes of expediting the military buildup, including one time when he waited until Daniels was on vacation to write a memo—one of Theodore's favorite ploys when he was assistant secretary. The peeved secretary should probably have expected that kind of insubordination from his upstart protégé. Before Franklin was appointed, Daniels consulted with Elihu Root, who had served as President Roosevelt's secretary of state, about the young man. "You know the Roosevelts, don't you?" Root said. "Whenever a Roosevelt rides, he wishes to ride in front."[25]

And so more and more, Franklin took on the aura of the Roosevelt heir apparent. He wasn't just stealing from the Colonel's playbook (while sitting at his old desk in the Navy Department). He was stealing from his illustrious cousin's life. Franklin tried to speak like his idol ("I'd like it bully well!") and look like him, having long ago taken to wearing Roosevelt's signature gold-rimmed pince-nez glasses. He lived in the same house that Theodore first occupied in Washington. In March 1916, Eleanor gave birth for the sixth and final time (though one child, the first Franklin junior, had died in infancy). That was not a coincidence. Ever since he was young, Franklin said he wanted to someday have six children, just like Uncle Ted. It's not entirely unreasonable to wonder if handsome, wealthy Franklin was initially attracted to dowdy Eleanor in part because she would open the door, and the bloodline, to her uncle. "By marrying Eleanor, whom TR himself called 'my favorite niece,' Franklin hoped to gain the instant access to the presidential family that distant kinship had always denied him," wrote FDR's biographer Geoffrey C. Ward. "His love for Eleanor was real, but her closeness to the immediate family of the man he admired most on earth must have been an important part of her dowry."[26]

During his first stint in Washington, Franklin developed another, and far more surprising, bridge to Oyster Bay. Alice might have complained about the menu at FDR's house, but she savored spending time with him. "I liked Franklin rather more than the rest of the family did," she said. "One could always have fun with him. And he was great to tease."[27] Franklin and Alice were very compatible: fun loving and social, quick-witted and a little ostentatious. (It was Alice who gave Franklin the first of what would become an FDR trademark: a Bakelite cigarette holder.)[28] She'd enjoyed him ever since they were teenagers, when they'd danced at Aunt Corinne's parties and she wrote him flirtatious notes. Now that they were neighbors after all these years, she knew how to get him to let his hair down. "Both Eleanor and Franklin could be very boring together, but not when he was without her," Alice said. "Then he asserted himself."[29]

They had plenty of alone time. Franklin often dined at Alice's place without Eleanor, who was so busy having children, running the household, and making her calls that in 1914 she'd hired a social secretary three days a week to handle her correspondence and schedule. The secretary's name was Lucy Mercer. At twenty-two, Lucy was an exceptionally poised and pretty young woman with sapphire-blue eyes and the smoky voice of a jazz singer. She'd come from a wealthy local family whose alcoholic father lost their respectability and their fortune. Aunt Bye once lived down the block from the Mercers, and when Eleanor needed help, she recommended Lucy, who was now supporting her mother and was only too glad to earn $30 a week lending a hand to a prominent family. Lucy proved to be a whiz at organizing Eleanor's life, sitting on the Roosevelts' living room floor surrounded by piles of invitations, letters, and bills.[30] Thanks to her Social Register lineage, she was also an ideal "extra" woman at social functions where the hostess feared that an unattached single man could turn into the jacket-and-tie equivalent of a rutting ram set loose in a herd. Even Mama liked Lucy. "Miss Mercer is here," Sara wrote to Eleanor when she joined Franklin on a navy trip to the West Coast. "She is so sweet and attractive, and she adores you, Eleanor."[31]

Lucy's unique combination of skills came in especially handy in the summers. Eleanor and the children routinely escaped from the sticky Washington heat to Campobello. Franklin would visit when he could (sometimes hitching a ride north on a navy destroyer), but he spent extended periods alone in Washington. In the summer of 1916, Eleanor and the "chicks" (as their parents called their children) were away well into September as a polio epidemic swept through the Northeast and the Roosevelts were desperate to keep the children out of harm's way. "The infantile paralysis in N.Y. and vicinity is appalling," Franklin wrote to Eleanor in July. "*Please* kill all the flies I left. I think it is really important."[32] In the meantime, Lucy was able to keep the Washington house in order as well as pitch in to help FDR. Apparently, she did that part of her job a little too well. Even the overwhelmed Eleanor noticed the chemistry between her husband and the flirtatious Miss Mercer. In the summer of 1917, as Eleanor was preparing to take the family back to Campobello for several weeks, she fired Lucy. The official explanation was that wartime left Eleanor with fewer social obligations and therefore less need for a social secretary. But no one was fooled by that, least of all Franklin. Only five days after Lucy lost her job with Eleanor, she found another—as Yeoman Third Class Mercer, posted to the office of the assistant secretary of the navy.[33]

Eleanor was understandably furious; she even considered canceling the Campobello trip. Of course, that would have looked suspicious and required some kind of explanation, not least to Mama. Besides, Franklin assured ER that she had nothing to worry about. "I really can't stand that house all alone without you, and you were a goosy girl to think or even pretend to think that I don't want you here *all* summer, because you know I do!" he protested the day after she and the children left Washington. "But honestly, *you* ought to have six weeks straight at Campo, just as *I* ought to, only you can and I can't."[34] To prove that he had nothing to hide, the next week Franklin wrote to her about a working-weekend cruise he threw together on the *Sylph*, the 124-foot presidential yacht. He had set sail for Hampton Roads, where he could review the fleet and explore the battleship *Arkansas*, as well as squeeze in a little swimming and al fresco dining along the way. The guests were President Wilson's personal physician (and his wife), one of Franklin's old Harvard buddies (and his wife), and a British diplomat named Nigel Law (who didn't have a wife). Guess who filled in as the "single" woman? "Such a funny party, but it worked out *wonderfully*!" Franklin wrote.[35] He didn't mention that Lucy looked fetching in her swimsuit.[36]

Franklin also neglected to tell Eleanor about another dinner party he had attended with Lucy, at Alice's house. Dinner at the Longworths' was an event, a performance, and a feast for the ears. As Eleanor said, everyone wanted to meet Alice. Alice, however, was mainly interested in visitors who were both acclaimed and capable of surviving the thrust and parry of the arena known as her dining room. "Whereas other Washington hostesses draw up their guest lists for compatibility, Mrs. Longworth chooses her guests for conflict," one writer observed. "A southern conservative will find himself seated next to a northern liberal, a dove next to a hawk. The food, the wine, the service, all have a turn-of-the-century elegance, but, like the perfection of the matador's costume, they presage the spilling of blood."[37] If that wasn't meant as a compliment, it should have been. Having grown up in a highly verbal and intellectually curious family, Alice found herself living in a town that was often allergic to conflict and controversy. Where was the challenge, the stimulation, in an evening with predictable politicians? If Aunt Bye kept books beside her bed as "mental manure," Alice did something similar with her dinner companions. Over the years, she would host the likes of Charles Lindbergh, Lady Astor, Lord Balfour, and Billy Sunday in their primes. Always the voracious reader, she especially stocked up on writers: Will Rogers was a favorite, as was Booth Tarkington. (Alice used to say that the characters in his novel *The Magnificent Ambersons* reminded her of another faded midwestern dynasty: the Longworths.) Dinner at Alice's wasn't unlike lunch with an equally quick-witted woman and her literary chums in New York: Dorothy Parker. Except the Algonquin crew really just amused each other. Alice also wanted to push her powerful Capitol Hill neighbors to open their minds a bit. No one else in town was doing that, which made dinner at Alice's a kind of golden meal ticket, despite the conversational quicksand. "As Cornelius Vanderbilt Jr. once said in a press dispatch about a dinner invitation of Alice Longworth's, such a thing is 'anent unto a command,'" said Alexander Woollcott, another Longworth regular.[38]

Tarkington happened to be at table one night in the summer of 1916 when cousin Franklin came to dinner.[39] Franklin, a rising star for the opposition Democrats, fit perfectly into Alice's pugilistic party plans. Except Alice's motives for inviting her cousin that particular night were naughtier than usual. Like many Washington insiders, she had heard that his relationship with Lucy mixed a good deal of pleasure with business. One day when she was out for a drive in the Virginia hills, she got her proof. She passed Franklin and Lucy in a car—alone. Naturally, Alice called to tease him as soon as she could. "I saw you 20 miles out in the country," she told him. "You didn't see me. Your hands were on the wheel but your eyes were on that perfectly lovely lady." Franklin somewhat cheekily replied, "Isn't she perfectly lovely?"[40]

Looking back, Alice claimed she didn't really believe anything untoward was happening between Franklin and Lucy. "It wasn't much of an affair, as good old Washington went," she said. "In those days in the summer, politicians bundled their families off to the mountains or seashore for the summer months and it was the usual thing for the paterfamilias to accumulate something attractive."[41] It might not have been the most innocent arrangement, but it wasn't necessarily sexual. And maybe it wasn't—yet. Would Franklin have given his notoriously loose-lipped cousin such a flip reply if he had anything to hide? (In fact, whenever Mercer arrived at the Roosevelts' home for a day's work, he would greet her by saying, "Ah, the lovely Lucy.")[42] "I do not think anything ever happened," Alice told Eleanor's friend and biographer Joseph Lash, adding that Lash should "put that in capitals."[43]

Whatever the truth, Alice's motives were hardly benign where her Hyde Park cousins were concerned. She'd never told Franklin that he'd have a date for the evening; when he arrived at the Longworths', Lucy was already there. It was sort of a purity test. If Franklin blanched, Alice would know the lusty truth. If he (and Lucy) played it cool, she'd at least have added an entertaining dash of tension to the meal. She'd have her dessert, too. People would undoubtedly gossip about the evening's most unconventional pair, and Alice knew that even a whiff of impropriety would sting puritanical Eleanor. Her most famous explanation for inviting Lucy and Franklin that night made it clear she wanted to hurt her first cousin: "He deserved a good time. After all, he was married to Eleanor."[44]

The big question, then, is why? Retribution, perhaps, for her fusty, do-gooder cousin's habit of making Alice look bad to her father, the one person she wanted most to impress. Or maybe Alice had another reason to envy Eleanor. Over the years, some Roosevelt relatives claimed that young Alice herself had been in love with Franklin and never fully recovered from having lost him to her less glamorous cousin. "Of course [Alice] denied it. But she was the one that was flirting with him long before my grandmother came on the scene," said Nina Roosevelt Gibson, one of Eleanor's granddaughters. "As they then grew older and she realized the impact that FDR was making—and Alice loved the spotlight—I'm sure in Alice's head she very well may have thought, *ooh, if I'd only* ..."[45] Eleanor herself sometimes seemed leery of Alice's intentions toward her husband. "I don't think Eleanor quite approved of my friendship with Franklin," Alice said.

> I remember running into him once shortly after they were married. It was in the lobby of a hotel in Boston where I was staying overnight and I asked him up to my room for a drink. Actually, it wasn't really my room. We just sat on a trunk in an alcove nearby and drummed our heels happily on it like leprechauns on a roof. Somehow Eleanor got to hear of it and was very annoyed and said

to Franklin, "No one would know that you were her cousin. You were seen going to a woman's room. I think it would be a good idea if you and Alice didn't see each other for some time."[46]

That said, Alice scoffed when an interviewer first confronted her with the idea that she had been in love with Franklin. "She looked startled, incredulous, a little delighted, a little as if she were thinking what was she going to do with this," Lash wrote. But she quickly came up with a reply. "I liked him of course, but he was a good little mama's boy," she said. "The sort of boy who was asked to the dance but not to the dinner."[47]

It's certainly true that Alice's taste never ran to good boys, as she was forced to acknowledge on a regular basis. Nick never did give up the hunt for other women. In fact, he did everything short of leaving the bedroom curtains open to flaunt his conquests. One day when he was sitting in the House chamber, a political foe walked by with what he thought was the perfect insult. He caressed Nick's bald head and said, "Feels just like my wife's bottom." Nick rubbed his own head and replied, "By golly it does, doesn't it?"[48] He had a habit of strolling away from his own dinner parties with a pretty lady and not returning for an extended period of time. It happened once with Nick's old flame Cissy Patterson, who, in the fog of fornication, made the mistake of leaving the Longworths' without her purse. The next day, Alice sent it back to Cissy with an appropriately caustic message. Cissy replied with a thank-you note—and a question. Had Alice also happened to find her silk stockings, which Patterson had stuffed between the couch cushions in the library, or the chewing gum that she stuck under the fireplace mantel?[49]

Alice got a measure of revenge via a wartime affair of her own, with a Cincinnati lawyer named Joe Graydon. No one has ever proven that they were unfaithful to their respective spouses; Alice and Graydon spent much of their time discussing philosophy, poetry, and religion. But the relationship, which lasted from about 1915 to 1919, was clearly inappropriate by the day's standards, as well as by their own. "I have been forced to the conclusion that it were best I should not visit in Washington in absence of affairs requiring my presence there," Graydon wrote to Alice in early 1918. "Please do not think I should not like to—or that I am unappreciative of your asking me: nor must you think any other whatsoever suspicious or horrid things as the cause why I am, I hope, disappointing you."[50]

Still, it must have been galling to watch her marriage wither while prim and proper Eleanor remained blissfully ignorant of her own husband's dalliance. Washington had already enabled Eleanor's weakness for grandly noble gestures. Alice was finding the temptation to stick a pin in her cousin's righteousness all the more irresistible. She was especially fond of retelling a story about a ball Franklin and Eleanor attended around this time at the Chevy Chase Country Club, along with his cousins Warren and Irene Robbins. Franklin and the Robbinses were having a wonderful evening drinking and dancing. Eleanor was not, and she wanted to make sure Franklin knew it. At about midnight, she announced that she was going to catch a cab and leave, but Franklin should stay and enjoy himself if he wanted. Franklin, refusing to go on his wife's guilt trip, partied on. He finally arrived home at around 5:00 a.m., opened the front door, and found someone sleeping in the vestibule—Eleanor. "Darling," Franklin asked, "what are you doing here?" In Alice's telling of the tale, Eleanor stood up like a "string bean that had been raised in a cellar" and explained that she had forgotten her key.[51] Why hadn't she come back to get his or gone to a neighbor? Franklin asked. "I knew you all were having such a glorious time," she explained, "and I didn't want to spoil the fun."[52] Eleanor got her guilt trip, and Alice got something more, the perfect epitaph for her killjoy cousin: Here lies Eleanor Roosevelt, literally a human doormat.

If Eleanor was aware of Alice's jabs—or, conversely, if Alice knew that her punches hit their mark—neither let on. But they clearly kept tabs on each other. "I saw Alice & had as satisfactory a talk with her as one is apt to have. Filled with noisy exuberance & no reality," Isabella Greenway wrote to Eleanor in the spring of 1916. "She was nevertheless refreshing & *un*changed (after not seeing her for eight years!) I had looked for stout dignity from numerous tales—but met old time lightness. She seemed to appreciate that you do your job in Washington a little bit better than anyone else."[53] Eleanor replied with just the sort of testy lecture that fed Alice's vengeance in the first place:

> Ethel told me you had seen Alice. Of course she isn't a bit changed
> & it is always entertaining to see her but now that I am older &
> have my own values fixed a little I can only say what little I saw
> of her life gave me a feeling of dreariness & waste. Her house is

charming, her entertainment delightful. She's a born hostess & has an extraordinary mind but as for real friendship & what it means she hasn't a conception of any depth in any feeling or so it seems. Life seems to be one long pursuit of pleasure & excitement & rather little real happiness either given or taken on the way, the "bluebird" always to be searched for in some new & novel way. I sometimes think that the lives of many burdens are not really to be pitied for at least they live deeply & from their sorrows spring up flowers, but an empty life is really dreadful![54]

Only six months earlier, Eleanor told Isabella Greenway that Alice had been "nice." With her sudden bitterness and emphasis on Alice's lack of "real friendship & what it means" and "depth in any feeling," it's hard not to wonder if Eleanor had become privy to more of her cousin's shenanigans than she let on.

———

Whatever ill will might have germinated in the family plot was quickly tamped down by something far bigger—the war. The United States formally entered World War I on April 6, 1917, and few families committed themselves more enthusiastically than the Roosevelts. All four of Alice's brothers enlisted. The baby, nineteen-year-old Quentin, went to sign up with his cousin Hall, Eleanor's brother. Neither of them could see well enough to enter the air force, though that's the branch they joined. "I think both Hall and Quentin must have memorized the card for the eye test," Eleanor said.[55] Theodore couldn't have cared less about how they got into the fight, as long as they got in. "I am more proud of you and of the other three boys than I can possibly put into words," he wrote to Archie. To prove his point, he bought a flag with a bold red border and four blue stars, one for each son fighting for his country, and hung it outside at Sagamore.[56]

The war had become Franklin's life too, but that wasn't good enough for Uncle Ted. TR repeatedly insisted that FDR quit his post at the navy and enlist, as he had done at the outbreak of the Spanish-American War. (Franklin tried; the brass in the military, aware of his central role in overseeing the naval bureaucracy, refused to let him go.) What's more, Theodore—approaching sixty, blind in one eye, and increasingly frail after grueling expeditions to Africa and South America—was itching to fight too. Just four days after Congress declared war, Theodore rushed to Washington in hopes of presenting his plan to President Wilson. He wanted to raise his own army division, something like the old Rough Riders and including some of the same men, and head to the battlefields of France. Franklin and Eleanor met him at the Longworths' on that afternoon in April 1917, then Alice drove with her father to the White House. The guard at the northwest gate let them right in—they were, after all, previous tenants—but without an appointment they couldn't get to Wilson. A week later, he tried again. This time, Theodore had asked Franklin to grease the skids, a tall order given that Wilson was Franklin's boss and Theodore had been Wilson's rival and harshest critic. But Wilson agreed to see him, and the former president arrived at the Red Room with his tail between his legs and Longfellow on his lips. "Mr. President, what I have said and thought," he conceded, "is all dust in a windy street if we can make your message good."[57] The two presidents spent forty-five minutes chatting amiably, perhaps more amiably than either had expected. "There is a sweetness about him that is very compelling," Wilson told an aide afterward. "You can't resist the man."[58] When Theodore left, he spent the rest of the day back at Alice's house, holding court with the press, a collection of ambassadors, and various congressmen eager to hear his battle plans. Wilson was actually in favor of sending TR to war, but his aides argued against it. One month and one personal plea on Roosevelt's behalf by the French prime minister, Georges Clemenceau, later, Wilson officially rejected Roosevelt's request. "I think the decision was a bitter blow from which he never quite recovered," Eleanor said.[59]

————

For all of Theodore's war hungering, he managed to overlook his own daughter's wan efforts. Even Alice admitted that her contributions paled next to those of women such as her brother Ted's wife, Eleanor Butler Roosevelt, who left their three young children at home in New York and went to France with the YMCA so she could be closer to her husband on the battlefields near Paris. "At that time, I was criticized for *not* serving my country," Alice said. "I mean, I dished out ice cream to soldiers coming through and things like that, but nothing very serious."[60] She preferred to make the most of her natural talents—giving dinner parties, for example.

Just because they didn't require much sweat and sacrifice didn't mean they weren't worthy, right? "I think it pleased the Washington that went to and gave dinners to feel that entertaining the representatives of the Allies had a recognized part in 'winning the war,'" she wrote. "Anyway, it was a far pleasanter form of 'war work' than canteens, Red Cross classes, and Liberty Loan drives."[61] Alice's biggest contribution to the war effort might have been a fashion statement. When the press went after her for going out to a dinner one night wearing silk, ankle-length pants under her tunic-like top, she turned it into a civic-minded campaign: "I urge all the ladies to wear pantalettes," she said. "They're comfortable, economical and save considerable cloth."[62] Just as she did with smoking or driving, Alice turned her nonconformity into a lifestyle upgrade for all women.

Alice's artful rationalizations didn't entirely stunt her more patriotic instincts. She sold Treasury bonds[63] and joined a committee to help government employees find housing in Washington.[64] She even invited Eleanor to serve with her. Then, when Eleanor started volunteering at the Red Cross canteen, a tin-roofed shed near Union Station where arriving soldiers could stop for a bite to eat, Alice asked to tag along. "Alice has been here twice in two days & to ask if I want her to work anywhere & I'm going to try to get her interested," Eleanor wrote to Isabella. "It is a pity so much energy should go to waste!"[65] Yet Eleanor knew Alice well enough to suspect that her enthusiasm would melt about as quickly as a Washington snowstorm, especially because Alice informed her that "she did not like scrubbing and ironing," as Eleanor said. "I'm taking Alice down to the canteen but I doubt if she does much and they told me they were almost afraid to take her on!"[66] In fact, Alice lasted all of two trips before quitting due to an ailment she jokingly called "canteen elbow."[67]

It's hard to say whether the heretofore unknown canteen elbow was related to Eleanor's finger condition, but it seems possible. One busy morning, Eleanor was using the bread-cutting machine to make sandwiches for the servicemen when she got distracted and gashed her finger. "There was no time to stop, so I wrapped something tightly around it and proceeded during the day to wrap more and more handkerchiefs around it, until it finally stopped bleeding," she said.[68] What was the point of Alice's even showing up? She knew she could never compete with a woman who spilled so much blood for her country.

And that was just a start. Eleanor already put in round-the-clock shifts at the canteen in often sweltering conditions ("I've come to the conclusion that you only feel heat when idle," she told Franklin).[69] She also paid weekly visits to the naval hospital bearing flowers and cigarettes for the wounded sailors, supervised forty groups of women who were knitting clothes to send overseas (while also knitting in "every waking moment"), and presided at the occasional Navy Department rally—all while overseeing the Roosevelt household, moving the children back and forth to Hyde Park and Campobello, and entertaining foreign dignitaries as the wife of the assistant secretary of the navy. The Food Administration even singled her out for her outstanding at-home rationing program, which earned her a small write-up in the *New York Times*. "Making the ten servants help me do my saving has not only been possible, but highly profitable," she explained modestly—though not modestly enough for Franklin.[70] "All I can say is that your latest newspaper campaign is a corker and I am proud to be the husband of the Originator, Discoverer and Inventor of the New Household Economy for Millionaires!" he wrote to her angrily. "Please have a photo taken showing the family, the ten cooperating servants, the scraps they saved from the table and the hand book. I will have it published in the Sunday Times."[71] With her own husband taking Eleanor down a peg, it's hard to blame Alice for her "elbow" and her conclusion: "I leave the good deeds to Eleanor."[72] Anyway, Eleanor didn't leave many undone.

On the other hand, Alice was only too happy to take on any naughty tasks that might arise, and it just so happened that one did. In the summer of 1918, the War Department suspected that a beautiful and wealthy young socialite named May Ladenburg was leaking American military secrets to the enemy. At the time, Ladenburg was the girlfriend of Bernard Baruch, a New York financier who was set to become chairman of the War Industries Board. The government believed that Ladenburg was charming (so to speak) information out of her lover. She and Baruch were mainstays on the Washington social circuit, so Alice naturally knew them both well. She had even attended parties at the N Street house that Ladenburg rented about a block away from the Longworths. When the Secret Service decided to bug Ladenburg's home in hopes of collecting incriminating pillow talk, they came to Alice for advice on where to plant the listening devices. She suggested, among other places, "not exactly a hammock but a kind of mattress on a swing" in an upper balcony—prime tryst territory. "I discovered that all I was being asked to do was to look over transoms and peep through keyholes. Could anything be more delightful than that?" Alice said.[73]

Well, actually, yes. In order to trap Ladenburg, the government also needed to create some phony military documents so they could track the source of her information (the Feds believed she was feeding the intelligence to an uncle in Vienna). The official charged with preparing the documents was none other than Assistant Secretary Roosevelt. Together, the partners in crime had the pleasure of eavesdropping on Baruch and Ladenburg's allegedly treasonous love nest. "We did hear her ask Bernie how many locomotives were being sent to Romania, or something like that. In between the sounds of kissing, so to speak," said Alice. Neither Ladenburg nor Baruch was ever charged with a crime. Nonetheless, Eleanor charged both her husband and her cousin with conduct unbefitting a Roosevelt. "Eleanor apparently knew about what was going on—as a great many people did—and years afterwards when Franklin was at the White House we were both chuckling about the incident one time and Eleanor said, 'You know, Alice, I have always disapproved of what you and Franklin were doing,'" Alice said. "Of course we were doing a most disgraceful thing in the name of looking after the affairs of the country, but it was sheer rapture!"[74] Did she mean the spying or the fact that she was joined on the dark side by her virtuous cousin Eleanor's husband?

———

The war naturally brought plenty of hardship, too. For the Roosevelts, the darkest cloud came on July 16, 1918, when the local Associated Press reporter showed up on Theodore's doorstep clutching a strange cable from France that read, "WATCH SAGAMORE HILL FOR—" For what? The censors had blotted out the rest. But Theodore felt sure it meant something had happened to one of his four boys. He asked the reporter to keep the mystery between the two of them for the moment, until they knew more. Theodore spent the evening with Edith as if nothing had happened. The next day before breakfast, the AP man returned with an unconfirmed report—it was young Quentin. He had been shot down over Chamery, France, deep behind enemy lines, and killed. Theodore went in to tell Edith and returned a half hour later with a public statement: "Quentin's mother and I are very glad that he got to the front and had a chance to render some service to his country and show the stuff that was in him before his fate befell him." Then the grieving parents climbed into a row-boat and paddled into the stillness of Oyster Bay.[75] If either Theodore or Edith felt morose, they sealed the lid on their grief like a tomb. Two days later, they were in Saratoga for the Republican State Convention, where Theodore went on as the scheduled keynote speaker. Still no official word about Quentin. Back at Sagamore three days later, some family friends who worked with the Red Cross dropped by with a delegation of visiting Japanese colleagues and asked the ex-president for a tour.[76] He took them to the trophy room and talked a bit about Japanese-American relations. On their way out, the neighbor, Trubee Davison, asked Roosevelt if he'd heard any more information about Quentin. "He said, 'Trubee, just 20 minutes before you arrived I received this telegram from President Wilson,'" Davison said. "Then he showed me the telegram from Wilson that spoke of Quentin's death. It was one of the most extraordinary exhibitions of control and courage I have ever seen."[77] Only those closest to the family could see through their steely curtain. "I dined with Alice last night & she says the family have been wonderful about Quentin," Eleanor wrote two weeks after her cousin's death. "He was killed instantly by 2 bullet holes in the head they have heard through Spain so he did not suffer & it is a glorious way to die but I know A. Edith & Ethel are suffering."[78]

Though her brother Hall ultimately returned safely, Eleanor suffered a different kind of loss at the hands of the war. She reveled in juggling her full plate of volunteering and managing the household, but that left her little time for Franklin. When she wasn't rushing from the canteen to the navy hospital, she was with the children in Hyde Park or Campobello. At the same time, Franklin was either sailing off to inspect naval bases or hopelessly trapped in Washington. "I do miss you so very much, but I am getting busier and busier and fear my hoped-for dash to Campo next week for two days will not materialize. Nor can I get to H. P. for Sunday, as I found my absence last Sunday has put me too far back," he wrote to her.[79] She had been petulant and suspicious about these sudden no-shows all summer, especially given how often Lucy turned up in Franklin's letters. Eleanor realized that her former secretary was still turning up in the Roosevelts' home, too, when she received a packet of paperwork in the mail from Lucy—even though Lucy had been fired weeks earlier. In August 1917, when Franklin entered a Washington hospital with a serious throat infection, Eleanor seized the chance to be alone with him. She left the children at Campobello and rushed home. The tone of Franklin and Eleanor's conversations there was alternately warm and strained, based on the letter she wrote to him on the return train trip back north: "I hated to leave yesterday. Please go to the doctor twice a week, eat well and sleep well and remember I count on seeing you the 26th. My threat was no idle one."[80]

The content of the un-idle threat remains a mystery. Some biographers believe she ordered him to stop making excuses and get up to Campobello by the appointed date or she would drag the brood back to Washington. (He did in fact show up as commanded.)[81] Others believe she actually confronted him about Lucy. "There was no mystery; she threatened to leave him," said their son Elliott.[82] But that seems unlikely. The truth is, despite her festering suspicions about Franklin and Lucy, Eleanor had adopted an astonishing see-no-evil attitude toward their relationship, even by her usual doormat standards. One day in the winter-spring of 1918, Eleanor was alone at home in Washington. Franklin had gone on a short trip to award some navy medals, and this time he took Mama and the two youngest boys, Franklin junior and John, with him. Eleanor spent the late afternoon listening to the wartime debates in the Capitol. She apparently also spent the day with Alice, who decided to have a fraught conversation with her cousin after the last hearing of the day. "On the way out I parted with Alice at the door not having allowed her to tell me any secrets," she said. "She inquired if you had told me and I said no and that I did not believe in knowing things which your husband did not wish [you] to know so I think I will be spared any further mysterious secrets!"[83]

Would Alice really have tattled on Franklin right in the Capitol rotunda? The larger question is why Alice, once again, acted so cruelly toward her oldest and once-dearest cousin—so cruel that she seemed determined to bulldoze her marriage. It wasn't just that Alice liked to make trouble for her own amusement, though that was certainly part of it. It was around this time that she became infamous on the dinner-party circuit for her braying Eleanor imitations. With her teeth thrust out, her jaw tucked in, and her voice ratcheted to a quivering upper register, Alice's take on Eleanor came across as something like a talking horse just out of a proper British finishing school. "Alice was venomous toward Eleanor," said Margaret Cutting, Hall Roosevelt's first wife. "I never saw anybody so vicious."[84]

But Alice didn't see it that way. She just thought Eleanor needed to lighten up. "She had so little enjoyment, so little amusement. She was so insecure about so many things," Alice said. "I've always laughed about the family, including myself. I'm a comic character too."[85] In fact, there was something almost protective about the way Alice confronted her cousin that day in the Capitol. She could easily have ratted Franklin out. Instead, she tried to lead Eleanor to uncover the truth for herself. If Franklin's relationship with Lucy really was an open secret around town, being the last one to know would make the situation that much more humiliating. Alice knew how it felt to be the subject of gossip. She had once been the most gossiped-about woman in the country. And she knew what it felt like to endure an unfaithful husband. If Franklin wasn't going to let his wife confront the situation on her own terms—rather than have the situation thrust on her when she least expected it—Alice was at least going to force his hand.

Instead of following Alice's lead, Eleanor once again buried her head and carried on her life as if nothing were amiss in her marriage. Franklin certainly couldn't get in much trouble in the summer of 1918. After months of badgering Secretary Daniels, he was finally being sent overseas to tour the troops in Europe. He sailed from Brooklyn on July 9 and spent two months in England, France, Italy, and Belgium. FDR might have been only an assistant secretary, but he was treated like royalty. He had a private forty-five-minute meeting at Buckingham Palace with King George V, who also sent regards to the family. ("He had just had a nice letter from Uncle Ted, thanking him for one he had sent at the time of TR's illness last spring," FDR wrote to Eleanor.)[86] He also met the prime ministers of England (Lloyd George), France (Clemenceau), and Italy (Orlando), along with a fleet's worth of admirals, colonels, and generals from throughout the Allied countries and a smattering of American politicians (Herbert Hoover, Fiorello La Guardia) who happened to be passing through. He even found time to squeeze in visits with a few relatives, including Roosevelt cousins Archie, Ted junior, and Ted's wife, Eleanor.

Naturally, Eleanor kept herself just as busy at home. She spent the first month alone in Washington, mostly slaving away in the canteen while the children were up in Hyde Park. "It was not an unusual thing for me to work from nine in the morning until one or two the next morning, and be back again by 10 a.m.," she said. "The nights were hot and it was possible to sleep only if you were exhausted."[87] At least she had some company. "Mrs. Wilson now has a uniform and comes to work fairly regularly," she wrote to Sara.[88] Eleanor did finally escape the heat for a few weeks in Hyde Park, taking a break only to attend the funeral of Aunt Corinne's husband, Douglas Robinson. She got word a few days later that Franklin would be heading home. Then, the day before his arrival, an urgent telegram arrived from the Navy Department saying that Franklin had contracted double pneumonia and that she should meet him at the dock in Hoboken with an ambulance. (Many others on board Franklin's ship were also gravely ill; a few had died and been buried at sea in the Atlantic.)[89] Naturally, Mama insisted on joining Eleanor to collect her boy. On September 19, the women and a doctor waited for Franklin, had him loaded onto a stretcher, then quickly delivered him to Sara's side of the house on Sixty-Fifth Street (Franklin and Eleanor had rented theirs out while they were living in Washington). "My husband did not seem to me so seriously ill as the doctors implied," Eleanor wrote later in her memoir, but plenty of other folks were worried.[90] "Dear Franklin, We are deeply concerned about your sickness, and trust you will soon be well. We are very proud of you. With love, Aff. Yours Theodore Roosevelt."[91]

If, in retrospect, Eleanor seemed blasé about her husband's condition, maybe it was because she was too angry to care how he had been feeling. After she and Mama put Franklin to bed, Eleanor set about unpacking his suitcases. As she went through his documents and tried to put them in order for him, she came across a stack of letters. They were from Lucy. She read them. The feeling was as stunning as being smacked across the face. "The bottom dropped out of my own particular world," she said, "and I faced myself, my surroundings, my world honestly for the first time."[92]

# Chapter 5

# THE BREAK BEGINS

I n December 1918, Theodore Roosevelt started talking about running for president again, which was surprising given that he was confined to a New York City hospital bed at the time. The Roosevelt men, for all their lust for life, were often betrayed by their bodies. Theodore had driven his especially hard, ever since he took up boxing as a way to beat back childhood asthma. His rough-riding adventures were the stuff of legend—and only the beginning. Right after leaving the White House, he and Kermit had gone on an African safari deep into the heart of darkness. The following year, father and son took on Brazil, where they explored an uncharted tributary of the Amazon (now called the Rio Roosevelt). They contracted malaria, and at one point Kermit almost had to leave his father behind in the jungle with a leg that had become so infected the ex-president couldn't walk. Now, at sixty, he was suffering with some combination of inflammatory rheumatism, vertigo, gout, lumbago, sciatica, anemia, and blindness in one eye. His doctors feared he would eventually be consigned to a wheelchair. "All right," the Colonel said after receiving that dour diagnosis, "I can work and live that way too."[1] A Roosevelt wouldn't let a mere wheelchair keep him from pursuing the White House.

Though he'd been ailing off and on for months, Theodore's hospitalization was preceded by a typical tornado of activity, including a series of speeches in early October that took him to Ohio, Missouri, Nebraska, and Montana. Quentin's death in July had been hanging heavily on him, and the Roosevelt cure for what ailed them was always action. On October 28, the day after his sixtieth birthday, Theodore delivered a two-hour speech (vetted once again by Alice) in Carnegie Hall that the *New York Times* called "savage." He was responding to a plea by President Wilson, made a few days earlier, to reelect a Democratic Congress that would assure passage of his fourteen-point peace plan. "He does not ask for loyalty to the nation," Roosevelt said. "He only asks for support of himself."[2] Roosevelt told the Carnegie audience that the fourteen points should be "emphatically repudiated" because they would fail to achieve "the peace of complete victory, a peace obtained by machine guns and not typewriters." The standing-room crowd frequently broke into the kinds of cheers you might hear at a boxing match: "Rub it in, Teddy!" Outside, several thousand more followers overran the sidewalks and the police.

The speech might have been a triumph, but the stress of delivering it slammed the man like a steer going down at a rodeo. Theodore's rheumatism (or gout, or whatever it was—the doctors were never sure) made one of his feet swell so badly that he couldn't get a shoe over it. He was ordered to stay in bed, as if that meant anything. Election Day was November 5, so he naturally ignored his doctors and dragged himself to a blacksmith's shop in Oyster Bay that served as the local polling place. Roosevelt got his wish; the Senate and the House both flipped to Republican. Even better, on November 9, Alice's old friend Kaiser Wilhelm II abdicated and fled to the Netherlands. Two days later, at precisely 11:00 a.m. on the eleventh day of the eleventh month, the armistice began.

———

Alas, November 11 was also the day Theodore landed in the hospital. He languished there for forty-four days, pondering a future somewhere between a wheelchair and the Oval Office. To prove his mettle to himself and the rest of the world, he maintained his usual, manic writing pace, from newspaper columns to the outline of his presidential platform. At one point, he wrote a five-page letter to his friend Rudyard Kipling, but before he could mail it, a letter from Kipling himself arrived. So Theodore wrote him four more pages and mailed them all.

The Colonel had begun to walk a little better by Christmas Day, and his doctors let him return home. Ted junior and Kermit were still in Europe recovering from their war wounds, but Alice, Ethel, and Archie met him at Sagamore, along with a dusting of snow that covered his beloved homestead like a welcoming blanket. There was no holiday from the joint pain, however. His wrist was so inflamed that he had to confine it to a sling and take arsenic injections to reduce the agony. He needed help shaving and had to dictate his letters and columns to Edith or Archie. By January 4, Edith became concerned enough to call in a full-time nurse and his retired White House valet, James Amos, the only person whom the president would allow to help him bathe and dress. He kept dictating— letters, editorials, corrections to a manuscript he'd written—but the pain had worsened on January 5 to the point where the nurse gave him a shot of morphine around midnight to help him sleep. He was staying in Ethel's old room that night, with Amos sitting near him by the coal fire. "James, will you please put out the light," Theodore asked just after the nurse left. Edith came to check on him at about 12:30 a.m. and again at 2:00 and found him sleeping peacefully; she didn't dare kiss him for fear of disturbing him. At 3:00 a.m., Theodore's breathing began to rev and fade like a sputtering car engine, and so loudly that it woke up Amos. He fetched the nurse. At 4:00 a.m., they summoned Edith, who rushed to her husband's bedside. "Theodore, darling!" she said. He didn't respond. He seemed to her to be "just asleep, only he could not hear." The doctors ruled that he died of a pulmonary embolism. On his nightstand were notes he had dictated to Archie, coordinating a lobbying effort in Washington. Among the condolences that began arriving in sacks the next day was one from Vice President Thomas Marshall. "Death had to take him sleeping," he wrote, "for if Roosevelt had been awake, there would have been a fight."

———

Theodore Roosevelt had died so suddenly, so unexpectedly, that most of the family received the grim news long-distance. Archie sent his brothers in France a cable as sharp and piercing as an arrow: "The old lion is dead." Kermit didn't get the message right away. He was away from his base, visiting a group of war correspondents in Koblenz at the time. The men there received word via the wireless and were about to break the news to Kermit when he stood up and asked to excuse himself because he wanted to read a letter he'd recently received from his father. No one had the stomach to tell him that "the old lion" was already gone.

Aunt Corinne, who had been scheduled to visit her brother at Sagamore that day, got a call at 6:00 a.m. from Edith. She arrived later that morning, and the two childhood friends "walked far and fast along the shore and through the woodlands he had loved." By the time they finished, near dusk, Sagamore was being patrolled by a fleet of guardian angels. "They must be planes from the camp where Quentin trained," said Edith. "They must have been sent as a guard of honor for his father."[3]

Though Alice had been home for Christmas, her father had seemed to be improving enough for her to return to Washington for New Year's. He had been the most significant presence in her life, the man whose approval or absence, feats or failures dictated most every decision she made. His passing before she could say good-bye left her speechless. She was reportedly "overcome by grief" at his funeral, but she never talked about her father's death.[4] Her most voluble response was a mere echo, a biblical allusion that came to mind after hearing of Archie's telegram to his brother: "The old lion perisheth for lack of prey, and the stout lion's whelps are scattered abroad."[5] In *Crowded Hours*, her autobiography, she skips from his Carnegie Hall speech to her postwar campaign against Wilson's peace plan. Just as Theodore Roosevelt's memoirs omitted any mention of his first wife's death, if Alice's memoir were your only source about President Roosevelt, you would never know he died.

Typically, Theodore's favorite niece worried about everybody's feelings but her own when she got the news. "I think much of Aunt Edith for it will leave her very much alone," Eleanor wrote to Sara, adding, "Another big figure gone from our nation and I fear the last years were for him full of disappointment."[6] Unfortunately, Eleanor couldn't offer her sympathies in person to Edith and her Oyster Bay family. She and Franklin were crossing the Atlantic and playing shuffleboard on the USS *George Washington* when the ship broadcast the radio report of Uncle Ted's death. It was Franklin's second voyage to Europe in the last six months. The first time, he had gone to assess the readiness of American naval forces and forge contacts with the Allies. Now he was going to close up shop two months after the armistice. The fact that he brought Eleanor along on this second sailing spoke less about the peaceful changes in Europe than about a shift in FDR's priorities. Last time he thought he was helping to save the world. Now he was hoping to save his marriage.

Despite Alice's hints, a town full of gossip, and enough of her own suspicion to have fired Lucy Mercer, Eleanor was by all accounts stunned when she harvested that bitter crop of love letters from Franklin's luggage after his previous European voyage. She did nothing at first, either out of shock or because Franklin was still so sick. But when she finally got up the nerve to confront him, letters in hand, the results were devastating. If he wanted a divorce, Eleanor told him, he could have one, though most of the family didn't know about her offer until many years later. "I remember one day I was having fun with Auntie Corinne. I was doing imitations of Eleanor, and Auntie Corinne looked at me and said, 'Never forget, Alice, Eleanor offered Franklin his freedom,'" Alice recalled. "And I said, 'But darling, that's what I've wanted to know about all these years. Tell!'"[7] After all, misery loves company. Alice had once offered her philandering husband a divorce, too.

Franklin did want out; he intended to marry Lucy. But while Eleanor initially seemed resigned, she was becoming more assertive and shrewd by the minute. After appearing to surrender to Franklin's wishes, she went behind his back and called in the heavy artillery: his mother. Sara was appalled at the notion of divorce. It had no place in her Victorian worldview. What's more, Eleanor had spent the last few years courting her mother-in-law. Despite their occasional tensions, they had grown closer. There's a genuine warmth pervading their letters, especially during these years of personal trials for Eleanor. "How lucky we are to have you and I wish we could always be together," she wrote to Sara. "Very few mothers I know mean as much to their daughters as you do to me."[8]

With Franklin's illness holding him captive in his mother's house that fall of 1918, Sara convened a meeting with her son and daughter-in-law to hash out the future. Like any smart parent, Mama knew that the surest way to push Franklin toward a divorce was to forbid him to get one. Instead, she simply informed her son that she would stop supporting him if he chose Lucy over Eleanor. He could never afford two houses, the various club memberships, a boat, and the children's upbringing on his salary and modest inheritance (Eleanor's $8,000 annual trust income was actually $3,000 more than what Franklin got from his father's bequest).[9] Life with Lucy would mean the end of his lavish lifestyle. To ensure that Franklin understood what was at risk, Louis Howe, his faithful consigliere, joined the tug-of-war. Facing the loss of his franchise player, Howe let Franklin know that divorce would vaporize his political career as well. He made sure Eleanor understood that too, in those moments when she seemed fed up with playing the good wife. "Louis did a selling job," Elliott said.

"Father wanted to give it up and mother felt betrayed and had a primitive outlook on it, but she came around because Louis convinced her."[10] With Mama and Howe lining up one hurdle after another—there was also Lucy's inconvenient Catholicism, which meant that her marrying a divorced man was highly unlikely—Franklin did what any clever and ambitious man would do. He broke off with Lucy and told her it was all Eleanor's fault. "She and Franklin were very much in love with each other," said Mrs. Lyman Cotten, Lucy's cousin and confidante. "I know that a marriage would have taken place but as Lucy said to us, 'Eleanor was not willing to step aside.'"[11]

Nonetheless, Eleanor got even with Franklin for the Lucy Mercer mess. As part of her agreeing to stay married, she forced Franklin to make a considerable sacrifice: their sex life. She was thirty-four. He was thirty-six. They never slept in the same bed again. While it's impossible to know if they remained celibate for the remaining twenty-seven years of their marriage, it's telling that Eleanor, who became pregnant on her honeymoon and gave birth to six children in rapid succession, had no more pregnancies. To the wronged wife, this frigid arrangement—something of a symbolic neutering—represented the ultimate punishment. At the same time, the end of their "marital relations" was no great loss to Eleanor. She later told her daughter, Anna, that she "had never been sexually fulfilled" and considered sex a "cross to bear."[12] When Eleanor caught a young Anna masturbating in bed, she tied her daughter's hands above her head to the bedposts.[13] Sex required a certain loss of control, of inhibition. Eleanor wasn't comfortable with those emotions anywhere, least of all in the bedroom.

Which isn't to say that she wanted no relationship with Franklin. On the contrary, she still cared for him, and he for her. "There was always an affection between them," wrote their son James. "After all, they had shared a lot and continued to share to the end."[14] Eleanor craved something like what Alice seemed to have with Nick in their similarly flawed but productive marriage. She wanted a partnership. "She demanded respect from then on," James said.[15] That trip to Europe in January 1919—in two adjoining cabins, not one—marked the beginning of their lives as equals. The seas crossing the Atlantic were horribly rough. Bernard Baruch, the object of Franklin and Alice's tawdry little reconnaissance mission, was on board and spent most of the time sick in his cabin. Livingston Davis, one of FDR's Harvard buddies who was also traveling with the Roosevelts, noted "whole dining room wrecked by heavy roll, also my breakfast landing on top of waiter's head."[16] It should have been torture for the sea-phobic Eleanor. Instead, she found herself sailing along comfortably. "I could sit at table, eat or dress or do whatever life required with a certain amount of assurance that I would get through the ordeal without being really ill!" she said.[17] Was it a coincidence that she found her sea legs just as she found herself on more equal footing with her husband?

Franklin did his utmost to embrace Eleanor's growing presence. During their thirty-five days abroad, they toured several stops along the French front lines, including battlefields in the Somme and Boulogne not often visited by women. She joined him to meet the president of France and numerous high-ranking soldiers while squeezing in visits with her injured cousins Ted and Kermit and a mini-reunion with her Allenswood classmates. The overall effect was like a vitamin $B_{12}$ shot of confidence. Unlike the infamous night when she slept petulantly on the doorstep awaiting Franklin's return from a late party, Eleanor dragged him away from a dinner one night at 11:00 when she noticed he was becoming "fascinated by Lady Scott"—then bragged about it to Mama in a letter.[18] To top it all off, the Roosevelts shared the ship home with President and Mrs. Wilson, lunching with him on the rare occasion when he deigned to mix with his shipmates, then riding the train together from Boston to Washington. "At every station cheering crowds greeted the President, even long after dark. My first experience of the kind and very moving, because the people seemed to have grasped his ideals and to want to back them," she said.[19] (A curious observation, given that she'd spent Inauguration Day 1905 with a president at least as popular as Wilson—Uncle Ted.) It's telling that in her autobiography *This Is My Story*, ER devoted more space to this European trip than to any other single incident. She titled the chapter "Abroad Together."

If Eleanor held a grudge against Alice for aiding and abetting the enemy of her marriage, she didn't show it. She invited the Longworths over for dinner regularly, as she always had. In many ways, the dynamic of their relationship was unchanged: it was still Alice the Imp and Eleanor the Audience. Alice was the main event at a dinner in October 1919 for Sir Edward Grey, an old friend of Theodore's and a former British foreign secretary, who was on a last-ditch mission to persuade President Wilson to compromise with the Republicans in order to ratify the League of Nations. "Lord G. said to Alice, 'I would like to have a list of the books which you have read and I've never heard of'! She really is extraordinary and kept us all entertained," Eleanor wrote to Sara.[20] The cousins clearly cared deeply about each other. Just before midnight on June 2, 1919, Alice and Nick arrived home from a party and were greeted at their door by a friendly local policeman she called Loftus. He wanted to tell the Longworths about an enormous explosion that had been reported just a few minutes earlier at the home of A. Mitchell Palmer, the controversial attorney general who had begun arresting perceived Russian sympathizers. (In fact, it was Palmer who deported Emma Goldman later that year, with the help of his eager new assistant, J. Edgar Hoover.) The Palmers lived at 2132 R Street NW. Franklin and Eleanor now lived at 2131 R Street, directly across the road. Nick, Alice, and Loftus jumped in the Longworths' car and drove the few blocks to the crime scene. They arrived to find shattered windows everywhere, chunks of the Palmer house missing, and anarchist literature strewn around the block. No one was hurt but the hapless perpetrator, who police believed might have tripped and fallen on the bomb while approaching the Palmers' front porch. "We went in to see Franklin and Eleanor," Alice said. "A leg lay in the path to the house next to theirs, another leg farther up the street. A head was on the roof of another house. As we walked across it was difficult to avoid stepping on bloody chunks of human being. The man had been torn apart, fairly blown to butcher's meat."[21] Like Alice and Nick, Franklin and Eleanor had gone out that evening and arrived home just minutes after the blast. "Finding me standing by the window, father embraced me so hard that, in my mind, I can still feel the ardor of it," James said. "Mother merely asked, 'Whatever are you doing out of bed at this hour, James?' as if a bomb exploded every hour."[22]

———

Yet despite their substantial family feeling, Alice and Eleanor continued to drift apart, like ill-fated siblings who found themselves fighting on opposites sides in the Civil War. Though Alice never spoke about her father's death, she became devoted to protecting his legacy. She blamed Wilson for her father's unexpected demise—a pulmonary embolism isn't exactly a broken heart, but Alice maintained that Wilson's refusal to allow Theodore to fight in France irreparably broke his spirit. She even kept a voodoo doll that resembled the president and often jabbed it with pins. Alice made a point to be at Union Station around midnight on July 8, 1919, when the president triumphantly returned to Washington after signing the Treaty of Versailles. "I wanted to see for myself what sort of reception he was given," she said. "It was a sparse crowd . . . There was very little cheering—such as there was had a treble quality, as women predominated."[23] (This was hardly a compliment. Alice was no suffragette, and she put little stock in opinions of the female persuasion.) The *New York Times* apparently watched the president's arrival from a different location: "Never in recent years has any other President received such a warm welcome at such a late hour. Not only were the crowds larger, but they were more demonstrative in their greeting and there was no mistaking their sincerity."[24] At least one person wasn't offering a warm welcome. When the president's motorcade drove past her, Alice jumped out of her car and stood on the curb to watch. Then she crossed her fingers, made the sign of an evil eye, and delivered a medieval curse: "A murrain on him! A murrain on him!"[25]

The fact that Franklin worked in the Wilson administration earned him and Eleanor a large black mark in Alice's book. It didn't help that Eleanor and Franklin had sailed home from Europe with Wilson in February 1919 as he carried the outline for the Treaty of Versailles, the blueprint for the League of Nations. Even though a wary U.S. Senate still needed to be persuaded to ratify the treaty, the Wilsonians were giddy at the prospect of forging what they believed was a landmark vehicle for world peace. "We heard nothing but the League of Nations and the great advantages of the League of Nations," said Sheffield Cowles, Aunt Bye's son who worked with FDR in Europe and also sailed home with him and Wilson. Once Sheffield arrived in Washington, he went to stay with his cousin Alice. When he told her all the rosy predictions he'd heard from Franklin, Eleanor, and the rest aboard the ship, Alice nearly blew his ears off. "I was surprised, from being in one milieu, in which the League of Nations was the ultimate and desirable thing to attain, to land in Alice's house where I found it was the absolute worst thing, in her opinion, that we could do for this country," Cowles said. "She immediately broke down my arguments in favor of the League. In fact, she completely changed me on it in no time at all."[26]

Alice might have chopped up young Sheffield's convictions like so much hamburger meat, but she wasn't really motivated by any grand geopolitical worldview. Although Theodore died before the final provisions for the league had been hammered out, she knew that he had planned to make defeating it a cornerstone of a potential 1920 presidential platform. After his unexpected death, Alice and the president's admirers clutched to the Gospel of Roosevelt as if it were some sort of political scripture. As with all scripture, Theodore Roosevelt's enormously complicated legacy was subject to interpretation. Over the years, his sharp, curious, and sometimes mercurial mind had explored and occasionally embraced contradictory stands on key issues. He might have rejected an international peacekeeping organization at the end of his life, but as early as 1910, when he traveled to Norway to accept his Nobel Peace Prize, he seemed to be arguing in favor of just such a body. "It would be a masterstroke," he said in Oslo, "if those great powers honestly bent on peace would form a League of Peace, not only to keep the peace among themselves but to prevent, by force if necessary, its being broken by others."[27]

When the outlines of Wilson's vision of peace came into focus with the league at its core, Theodore turned skeptic. In part, he had qualms about who would be allowed to join and when, as well as some concerns about the potential for U.S. membership to infringe on national sovereignty. Most threatening, though, he worried that the league could ultimately entangle the United States in a foreign war. This was a somewhat ironic concern coming from one of the loudest cheerleaders for American involvement in World War I, not to mention the man whose own proposal had called for the use of force where necessary to keep the peace. In short, while TR was very much an internationalist who embraced the concept of a league, nothing could convince him that the hated Wilson—the man who personally barred his way to battlefields of Europe—could be trusted with the job of establishing it.

That distrust, even loathing, of Wilson was one of the legacies Theodore bequeathed to Alice. Well after her father's death, she was still doubting that anyone could abide the man. In 1920, Ethel Barrymore was in Washington performing in a play called *The Twelve-Pound Look*, and Wilson was in the audience one night. Traffic was tied up for blocks after the curtain, delaying Barrymore's dinner date with Alice. "I couldn't get out of the theater any sooner because there was such a terrific crowd around it waiting to see Mr. Wilson leave," Barrymore explained. "Who?" Alice asked. "When I told her, she wouldn't believe me. She hated Wilson so bitterly that she simply couldn't believe that a great crowd had waited just to see him pass."[28]

Even before Wilson returned from Paris with the draft of the Treaty of Versailles, a group of senators and representatives from both parties had focused their collective firepower. They called themselves the Irreconcilables because they wanted to make clear that they would never accept the league under any conditions (as compared with another faction, the Reservationists, named after Senator Henry Cabot Lodge's Twelve Reservations, which, had they been adopted by President Wilson, might have allowed this Senate faction to support the treaty). Alice spent hours and hours each day listening to the Irreconcilables' broadsides in various committee rooms and on the House and Senate floors. Some nights she stayed glued to her chair in the Capitol galleries until well past midnight. Other times she would pile in a car with a handful of Irreconcilables and drive around town plotting the next move. Her influence was soft—it would be another year before the Nineteenth Amendment gave women the right to vote—but real. She frequently entertained the men at her house for a strategy-planning dinner, where her strong and strident voice was heard just as loudly as the men's. Sometimes she was enlisted to lobby a Reservationist personally. When President Wilson began a nationwide speaking tour to drum up popular support for the league, one of his arguments was that Theodore Roosevelt himself had been a supporter.[29] To kick that claim to the curb, Senator Lodge asked Alice to write an open letter denouncing that as a "gross misrepresentation."[30] (Five decades later, she shamelessly contradicted herself. "We were always for a League of Nations, because my father had started it in this country in his Nobel Peace Prize speech," she told one interviewer.[31] Just not Wilson's league.) Soon enough, the Irreconcilables gave Alice her own nickname: the Colonel of the Battalion of Death.

If Wilson was the common enemy, the league battle also supplied Alice with a rather close friend. Though she would sometimes pull up a chair in the House to hear what her husband had to say, she gravitated to the Senate Foreign Relations Committee and Idaho's fiery orator William Borah. Borah was an unlikely man for Alice to support. They had been adversaries since 1912, when she picked a fight with him in the dining car of a train out of Chicago because he had refused to abandon the GOP in favor of her father's Progressive Party. By the same token, Borah had frequently backed Wilson in the run-up to the war, and support for Wilson was her political third rail. But Borah prided himself on being someone who didn't let party or politics interfere with ideals. His reputation for being contrary was downright infamous. When Calvin Coolidge heard one day that the senator was horseback riding, he quipped that "I doubt it, because I have always understood that a horseback rider has to go in the same direction as his horse."[32]

Yet Alice always respected freethinkers—especially when they agreed with her. As soon as Wilson revealed his vision for the League of Nations in his famous Fourteen Points in January 1918, Borah joined the Irreconcilable opposition. Borah himself was nicknamed the Lion of Idaho, a nod to both the mane of unruly hair on his overlarge head and his deep growl of a voice. He was the matinee idol of the Capitol. His grand and literate speeches, rehearsed down to the syllable (often while riding his favorite horse, Jester, through Rock Creek Park), drew overflow crowds to the staid halls of the Senate. Clarence Darrow, who faced off against Borah in the sensational 1907 trial of a man accused of blowing up the former governor of Idaho on his own front porch, called Borah "the ablest man" he ever faced (though Darrow still won the case).[33] Alice was smitten every time he opened his mouth. "Occasionally I did not entirely agree with what Borah said, or rather with the slant he gave some question," she said, "but he had a quality of earnest eloquence combined with a sort of smoldering benevolence, and knew so exactly how to manage his voice that before he finished I was always enthusiastic."[34]

Somewhere along the way, her enthusiasm spread to the other parts of his body. It wasn't surprising that they became lovers. Borah was very much Alice's type. Older (by almost two decades), intellectual, and with a love of literature, the Lion of Idaho once again satisfied her daddy issues: "Lion" was also one of Theodore's nicknames. Like all the men in her life, Borah was as masculine as a ram. When he was offered a cup of tea by a hostess once, he answered, "Do I look like a man who drinks tea?"[35] He chased women like an animal, too, though his wife, Mary, was either oblivious or resigned. It was Mary Borah with whom Alice had gone calling the day she refused to get out of the car, which raises the question: Was Alice trying to deflect attention from her affair with Borah by flaunting her friendship with his wife, or was she just being her usual devilish self?

In small-townish Washington, the gossiping class aired its suspicions about Borah and Alice with relish, both in whispers and in print. It didn't help that the ascetic Borah—he would later become a leading defender of Prohibition—almost never went to parties except for those thrown by one of two women: Alice or her old friend, rival, and panty depositor, Cissy Patterson, who was now known as Countess Gizycka by virtue of her foundering marriage to a wealthy Polish count. Like two fancy poodles sniffing around a Great Dane, the princess and the countess again found themselves fighting for the same powerful man. At the 1920 Republican convention in Chicago, Cissy put Borah up in the house she'd rented, then salivated all over him in a story she wrote for the *Chicago Herald and Examiner.* "He picked up and held that audience in his hands as expertly and delicately as a woman might hold a peevish child," Cissy said about a nominating speech he made on the floor. (It's worth noting that while the Pattersons owned the *Chicago Tribune,* Cissy, ever the troublemaker, had gone to work for the rival *Herald and Examiner,* where along with her byline she was trumpeted as "Sister of the Editor of the *Chicago Tribune.*")[36] The stories linking Cissy and Borah were numerous, hilarious, and often apocryphal. One of the most widely circulated had Borah arriving at a Longworth party, only to disappear upstairs with Cissy. If that sounds familiar, so was the postmortem: Alice allegedly found several of Cissy's hairpins in the library and returned them to her with a note. Only this time, instead of wondering if Alice had found her silk stockings in the couch, Cissy replied by asking if she'd discovered her underwear—in the chandelier.

Just as with their last love triangle, Alice got her man in the end. Her most triumphant moment might have come on November 19, 1919, when the Senate convened to vote on the Treaty of Versailles after four months of debate. Alice and her closest friend, Ruth Hanna McCormick[*] (whose husband, Medill, was a first-term senator from Illinois), sat in the family gallery from the opening gavel until 11:00 p.m. "It was the greatest crowd I have ever seen there," Alice said.[37] As an acknowledgment of his moral and oracular authority, Borah was given the penultimate speech. He lec-

---

[*] Ruth Hanna McCormick Simms (1880–1944) was the daughter of Republican powerhouse and McKinley-backer Senator Mark Hanna. Alice's lifelong friend and close confidante, Ruth married wealthy journalist and politician Joseph Medill McCormick in 1903; he committed suicide shortly after Paulina Longworth's birth in 1925. Ruth then married Representative Albert Gallatin Simms. She served one term representing Illinois in the House of Representatives from 1929–1931, then left the House for an unsuccessful bid to represent Illinois in the Senate.

tured for two hours, invoking Monroe, Lincoln, Washington, Jefferson, and Frederick the Great, all the while addressing himself directly to President Wilson. "Sir, since the debate opened months ago, those of us who have stood against this proposition have been taunted many times with being little Americans. Leave us the word American, keep that in your presumptuous impeachment, and no taunt can disturb us, nor decompose our purposes."[38] When Borah finished, that old salt Senator Lodge was reduced to tears. The Senate voted down Wilson's plan 53 to 38, the first time it had ever rejected a peace treaty. To celebrate, the Irreconcilables repaired to their unofficial headquarters: Alice's dining room. "Mrs. Harding cooked the eggs," Alice said. "We were jubilant."[39] Alice and Borah drove there together.

———

The Democrats weren't ready to give up on their dream for the league just yet—far from it. Although Wilson had suffered a debilitating stroke in October that left the presidency largely in the clutches of his manipulative wife, Edith, his followers carried on in Washington and beyond. At the Democratic National Convention in San Francisco in the summer of 1920, support for the league was as thick as the field of candidates. Twenty-four men lined up to run for president, including the governors of New York, New Jersey, and Ohio. FDR was a delegate for New York's Al Smith, but when he dropped out, Roosevelt switched his support to the former secretary of the Treasury William Gibbs McAdoo. McAdoo also happened to be Wilson's son-in-law, and Franklin had been almost ostentatiously loyal to Wilson. Upon entering the Civic Auditorium on the first day of the convention, the delegates were greeted by an enormous American flag—at the time reported to be the largest flag ever created—hanging from the ceiling like a billboard. As a small marine bugle band played "The Star-Spangled Banner," the flag began to rise as if Houdini himself were pulling the strings. Slowly, the real star of the show appeared behind: a large oil painting of Wilson, glowering in a spotlight. "It was not a very good picture, rather red faced and staring and frightened, but it served as a symbol of the man in the White House, and the cheering burst out," wrote Heywood Broun in the *New-York Tribune*. "Or if it didn't burst, at any rate it began."[40] Like Broun, Franklin thought the crowd's tribute to their semi-fallen hero seemed tepid, especially among the New Yorkers.

"Somebody must make a move," Franklin told Smith. And with that, FDR leaped up from his seat in the hall, grabbed the "New York" placard from the surprised delegate who was carrying it, and led a merry, mini-band of six New Yorkers on a march around the auditorium.[41]

FDR turned up in many surprising places in San Francisco. Before leaving Washington for the convention, he had told a navy admiral that he was having trouble finding a hotel room in San Francisco, a dubious claim given that the states almost always reserved blocks of rooms for their delegates. Still, he managed to get himself berthed on the battleship *New York*, which provided a none-too-subtle salute to his wartime pedigree. (As did the grand reception he threw for his fellow Empire State delegates on the ship's quarterdeck.) Not that the Democrats needed any reminders. The Roosevelt name had long popped up in the paper more than any assistant secretary had a right to expect, whether it was coverage of his countless naval base visits or of his breathless, on-the-scene reporting at the Palmer bombing. The convention boosted his standing even further. Two days after his placard-grabbing stunt, FDR hurdled over several rows of chairs on his way to the podium to second Smith's ill-fated nomination—a dynamic contrast to the disabled president who was about to be replaced. The Democrats ultimately picked Governor James Cox of Ohio, though it took forty-four ballots and six long days and nights to settle on a nominee. Cox, a newspaper publisher from Dayton, hadn't attended the convention, and when he was reached by phone, the big question was obviously about his choice of running mate. "Naturally, I've been thinking about this a good deal," Cox said, "and my choice is young Roosevelt."[42]

———

Franklin had many traits to recommend him: he was from the country's most populous state, his pro-league stand would offset Cox's relative indifference, and he was strongly anti-machine. But perhaps the biggest reason was the first one Cox mentioned in that phone call: "His name is good." As the decided underdog, Cox could do worse than attach himself to a political dynasty, not to mention one rooted in the other party. The press naturally made much of Franklin's similarity to Uncle Ted. "Roosevelt Career like That of Cousin; Both Served in State Legislature and as Assistant Secretary of the Navy," was the headline on one *New York Times* story.[43] Another, two weeks later, noted that "The name Roosevelt is an inspiration, and the name of Franklin D. Roosevelt suggests to the popular imagination many of the things for which in public, social, and civic life Theodore Roosevelt stood, and with which he was identified."[44] The weekly newsmagazine the *Outlook*, for which Theodore Roosevelt had frequently written, joined the bandwagon, calling Franklin "a gentleman of liberal culture, of high character, an able and upright public servant who possesses not a few of the political and personal qualities of his distinguished cousin, Theodore Roosevelt."[45] He was like Uncle Ted in one other way, too: as a leading contender for governor of New York, Franklin was a potential thorn for the state's political bosses. They permitted his VP nomination largely to get him out of their hair.

Still, no one was more surprised by Franklin's sudden rise than the Roosevelts themselves. Eleanor, who had taken the children to Campobello for the summer as usual, heard the news not from her husband but in a telegram from Josephus Daniels. She didn't know what to think. "I am sure that I was glad for my husband, but it never occurred to me to be much excited," she said.[46] Joy had never been one of her primary colors, and the Lucy affair was still darkening her mood. "This past year has rather got the better of me it has been so full of all kinds of things that I still have a breathless, hunted feeling about it though for the moment I am leading an idle if at times a somewhat trying life!" she told Isabella Greenway.[47] A month after that letter, Eleanor's grandmother Hall passed away. Six months later, the converted Manhattan stable house where her mother's sister Pussie lived caught fire. Pussie and her two young daughters died. All told, Eleanor was hardly prepared for the rigors of a national campaign on any level. At one point, Louis Howe sent her an urgent request from Washington. "Papers are demanding your picture. Is there one at the house here that I can have copied?" Eleanor's reply: "Are no pictures of me."[48] Of course, that was not even remotely true. She'd been photographed plenty of times, including the previous year by United Press International, which circulated the shot nationwide. But Eleanor's default mode was still to play the shrinking violet, and in this case at least she got her wish to fade away. A few days after Howe's plea, the New York *Daily News* ran a full page of photographs featuring "glimpses" of the new vice presidential nominee in various locations. It included a large picture of a woman in a black hat and white fur collar over a caption that read, "Roosevelt's wife is one of the leaders in Washington society." The problem was, the woman in the picture was not Eleanor.[49]

She didn't stay anonymous for long. Franklin embarked on the kind of whistle-stop campaign that would have made Uncle Ted proud: thirty-two states and more than a thousand speeches in three months. For the last four weeks of the tour, Eleanor went along for the ride, from Colorado to New York. The Nineteenth Amendment, giving women the right to vote, had just been ratified on August 18, 1920, and suddenly politicians realized that the polling booth was no longer a boys' club. Eleanor's presence would help Franklin appeal to women voters (though in point of fact, Eleanor never worked for the suffrage movement and only supported the Amendment after Franklin did). But traveling around on Franklin's private railroad car—which doubled as a rolling campaign office, dormitory for staffers, and speaker's platform—made her feel even more awkward than usual. By day, Franklin shook hands and delivered speeches while she sat nearby gazing and smiling and as lifeless as a mannequin. Wives had rarely traveled with their candidate-husbands before. Eleanor became the prototypical adoring spouse, the kind who became a fixture on every politician's campaign. The evenings weren't much better. The men stayed up late on the train, writing speeches, smoking, and playing cards. ER went to sleep in her stateroom, seething at FDR. "I was still a Puritan," she said. "Little did I realize in those days how much he received through these contacts and how impossible it would have been for him, after the kind of days he was putting in, to go to sleep placidly."[50]

After only a few days on the trail, she was planning to quit and head home because twelve-year-old Jimmy had become sick and ended up in the Groton infirmary. But Franklin said the three magic words that Eleanor could never resist: "I need you."[51] The job of actually using her, however, fell to Louis Howe. Howe had stayed as loyal as a puppy throughout FDR's stint at Navy, working as both a publicity guru and all-around problem fixer. Eleanor had learned to tolerate his filthy appearance and influence with her husband, but she'd never really accepted him. During those four weeks on the campaign train, that changed. When Howe saw that Eleanor felt marginalized, he made a point of drawing her into the action. He would knock on her stateroom door and ask her opinion on the draft of a speech or chat about current events. At campaign stops, he began to introduce her to the political reporters. They were charmed by her frankness. Perhaps because she was so obviously out of her element—a woman among men, a city girl in the heartland, a blue blood blending with the working stiffs—she let her guard down in ways she almost never had before. She enjoyed when the reporters stood in the back of the room and made faces, trying to make her laugh "when Franklin was making the same speech for the umpty-umpth time."[52] Sometimes they even made fun of the way certain women on the stump flirted with her tall, charming husband. "One of the standing jokes of that campaign has always been a reference to the day in Jamestown and certain photographs which were taken of lovely ladies who served luncheon for my husband and how they worshiped at his shrine," Eleanor remembered. "He has had to stand much teasing from the rest of the party about this particular day."[53] In the not-too-distant past, humorless Eleanor would never have found humor in a topic like women on the prowl—*especially* in a topic like women on the prowl. Now she had joined the party.

Franklin and Eleanor weren't the only Roosevelts on the campaign trail in 1920. The Oyster Bay side of the family had never taken "Feather Duster" seriously and were at least as shocked as Eleanor when Franklin landed on the national ticket. It was around this time that mild-mannered Edith began to carp that "Franklin is nine-tenths mush, and one-tenth Eleanor."[54] She and the rest of the Oyster Bay family insisted that Franklin was shamelessly trading on their name, just as he'd lifted so much else from Uncle Ted's résumé. Many voters assumed that FDR was TR's son, and the Democrats did little to set the record straight. In fact, they tried to muddy the issue as much as they could. "At the recent Democratic rally on Boston Common not one of the various speakers mentioned the name of Woodrow Wilson," the *Boston Herald* wrote in an editorial. "But the memory of Theodore Roosevelt was consigned to no such oblivion. Somebody with a keen ear counted no fewer than 63 allusions to his wise and humane statesmanship, his progressive ideals, and his staunch Americanism."[55]

The fact that FDR and Cox were campaigning as proud supporters of the League of Nations—Theodore's late-in-life whipping boy—made the Roosevelt name game all the more infuriating in Oyster Bay. "Mama is wild over Nick L having called you in a speech a 'denatured Roosevelt,'" Eleanor wrote to Franklin.[56] Alice found an even more novel way to go after Franklin. She had never campaigned for anyone but her father and her husband, and Warren Harding, who was running against the Cox-Roosevelt ticket, was hardly her type. "To call him second-rate," she said, "would be to pay him a compliment."[57] But she offered the Republican nominee a deal. She and the rest of the family would publicly support him if Harding agreed to appoint her brother Ted assistant secretary of the navy—take that, Franklin—and later support Ted for governor of New York.

Alice knew that Harding loved a good horse trade. Back in 1912, just as Nick was agonizing over how to navigate the Taft-Roosevelt presidential face-off, Harding had the nerve to offer Nick help in becoming governor of Ohio, with the tacit understanding that Nick would back Taft over Theodore Roosevelt, his own father-in-law. Alice, standing right next to her husband, chewed out Harding before Nick could even reply. "One could not accept favors from crooks," she told him. "I must say it was a little obtuse and raw of Harding to make that offer to Nick in my presence. Insight and taste, however, were not his strong points."[58]

They apparently got over their spat, because Alice made front-page news in early September when she said she'd begin campaigning for Harding in Maine. She forgot one thing—to show up. The same thing happened in October in southern Ohio. Alice blamed the no-shows on her abject fear of public speaking. Fortunately, other members of the family were less easily rattled. Aunt Corinne, who had just seconded the failed Republican presidential nomination of Leonard Wood (becoming one of the few women to address a major party's national convention), took to the stump on a swing through the Midwest. "I am behind Senator Harding and Governor Coolidge," she said, "because I believe them to be 100 percent American, of true patriotism, who have not failed to show marked efficiency and ability in public office."[59] Corinne's praise for the VP candidate Coolidge was clearly a slap at the VP candidate Roosevelt. It hurt even more seeing how Franklin's half-niece, Helen, was married to Corinne's son, Douglas. FDR had been an usher at their wedding fourteen years earlier.

But the main attraction in the FDR hit parade was Alice's brother Ted. Theodore had always envisioned his oldest son becoming his political heir, even though living up to his father's expectations had terrified Ted junior since he was a kid. The president himself admitted that he'd probably given his eleven-year-old son a sort of "nervous breakdown" by pushing him too hard; one of his extended stays with Auntie Bye was meant as a way for him to be "treated"—the treatment apparently being a respite from his father.[60] "The disadvantages of being a great man's son far outweigh the advantages," said Ted's wife, Eleanor. "At twenty-five he was compared with his father at fifty and found wanting. He was always accused of imitating his father in speech, walk, and smile. If he had taken this seriously and tried to alter himself he would have been unbearably self-conscious."[61]

What Ted really wanted was to be a soldier. He had spent a few months after the war in Paris helping to establish the American Legion, then returned to the United States in March 1919 and published a memoir profiling his fellow men in uniform, *Average Americans*. Within days, the newspapers were suggesting a career change. "Many Republicans believe that young Mr. Roosevelt has a political future as promising as was his father's when the latter first started political life ... If he should be elected President of the [New York City] Board of Aldermen, there is no reason why Mr. Roosevelt should not go higher, Republican leaders assert ... [T]hey already see him the Mayoralty candidate of the party in 1922."[62] Good soldier that he was, Ted couldn't ignore the calls to political duty, especially in the shadow of his father's death. Instead of running for office in heavily Democratic New York City, Ted followed his father's path to the New York State Assembly, running from his parents' home in Oyster Bay. He won by the largest margin ever recorded in that district. He made his mark with his very first floor speech, in which he fiercely defended five assemblymen who had been expelled from the legislature because they were avowed socialists. "We abhor the doctrines of the Socialist Party," Ted said. "[But] we must not let justifiable dislike force us to commit a crime against representative government."[63] It was just the kind of in-your-face defense of the underdog that his father would have relished. And his cousin Franklin, too.

———

Ted was running for his second term in the assembly when Franklin hitched a ride on the 1920 Cox ticket and threatened to establish himself as the new Roosevelt commander in chief. Ted scurried to the barricades, quitting his own reelection campaign and forcing his wife, Eleanor Butler Roosevelt, to stump for votes in his place. "I was appalled," Eleanor Butler said. "'Ted! I can't possibly do that. I never heard of such a thing!'" To which he replied, "Why, of course you can. You've got to! Constituents don't like to feel neglected."[64] By mid-August, the Republicans had sent Ted junior out to tail FDR across the country like a policeman on the trail of a fugitive, following him from stop to stop. "The Republican managers are afraid that voters out West will get the impression that the Democratic Roosevelt is really the son of the late Colonel and that the progressively inclined will rally to his support," the *New York Times* explained.[65] Ted's attack plan was simple: to take a hatchet to the Roosevelt family tree. "He is maverick," Ted told a crowd filled with former Rough Riders in Sheridan, Wyoming. "He does not have the brand of our family."[66] This might well have been the first time in national politics that anyone campaigned almost exclusively against a party's *vice* presidential nominee.

Of course, the election of 1920 was less about the four men running for office now than it was a referendum on eight years of Wilson and his professorial hectoring on war and peace. In that respect, the Democrats were doomed. Harding and Coolidge pummeled Cox and Roosevelt, taking 60 percent of the popular vote (the biggest popular-vote landslide since the 1820s) and 404 electoral votes to 127 for the Democrats. With those kinds of numbers at the top of the Republican ticket, Ted junior triumphed easily in his assembly race, despite going AWOL from his own campaign. If Franklin and Eleanor harbored any ill will against their victorious Oyster Bay cousins, they didn't seem to show it. By July 1921, they had mended their differences enough to join in a pre-wedding dinner for Sheffield Cowles, Auntie Bye's only son, at Oldgate in Connecticut. Franklin did have a bit too much to drink, but hearty partying was a Roosevelt family tradition. So was Eleanor's reaction: she was appalled. It was just like old times.

At least for Eleanor. For Alice, the election of 1920 was her first without the strong hand of her father. Her success in helping topple the League of Nations earned her a place in Washington's power elite, as much as a woman could claim such a thing. She was among a handful of Republicans invited to consult with Harding on his possible cabinet choices, and the only one who had the nerve to warn him against selecting his unscrupulous campaign manager, Harry Daugherty, as White House chief of staff. (Harding ignored her.) She'd become a confidante to countless other Republican politicians eager for her keen insights and unparalleled access. She had also earned herself a designated seat in the senators' family gallery, even though she had never had a relative in the Senate. "One morning [the Kansas senator] Charlie Curtis telephoned that the rules had been changed to give 'immediate members of ex-Presidents' families' the privilege of that gallery," Alice wrote. "When I got to the Senate, he took me up. In a few minutes, [the New Hampshire senator] George Moses joined us to say that as the Senate rules had been changed for me, would I perhaps like the Constitution changed too?"[67] Washington, the *New York Times* said, had become "a world where Alice Roosevelt Longworth would spend all of her days leaning over the railing of the Senate gallery—and then by night proceed to invite to dinner the senator whose argument she wanted to answer back—and under the glamour of her tingling personality and 100% French evening dress and under the soft allurement of candle light tell him how she'd vote on that measure."[68]

Not all of Alice's powerful friends needed to win an election to claim their seat at the table. She had long been close to Evalyn Walsh McLean, who owned the two most precious gems in town: the *Washington Post* and the Hope Diamond. (The McLeans also owned Nick's hometown *Cincinnati Enquirer*.) Nick and Alice had spent the first few days of their honeymoon at the McLeans' house, a seventy-five-acre estate in northwest Washington called Friendship. Evalyn claimed that Alice's own friendship with Borah became something more serious at her place as well. They were there for Easter brunch in 1921 when Alice pushed back from the table, stood up with the imposing senator from Idaho, and brazenly disappeared with him on the grounds (which wasn't hard to do, given that Friendship enjoyed its own eighteen-hole golf course, stables, cast-iron swimming pool, and Italian gardens). McLean was as eccentric as she was rich. At a birthday party once, she let the guest of honor parade around wearing the Hope Diamond—the guest in question was her dog Mike, who had the 45.52-carat blue gem attached to his doggy collar. But even McLean thought Alice had gone too far by romping with Borah right under the noses of the ne plus ultra of Washington society. "Alice, you are a fool. You are hurting your reputation," McLean told her once she and Borah had emerged from Friendship's garden of Eden. To which Alice replied, "I am a Longworth. I can do as I please." At the White House Easter egg roll the next day, Alice made clear that she'd informed Nick about everything and had no intention of turning back. "I am absolutely independent now," she told Evalyn, "and I am going my own way."[69]

Alice was hardly in any danger of becoming a pariah, as McLean must have known. In addition to all her other iron-clad Capitol connections, she had long been friendly with the new First Lady (and fellow Ohioan),

Florence Harding. Two strong women eager for influence and the spot-light, Alice and Florence had an up-and-down relationship. Alice mocked Mrs. Harding's broad midwestern accent and lack of style. "She was a nervous, rather excitable woman whose voice easily became a little high-pitched, strident," Alice said. "She usually spoke of Mr. Harding as 'Warren Harding.' It is impossible to convey her pronunciation of the letter R in print. Something like Wur-r-ren Ha-ar-r-ding."[70] Florence thought Alice acted as if she thought she had a lifetime lease on the White House, which was probably true. "The Hardings never liked me, and I can hardly blame them. One of their intimate friends once asked me if I realized that when I spoke to the President my manner was condescending, if not actually contemptuous."[71] But Alice knew enough to play nicely with the current lady of the White House, and the three of them (along with McLean) bonded over their fascination with mysticism. (Evalyn and Florence were especially fond of a fortune-teller named Madame Marcia, who made reg-ular visits to the White House with her crystal ball.) When the Hardings held a grand public reopening of the White House on March 8, 1921—a flamboyant retort to the Wilsons, who had kept visitors away on account of the war and the president's declining health—Alice was among the first to arrive. The man on her arm wasn't her semi-estranged husband or even Borah. It was her brother Ted, the incoming assistant secretary of the navy and the vessel into which she was now pouring her accumulated clout.

———

Eleanor was also declaring her independence—from Mama. Distancing and occasionally defying her mother-in-law had been a gradual process throughout her time in Washington. Not long after she'd arrived, Eleanor fired her entire domestic staff, all of whom had been hired by Mama—and all of whom were white, as they were in most proper northern households. Eleanor replaced them entirely with African-Americans. It wasn't exactly the kind of socially progressive statement she'd make in later decades. "Well, all my servants are gone and all the darkies are here and heaven knows how it will all turn out!" she wrote to Mama.[72] (Though very much a product of her time and class, Eleanor would grow more aware of the insensitive use of such racially charged terms.) The truth was, black servants were paid less than white ones, and Eleanor was always looking to be frugal despite the family's relative comfort. But she also clearly sought to swerve from the path that her mother-in-law had chosen for her. ER wasn't afraid of Sara anymore. In fact, she sometimes seemed to relish the fight. "Mama and I have had a bad time," she wrote to Franklin after the two had crossed swords over the children. "I should be ashamed of myself but I'm not."[73]

As it happened, Franklin, Eleanor, and the kids had to move into Mama's half of the Sixty-Fifth Street house when they returned to New York after the failed 1920 campaign because their side had been rented out for six more months. But Eleanor spent relatively little time there. She couldn't sit at home anymore, not after all she'd accomplished, and endured, in the last five years. "I did not look forward to a winter of four days a week in New York with nothing to do but teas and luncheons and dinners to take up my time," she said. "The war had made that seem an impossible mode of living."[74] So she turned herself into a one-woman self-help course. She took classes in cooking, shorthand, and typing. "My mother-in-law was distressed and felt that I was not always available, as I had been when I lived in New York before," said Eleanor. So she agreed to attend weekly knitting classes with Sara, too.[75]

Not long after she'd returned to New York, an acquaintance from Washington named Narcissa Vanderlip stopped by. Vanderlip was the president of the New York chapter of the League of Women Voters, which had been formed only a few months earlier. She had worked with Eleanor on a few war-relief projects, and she was impressed by ER's tirelessness and managerial ability. Would Eleanor like to join the board of the league? Her experience in Washington and on the recent presidential campaign would make Eleanor an excellent person to monitor any national legislation that would be of interest to women, Vanderlip said. Eleanor, being Eleanor, begged off, explaining that "I would be interested but doubted my ability to do this work."[76]

Vanderlip, whose husband, Frank, was president of the National City Bank (later to become Citibank), didn't fall for that. To help Eleanor get up to speed and over her nerves, Vanderlip assigned a young lawyer named Elizabeth Read to study the *Congressional Record* with her, teaching Eleanor how to track bills for the league. In January 1922, Eleanor traveled to Albany as a Dutchess County delegate to the state's League of Women Voters convention. In April, she went to Cleveland for a national League of Women Voters convention. Despite a large number of Republicans, the

League of Women Voters was also strongly behind the League of Nations, which made ER's connection to the new organization that much stronger. When she wrote to Franklin from the league convention in Cleveland, she almost seemed to feel guilty for enjoying herself. "Much, much love dear," she said, "and I prefer doing my politics with you."[77]

But Franklin wasn't doing much politics anymore. After losing the 1920 election, he took a job as vice president of the Fidelity and Deposit Company of Maryland. Like so many of the Roosevelt men, including Uncle Ted, he was a lousy businessman. He was clearly frustrated to be out of politics, which is why he kept Louis Howe on the payroll, poking around for ways to get FDR back in the game. In the meantime, that party for Sheffield Cowles wasn't the only time in recent months that he'd spent an evening drinking as if he were still a Harvard student. Eleanor had hoped to save Franklin from himself by ensconcing the family at Campobello for most of the summer of 1921, and she'd invited a rotating slate of houseguests, including the Howes, a Romanian diplomat, and Elizabeth Asquith Bibesco, the daughter of the British Liberal Party leader. But in July, the Senate Subcommittee on Naval Affairs accused FDR and Secretary Daniels, in a shockingly detailed six-hundred-page report, of covering up a program where sailors at a naval facility in Newport, Rhode Island, were encouraged—and perhaps forced—to seduce other men in order to expose suspected homosexuals in their ranks. The *New York Times* said that the details were of an "unprintable nature." Daniels and Roosevelt were forced to head to Capitol Hill for a long, stressful day testifying in front of the committee to clear their names.*

Franklin seemed tired when he returned to Canada from Washington, but the sea always lifted his spirits, even on the cold and foggy morning of August 10, when he took the children and Louis sailing on the Bay of Fundy. This being a Roosevelt family outing, it was hardly relaxing. The family went fishing for cod, then for a swim in the frigid bay. They even helped tamp down a forest fire with the help of some pine branches. By the time they returned to the house that afternoon, Franklin was feeling chilled and tired. The next morning he felt worse. His limbs dragged and

---

* They only partially succeeded. Though Daniels and Roosevelt denied any knowledge of the plan's details, many people didn't believe them. The Senate committee, in a report issued in July 1921, called the men's role "reprehensible." *New York Times*, July 20, 1921.

he had a fever. By the next day, he couldn't move his legs at all. An eminent doctor from Philadelphia came to examine him on August 12 and diagnosed a blood clot. "The doctor feels sure he will get well but it may take some months," Eleanor wrote to Franklin's half brother, Rosy. Franklin was eager to return to New York, and the doctor thought he could go some time after September 15, when the heat in the city subsided. And the doctor advised Eleanor to take one more precaution for the trip home. "It may have to be in a wheelchair," he said.

# Chapter 6

# THE SINGING TEAPOT

L ouis Howe desperately wanted to keep news of Franklin's condition away from the press—and the voters. A second doctor, this one an orthopedist, had examined Franklin and diagnosed him with polio. The doctor wasn't sure yet how severe the case was; there was a chance that FDR might walk again. But Howe worried that the slightest hint of a debilitating illness would end FDR's political career. So once the doctors gave permission for Franklin to return to New York, Howe devised a plan to sneak him home as if he were contraband. To get Franklin off tiny Campobello without hiring an ambulance or alerting the authorities, six men strapped him on a stretcher and carried him across a stony beach and up a gangway to a motorboat for the two-mile trip across the bay to Eastport, Maine. From there, Howe had arranged for a private railcar—compliments of Franklin's uncle Lyman Delano, a railroad magnate—to take him back to Manhattan, but the men had to slip his limp, prone body through the train window, rather than maneuver him around the narrow train corridors. Howe had already stocked Franklin's room with enough pillows to prop him up so he looked as if he were sitting, in case anyone could see through the window. Just to be sure, he also put a festive fedora on FDR's head, one of his signature cigarette holders in his mouth, and the Roosevelts' Scottish terrier, Duffy, in his arms. He looked as if he were out for a leisurely journey home.[1]

Even a media wizard like Louis couldn't make this kind of story disappear, however, and sure enough reporters had staked out Grand Central

Terminal on September 15 to wait for FDR's train. In that morning's paper they had reported (via Howe's misleading tips) that Franklin was feeling "better" after having been "seriously ill."[2] Now Howe adjusted the narrative, which in the next day's paper became "F. D. Roosevelt Ill of Poliomyelitis," but of a mild strain causing "the loss of the use of both legs below the knees."[3] Strictly speaking, that was true; his lower legs had stopped working. But so had his upper legs and the rest of his body up to his chest, including, for a time, the muscles controlling his bladder and bowels. The spinning continued: "You can say definitely that he will not be crippled," his doctor, George Draper, was quoted as saying. "No one need have any fear of permanent injury from this attack."[4] Even more shamelessly, that very day Howe had Franklin write a letter—actually, Howe ghostwrote it himself, over Franklin's signature—to Adolph Ochs, the publisher of the *New York Times*, that referred to the paper's unwittingly misleading story about his illness. "While the doctors were unanimous in telling me that the attack was very mild and that I was not going to suffer any permanent effect from it, I had, of course, the usual dark suspicion that they were just saying nice things to make me feel good," the letter said, "but now that I have seen the same statement officially made in the New York *Times* I feel immensely relieved because I know of course it must be so."[5]

The public bought the whole thing. Even folks who seemed unlikely to sympathize with Franklin expressed their encouragement. "Dearest Eleanor," wrote Ted junior, who only a few months before was telling anyone who would listen that Franklin was a "maverick" who didn't belong in his family. "I have just heard of Franklin's illness. I am so sorry. I hope it will turn out to be but of a short duration and that he may be soon well again. Meanwhile, I know just how very hard it is for you. It is after all those who love us that suffer more when we are sick than we do ourselves. I think of you constantly. Will you give my best to Franklin and tell him 'good luck' from me. Affectionately, Theodore Roosevelt."[6] It was a remarkably gracious note from across the family divide. Then again, it was easy for the Oyster Bay clan to be gracious now. They had just won the war of the Roosevelts. For all their fear of Franklin usurping the family name and its claim to power, their rival was now effectively finished. He might not have meant to gloat, but it's telling that Ted junior wrote his note to Eleanor on stationery embossed across the top with "The Assistant

Secretary of the Navy." The Oyster Bay Roosevelts had wrestled that precious perch back from the upstate upstart.

————

Despite his steady climb up the political ladder, Ted junior was still not much of a politician. The job of guiding his career belonged to Alice. "Although her brothers are striving mightily to do credit to their name, and carry the titular honors, nevertheless it is Alice Longworth who is the true bearer of the Roosevelt tradition," said one paper. "Her friends say she possesses more than her share of the family personality, ability, intellect and courage."[7] After Ted and his wife, Eleanor, moved the family to Washington, he and Alice lunched together almost daily, played poker weekly (often with the Hardings), and plotted his future constantly. He relied on her completely. After Alice went on an extended European trip in 1923, Ted could hardly wait for her to return. "I have missed her more than I can say," he wrote in his diary. "It will be like rain falling on parched ground to have her back here again with me."[8]

Ted was actually one of three potential tickets back to the White House for Alice, along with her husband and her lover. Rather than dissipating her potency like so much watered-down gin, Alice's ubiquity—she had a man in the House, a man in the Senate, and a man in the administration—only magnified her claim to influence. Some of her clout was obviously trivial. "The saying is in Washington that the Senators have formed the habit, upon coming into the United States Senate chamber at noon, of looking up to the family gallery, to the left from the Vice-President's chair, to estimate the temper of business for the day," wrote one reporter. "If Alice Roosevelt Longworth is in the gallery—her usual place is in the front row—they take off their coats, figuratively speaking, of course, and prepare for a 'hot day.'"[9] Others claimed her power was more substantial. She got credit for the defeat of a treaty that would have required the U.S. to pay Colombia $25 million as restitution for having finagled Panama's independence in order to build her father's cherished canal. Not long before his death, Theodore had called the restitution plan "blackmail," which explains Alice's involvement: her causes were almost invariably his. That said, while she might have helped the Senate sink the plan during the Wilson administration, it sailed through under Harding.

Alice's true authority was difficult to gauge because it wasn't the type that left a paper trail or even fingerprints. She never cast a vote on legislation, rarely made a speech. Instead, she merely whispered into the ears of the country's most influential men. But in Washington, proximity to power was almost as good as the real thing. In February 1922, the Massachusetts representative Charles Underhill was complaining to an audience at a local chamber of commerce meeting about how ignorant some of his colleagues back on Capitol Hill could be. Exhibit A was a conversation Underhill overheard between two congressmen discussing an upcoming celebration of Massachusetts's favorite son, the poet Henry Wadsworth Longfellow. The whole idea of a tribute, one of the politicians complained, was ridiculous. "Why, nobody ever heard of Longfellow," the congressman said, "until he married Alice Roosevelt."[10]

Her stock rose again in 1923, when Nick became House majority leader, though some people thought she merited a more vaunted position. "When folks wonder why Nicholas Longworth does not run for the Senate, it is whispered that his wife will not let him," said one paper. "She wishes to be senator herself. And certainly few people know more about the job of being a senator than she."[11] She had also developed an unusual talent for capitalizing when a president died in office. It happened again on August 2, 1923, when Harding, who was enduring the first drips of the Teapot Dome scandal, died of a heart attack in San Francisco. While Alice had long dismissed Harding as "just a slob," she had cultivated a nice relationship with Vice President Coolidge. They were both boxing fans; she joined his group on a private train to see Jack Dempsey defeat the Frenchman Georges Carpentier in New Jersey in July 1921, then played cards with him on the trip back home. "Coolidge whipped us with pinch paste playing poker," she remembered.[12] Coolidge was close to Borah too, or at least close enough to ask the Idaho senator to be his running mate in 1924. Borah's reply: "For which position?"[13]

———

Alice was so busy laying track for the future she never realized she was about to be run over by a man in a wheelchair. It was natural to assume that Franklin's days as pretender to her father's throne were over. Most everyone else did, and because she kept her distance during his long rehabilitation—Edith, Aunt Corinne, Aunt Bye, and Ted junior all wrote notes when they got word of Franklin's illness, but not Alice—she had no reason to look over her shoulder. But Eleanor and Louis Howe thought otherwise. Howe had believed, since their first meeting at the 1912 Democratic convention, that Franklin would one day become president, and he wasn't about to let a little paralysis change that. Back in New York, Howe moved into the Roosevelts' Sixty-Fifth Street house—or, more precisely, he moved into their daughter Anna's bedroom on the third floor, while she decamped to a smaller room on the fourth. Anna was furious, as only a dispossessed teenager can be. "For years, all of us thought that Louis Howe was just kind of a nuisance," said Anna, who got into enormous shouting matches with her mother, followed by extended periods where they wouldn't speak, while Howe lived with the family. "I was very jealous of him." [14]

Eleanor was never the most intuitive of mothers; now she became almost oblivious. She was simply too busy, too harried, to be bothered by how miserable her children had become. Sara was adding fuel to the children's animosity, but the newly emboldened Eleanor cared less and less about her overbearing mother-in-law's opinion about Howe, or anything else. "Various members of the family thought it was their duty to criticize the arrangements which I had made, but that never troubled me greatly, for I realized that no one else could plan our very complicated daily lives," Eleanor said. [15] She herself was sleeping in one of the boys' rooms, having given up her own bedroom for Franklin's nurse. After all, sacrifice and duty were her specialties. "It is impossible to assess ... the emotions of Mother as she compelled herself to perform the necessary physical tasks on the body of the man whose intimate touch was only a memory," said their son Elliott. "He had to be bathed and rubbed to guard against bedsores. With Louis panting from the effort of helping her, he needed to be lifted and turned. All his bodily functions were paralyzed now. Catheters and enemas had to be used to do the work of powerless muscles." [16]

Eleanor and Louis—in only a few years their relationship had evolved from wariness to friendliness to something that looked a lot like devotion. With Franklin's political future now resting in their hands, Eleanor put herself entirely in Louis's, sometimes literally. Anna once walked into a room in their house and found her mother curled up at Louis's feet while he lovingly brushed her hair, almost as if she were his daughter. "He probably cared for me as a person as much as he ever cared for anyone and more than anyone else has," Eleanor once said. [17]

That might well have been true, but it was also a by-product of his larger goal: saving Franklin. Howe thought the way to do that was with a steady stream of news, visitors, and contact with the outside world, all of which would stop him from sinking into despair while keeping his name in play. Eleanor could help with all of that, especially if she lent a hand in the Roosevelt family business—politics. Howe encouraged her work with the League of Women Voters and pushed her to get involved with Democratic Party initiatives. When a woman named Nancy Cook, the executive secretary of the newly formed Women's Division of the New York State Democratic Committee, called out of the blue to ask if Eleanor would speak at a fund-raiser, Louis went into full Pygmalion mode. By now he had seen that inside ER's mousy exterior was a lion ready to roar, even if she needed elocution lessons. She made the speech, all the while gripping the podium as if she were enduring an earthquake. "I trembled so that I did not know if I could stand up, and I am quite sure my voice could not be heard," said Eleanor.[18] In fact, the speech was a success, and she was soon asked to do more. Her mentor rarely left her side. "Louis Howe went with me and sat at the back of the audience and gave me pointers on what I should say and how I should say it," Eleanor said. "I had a bad habit, because I was nervous, of laughing when there was nothing to laugh at. He broke me of that by showing me how inane it sounded. His advice was: 'Have something to say, say it, and sit down.'"[19]

She didn't sit for long. Eleanor's fledgling friendships with women activists led to an ever-expanding web of commitments; suddenly everyone wanted Eleanor to play on her team. She joined the Women's Trade Union League and attended the International Conference of Working Women in Washington. She co-founded a monthly newsletter (which Howe edited, naturally) called the *Women's Democratic News* that reported on projects involving the party's female members. She even learned to drive, albeit with middling results. "I might as well own up at once that I had two accidents," she wrote. "I drove into the stone gatepost of the Hyde Park Avenue [entrance] because I tried to turn while going too fast. [And] I backed the entire family downhill, off the road and down a steep bank and came to a stop because I struck a tree."[20] She neglected to note that, like Alice, she had a lead foot that earned her a $10 speeding ticket on her way home from speaking to the Democratic women of upstate Chenango County. She was becoming less fearful by the day, in every aspect of her life. "The more she got involved in helping father," said Anna Roosevelt, "the more she gained her own self-confidence."

Her personal relationships took on a new intensity as well. The young woman who had been terrified of dances and parties suddenly found her card filled with friends and admirers. She spent many evenings discussing politics and reading poetry in the Greenwich Village apartment of Elizabeth Read, the young lawyer she met working with the League of Women Voters, and her lover, Esther Lape. Nancy Cook's female lover, Marion Dickerman, was a teacher involved in advocating for various social causes, and Eleanor invited the couple to Hyde Park for weekends. Rose Schneiderman, a leader of the Women's Trade Union League, schooled Eleanor and Franklin on workplace issues over dinners and visits in New York and Hyde Park, sometimes joined by her girlfriend. Eleanor made friends with plenty of straight women too, including Elinor Morgenthau, a Dutchess County neighbor (and wife of FDR's future Treasury secretary, Henry), and Caroline O'Day, who later became the first female Democrat elected to Congress from New York. But the number of lesbians in her sphere could hardly escape notice. Whether Eleanor initially knew of their sexual orientation is an open question, but if so it wasn't a mystery for long. FDR and Howe referred to Eleanor's lesbian friends as "she-males." Alice called them "female impersonators" and mocked her cousin's friendships, though she didn't seem to be passing judgment on homosexuality per se. "My cousin Helen had a horrible story—a delightful story—of being once in an adjoining room to one in which Eleanor and a couple of her female impersonators were having a pillow fight (apparently they used to leapfrog a lot as well)," Alice wrote. "She had not had a very happy childhood, so of course it was nice for her to have some vigorous companions who adored her. Couldn't be better. More strength to all of them. Pillow fights were obviously as jolly a form of communication as any."[21]

Fun and games weren't the stock-in-trade of the "impersonators," however. The League of Women Voters, the Women's Trade Union League, the Women's Division of the New York State Democratic Committee—this constellation of rising women gave Eleanor the sense of purpose and camaraderie she hadn't enjoyed since her days at Mlle Souvestre's boarding school. The lesbianism, at least the sexual component, was beside the point. Eleanor was developing an affinity for strong, passionate women who didn't need a man in their lives to find meaning. Howe might have opened Eleanor's eyes to her own potential, but her female friends encouraged her to work on her own behalf, for the causes that mattered to her, regardless of their utility to her husband. "She thought through her position on such issues as women's rights, labor, welfare, so that when Father went back into public life, she had such definite opinions of her own, she could pester the hell out of him," said their daughter, Anna.[22]

————

If Alice made light of Eleanor and her female friends, perhaps that's because she had a front-row seat when they first stepped onto the national stage—and tried to revive a prime piece of Alice's roadkill. By 1923, Alice's Irreconcilables thought they had buried the League of Nations, but a Dutch-born man named Edward Bok wasn't ready to let it go so easily. Bok had been the editor of the *Ladies' Home Journal* and the author of an autobiography called *The Americanization of Edward Bok*, which won the Pulitzer Prize in 1921. The book is filled with the kinds of up-by-his-bootstraps life lessons often told by humbly successful immigrants, from the fateful boat ride to America and impoverished youth in New York to his baby steps in publishing and transformation of the *Ladies' Home Journal* into the first magazine with a circulation of more than one million. He prided himself on being a sort of spur to the flank of his adopted country. He also credited his devotion to philanthropy and public service to a Dutch-American friend: Theodore Roosevelt.

Roosevelt drops into *The Americanization of Edward Bok* so often he is practically its co-star. "Bok felt somehow that he had been given a new draft of Americanism: the word took on a new meaning for him; it stood for something different, something deeper and finer than before," Bok wrote about his first meeting with Theodore. (Bok wrote the book in the third person, which makes it feel both faux humble and pretentious at the same time.) "And every subsequent talk with Roosevelt deepened the feeling and stirred Bok's deepest ambitions. 'Go to it, you Dutchman,' Roosevelt would say, and Bok *would* go to it. A talk with Roosevelt always left him feeling as if mountains were the easiest things in the world to move."[23]

But Bok was no Roosevelt, and he perhaps underestimated the size of the mountain he chose to climb on July 1, 1923. That was the day he announced what he called the American Peace Award, which he thought would pick up where the defeated League of Nations fell short. The award was an elaborate contest that asked people to submit a master plan for how to "achieve and preserve the peace of the world."[24] A big job—with an even bigger payoff. Bok put up a whopping $100,000 ($1.3 million in 2015 dollars) as prize money, half awarded to the winner upon selection of his or her proposal by a panel of seven expert judges, half paid when the Senate or the American people voted to make it law. Overall, 22,165 plans were submitted. Keeping with Bok's quaint belief that "peace is primarily a woman's problem; she takes it as her own more than a man does," he appointed Esther Lape, Elizabeth Read's lover, to oversee the entire process. The first woman Lape asked to be her deputy was Read's industrious friend from the League of Women Voters: Eleanor Roosevelt.

It was a perilous assignment, kindling for firestorms in Congress and the papers. Bok was a foreign-born private citizen who seemed to be attempting to influence American foreign policy with a come-on that was equal parts patriotic and mercenary. "The audacity of the propagandists who are financing and directing this attempt to misrepresent public opinion is astounding," wrote the *Washington Post*. "There is something in this propaganda which resembles the amazing expertness of European propaganda systems during the war."[25] Even before the winner was named, the Senate Special Committee on Propaganda moved to investigate whether Bok had attempted to "control public opinion and the action of Congress upon legislative matters through propaganda or by the use of money, by advertising, or by the control of publicity." It just so happened that the Propaganda Committee included a few of Alice's closest Irreconcilable friends: Senator James Reed and Senator George Moses. Their distrust of the peace award wasn't surprising, given how Bok's idea seemed to be built with spare parts from the League of Nations. He even seemed to be correcting his hero Roosevelt's insistence on "a peace obtained by machine guns and not typewriters" when he explained his motivation: "Wars are not voted upon, but peace can be, and perhaps the next war will go to a vote."[26]

But if the battle lines were familiar, this particular skirmish featured a new duel: Alice versus Eleanor. On January 21, 1924, they faced each other in the middle of a packed Senate hearing room as the Propaganda Committee convened three days of hearings on Bok's peace award. Alice would have been staring down from her post up in the family gallery if the hearing had been in the main Senate chamber. In the smaller committee room, she had an even better seat: a large leather couch placed "in a privileged corner" of the senators' own section—right behind Senator Reed.[27] That not only kept the princess away from the riffraff; it gave her a direct view of Eleanor.

Eleanor seemed far less comfortable in her surroundings. She knit constantly and said nothing. Other than her white gloves, she arrived wearing all black. Even the large black ostrich feather that stuck out the back of her bowler-type hat made her look as if she were heading to a funeral. But she sat with Lape and Narcissa Vanderlip, Lape's other deputy, front and center at the witness table. "Maybe that's why [Alice] was so well-behaved," Lape told Lash years later, noting that Alice kept remarkably quiet on her couch. "I remarked," Lash said, "that I did not think that ER's presence would have restrained her."[28]

The hearings featured enough fireworks without Alice's usual dramatic tendencies. The anti-League forces, led by Reed and Moses, were determined to prove that Bok had stacked his judging committee with pro-league activists (though it's hard to see the crime in that). At one point, Reed—chomping on a black cigar and clenching his fists as if he were just itching to throw a punch—questioned Lape with such ferocity that two Democrats on the committee warned him to back off. Not that Lape needed any help. The people in the courtroom gave her an ovation when she finished sparring with the men. "Miss Lape proves match for hecklers at Bok Prize hearing," reported the *New York Tribune*. "Emerges victor in contest of wits."[29] By the time that Charles Levermore, a retired college president and a longtime peace activist, was named the award's winner in early February, the Propaganda Committee had lost any hope of scoring political points and had quietly disbanded. Eleanor might never have said a word during the proceedings, but she had clearly arrived. The woman who only three years earlier could not produce a single photograph of herself had now turned up on the front page of the *New York Times*. She turned up someplace else, too: her appearance before the Senate committee earned the first entry in what would become a voluminous FBI file.

Typically, Eleanor downplayed any credit to the point of obsequiousness. "You need not be proud of me dear," she wrote to FDR after the hearings were over. She had already moved on to fund-raising for her various political organizations and preparing to make a presentation at the 1924 Democratic National Convention that June on the Women's Division's political concerns. "I'm only being *active* till you can be again. It isn't such a great desire on my part to serve the world & I'll fall back into habits of sloth quite easily! Hurry up for as you know my ever present sense of the uselessness of all things will overwhelm me sooner or later!"[30] Of course, she was now about as likely to be overwhelmed as a herd of elephants.

———

One reason Alice didn't put up a better fight at the Propaganda Committee hearings was that they weren't the only match on her Capitol boxing card that week. She was also shuttling to hearings before the Senate Committee on Public Lands, an otherwise unglamorous setting except that in January 1924 the public land in question was a government oil field in Wyoming named Teapot Dome. Alice would have deposited herself at the Public Lands Committee hearings under any circumstances. Teapot Dome was already shaping up to be one of the biggest political scandals in American history, a tale of cabinet members accused of selling exclusive access to public property for their own gain. But Alice had an uncomfortably personal connection to Teapot Dome. Two of her little brothers—Ted and Archie—were being called as witnesses in the case, threatening their careers and the pristine Roosevelt family name.

The Roosevelts' deep and complicated connection to Teapot Dome began years earlier. Teapot (named for the shape of a boulder that dots that Wyoming landscape) was one of a handful of oil-rich tracts set aside by the government in the wake of World War I as vast reserve fields. In 1921, Secretary of the Navy Edwin Denby, Ted junior's boss, agreed to transfer jurisdiction of reserves in Wyoming and California to the Department of the Interior and its secretary, Albert Fall. Fall then secretly agreed to lease exclusive access to the Wyoming fields to the Mammoth Oil Company, which happened to be where Ted worked as a director prior to becoming assistant secretary of the navy—and where Archie Roosevelt was still employed as the vice president of international operations. In appreciation of Fall's assistance, Harry Sinclair, Mammoth's owner, delivered a gift of six heifers, a bull, two boars, four sows, and a Thoroughbred horse to the interior secretary's New Mexico ranch. A California oil company owned by Edward Doheny got a similar sweetheart deal and "lent" Fall $100,000, which Doheny had wrapped in paper, stuffed into a little black bag, and delivered (by his own son, Edward junior) to Fall's Washington apartment.

At first, the folks most outraged by these shady arrangements were the competing oil companies that failed to get their greasy-palmed piece of the action. In July 1922, one of those companies, Mutual Oil, went ahead and set up a wildcat rig at Teapot Dome. Sinclair promptly appealed to his man Secretary Fall, who in turn appealed to the navy for help. As luck would have it, Secretary of the Navy Denby was traveling at the time; Assistant Secretary Roosevelt was in charge. Ted issued an order for all "squatters" to leave Teapot Dome, then sent a contingent of marines to dispatch them—all the while letting the press know, in advance, what was coming. When Fall sent a commendation to the marine commander who drove off the unauthorized drillers, Ted junior added in his own handwriting, "You did excellently and confirmed our pride in the ability of the Marine Corps to measure up to whatever it was put up against—T.R."[31]

It's possible that at the time Roosevelt didn't know the sordid nature of the deal he defended, but he would soon enough. As the Public Lands Committee continued its Teapot Dome hearings in January 1924, Archie called Ted from New York and said, "Of course I may be wrong, but I'm afraid there's been dirty work at the crossroads on this oil business. I don't want to talk on the telephone. When are you coming to New York?" Archie wasn't always the sharpest tool in the Roosevelt drawer, perhaps as a result of his wartime experience that left him occasionally disoriented. "I thought that the Sinclair Company wanted me because I was such a brilliant young man," he said once he realized the extent of the Teapot mess. "I didn't know that they had hired me because my father's name was Theodore Roosevelt and they believed they could use that name."[32] To his credit, Archie immediately resigned from Mammoth when his suspicions about "dirty work" grew too putrid to ignore. The other two men in Alice's brain trust, Borah and Nick, then advised him to voluntarily testify before the Public Lands Committee.

Archie arrived in Washington on January 23, and he brought his own cheering section. "Beside Archie and his wife, there was his bald but beautifully dressed brother-in-law, Nicholas Longworth, his unbeautiful brother, Theodore, and his wife," said one paper. "It was as tense a scene as has been witnessed in Washington in a long time and the Roosevelts were the center of it."[33] Naturally, Alice was there too; as luck would have it, the Bok committee didn't meet that day. If Eleanor had arrived at the Capitol dressed in unobtrusively basic black, Alice, as was her wont, took the opposite tack. She wore crimson from her hat to her gown. The only exception was a heavy, gold-chain necklace. "It and her dead-white face and hands were the only things not red about her," the *Baltimore Sun* said.[34] Now that her side of the family was in the hot seat, Princess Alice transformed herself into Washington's own Mary, Queen of Scots, preparing to be martyred.

For all that, it didn't take long for Archie to exonerate himself. He explained to the committee that what compelled him to quit the oil company was a conversation with G. D. Wahlberg, Sinclair's personal secretary, who admitted that his boss had bribed Secretary Fall with $68,000. Ted, however, wouldn't escape so easily. In March 1924, Congressman William Stevenson of South Carolina learned that Ted's wife, Eleanor, owned a thousand shares of Sinclair stock, which had shot up ten points thanks to its Teapot Dome lease. Stevenson, on the floor of the House, called for Roosevelt's resignation from the navy while sideswiping Eleanor Butler's integrity in the process. Ted immediately vowed to take matters with Stevenson into his own fists, which prompted a quick phone call from his older and wiser sister. "Ted? I hear you're going to beat up Stevenson," Alice said. "Yes, of course he deserves it . . . I know he's a rat. By the way, he's a little elderly man and wears glasses. Remember to have him take them off before you hit him."[35]

Ted backed down, but Alice let fly with her own one-two punch. First, she lobbied her poker buddy President Coolidge to intercede on Ted's behalf with the Senate. When he refused, she got her husband and her lover to defend Ted on the floor of their respective houses. Ted was ultimately exonerated on the strength of one piece of unmanly evidence. It turned out that while he had been a member of the Mammoth Oil board as recently as 1921, Roosevelt didn't personally make any money when the company's stock rose. That was because he had put his wife in charge of all the family finances, and she had sold their thousand shares in Sinclair in December 1921—at a loss.

———

The Oyster Bay Roosevelts weren't the only ones hanging on every Teapot Dome development. By 1924, FDR's health and strength had improved enough for him to take an active part in politics again. He knew that Ted had been working hard to seal the deal his sister had made for him to become New York governor in 1924. It was, after all, an essential launching pad. The incumbent governor was almost always on the short list of consideration for the national ticket; it had been a stop on his father's road to the White House, too. It was also the job Franklin thought could be his, before polio intervened. Instead, it was Ted who spent hour after hour awarding blue ribbons at countless county fairs, observing obscure Masonic Lodge anniversaries, and trekking to small towns from Long Island to Niagara Falls. Few events in New York didn't merit a visit from the assistant secretary of the navy. Speculation about his future was soon rampant: Ted for governor . . . Ted in the VP slot with Coolidge. Teapot Dome could still put a stop to all that, if the Hyde Park side was lucky. "I am sending you clippings from which you will see that little Ted appears to be down and out as a candidate for governor," Louis Howe said gleefully in a letter to FDR. "Politically he is as dead as King Tut, at least for the moment."[36]

While Howe was counting the minutes until Ted's political demise, he was also plotting Franklin's resurrection. Governor Al Smith of New York was attempting to become the first Catholic president, and he asked Franklin—a Protestant who was popular with labor voters—to deliver his nominating speech at the 1924 Democratic National Convention in New York City. Even though his legs were as useless as toothpicks, FDR spent weeks training to maneuver on his own—long enough, at least, to lock his legs in heavy metal braces, hoist himself up on a pair of crutches, and hobble across a convention stage, first on the shoulder of his son James and then, for the final fifteen agonizing feet, all alone. FDR's Happy Warrior speech on behalf of Smith—"This is the Happy Warrior, this is he, whom every man in arms should wish to be"—sent the hall into a wild ovation. The applause wasn't for the man being nominated; Smith ultimately lost to the congressman and diplomat John W. Davis on the 103rd ballot. It was for the speaker: FDR, the irrepressible fighter who had just willed his way back from the political dead.

What most people had only started to notice, however, was that FDR wasn't the only happy warrior in the family. A few months after his electrifying speech, Eleanor herself took to a stage in Syracuse to second the nomination of Al Smith—for governor again, Smith's consolation prize.

Her speech, too, was a highlight of the convention, and no less for the fact that Smith's opponent was, as Alice had long planned, Ted junior. He had secured the state's Republican nomination just the day before. "Of course Smith will win," Eleanor told the Democratic faithful. "He could not do otherwise when the Republican convention just did all it could to help him" by nominating her cousin. One newspaper said her zinger "raised a howl of laughter."[37]

Ironically, Ted's positions were often quite close to Eleanor's, especially on social issues. His unpopular support, on free-speech grounds, of five socialist New York state assemblymen presaged Eleanor's stance during the Red Scare of the 1950s. At a time when racial intolerance haunted the nation, Ted's unambiguous positions stood in contrast to many leading Democrats', including those of President Wilson, who actually resegregated the executive branch that had been integrated by Theodore Roosevelt. One reason the Democrats took 103 ballots to nominate the former West Virginia congressman John W. Davis for president in 1924 was the strong but divisive Klan support for his opponent William McAdoo. Ted took up the issue on the stump in New York City: "No race, no religion must ever be permitted to come up when American is meeting with American. The Ku Klux Klan or any other organization which endeavors to do otherwise is committing an un-American act."[38] Race would remain a constant theme in Eleanor's life as well, helped in large part by the educator Mary McLeod Bethune, whom she met in 1927, and countless other activists over the years. As she said later in a famous essay she wrote for *Ebony* magazine, "Some of my best friends are Negro."[39]

But politics makes both strange and estranged bedfellows, and with the Oyster Bay and Hyde Park Roosevelts politics usually acted like a hot knife slicing through a stick of butter. There were less than six weeks between the New York state Republican and Democratic nominating conventions in late September and Election Day on November 4. If Eleanor was going to block "little Ted" and therefore keep Franklin's path to the governor's office open, she had to hurry. On September 30, the Republicans announced that Ted junior would travel to every corner of the state in a specially equipped campaign train. Over the next week, Eleanor gathered many of her allies from the Women's Division of the New York State Democratic Committee (along with Howe) at Hyde Park. The first public hint of their emerging strategy came in a campaign booklet the group published on October 12 that included a Q&A section worthy of a late-night talk show monologue. "What is Teapot Dome?" it asked. "A large body of government oil completely surrounded by Republican cabinet officers."[40]

Oil, of course, spreads easily and soils everything, and Eleanor and her cronies were more than happy to help that process along. Their vehicle was, in fact, a car—a large blue Buick with the words "For Honesty and Efficiency Vote for John W. Davis and Alfred E. Smith" painted on the side. It came to be called the "singing teapot," though it neither sang nor brewed tea. It was, however, fitted with a makeshift teapot constructed of white canvas and stretched over a six-foot wooden frame. It even belched steam. The allusion to Teapot Dome was clear enough, but in case anyone missed the point, a press release explicitly credited Eleanor as the architect of the entire enterprise—and pointed out that she was the first cousin of the Republican nominee.

Eleanor also took a page right out of Ted's own game plan. Much as he had shadowed Franklin in 1920 to denounce him as a "maverick," the singing teapot was scheduled to nip at Ted's campaign footsteps. It worked the state in a sort of triangle: beginning in New York City, then due north up the Hudson almost to the Canadian border (with an overnight stop at the Roosevelts' Springwood estate in Hyde Park), then west along the southern edge of Lake Ontario to Buffalo, then finally back toward New York City for a celebratory dinner at Franklin and Eleanor's town house. The punishing itinerary called for 218 stops, sometimes as many as 14 in a day. In the smallest towns, the teapot was allowed only five minutes to park, distribute literature, and move on with a few belches of steam for good effect. There was no time to waste. For the launch event on October 20 in Manhattan's Pershing Square, the president of the city's Board of Aldermen, Murray Hulbert, was asked to make a bon voyage speech. He was in the middle of his prepared remarks as the noontime departure arrived. Whistles and horns sounded, the crowd cheered and surrounded the teapot, and soon Hulbert was left alone on the speaker's platform. The Republican press made much of the "disorganization of the Democrats" and the insult to the Democrat Hulbert, who promptly vowed to give no more speeches on Smith's behalf. But the moveable beast was proving its PR value before its journey had even begun.

It made news everywhere it went, including deep inside Republican territory. "The Singing Teapot Dome car of the Democrats visited Fulton on Friday evening and held an open air meeting," wrote the *Fulton Patriot*. "It was a notable campaign venture in the interests of the Democratic ticket, and the ladies in charge made a good presentation of their side of the arguments. However, Fulton and Oswego Counties will not follow the ideas presented to any large extent."[41] It even made news when it did not show up: on October 23, the Ogdensburg *Republican-Journal* ran the headline "Teapot to Sing Across North Land—Davis and Smith Women Campaigners Not Coming Here."[42] It's hard to know if the paper was boasting or brooding.

If the opposition press went easy on them, perhaps that's because Team Teapot was exclusively female. Florence "Daisy" Harriman, a prominent socialite, suffragist, and social reformer, always spoke on behalf of the national ticket. Harriet May Mills, who had been the Democratic nominee for secretary of state for New York in 1920, spoke for Governor Smith. Taking turns driving and distributing campaign literature were the daughters of three prominent politicians: Elia O'Day, whose mother, Caroline, was the future congresswoman and a longtime ally of Eleanor's; Governor Smith's daughter Emily; and Eleanor and Franklin's daughter, Anna. "I spent all of my time explaining how Emily Smith and Anna Roosevelt could be in the same party," said Smith, "because Franklin Roosevelt was so unknown at the time. They only knew of Theodore. They didn't realize there was a Democratic branch of the Roosevelt family."[43] The trip itself was paid for by Henry Morgenthau's wife, Elinor. The one person who did not bear witness to the teapot's triumphs was Eleanor herself. She campaigned with Governor Smith while the teapot steamed through other parts of the state, though she returned to Manhattan to host an end-of-tour dinner at the family's Sixty-Fifth Street town house with Franklin. Beyond that, FDR decided not to involve himself in Eleanor's shenanigans. To put a safe distance between himself and the mudslinging, he spent most of October convalescing in Warm Springs, Georgia.

Besides, this was Eleanor's battle. She was clearly proud of the whole endeavor. Her one documented ride in the singing teapot was a side trip she and the ladies took to show off their new toy to Auntie Bye in Connecticut. Apparently, Eleanor forgot that Bye was also Ted junior's aunt, and she was none too pleased by her troublemaker niece, even if she didn't say it in so many words. "I just hate to see Eleanor let herself look as she does," she wrote to her sister, Corinne. "Though never handsome, she always had to me a charming effect, but alas and lackaday! since politics have become her choicest interest all her charm has disappeared, and the fact is emphasized by the companions she chooses to bring with her."[44] Two days before Election Day, Eleanor debated Frances Parsons, a Republican activist, at Town Hall in New York City. Parsons scolded her for using the teapot as a symbol against Ted when he had been "completely exonerated," but Eleanor refused to back down. Her cousin, she insisted, was "a personally nice young man whose public service record shows him willing to do the bidding of his friends."[45]

Years later, Eleanor would call the singing teapot, semi-apologetically, a "rough stunt," which she chalked up to getting swept up in the political battle. But it was clearly more than that. It was a way for her to flash the steel she'd acquired in her velvet glove, to show the world that she was no longer willing to be just a mousy mother of five. There was a dash of vindictiveness about the teapot, too. ER wanted to settle scores: with Ted junior for going after her husband as a "maverick" in 1920 and with the rest of her Oyster Bay relatives, who thought she was too ugly or timid to ever amount to much. Blindsided by her cousin's hidden cunning, Alice was struck virtually speechless. Her reaction was simply to say "it was a base thing to do," along with a threat: "Like the Republican elephant I am, I never forget."[46]

Anyway, Eleanor wouldn't have let her cousin forget. As the years went on, she eagerly, and uncharacteristically, boasted about the tour's dirty tricks. In her autobiography, she wrote that the singing teapot "led the procession of cars touring the state, following the Republican candidate for governor wherever he went!"[47] Alice went further, placing Eleanor in the car during the tour. In fact, while the teapot inevitably visited some of the same towns in which Ted junior had earlier campaigned, their teapot and his train never got to within seventy-five miles of each other. And though Eleanor was clearly the driving force behind this "rough stunt," there is no contemporary evidence that she accompanied it on the tour, much less spoke from it.

For a family that built its political identity on being straight shooters, they often lost track of the truth when it came to each other. Why the white lies? Maybe it was bragging rights, a by-product of growing up in a hypercompetitive family. The problem was that the Roosevelts were, for many years, America's First Family. Their various tall tales got amplified in the national gossip mill, and those echoes didn't help family unity, especially with two cousins as evenly matched in their histories and fame as Alice and Eleanor.

But to a certain extent, the facts didn't matter. The singing teapot made sure no one forgot Teapot Dome. In a year where President Coolidge, a Republican, carried New York by 870,000 votes, Ted lost to Smith by a margin of 100,000. His political career had evaporated like the steam belching from the singing teapot, and the Oyster Bay side of the family lost its best hope for a return to glory. They wouldn't give up fighting, of course, especially Alice. She still clung to the dream of returning to the White House through what you might call the back door—on the arm of either her husband or her lover. But before she could even begin to plot her next move, she had to tend to a bit of personal business that would stun Washington and beyond.

# Chapter 7

# NEW ROLES

---

I n elected Washington, the only thing harder than keeping your job is keeping a secret. Franklin could testify to that, though he and Howe did better than most. Finding a picture of FDR in a wheelchair is still a rarity. Alice played her own cat-and-mouse games with the press corps—more of them, given her gossip-magazine level of fame. But she didn't always prevail. In 1915, the papers reported on an illness that she'd clearly hoped to keep to herself: "It was learned today that Mrs. Nicholas Longworth, formerly Miss Alice Roosevelt, has been confined for the last days at the home of Mrs. Cornelius Vanderbilt, Fifth Avenue, with a severe attack of the mumps." One paper then delivered Alice's version of a non-denial denial: "A servant of the Vanderbilt home brought back the following message to a reporter who called there today: 'Mrs. Longworth does not want her mumps to get in the paper.'" Sorry about that, Mrs. Longworth.[1]

However, there was one big secret she managed to keep from everyone—except the president of the United States. In July 1924, the Coolidges lost their sixteen-year-old son, Calvin junior, to a freak accident. He had developed a blister on one of his toes after playing a match on the White House tennis court. The toe became infected, and the infection spread, killing him within a week. The Longworths and the Coolidges had become friends over politics, poker, and boxing matches, so when Alice had some news she thought might cheer them up, she called the White House and asked to come over. Mrs. Coolidge had a busy official schedule that day, including a lunch, along with the president, for a large women's organization, so she tried to beg off. Alice, being Alice, wouldn't hear of it. She arrived shortly after 10:00 a.m., flitted up to the First Lady's room, and announced she was going to have a baby. Then she flitted back downstairs, hugged Ike Hoover, the old White House head usher, and departed.

If nothing else, Alice's surprise made for lively table talk at the women's luncheon later that November day. One guest asked Mrs. Coolidge when Alice's baby was due. "Now, if that isn't like me!" she replied. "In all the excitement, I just forgot to ask."[2] With that, President Coolidge picked up a nut off the table and muttered blandly, "Some time in February, I understand." The ladies were shocked, and none more than Mrs. Coolidge. "Well, how would you like to live with a man like that?" she said. "He had known it for two weeks and never a word said he to me!"[3] Which just goes to show: being pals with a man known as Silent Cal had its advantages.

Mrs. Coolidge obviously wasn't the only one who had her hair blown back by Alice's news. The reporter who called Alice later that day to confirm the story seemed scared half to death. "Excuse me, Mrs. Longworth," he stammered. "I apologize for asking you this question, but are you pregnant?" "Hell yes!" Alice shot back. "There's nothing to be ashamed of." The reporter's hesitation was understandable. After all, Alice was hardly the maternal type. What's more, when news of her pregnancy broke, she was forty years old.

As much as she might pretend otherwise, Alice worried quite a bit about what people would say regarding her "condition." Her close relationship with Borah was one of the worst-kept secrets in the city, though she obviously wasn't expecting to get pregnant (and probably assumed, at the age of forty and after twenty years of childless marriage spiced with a few affairs, it wasn't going to happen). "Poor Alice. She feels humiliated about the baby and dreads what people will say," her best friend, Ruth Hanna McCormick, wrote in her diary. "Nick will have a hard time of it for a while, and so will Alice. Everyone will gossip about it and then I hope it will be forgotten for a while."[4]

Everyone did gossip, starting with her own family. When Edith heard that she was going to be a grandmother again, she wrote in her diary the French word *bouleversé* ("stricken" or "shattered"). After all these years, prim and proper Edith could still be shocked by her brazen stepdaughter.

"Alice's news," Edith wrote a few days later to Aunt Bye, "was rather a blow."[5] She apparently knew, or assumed, something Nick did not. When Nick talked to Alice's brother Kermit about the baby, Kermit was surprised by the expectant father's untempered joy. "[Nick] seems very much pleased about it," Kermit wrote to his wife, Belle. "I imagine Sister is doing a great job of bluffing when she talks as she does."[6] When Congress went back into session in early December, all eyes were on Alice—and she knew it. Rather than take her normal seat overlooking Borah in the Senate chamber, she chose to station herself near Nick in the front row of the House family gallery. (Almost as remarkable, sitting with the House meant she couldn't witness the Senate's tribute to her great friend Henry Cabot Lodge, who had died less than a month earlier.) At a time when the press gave considerable deference to the privacy of the famous and powerful, most reporters winked at the truth. They would refer to Borah as Alice's "good friend" or "great admirer"; the one reporter who referred to Alice as "his most intimate friend" didn't have the nerve to include a byline.

———

Propriety—wasn't that supposed to be Eleanor's territory? As they crossed into their forties, the cousins suddenly started to resemble each other, at least around the edges. Just as Alice began to fret about public opinion, Eleanor became more comfortable kicking it aside. On a lovely late August afternoon in Hyde Park, Eleanor and Franklin went on an outing along a stream a few miles away from Springwood, joined by what she called a "gay party of picnickers." In retrospect, that was an apt description, given that their companions were her lesbian friends Nancy Cook and Marion Dickerman. The couples had become close; Franklin playfully called Nancy and Marion "the girls," referred to himself as "Uncle Franklin," and designated the foursome "our gang." With the burbling Fall Kill Creek supplying a sort of natural mood music, Eleanor began to lament the end of summer and what would likely be the gang's last picnic before Sara mothballed the house for the winter. The "girls" agreed. Franklin, however, wasn't having any of it. "But aren't you girls silly," Franklin said. "This isn't Mother's land. I bought this acreage myself."[7] In that instant, a plan was hatched. "Why shouldn't you three have a cottage here of your own, so you could come and go as you please?"[8]

Within days, Franklin wrote to a contractor friend, explaining the assignment: "My missus and some of her female political friends want to build a shack on a stream in the back woods." Before long, he had deeded the land to the three women, appointed himself general contractor, and managed construction of a one-story, Dutch-style stone building complete with swimming pool and gardens. He gave it, too, a wry nickname: "the honeymoon cottage." FDR was referring to its cozy, bucolic, away-from-it-all charm, but whether he meant to or not, the literal meaning could apply as well. The women ordered personalized stationery that read, "Val-Kill Cottage" (taking the Dutch translation of the nearby creek's name). Eleanor monogrammed the bath towels and linens herself with the initials EMN, for Eleanor, Marion, and Nancy. She only had a room in what became Nancy and Marion's permanent home, but this was very much their place. When the house was still under construction, the women became frustrated by Franklin's micromanaging of the project, so the ladies loaded John, FDR Jr., and two other boys into a big blue Buick they'd bought together and took off for a camping trip to New England, Quebec, and Campobello. At one point when they couldn't find a campsite, they pulled up to a farm and Eleanor asked if they could pitch their pup tents for the night. "Where are your husbands?" the farmer asked her. "Mine is not with me and the others don't have husbands," she replied. "I don't want women of that kind," he said. And so they piled back into the Buick and left.[9]

Eleanor didn't care what the farmer, or anyone else, thought. Nancy and Marion helped her feel free. With them, she could leave behind her obligations as wife, mother, and daughter-in-law. Their friendship was based on shared values rather than on bloodlines or class. That became even more evident when the three women decided to go into business together. In 1926, they established Val-Kill Industries, a factory focused on reproductions of Early American wood furniture, along with a few products created on a metal forge and a small loom. Their idea was to use Val-Kill as a sort of progressive workers' commune, in hopes of providing economic support to rural tradesmen who were finding it increasingly hard to survive in America's changing economy. As a business, it was a failure. Val-Kill never employed more than thirty craftsmen, and Eleanor had to sink more and more of her own funds into the project. "In fact, I was probably one of the best customers the shop had, because I bought various pieces of furniture as wedding presents and gifts for other occasions," she said.[10] But the experience was invaluable. Val-Kill was Eleanor's first real attempt at community building and economic engineering, both of which would play a role on a larger scale during the New Deal just a few years later. "Val-Kill," Eleanor would say, "is where I used to find myself and grow."

Even by the permissive standards of the Roaring Twenties, Eleanor's keeping house with two unabashed lesbians was a remarkably bold—and, to some, confusing—idea. Sara was completely perplexed by the arrangement. "Can you tell me why Eleanor wants to go over to the Val-Kill cottage to sleep every night," she asked one of Eleanor's friends. "Why doesn't she sleep here? This is her home."[11] Of course, that was the other reason the previously conventional Eleanor, who only a few years earlier had devoted herself to the arcane Washington practice of "calling," was suddenly building her own little Bohemia on the Hudson. She never felt at home at Springwood, and Sara never could see it. But Franklin did. However estranged they had become romantically, Franklin and Eleanor still cared deeply about each other's happiness. Besides, he knew that helping his wife acquire a room of her own would buy him a much-needed dose of domestic tranquillity. In that sense, Val-Kill was indeed Eleanor's "honeymoon cottage." It offered her, for the first time in her adult life, a chance to live by her own rules, pursuing her own priorities and dreams.

———

Despite the family's initial trepidation about Alice's pregnancy, she soon found herself in a familiar spot: thumbing her nose at society with impunity. The minute the news broke, the press began acting as if the royal family had just trumpeted the next heir to the throne, rumors be damned. "She is still the Princess Alice and she succeeds by means which would be the ruin of others to attempt," wrote *The New Yorker*.

> She does no official entertaining, gives no large parties, returns no calls. She breaks every rule in the book and in Washington the rules count. Yet an invitation to the Longworths is more prized by the discriminating than an invitation to the White House ...
>
> If she does not feel like dressing, Alice—not the butler—may receive her guests at the door in a Chinese silk outfit something like a swell set of pajamas. She will sit on her feet on a tiger skin before the fire and smoke while Nick, after a wearing day on the floor of the House, fiddles with complete abstraction.[12]

With similarly fawning reports being filed from all over the country, Alice felt secure enough of her place in the pecking order to really tweak the gossipmongers. She told Nick she wanted to name the baby Deborah—as in *de* ("of," in French) Borah. He was not amused. "With all the gossip going around, why would you want to name her De-Borah?" he asked.[13] They decided on Paulina, after Alice's favorite saint.

Despite Nick's comment, it's hard to believe he didn't have suspicions about Paulina's paternity, given the Longworths' long-running estrangement and the incessant rumors. (Best joke at the time: What do the Longworth baby and a brand new parquet floor have in common? Neither have a bit of Nick in them.) Or maybe he knew the truth and just didn't care. Nick's House colleagues gave him a heartfelt standing ovation when the Associated Press first flashed news of Paulina's birth on February 14, 1925. True to the baby's quasi-royal lineage, the entire country seemed thrilled about the "Valentine Baby," as Paulina became known. "For every newspaper it was a front page story," wrote *The New Yorker*, which added an observation that must have warmed Alice's vindictive little heart: "No such romantic glamor spun about the children of the Wilson girls, even though those happy events took place in the White House itself, and the grandfather of the youngsters was President. The nation reserved its rejoicing for the delivery of an heir to the Princess Alice; for the daughter of T.R."[14]

Paulina became a regular visitor to the House, sitting on Nick's knee and smiling for the cameras while the proud papa beamed right back at her. Before her first birthday, Nick was elected Speaker of the House, his popularity boosted in part as the father of the country's most famous infant. By 1926, the pundits speculated that Nick would run for president. They also speculated about where he got the idea: "In the nimble brain of that uncomfortable woman, Alice Roosevelt Longworth. Every move Nick makes is colored Alice blue ... [She] has the finesse of a fencer. Also of a boxer, billiardist, bridge player and every other art requiring tact, discrimination and judgment."[15] Even for wealthy women at the time, motherhood meant signing up for a lifetime of assignments and obligations tied specifically to the welfare of the family. Not for Alice Longworth. For her, motherhood merited a promotion to more important, less homebound pursuits. "It is no exaggeration to say that she shapes national policies, executive and legislative—not all policies, of course, but those she is interested in, and her interests are very wide."[16] In 1926, she was "virtually assured" to become the Republicans' national committeewoman from Ohio—until she took her name out of contention. "I am convinced that the duties of national committeewoman are not in my line," she said somewhat vaguely.[17] In February 1927, she landed on the cover of *Time* magazine for no other accomplishment than being deemed "the most popular lady in the land." She made news when she was paid $5,000 (roughly $68,000 in 2015 dollars) to appear in a Pond's cold cream ad and again when, for some bizarre reason, the appendix she had removed in 1907 turned up in possession of the U.S. government, preserved in a bottle of alcohol. No matter how brightly Nick's star shone, Alice's made it look paler. Even the possibility of Nick's becoming president was examined through the lens of his wife: How would she behave as First Lady? How would she feel about moving back into the White House? Would Paulina be as mischievous as First Daughter Alice? When Nick declared that he wouldn't run for the White House after all, guess who got the credit: "Alice Rules 'Nick' Out."[18] Adding to poor Nick's humiliation: that paper suggested that Alice's preferred ticket was Borah for president, with her brother Ted for VP. Unfortunately for Nick, that was probably true.

————

The rest of the country was so busy beating the drums for Alice even she didn't hear the footsteps approaching from Hyde Park. Eleanor clearly regretted running over her cousin Ted with the singing teapot; she tried to mend their relationship and never played that dirty again. But the 1924 campaign kindled a newly competitive, even combative, spirit in her, and like any recent convert she embraced her new assignment with the zeal of a missionary. When Franklin's half-niece, Helen Roosevelt, came to visit Hyde Park with her husband, Theodore Robinson (Aunt Corinne's proudly Republican son), in the fall of 1925, she found herself playing referee. "Eleanor also has become so rabid," Helen wrote to Aunt Corinne, "that I see perfectly that I shall be a continual 'buffer' during the entire visit and am preparing to leap actively into all breaches at any moment."[19] Eleanor became a leading voice for the forty-eight-hour workweek and gradually took up almost any women's rights issue. She spoke on the radio, hosted antiwar lunches, and wrote prodigiously for the *Women's Democratic News*. She made a splash after she was arrested for disorderly conduct while picketing alongside striking box fabricators in New York, and she kicked up a storm with an article she wrote for *Redbook*: "Women Must Learn to Play the Game as Men Do." All of a sudden she was being compared favorably with a certain male Roosevelt—Uncle Ted. "There is something about that smile that is reminiscent of her illustrious uncle, while the droop in the outer corner of her eyes likewise reminds one of the former President," wrote the *New York Times*.[20] Eleanor was soaring at last—and in more ways than one. She had always loved the idea of flying, and she persuaded her friend Amelia Earhart to give her pilot lessons. FDR, who was never comfortable with air travel, finally convinced her to stop.

Of course, with every speech and handshake, she was also helping raise FDR's profile, even while he spent a good deal of time at his Warm Springs spa, determined to walk. As the 1928 election approached, FDR's mentor, Governor Al Smith of New York, decided to run for president again, and he asked Franklin for a repeat performance as the man who introduced the "Happy Warrior" to the Democratic convention four years earlier. This time Smith got the party's nomination, but even he realized he was a long shot in the general election, given that the Republicans had presided over a roaring economy for the last eight years. It didn't help that Smith was a Roman Catholic, a sixth-grade dropout, and the purveyor of a New York accent as thick as the mustard on a Coney Island hot dog. His opponent, Secretary of Commerce Herbert Hoover, was an upright and fastidious Quaker whose work coordinating Europe's postwar relief efforts had made him so popular the Democrats had briefly talked of drafting him. Smith was worried enough about carrying his home state that he begged Franklin to run for governor in the hopes that the Roosevelt name would attract enough votes to carry New York for the both of them. The scheme didn't quite go down as planned. Smith got buried in the national election, losing forty states, including New York, while Franklin squeaked by with the narrowest of margins. Another election, another move into one of Uncle Ted's old houses.

Two days after Franklin's victory, Eleanor unexpectedly played against the good-wife type again. When a reporter asked her if she was excited that her husband was now governor-elect, she came at him like a snapping turtle. "No, I am not excited about my husband's election," she said. "What difference does it make to me?"[21] Eleanor knew that moving to the governor's mansion in Albany meant she'd have to leave behind many of her own political projects—as with children, the wives of elected officials were supposed to be seen and not heard. She stepped down as the editor of the *Women's Democratic News* and started to turn down speaking requests. Instead, she spent a good deal of her time commuting four hours to New York City, where she taught English literature and history at the Todhunter School for Girls, which she had purchased in 1927 with Marion and Nancy. Remembering how Mlle Souvestre had had such a profound impact on her life, Eleanor embraced teaching as an opportunity to do the same for a new generation of young women. Like her mentor, Eleanor challenged her students—most of them wealthy, spoiled, and maddeningly incurious—to discover and be themselves, not what society expected them to be. She especially wanted them to be aware of the great injustices around them and to try to change society for the better. In what would become her signature approach when she became First Lady, her classes took frequent field trips, venturing to outposts few teachers today would dare visit: a police lineup in a local precinct, a soup kitchen, and the worst kind of housing project she could find. "They need to know what bad housing conditions mean and then I would like them to see as model a tenement as possible in a bad neighborhood."[22] One of her favorite final exam questions was, "In what ways are negroes kept from voting in the South?" It would be at least twenty years before most Americans would even begin to think about voter suppression.

While Eleanor was teaching social studies to the privileged young ladies of Manhattan, Alice decided to offer her own history lesson to Washington society. The same arcane social rules that governed the ritual of "calling" also dictated the seating chart at formal affairs. Who would sit to the right and the left of the host, or next to the Romanian ambassador, or the junior senator from Arkansas? All of it was determined by long-standing rules of protocol. The wife of the president naturally took precedence and received the best seating in the house (next to the host or the most honored guest), followed by the wife of the vice president and the wife of the Speaker. But what if the vice president didn't have a wife and instead used his sister as a stand-in? Would she take precedence over, say, the actual wife of the Speaker?

That was the question with President Hoover's No. 2, a sixty-nine-year-old Kansan named Charlie Curtis. Vice President Curtis was a

widower, which meant he needed to anoint an official hostess and dinner companion for formal Capitol Hill functions. The fact that he had
asked his half sister, Mrs. Dolly Gann, to do the honors at first seemed
insignificant—until Alice begged to differ. When she and Speaker Longworth learned in early 1929 that Dolly Gann would be seated ahead of
Alice at a dinner thrown by Eugene Meyer, the publisher of the *Washington Post*, Alice called to say the Longworths wouldn't be coming after
all. The Dolly Gann Affair was born, and while a fight over place settings
may sound ridiculous now, it burned up Washington for a year full of
tit-for-tat snubs and hubbub. "This new turmoil over matters of social
precedence has divided Washington into two hostile camps, just as the
Wars of the Roses of the 15th century divided the aristocracy of England
into two great groups," one paper panted.[23] Invitations were accepted and
then refused. Editorials were written and then debated. Finally, about six
months after the first eruption, the State Department* ruled that Mrs.
Gann did indeed outrank Mrs. Longworth. Some Solomonic dignitaries then took to scheduling twin dinners so that Dolly could preside at
one and Alice at the other. Even Will Rogers lent his satirical voice to
the shouting match, in an open letter to the *Los Angeles Times*: "Had dinner with Mrs. Longworth and sat by Mrs. Gann in the Senate gallery
today and had a fine chat. So got everything fixed up between Alice and
Dolly. Alice is to have preferential seating relief on Mondays, Wednesdays
and Fridays, and Dolly on Tuesdays, Thursdays and Saturdays. Sundays is
neutral."[24]

The irony of Alice Longworth suddenly standing up for decorum certainly wasn't lost on anyone: "Especially it is a relief to the recalcitrants
to have Mrs. Longworth appearing in the role of leader in defense of the
old-established social-official, or official-social, order. It is a fact all the
more impressive because so novel. Always Mrs. Longworth has ignored,
even defied, precedent, in the matter of paying and receiving calls, giving
and accepting invitations, even keeping an open house on New Year's Day,
as every Speaker's wife before her always did, and as she never has done."[25]

---

* The Department of State had the unenviable task of resolving these semi-weighty matters
because of the complexities involved in hosting the representatives of foreign governments.
In a feat of exquisite timing, the Office of the Chief of Protocol was established on Febru-
ary 4, 1928, just before the Dolly Gann Affair exploded. Five and a half decades later, Selwa
Roosevelt (daughter-in-law of Alice's brother Archie) would hold that position during the
Reagan administration.

It's fair to say that while protocol might have been the tinder that ignited the whole affair, it was really Alice who fueled it. Being the most famous woman in Washington had its price: "The part which Mrs. Longworth plays on Capitol Hill, the prestige she commands throughout Washington, is, of course, resented by other Congressional wives, most of whom lead a dull and pompous existence in the red-plush drawing rooms of the second class hotels which cluster around the Hill, or attend excessively stodgy teas, the guest lists of which they phone at great lengths to society editors. It was natural, therefore, that a large number of these estimable ladies should have sided with Dolly Curtis Gann in the social-precedence war against her more charming and socially-powerful opponent, Alice Longworth."[26]

Yet the silliest part of the feud wasn't Washington's juvenile reaction but Alice's. She insisted, for years afterward, that she had about as much interest in snubbing Dolly Gann as she did in a quiet game of checkers. The whole thing had really been Nick's crafty way to back out of a "dry" dinner party when he could. "There never was any row," she wrote four years later, in *Crowded Hours*. "Anyone who knew me was aware that rank and conventionality were things I always fled from and shirked."[27] But she certainly acted as if she cared. If she didn't, a single public comment to that effect would have dissolved the feud instantly. Instead, she let her actions do the talking. The week after the State Department ruled in Dolly's favor, Alice made a point of pulling out of a White House dinner honoring the British prime minister, setting off yet another round of coverage. The truth is, she liked playing the game, especially because she was writing the rules. With her impeccable sense of publicity, she knew exactly how to stoke the press for her own amusement, right down to the end. In December 1930, when she had apparently had enough, Alice made a point of showing up at one of the biggest functions of the year, the annual White House Diplomatic Reception, knowing full well that Dolly would be there on the vice president's arm. When they saw each other, the two women immediately smiled and held hands. Alice seemingly put the lid on the whole episode with her cheerful greeting: "Hello, Dolly!"[28]

There was ample reason for green-eyed Washington to go after Alice Blue Eyes. The press treated her with more deference than any woman in town. "Heavy politics are played at the Longworth house and Alice sits in. The Longworth place is the closest thing to a salon that Washington has. Alice Longworth never made a speech in her life and never gave an interview. She was not a suffrage advocate, never joined a women's club, never is a sponsor for or a member of the 'honorary committee' of this or that great movement . . . Yet in her imperceptible way she is one of the most influential women in Washington. She knows men, measures, and motives; has an understanding grasp of their changes."[29] Sometimes she came across as a superhero, even if the stories sounded apocryphal. When the Republicans were missing a crucial member before a close vote in the Senate, Alice was said to have been the only person with the nerve to march into the unnamed senator's house, rouse him from a drunken stupor, pack him into her car, and get him to his desk in time to raise a wobbly hand in favor of the bill. When asked by a portly matron during a fashionable party how she kept her figure, she was said to have pinned her skirt tightly around her legs and launched herself into a headstand. "Girth control!" she told the flabbergasted woman. It was also during this time that her character-defining quips started to become the stuff of legend. The one that launched her viper-tongued reputation came at the expense of her friend and confidant, Calvin Coolidge: "He looks like he was weaned on a pickle."

The one person who didn't buy the Longworth lore—or at least pretended not to—was Alice. "At intervals legends grow up that certain women have political power, that they influence votes on legislation," she wrote. "Such a role is from time to time attributed to me, and a legend is what it amounts to—totally absurd and without foundation in fact."[30] The problem is that she protested too much. She denied credit for most everything, from the Gann feud right down to the pickle quip. "I heard that at my dentist's office," she insisted, sounding like someone who had been caught passing a nasty note behind the teacher's back. "But didn't it describe him exactly?" Alice's modesty did have some basis in truth. Two close friends, Isabella Greenway and Ruth Hanna McCormick, became members of Congress themselves, something Alice never even considered. But there was a good bit of self-preservation in her humility. She had the unfortunate habit of overshadowing the powerful men in her life. It's telling that when the *Los Angeles Times* blamed Alice for removing Nick from presidential consideration in 1927, it also noted that she had thrown her weight behind Borah. He, too, was often described as being "advised" by her, but then again so was half of Washington. "Mrs. Longworth, who is regarded in capital circles as having inherited more of the 'T.R.' flair for politics than any of her male line, is expected to breathe some life into the drawing-room caucuses which are indulging in President-making when she re-opens her Massachusetts-avenue house within a few days," the *Times* said. "Those who know best the ways of the capital hesitate to challenge even for an instant the power Mrs. Longworth wields."[31]

Her brother Ted got the worst of it, probably because she exerted so much of her influence on his behalf. She had bargained hard with Harding to get his support when Ted ran for governor of New York in 1924, only to have Harding die before he could lift a finger. In 1929, she asked Hoover to appoint Ted governor of the Philippines. When that fell through, she tried again for Puerto Rico, piling him and her friend (and now congresswoman) Ruth McCormick into her car and delivering them personally to the White House for a final vetting. The newspaper headline: "Sister Helps Clear the Way for Roosevelt." Ted got the job and did well enough in Puerto Rico to capture that posting in the Philippines in 1932, but Alice stole his thunder yet again. "If some Roosevelt must be sent to Manila, why not the famous 'Princess' Alice?" whined the *Philippines Free Press* when news broke of Ted's appointment. "Her executive ability is on a par with her brother's, and she seems to have inherited some of the political acumen of her Presidential father. By all means, if we must have a Roosevelt, let it be Alice."[32]

———

In Alice's defense, upstaging their men—intentionally or not—ran in the Roosevelt family. Unlike Alice, Eleanor wasn't reluctant to leave her fingerprints on her pet projects. As much as she had dreaded abandoning her progressive causes when she moved to Albany, she discovered that she'd come too far to fade away now. In between her work at the Todhunter School and the endless ribbon cuttings, society teas, and various photo ops that fell to the wife of a politician (and especially of one eager to keep his paralysis out of the public eye), Eleanor slowly edged her way back onto her soapbox. She worked to raise money for underfunded schoolteachers, wrote newspaper opinions about the proper role of women in the home and workplace (including calling for a minimum wage for women), supported striking dressmakers, denounced lengthy prison sentences for minor crimes, and even waded into two of the most heated issues of the day: birth control and Prohibition.

If there was any question that her shrinking-violet days were history, it was answered at the small town of Lake Placid, New York. In February 1932, Lake Placid opened its frosty doors to the third Winter Olympics; Franklin, as governor of the host state, presided over the opening ceremony. With one eye already on the upcoming presidential election, he used his moment on the world stage to make a Wilsonian plea for global peace and cooperation. Unfortunately, his big moment was almost eclipsed when Eleanor struck up a conversation at lunch with a member of the American bobsled team. Before anyone could stop her (and long before the issue of liability insurance would have scuttled the fun), she had agreed to strap herself onto a two-man bobsled and take the plunge. In the next day's paper, her joyride got nearly as much space as Franklin's speech: "The sled passed through the 'zigzag,' a double series of curves, and a few moments later was visible streaking down the mountain side and into the final curve. It shot up the wall of ice and down again and then raced under the finish bridge and up the slope to a standstill. Smiling, Mrs. Roosevelt removed the leather helmet which sledders use, and came back through the snow, chatting with her companions."[33] Somewhere, Uncle Ted was smiling right back at her.

When it came to making the actual decisions of government, however, Eleanor went out of her way to underplay her clout. As with Alice, nothing could have been further from the truth. Her role as Franklin's unsung adviser began in earnest when they moved to the Governor's mansion in Albany. It turned out that Alice and her Oyster Bay family weren't the only ones who regarded Franklin as a lightweight. Having lost the presidential election but succeeded in getting his apprentice elected governor, Al Smith still expected to run New York State. He insisted that FDR reappoint most of his administration and imagined that Governor Roosevelt would spend most of his time floating in the healing waters of Warm Springs while Smith controlled the government by proxy. Franklin did keep much of the Smith team intact, with two notable exceptions: Robert Moses, the legendary urban planner and builder, and Belle Moskowitz, Smith's closest adviser. Smith's expectation regarding Moses was absurd, given that the power-hungry Moses had been openly contemptuous of Franklin when they worked under Smith, especially when the parks commissioner refused Roosevelt's request to find a job for Louis Howe.

Belle Moskowitz, however, was the sort of gutsy, hardworking, and skilled woman that Franklin, and particularly Eleanor, would have been expected to welcome onto their team. Franklin was all for her. It was Eleanor, he said, who objected:

> Eleanor said to me, "Franklin, Mrs. Moskowitz is a very fine woman. I have worked with her in every campaign. I never worked with anybody that I liked to work with better. She's extremely competent . . . I think a great deal of her and I think we are friends. But I want to say this to you. You have to decide, and you have to decide it now, whether you are going to be governor of this state, or whether Mrs. Moskowitz is going to be governor of this state. If Mrs. Moskowitz is your secretary, she will run you. It won't hurt you. It won't give you any pain. She will run you in such a way that you don't know you're being run a good deal of the time. Everything will be arranged so subtly that when the matter comes to you it will be natural to decide to do the thing that Mrs. Moskowitz has already decided should be done."[34]

This was clearly not the same Eleanor who had silently emptied the men's ashtrays and refilled their drinks when the state senator Roosevelt was in Albany sixteen years earlier. She had become a keen political observer and cunning enough to separate her personal fondness for Moskowitz—and her natural inclination to support a woman—from the risk Moskowitz posed to her husband. Four years before they moved to the White House, the seed of the Roosevelts' unprecedented political partnership had started to take root.

The Longworths had long ago mastered the art of the business-only marriage, despite such obstacles as the daughter that at least one of them knew did not belong to them both.[*] Ultimately their exile from power was caused by something far bigger than anything they could control. When the stock market crashed and took the rest of the economy with it in October 1929, much of the country, understandably, blamed the Republicans. They were the party in power and had been for the entire

---

[*] That Borah was Paulina's biological father was long suspected but not confirmed until 2007, when unprecedented access to Alice and Borah's personal correspondence was granted to Alice's biographer. In many of the letters between them they employed a simple code that, deciphered, makes clear that Borah was aware that he was a father and was genuinely concerned for and fond of his child. See Cordery, *Alice*, 287.

decade. Even as the economy swirled ever closer to the sewer, President Hoover stuck to his belief that the government shouldn't interfere, while progressive politicians such as Roosevelt experimented with a host of aggressive policies that would later be expanded during FDR's presidency, such as unemployment insurance and a form of social security. In the election of 1930, the Republicans lost forty-two House seats, putting them in a virtual tie with the Democrats. Even if the GOP somehow managed to hold on to its majority, its members seemed ready to ditch their leadership. "Perhaps this is the last time I will address you from this rostrum," Nick told his members on the last day of the Seventy-First Congress. Then he played his own elegy on the House piano.

Alice and Nick did their best to keep up their spirits and appearances. As per tradition, they hosted the annual Speaker's dinner for the president and the First Lady, during the week before Christmas. In February 1931, they threw themselves a twenty-fifth-anniversary party. Alice, perhaps pining for her glory days, asked the guests to come dressed in clothes from 1906. She herself wore a gold silk gown plucked straight from her trousseau, along with the same profusion of jewels she wore at her wedding (plus a new diamond tiara in the place of an orange-blossom wreath). Despite the usual, effusive coverage in newspapers across the country, Nick wasn't feeling like himself. At sixty-one, he was in as bad shape physically as he was politically, a lifetime of drinking and partying finally taking a toll. He'd had a head cold that lasted several weeks, and in April he took a trip to Aiken, South Carolina, to shake it. He was sure to feel warmer there, given that he'd be staying in the winter home of his current mistress, Mrs. Laura Curtis.* (Mr. Curtis, in the style of the times, politely looked the other way.) Whatever her good qualities, Laura was apparently a lousy nurse. Nick's cold morphed into pneumonia, and she called for Alice, who arrived on April 8. The next day, Nick was dead.

Alice arranged for a special train to take the body back to Cincinnati— special, in part, because among the passengers keeping vigil over Nick's corpse were Mr. and Mrs. Curtis as well as a woman named Alice Dows, another of Nick's great loves. "[Alice] asked me to go with her," Dows said. "Oh, it was very moving. Particularly the way Alice treated me, as

---

* Ironically, Aiken was also home to another political mistress, Lucy Mercer Rutherfurd. It was from Aiken that she would travel, unbeknownst to Eleanor, to join FDR at Warm Springs in 1945.

if *I* was the widow, which I suppose I was."[35] The president and the vice president also attended the Cincinnati funeral. Franklin and Eleanor did not but issued a formal statement of condolences, noting that they were "deeply grieved to learn of the death of Speaker Longworth, because both of us have known him since we were children."[36] The widow—the widow Longworth, that is—seemed to bear up just fine. "Nick's death was very sad and will be a real blow to the Republican party," Kermit wrote to his wife's sister. "Sister has been extremely plucky about it and I think will go on with her life in the same way, dividing up her time between Cincinnati and Washington."[37] In an interview many years later, Alice was asked what she remembered most fondly about Nick. She said she couldn't think of anything.

For Alice, the more wrenching funeral came four months later, when Aunt Bye, at age seventy-six, died in Connecticut. If she wasn't a celebrated pillar of the Roosevelt family, she was certainly the cement that kept the foundation in place. She was brother Ted's greatest confidante, orphaned Alice's savior, and young Eleanor's lone source of consistent support and affection. She'd introduced Sara Delano to James Roosevelt, raised Rosy Roosevelt's motherless children, and in her later years—when she was deaf, confined to her wheelchair, and yet still the liveliest conversationalist in the room—gave Franklin companionship in his disability. When it came to the Roosevelt women's ability to outshine their men, Bye created the template. "I used to think she might have governed an empire, either in her own right, or through her influence over a king or an emperor," Eleanor wrote, ten years after Bye's death.[38] Other than Franklin, who couldn't get away from Albany, all the surviving members of the family made the trip to Bye's house for her funeral: Sara Roosevelt (age seventy-six), Edith (seventy), Aunt Corinne (sixty-nine), Joe and Stewart Alsop, and of course Alice and Eleanor. There was something fitting about Aunt Bye's knitting the entire family together—and something sad. Within a year, the election of 1932 would drive a wedge between the family's two branches from which they would never fully recover.

―――――

War was declared even before Franklin's candidacy. After Governor Roosevelt won reelection by a landslide in 1930, his name was on every pundit's presidential short list, and his Oyster Bay relatives began planning their Armageddon. "Well, as far as I can see, the ship went down with all on board," Ted junior wrote to Edith. "Your cousin Franklin now, I suppose, will run for the Presidency, and I am already beginning to think of many nasty things to say concerning him."[39] The issue wasn't so much FDR's big-government ideals, though the Republican Roosevelts didn't cotton much to them. This was really about bragging rights, about retaining their claim to the hallowed Roosevelt name, much as it was when Franklin ran for vice president in 1920 and Ted junior rode around the country declaring that his cousin didn't have the "brand" of their family. "We behaved terribly," Alice admitted many years later. "There we were—*the* Roosevelts—hubris up to the eyebrows, *beyond* the eyebrows, and then who should come sailing down the river but Nemesis in the person of Franklin. We were out. Run over ... It was complicated by the fact that my brother Ted had been brought up by my father to follow in his footsteps, which was very tough, and then to see Franklin follow in those same footsteps with large Democratic shoes on was just too terrible to contemplate!"[40]

On both sides of the family divide, the Roosevelt women eagerly hit the road in 1932. Edith hadn't set foot in the White House since she left it in March 1909, but she showed up for a party celebrating President Hoover's re-nomination, along with Ethel and Alice. She still didn't say much. When a reporter asked the famously tight-lipped former First Lady for a statement, she replied, "I haven't talked for the press, not in 71 years, and it's too late to begin now."[41] But when she returned home to Long Island, she wrote to Ted in the Philippines and gave him a full report, at least as she saw it. "As far as I can tell there is no enthusiasm for Franklin," she wrote optimistically, even sharing a sample of opinions from her still-voluminous mailbag: "One woman wrote, 'He has made a poor governor so why should he make a good President?'"[42]

Having long insisted she was too shy to speak in public, Alice managed to steel herself and tackle the role of Oyster Bay mouthpiece. She spent much of her time, ironically, in Nick's backyard, despite having spent her married life escaping from Ohio whenever possible. Alongside First Lady Lou Henry Hoover, Alice appeared at numerous rallies and parades. At one point when they crossed over the Ohio border, Mrs. Hoover was able to coax Alice to the front of the train platform and greet the crowd, though it's hard to imagine Alice convinced many of them when she announced, "I'm glad to see my fellow Buckeyes!"[43] She did better three days later at a Republican women's rally in Columbus. "I was so carried away with the enthusiasm and spirit of the meeting that I just had to talk," she insisted.[44] But unlike her father, whose written speeches were so hefty they could literally stop a speeding bullet, Alice kept her pitch to a mere thirty-one words: "The Democrats can't get away with blaming the Depression on President Hoover. Because the people are realizing this and waking up to that fact, President Hoover will be re-elected November 8."[45]

Alice might have gathered enough courage to speak publicly, but she didn't dare tell voters what really motivated her. "I wasn't so much for Hoover," she said years later, "but I was against Franklin, in that nasty way that an Oyster Bay Roosevelt felt about it."[46] The ill will didn't only emerge in the political arena. Long before the 1932 campaign took shape, Eleanor had begun constructing a sort of valentine to her father, Elliott: a collection of his letters written while he was young, sober, and still the most promising of the Roosevelt boys. Aunt Corinne, Elliott Roosevelt's last-surviving sibling, suggested that Scribner's might publish the letters. "They looked them over very carefully and wrote me a nice note about them but said that they did not think they could publish them before Christmas," Eleanor wrote to her aunt. "I asked Mr. [Louis] Howe to see Mr. Scribner and it then developed that he was very nervous on account of being great friends with Alice, Aunt Edith, and you, for fear if he published them at this time they would in some way be considered a political document and he would be accused of playing up the enemy camp."[47]

In fact, Aunt Corinne was one of the few Oyster Bay relatives who refused to go after Franklin. She had been active in Republican politics for years and actually campaigned for Hoover in 1928 against Al Smith. In early October 1932, the New York State Republican Party named her as a Hoover "elector," a largely ceremonial position that involved formally registering a state's vote in the Electoral College. The next day, she refused the party's offer. "You must understand why I cannot comment on the national campaign," she said at a Republican event. "My own beloved niece is the wife of the Democratic candidate. She is the daughter of the brother who was closer to me in age than Theodore. For her I have the deepest affection and respect. So much as I would like to pay the highest tribute to President Hoover, I cannot do so in this campaign."[48]

Eleanor certainly appreciated the support from at least one limb of her family, even as she insisted she didn't hold anything against the others.

"Many thanks for both your notes," she wrote to Corinne Alsop, Aunt Corinne's daughter and another relative who refused to enter the fray. "As you know, I haven't the slightest feeling that anyone should work for any party they don't believe in, but I do know that I can always count on your personal affection and it was very dear of you to write. Franklin appreciated it as much as I do."[49]

On the other hand, Eleanor was almost too busy to notice what Alice and the others were saying. In July 1932, she flew with Franklin to the Democratic National Convention in Chicago. He was the first major-party candidate to break with the received wisdom that accepting the nomination in person was somehow unseemly; his dramatic appearance at the podium in front of the delegates was cleverly designed to show him as a man of emphatic action, and not one hobbled by polio. Eleanor was soon to become the most widely traveled and prominent wife of a nominee. It would be difficult to overstate her importance to her husband's campaign as she trekked around the country with a particular focus on women's groups, reaping the benefit of the ties she had cultivated as New York's activist First Lady. As if that weren't exhausting enough, Eleanor insisted on driving herself to many campaign stops, though Franklin demanded she travel with the New York state trooper Earl Miller in the passenger seat and a handgun in the glove compartment. Somewhere along the way, she developed an unusual technique for battling fatigue: she could fall asleep anywhere and almost instantly if the situation didn't require her full attention. Sometimes that meant in the middle of a quiet conversation; sometimes she managed to ignore an enormous amount of noise. The family had been campaigning in Chicago on October 1, and because the New York Yankees happened to be in town facing the Chicago Cubs in game three of the World Series, Eleanor decided to treat the family to a game. This particular contest would go down in baseball history as the one where Babe Ruth, being heckled mercilessly by fruit-throwing Chicago fans, pointed to the center field bleachers and proceeded to deposit a home run in that very spot, 440 feet away. The New Yorkers in the crowd went wild. Well, all but one: "Mrs. Roosevelt sat between her husband and Jimmy, squeezed in so tightly that she could not have fallen over even if she had collapsed," said Lorena Hickok, an Associated Press reporter assigned to cover the Roosevelts. "I noticed that her head had dropped forward, and, on the way out of the ball park, Jimmy told me his mother had slept through the entire game."[50]

With the election approaching and Hoover still sinking, the Oyster Bay family got desperate. On Halloween night 1932, Edith unglued her lips and showed up at New York's Madison Square Garden to introduce Hoover to thousands of rallying Republicans. On November 3, just five days before the election, Alice broke down and made her first national radio address, which turned out to be as preposterous as it was momentous. She argued that the Democrats not only lied when they blamed Hoover for the Depression; they also insulted the voters, who obviously knew a specious argument when they heard one. "They belittle the intelligence of the average citizen," Alice claimed, "and I, as an average citizen, resent it." When Alice Roosevelt Longworth was willing to refer to herself as an "average citizen," hope was clearly lost. On November 8, Franklin won forty-two states, Hoover only six.

The battle might have been over, but the war was just beginning. Ted junior, who had been governor-general of the Philippines for less than a year, realized his days in Manila were numbered. When a reporter there asked how he was related to the president-elect, Ted replied, "Fifth cousin, about to be removed." (And removed he was. In fact, the boat carrying the retiring governor and his wife back to the United States on March 22 hit the rocks and ran aground off the southern Philippines. It was an apt metaphor for his foundering political career.) In Washington, the Oyster Bay side began to panic about an eighty-five-acre island in the Potomac River that had recently been purchased by the Theodore Roosevelt Memorial Association. The plan had been to turn the land, which sat in the shadow of the ten-year-old Lincoln Memorial, into the home for some sort of tribute to TR. Now that the wrong Roosevelt was about to enter the White House, the Oyster Bay family quickly arranged a ceremony so that they could present the island to the lame-duck president, Hoover, rather than to President-elect Roosevelt. They sent Alice to the White House to do the honors.

Of all the Oyster Bay relatives, Edith was the most incensed by the notion of a second president Roosevelt. In a letter to Ted's wife, she complained bitterly after a stranger "asked if I was the mother of the President. I furiously said no, the widow of one whose mother had been dead for fifty years. I wish Franklin would drop Mr. Roosevelt and retain Mr. Delano."[51] She wasn't all that happy with her son Kermit, either. Kermit had long been the closest to the Hyde Park family, having bonded a few years earlier when his daughter Clochette had a brush with polio. He had warmly congratulated Franklin and Eleanor after both of FDR's gubernatorial elections and again after his presidential win. In fact, he joined Franklin and some friends on the philanthropist-tycoon Vincent Astor's yacht *Nourmahal* for a ten-day, preinaugural cruise around the Bahamas. The *New York Times* promptly ran the headline "Rift Between Roosevelt Families Bridged," which wasn't exactly true. When a reporter asked Edith why Kermit was yachting with the president-elect, she answered, "Because his mother wasn't there."[52]

When the *Nourmahal* docked in Miami on the evening of February 15, a suntanned Franklin was greeted by cheering crowds on the dock. He stopped to deliver a few off-the-cuff remarks, but before he was finished, an unemployed Italian bricklayer named Giuseppe Zangara fired five shots at him. A woman standing in front of Zangara grabbed his arm at the last second. He missed Roosevelt, but he hit Mayor Anton Cermak of Chicago in the stomach; Cermak would linger for three weeks before dying from his injuries. "Those things are to be expected," Eleanor told the children when she got the news, an astonishingly calm reaction that would reverberate twelve years later when she was summoned to the White House to be told of Franklin's sudden death.[53]

Less than a week after the assassination attempt came the news that Aunt Corinne had died. Eleanor had just seen her at a party honoring the incoming First Lady at the Waldorf-Astoria hotel. Delighted by her favorite niece's success, Corinne, seventy-one, had trekked from her home in upstate New York into the city despite having a minor respiratory infection. But her condition worsened quickly after that, and she died exactly one month later. The fractured family, thrown together sooner than anyone had expected, behaved admirably at the funeral service, with Alice, Eleanor, Franklin, and many Oyster Bay cousins attending. It might have helped that Edith, Ted junior, and his wife, Eleanor, were still away in Asia at the time. Or maybe the temporary truce was just a tribute to Corinne's place in the family. "One wanted to tell her everything," Alice wrote in her memoirs, "sure of her perfect comprehension and response, whether it was a serious problem or indulgence in family malice."[54] Without her aunt applying the brakes, Alice would now be free to indulge her taste for family malice at even greater speed.

# Chapter 8

# IN THE ARENA

The president might have insisted that "the only thing we have to fear is fear itself," but he evidently forgot to check with his wife first. Eleanor was something of a nervous wreck on March 4, 1933, her first Inauguration Day as First Lady. In large part that was because she had to fly solo for much of it. She and Franklin drove in separate limousines to pick up the sullen and semi-mute Hoovers for the ride from the White House to the Capitol, the men in the first car, the wives following. Eleanor wore a velvet dress in a lovely shade of lavender (which the press immediately dubbed "Eleanor Blue"), a short overcoat, and an inconspicuous little bowler hat. They hardly kept out the chill on that raw and windy Saturday. Eleanor stood, shivering and apprehensive, as Franklin leaned on their son James's shoulder and walked deliberately from the East Portico of the Capitol out to the center of the inauguration platform, 146 daunting feet away. While his landmark "fear itself" speech took only fifteen minutes, the ensuing parade stretched for six miles and several hours. "The crowds were so tremendous, and you felt that they would do anything—if only someone would tell them what to do," Eleanor recalled. "It was very, very solemn, and a little terrifying."[1] The president wouldn't budge until the last of the forty marching bands had filed by, but she had to leave early to get back to the White House to greet the one thousand guests expected for afternoon tea and sandwiches (though three thousand actually showed up). Later that night, she would leave Franklin behind again to attend the inaugural ball. Eleanor had already tried to back out of the traditional gala, claiming she wanted to show respect for FDR's attorney general designate, Senator Thomas Walsh, who had died suddenly two days before the inauguration, as well as Mayor Anton Cermak, who was still in a coma after the February 15 assassination attempt against FDR. (Cermak died two days later.) But Louis Howe reminded her she had a duty as First Lady not to disappoint her husband's loyal supporters, so the woman who had dreaded dances and cotillions her entire life put on her silver lamé ball gown and headed off to do her social-minded duty.

And that was the easy part of the day. In between the parade and the gala, she had endured the most fearsome event, when the extended Roosevelt family arrived to celebrate its latest White House triumph. There were seventy-five of them in all for a buffet dinner, and not a drop to drink. (Prohibition wasn't repealed until the following December.) The invitation list was drawn up by Sara, who sat near her Franklin in the small drawing room, swollen with pride and expensive jewelry, waiting to welcome the guests. Eleanor discarded the usual First Lady protocol and greeted the visitors herself at the door, among them cousins Teddy and Helen Robinson and Archie Roosevelt from her side; cousins Lyman and Laura Delano, Uncle Fred Delano, and Aunt Kassie Collier from his. And then came Alice.

At first, no one knew exactly how to react. After all, this was a party for a victory she'd tried to snuff out like a kitchen fire. The indomitable Sara chatted with her amiably; Alice had the good sense to limit her conversation to praising the current president Roosevelt, as opposed to the previous one. Then she walked over to Eleanor, who had been such a remarkably approachable presence at the day's various events that the Associated Press wrote a gushing story with the headline "Mrs. Roosevelt Shatters Traditions in a Single Day."[2] Alice, however, thought her cousin could still use a few pointers. "You'll be able to learn after a while how to handle affairs like this," she told Eleanor, glancing around the roomful of their collective kin. "I'll help you if you like."[3] Not everyone appreciated Alice's condescending brand of goodwill. "Mother expressed her thanks, her nervousness mounting under her cousin's patronage," said Eleanor and Franklin's son Elliott. "Almost two years of widowhood had done nothing to curb [Alice's] style or her irresistible compulsion to lord it over Mother."[4]

Alice's lifetime claim on the White House was as strong as ever in 1933. She didn't only drop by on Franklin's first day. She had also been there the day before to visit the previous residents—the Hoovers. Alice said she wanted to take eight-year-old Paulina over to say good-bye, but there was clearly a dose of morbid curiosity in her motivation. "They looked like figures from waxworks, they looked so unalive. Poor, stiff, bruised, wounded," she said. "That was the third of March. The next night—dinner at Franklin's! Dinner at the White House! Riots of pleasure! All of us there, all of us having a good time. It couldn't have been a more incredible contrast. The overwhelming of the defeat and then the triumph of a very gay first family."[5]

Alice must have been in a very small circle of people in history who were invited to visit the outgoing president on his last day in office and the man who defeated him on his first. The fact that she showed up to celebrate with the extended family wasn't entirely shocking, though given her rabid support for the Republican ticket it was a little like a player from the losing Super Bowl team dropping by the winners' locker room to guzzle champagne. In the years that followed, what surprised and puzzled onlookers, and frequently annoyed Roosevelts on both sides, was that Alice kept coming back. Faced with the grim reality of now being an "out-of-season" Roosevelt (a phrase coined by Alexander Woollcott), she had two options for dealing with the rise of her Hyde Park relatives: make peace with them (as her brother Kermit did), or take a vow of ice-cold hostility (her brother Ted's route). Alice never liked playing by other people's rules, so naturally she chose both options. She cursed nearly every one of Franklin's policies and mercilessly mocked Eleanor, all the while accepting virtually every invitation to the White House. That seeming vacillation—playing friend and foe—surprised some folks, given Alice's habit of turning political differences into something very personal (as Presidents Taft and Wilson and her collection of voodoo dolls could attest). The more belligerent members of her immediate family were disgusted by her willingness to associate with the White House usurpers. "I could not help feeling that it was like behaving in like fashion to an enemy during a war," said Alice's devoted brother Ted, who rarely disagreed with her on anything. "More so, for enemies generally only fight for territory, trade, or some material possessions. These are fighting us for our form of government, our liberties, the future of our children. I did not expect Kermit to see—for that's his blind side. But I did expect her to see this, for she's acute and her life has been politics."[6]

From a conservative standpoint, Ted's apocalyptic whining was certainly justified. Within what came to be called "the first hundred days" of his administration, President Franklin Roosevelt set about expanding and changing the government more radically than any president before or since. From March through June, he let loose with a fusillade of legislative initiatives, fifteen in all and some of them still in effect eight decades later: the Federal Deposit Insurance Corporation, the Tennessee Valley Authority, the Federal Securities Act, the Civilian Conservation Corps, the Public Works Administration, the National Recovery Administration, and the Home Owners Refinancing Act, to name just a few of the pillars of the New Deal.* The Emergency Banking Act, which closed banks nationwide to forestall a run on deposits, was rammed through Congress so quickly the members of the House had to listen to the clerk's reading of the draft to know what they were voting on because the bill hadn't been printed yet. "Congress doesn't pass legislation anymore," Will Rogers quipped. "They just wave at the bills as they go by."[7]

Eleanor would often spend part of the day observing the congressional chaos from one of the family galleries, briskly knitting all the while. Watching the legislative process had been a favorite spectator sport since her days with the League of Women Voters. She had already spent more time on the Hill than any First Lady had, perhaps more than all of the previous First Ladies combined. That said, she was hardly the first president's wife with her own life and interests. Her immediate predecessor, Lou Henry Hoover, had been a Stanford-educated linguist, the president of the Girl Scouts, and on the board of the National Amateur Athletic Association. As First Lady, she made periodic radio broadcasts on what would have been called "women's topics" and even found herself in the middle of a firestorm after she invited the wife of the Illinois representative Oscar De Priest, the first black congressman elected in the twentieth century, to the White House for a tea with other congressional wives.†

---

* It was not a coincidence that the name given to FDR's policies, "the New Deal," sounded a lot like President Theodore Roosevelt's "Square Deal" of three decades earlier. Many New Deal programs could be traced directly back to the progressive initiatives of that earlier era; much to Alice's chagrin, Franklin continued his eager appropriation of her father's legacy throughout his presidency.

† Though the president was consulted and supported his wife's decision to invite Jessie De Priest, it was Mrs. Hoover who earned the brunt of the criticism. Newspapers throughout the South vilified her, and several state legislatures issued formal condemnations of her.

But Mrs. Hoover generally kept her distance from political issues, and she steadfastly refused to give interviews. She thought of her job much as the women before her did: an apolitical social appendage to the president.

Eleanor apparently expected to follow the same below-the-radar path as the rest. "I knew what traditionally should lie before me; I had watched Mrs. Theodore Roosevelt and had seen what it meant to be the wife of the president, and I cannot say that I was pleased at the prospect," she said.[8] Her enforced vow of monotony lasted exactly two days into Franklin's term. On the Monday after the inauguration, Eleanor conducted a press conference in the Red Room. That was noteworthy on its own; no First Lady had ever held her own White House press conference before. Eleanor also added a twist: she only allowed female reporters to attend. It was her form of affirmative action, a way to underscore the disadvantages women faced in most professions, including the media.[*] The first conference attracted thirty-five female reporters, some of whom had to sit on the floor because there weren't enough chairs. Eleanor arrived carrying a box of candied fruit and passed it around as if she were hosting a neighborhood bridge party. There was a decidedly clubby feeling at her conferences. She focused on topics she felt would interest women and pledged not to answer anything blatantly political, which she insisted was the president's realm.[†] When she seemed to stray too close to hot-button territory, it was the women reporters who would sometimes caution her by yelling out, "Oh, Mrs. Roosevelt, you'd better put that off the record!"[9] The female press corps developed a strong (and some would say unprofessional) sense of loyalty, even devotion, to her. They had a vested interest in her success, not only because she gave them unprecedented access, but because she was, in some respects, one of them, a woman trying to make her way in a male-dominated world. Eleanor stuck to her women-only rule for the next twelve years almost without exception. Her last press

---

[*] At the time, there were no women assigned to cover the president. The first female correspondent assigned to the White House by a news service was Helen Thomas, at the start of the Kennedy administration. Women weren't allowed to join the National Press Club until 1971.

[†] Once again, Eleanor was inspired by her famous uncle. TR realized, as few had before him, the importance of using the press to get *his* story out to the public on *his* terms. During his tenure as governor of New York, journalists were rounded up every day at 11:00 and 5:00 for a press conference. "It is not often that he tells much that is of importance, but he is listened to most carefully." "A Day with Gov. Roosevelt," *New York Times*, April 23, 1899.

conference as First Lady was held on the morning of April 12, 1945. The president died that afternoon.

On her first tour of duty in Washington, when Franklin was assistant secretary of the navy, Eleanor was terrified to color outside the lines of protocol. Now she was like a high school senior who gleefully flouted the rules. She was the first First Lady to attend the Congressional Club tea, a welcoming event for the wives of new members of Congress, and the Women's National Press Club dinner, an off-the-record society affair featuring satirical skits of prominent Washington women. Alice was at the National Press Club dinner too, and she got to see herself mocked twice. The first skit featured her and Dolly Gann frolicking to the tune of "Hail, Hail, the Gang's All Here," which ended with them singing, "Where the hell do they sit now?!" The second skit didn't mention Alice by name. In it, a woman identified only as "Mrs. Democrat" is eager to talk to her friend "Mrs. Republican." At first, the slightly dotty Mrs. Democrat dials her at National 1-4-1-4, only to discover that she's called the White House—and it's her own number now. Mrs. Republican's number is actually Deflator 0-0-0-0. Everyone in the room knew whose sharp Republican tongue was the best "deflator" in Washington.

Eleanor even broke the First Law of First Lady Dynamics: she disagreed with her husband's policy—in public. The second piece of legislation FDR signed (after the Emergency Banking Act) was called the Economy Act, a far-reaching, budget-slashing tool that cut defense spending, veterans' pensions, and the salaries of federal employees (including the president's). It also stipulated that when both halves of a married couple worked for the government, the woman's job must be eliminated first, regardless of the couple's respective departments or positions. Men, after all, were supposed to be the breadwinners; women's salaries were an expendable luxury. Eleanor was outraged. She called the provision a "very bad and very foolish thing" at her press conference (so much for staying apolitical).[10] The president didn't budge, and Eleanor was forced to pipe down, at least temporarily. Four years later, when Congress repealed the law, she applauded—and made a prescient prediction. "It seems to me that the tradition of respect for work is so ingrained in this country that it is not surprising that fathers have handed it down to their daughters as well as to their sons," she wrote. "I wonder if we are not going to feel more respect in the coming years for the women who work and give work to others, than for the women who sit at home with many idle hours on their hands."[11]

Eleanor's experience with the Economy Act taught her that she'd do better to take more nuanced stands in public while applying her activist muscle behind the scenes. In the depths of the Great Depression, of course, there was no shortage of worthy causes she was pining to champion. In the summer of 1933, Eleanor's journalist friend Lorena Hickok, now working at Eleanor's behest as a sort of roving reporter on poverty with the Federal Emergency Relief Administration, sent her a report on Scotts Run, West Virginia, a coal-mining community in the northern corner of the state near Morgantown. The area had become a wasteland of unemployed miners and their families, many of them blacklisted by the big coal companies after daring to try to organize a union. Hickok told Eleanor that Scotts Run was "the worst place I had ever seen. In a gutter, along the main street through the town, there was stagnant, filthy water, which the inhabitants used for drinking, cooking, washing, and everything else imaginable. On either side of the street were ramshackle houses, black with coal dust, which most Americans would not have considered fit for pigs. And in those houses every night children went to sleep hungry, on piles of bug-infested rags spread out on the floor."[12] A group of Quaker volunteers did what they could to feed and clothe the desperate residents, but the combination of the Depression and the languishing mining industry had dealt the area a deathblow. On August 18, Eleanor drove the 225 miles from Washington—alone, but with FDR's blessing—to see the place for herself. She was still relatively unknown, at least in this corner of rural America, and she was able to travel without being recognized. The Quakers took her from one hovel to the next, where she gathered the people's heartbreaking stories and brought them back to Washington in search of a lifeline.

Using her experience with Val-Kill Industries as an example, Eleanor persuaded Franklin to fund a kind of collective in West Virginia through the New Deal agencies. Working with the Department of the Interior, she helped construct a plan to purchase a twelve-hundred-acre farm from the nearby Arthur family and construct a small community. Arthurdale ultimately included more than 160 houses, a school, and several community buildings, along with factories and enough farmable land to make the new Arthurdale residents self-sufficient. Eleanor was a frequent and hands-on visitor. She personally chose the refrigerators for each of the houses and ultimately befriended many of the settlers, attending their square dances and graduations and often writing and speaking about the community's progress. Over time, Arthurdale would become a prototype for more than fifty planned communities developed across the country under the auspices of the Subsistence Homesteads Division of the Department of the Interior.

And yet Arthurdale would prove to be a source of both inspiration and frustration for Eleanor. She donated a significant amount of her radio earnings to the Quakers' efforts there. She also involved many of her friends, including the financier Bernard Baruch, encouraging them to open their hearts—and their wallets—to the cause. The downside of her very public activism was that Arthurdale became a lightning rod for congressional critics, as well as for certain factions within her husband's administration. In a rush to show quick progress, the government made numerous, often expensive, mistakes, such as purchasing prefabricated houses that couldn't withstand West Virginia's harsh winters and ultimately needed to be replaced.* In 1941 alone, the government spent an estimated $2.5 million on Arthurdale ($40 million in 2015 dollars), an exorbitant amount to lavish on one small community at the height of the Depression. Not long after that, the government sold the town back to the residents, and at a considerable loss. Still, Eleanor was tremendously proud of Arthurdale, and she would never apologize for her work there. "There is no question that much money was spent, perhaps some of it unwisely," she said. "Nevertheless, I have always felt that many human beings who might have cost us thousands of dollars in tuberculosis sanitariums, insane asylums, and jails were restored to usefulness and given confidence in themselves."[13]

Eleanor brought a similar commitment to the advocacy of the arts through the Works Progress Administration (WPA), the multiyear, multibillion-dollar public works omnibus that oversaw the construction of thousands of public buildings and bridges and more than half a million miles of road. Eleanor was a tireless champion of all aspects of the WPA, but its arts-related initiatives received her special attention, another vestige of the influence of Mlle Souvestre. Jackson Pollock, Thomas Hart Benton, Orson Welles, Burt Lancaster, and John Houseman were among the

---

* At the onset of World War II, when the costs of the various federally administered New Deal housing projects were examined, the per-house cost at Arthurdale was assessed at $16,635, significantly higher than the average cost of $9,691. Lash, *Eleanor and Franklin*, 416.

thousands of artists who were, at some point, employed by the WPA. This kind of big-ticket public funding naturally touched off its own wave of controversy and debate: paying for theater when people are hungry and overtaxed? Alice was among the program's fiercest critics, deriding the entire WPA as a boondoggle designed to buy votes and reward constituencies at public expense. "The New Deal practice of 'political clearance' reaches into the life of the humblest worker on W.P.A. projects," she wrote. "They are told that they are working on Roosevelt jobs, that they are being paid with Roosevelt money, and that in order to hold down those jobs and get that money they must electioneer and vote for Roosevelt. They are threatened with dismissal if they fail to contribute out of their meager pay to the New Deal campaign funds. The bare existence of these men and their families depends on what they can earn. No one can learn of the intimidation ... they are subject to without feeling a wave of hot indignation. It is playing particularly vicious politics with human need."[14]

As the 1936 election season loomed, Alice was commissioned by her father's old friend Edward Bok to write a piece for the *Ladies' Home Journal* titled "The Ideal Qualifications for a President's Wife." Journalistically, it was inspired casting. And yet, Alice passed up the chance to go after her cousin directly. Instead, she shared memories and tame observations of the First Ladies she had known, starting with Mrs. Cleveland, Mrs. McKinley, and of course her own stepmother. When it came to Eleanor, Alice applied far more charm than smarm, giving her ample credit for using her White House perch in bracingly new ways. She took a poke or two at her cousin, but she wrote in a sort of invisible ink, focusing on Eleanor's means—her noblesse oblige and obsession with saving the world—rather than her actual policy choices. "She travels thousands of miles investigating conditions in all parts of the country, doing on a tremendous scale what the lady of the manor did in other days when she looked after the tenantry," Alice wrote. "She makes as many speeches as the President, if not more. She is here, there, and everywhere, gracious, friendly, interested, always with something to say."[15] If Eleanor was overstepping her boundaries as the president's wife, Alice certainly wasn't going to say so directly, even as she reminded readers that the First Lady was still fair game. "There is always the possibility," she warned, "that people will say, 'We didn't elect her. What is she horning in for?'"[16]

Eleanor horned in because, like her Uncle Ted, she knew the value of a bully pulpit. A meeting with the First Lady, or just her brief presence at an event, could shine a light on an issue or problem she cared about. She spent considerable time and energy visiting with schoolchildren, labor representatives, women's groups, and social service organizations. And her activities were not just "events" staged for public consumption. She was now a seasoned political veteran who coached, mentored, and organized everywhere she went. She knew the importance of getting women and fellow progressives into key roles in the committees and party infrastructure that generated policy, selected candidates, administered patronage, and turned out the vote. In addition to her own priorities, she continued her now-familiar role as her husband's stand-in. In New York, as the wife of a governor in a wheelchair, she was obligated to travel from one corner of the state to the other; as the wife of a president in a wheelchair, she had to do it on a national scale. In one thirteen-day period in June 1936, she trekked from New York to Chicago to Des Moines to Fulton, Kentucky, to Little Rock to Fort Worth to Grayville, Illinois, to Indianapolis and finally back to New York.* In her first year as First Lady, she logged thirty-eight thousand miles (and even more the next).[17] She was the first First Lady to travel by airplane, though she was perfectly happy using less stylish modes of transportation. She frequently spent the night on a train, sometimes sleeping in her seat if a sleeper car wasn't available. "I do not mind riding in day coaches," she wired the reception committee in Jackson, Mississippi, when it began hunting for a sleeper train for her trip there. "Please do not put yourself or the railroad to extra expense."[18] She didn't like being fussed over by anyone, really. On March 15, 1933, she went to New York City to visit the Women's Trade Union League and to speak to her old students at Todhunter. It was one month to the day after the assassination attempt on Franklin in Florida, and she noticed a small army of police milling around at her first appointment. "I don't want to be guarded, please go away," she said. "No one's going to hurt me."[19] When the police wouldn't budge, she called Louis Howe, who called the NYPD and persuaded them to back off. She spent the rest of the day in the city traveling by cab—without an official escort. In November 1933, she made the cover of *Time* magazine (more than six years after Alice earned that

---

* In addition to having the White House as her official residence during her husband's presidency, Eleanor used a variety of home bases in between road trips, including Val-Kill, Springwood, an apartment in New York City, and any number of friends' spare bedrooms.

honor). The apt headline was "Eleanor Everywhere." "As every reader of newspapers is by now aware, Franklin Roosevelt's Eleanor uses No. 1600 Pennsylvania Ave. less as a home than as a base of operations," the story said. Though it included the requisite biography and quotations, almost half the story was a list of her many activities—so many that by the end of the piece, the *Time* reporter seemed exhausted: "Such a routine would soon put many an ordinary woman in a sanitarium. Mrs. Roosevelt is no ordinary woman."[20]

Perhaps just as remarkably, she now traveled without regular guidance from her most faithful adviser. Louis Howe's health had been failing for years, and now that he'd successfully masterminded the election of President Roosevelt, he seemed to slip further. Howe spent most of the winter of 1934 confined to his room in the White House—the Lincoln Bedroom—battling pneumonia and the flu. Keeping him quiet enough to recuperate was no easy task. At one point, the White House staff was instructed to hide his pants, as a way to discourage him from heading downstairs to work. "It's an outrage for doctors to make such a handsome man as I receive visitors before I get my makeup on," Howe said.[21] Eleanor visited him every day, and Franklin came nearly as often. But Louis still managed to sneak out. He often hijacked one of FDR's wheelchairs and conducted himself to the Oval Office for a chat with the boss. In the summer of 1934 he turned up all the way across the country in Portland, Oregon, to meet the president after a tour of the Pacific and join him for the trip home.

But by March 1935, he was down again, presumably for good. His wife, Grace, who lived most of the time at the Howes' home in Fall River, Massachusetts, hurried to Washington, as did their daughter, Mary. Franklin and Eleanor both canceled scheduled trips, and a train was ordered to stand ready at Washington's Union Station to take Louis home to be buried. His comatose body was put into an oxygen tent. "No hope beyond twenty-four hours," Mary wrote to her husband on March 19. At 5:00 p.m. that same day, Louis suddenly opened his eyes, like a cat on his ninth life. "Why in Hell doesn't somebody give me a cigarette?" he barked.[22] A few days later, his doctors caught him red-handed with another one of his vices. "Do you know what that little boss of yours has done now?" one of the doctors reported to Howe's longtime assistant, Lela Stiles. "While we were out of the room this morning he reached out under the oxygen tent for the telephone, called Harry Hopkins* and talked to him for 15 minutes."[23] (Louis was also known to place a tented call to his bookie.) The doctors and the Roosevelts were only able to relocate him to the far more suitable naval hospital when the electricity was turned off in the Lincoln Bedroom during a large-scale renovation of the White House. Naturally, he insisted on having a direct line to FDR installed in his hospital room.

Eleanor and Franklin visited him there regularly, too. Sometimes Franklin would bring a guest to amuse him. "Felix and I were discussing your case on the way down here," FDR said after arriving one day with the future Supreme Court justice Felix Frankfurter. "We've decided that it's unconstitutional."[24] More often than not, the president would go alone to consult with the man who had been his most stalwart adviser and confidant for more than twenty years. The rise of Hitler, the upcoming State of the Union speech, strategy for the 1936 campaign—Louis might have left the building, but he was still very much at the center of the White House. As the end grew nearer, Eleanor stopped by every day to check on him. On April 18, 1936, they were both out: Franklin telling jokes at the annual Gridiron Club dinner (an all-male affair in those days) and Eleanor hosting the club members' wives. They got the news when they returned home just after midnight that Louis had died in his sleep. The president immediately canceled all his appointments for the upcoming week and had the flag of the White House lowered to half-staff. Eleanor planned the funeral service in the East Room and all the details for the burial in Massachusetts. In a family that made a point of affecting indifference to death, she realized immediately that she couldn't shrug off the loss of Howe. "I think I felt Louis would always be an invalid but still always there," she wrote to Hickok on the day after he died. "He was like a pitiful, querulous child but even when I complained I loved him and no one will ever be more loyal and devoted than he was."[25] She, too, was devoted to the end. Her penultimate My Day column was largely devoted to Louis. It was published on September 24, 1962, less than two months before Eleanor died.

———

* Another of FDR's "brain trust" and Howe's eventual successor as the president's chief adviser.

The *Time* cover story had been published to coincide with the release of Eleanor's book of essays called *It's Up to the Women*, an odd mix of platitudes ("For every normal human being, fresh air is essential") and impassioned arguments about the role of women in the country and the world. She wasn't the only Roosevelt moonlighting as an author. The same week that Eleanor's book was released, Alice published her long-awaited autobiography, *Crowded Hours* (a favorite phrase of her father's). Derived in large part from a series of articles Alice had written for the *Ladies' Home Journal*, *Crowded Hours* was a fairly bloodless political memoir. To her credit, she insisted on writing it all herself—no ghostwriter—though she did have the services of Maxwell Perkins, the legendary editor who worked with Hemingway and Fitzgerald. Still, she devoted the majority of the book to the events leading up to the torching of the League of Nations, her personal house of horrors. She never mentioned the death of her father, her husband, or her brother Quentin, or anything at all about her daughter, Paulina. For the rare personal anecdote, she reached all the way back to her childhood at Sagamore Hill and her whirlwind 1905 trip to Asia. To explain her decision to omit almost everything after 1921, Alice provided one of the strangest rationalizations ever conjured by a memoirist. "The past twelve years, it seems to me, are too much in the middle distance, not far enough away, or not near enough to write about with much detail," she explained.[26] She didn't even cough up many of her legendarily wicked bons mots. The best she could do was excuse Harding for the Teapot Dome scandal—"Harding was not a bad man," she wrote. "He was just a slob"[27]—and poke her cousin Franklin, albeit mildly. "The President has the name of Roosevelt, marked facial resemblance to Wilson, and no perceptible aversion to the policies of Bryan. [In Alice's world, there was still no greater insult than to be likened to Wilson.] The New Deal, which at times seems more like a pack of cards thrown helter skelter, some face-up, some face-down, and then snatched in a free-for-all by the players, is going on before our interested, if puzzled eyes."[28] Still, the book sold well, in large part because Alice had said so little for the record over her thirty-plus years of celebrity.* *Crowded Hours* was at the top of the nonfic-

---

* The *New York Times* called *Crowded Hours* a "sparkling flood of reminiscence" and included it on its list of the best books of 1933, right along with *The Autobiography of Alice B. Toklas*. ("Gertrude Stein, articulate at last," the *Times* said.)

tion best-seller lists for every city east of the Mississippi on November 13, 1933. That was the week Eleanor's book hit the stands. *It's Up to the Women* only made the list in Washington, where it beat out *Crowded Hours* for the top spot.[29]

As it turned out, the cousins' books were only an introduction to what became a long-running media sparring match. The next round, ironically, was touched off by Will Rogers, world-famous actor, writer, vaudevillian, and wit. Rogers was one of a handful of prominent people who was a friend equally to Alice and to Eleanor. In August 1935, the fifty-five-year-old Rogers was touring Alaska with the famed aviator Wiley Post when their plane crashed on takeoff, killing them both. His column, *Will Rogers Says*, had been a fixture in American newspapers for thirteen years, read daily by forty million people. Suddenly the McNaught Syndicate needed another pithy, informed, well-known writer to fill Rogers's space.[*] McNaught's founder, V. V. McNitt, thought Princess Alice was just the woman for the job. He was a fan of *Crowded Hours*, and it had done well enough to suggest that the country wanted to hear more from her. The trouble was, as much as Alice admired writers, she didn't enjoy writing. The drudgery didn't appeal to her, though she'd never say that in so many words. "I shall never write another book," she'd later joke. "My vocabulary is too limited."[30] But McNitt pursued her for months, and he finally prevailed on her to write a few sample columns, to see how she would respond to working on a deadline. "They have been frankly partisan, loudly anti–New Deal," *Newsweek* reported in a piece detailing the genesis of her column. "But since two-thirds of the nation's newspapers are normally Republican and three-fourths of them are against the New Deal, McNaught should not find this a drawback."[31] In fact, Alice's appeal was strong enough that more than seventy-five newspapers bought her column sight unseen.

What Alice Thinks[†] debuted in January 1936, and just as McNitt had hoped, she zeroed in on all aspects of the New Deal. Her topics ranged from the latest farm bill to praise for a speech by the former New York

---

[*] During the 1930s, McNaught's impressive talent pool included Al Smith, Walter Winchell, Dale Carnegie, and even Albert Einstein, who produced a grand total of one syndicated piece.

[†] Alice's column ran under several names in addition to What Alice Thinks during its brief life. Among these were Chatting with Alice Longworth, Alice Longworth Says, and even the unfortunate Alice Longworth's Terse Comments on News Events.

governor Al Smith (who by this time had angrily broken with FDR, his former protégé). She bemoaned, with undisguised envy, FDR's mesmerizing speaking voice and speculated about which Republican would step into the ring against her cousin in the next presidential election.

But while Will Rogers had been the quintessential everyman, a master at bringing the high-and-mighty down to the level of the average Joe, Alice was such a deep Capitol Hill insider that she was practically entombed. In What Alice Thinks, she would launch into an attack on boondoggles at Passamaquoddy, the recent speech by one Ernst Hanfstaengl, or the persecution of General Hagood, all with the assumption that her readers were as in the know as guests at her legendary dinners. If you had to ask "who?" you simply didn't belong around her table. Less than two months into her run, folks in the Washington–New York media axis were wondering just what *was* Alice thinking? "Frankly, I can't understand how so colorful an individual as I have always thought Mrs. Longworth to be, can produce such conventional and uninteresting copy," M. V. Atwood, an editor at the Gannett Newspapers, wrote to McNitt. "It seems to me it has no value except the value of her name."[32] She would occasionally draw blood, as McNitt had hoped, but her cuts tended to be superficial and hamhanded. It was hard to miss her dig at FDR's paralysis when she described Al Smith's feud with the administration like this: "The Governor's threat to 'take a walk' gives a violent palsy to administration forces."[33]

What Alice Thinks looked all the more ponderous next to the debut of a column by another celebrated Washington woman: Eleanor. The First Lady had considerably more editorial experience than Alice. She had published three books, written columns for the *Women's Democratic News* and *Good Housekeeping*, earned bylines in numerous magazines, including *Redbook*, the *North American Review*, *Modern Screen*, and *Women's Journal*, and edited a magazine called *Babies, Just Babies*. When word spread that a column from Alice was in the offing, the editors at the United Feature Syndicate were eager for a column by Eleanor that could compete. But they weren't sure that the multitasking and peripatetic First Lady could pull it off. They asked her to write a series of test columns so they could shop them to newspapers, and several editors critiqued her submissions. Monte Bourjaily, the general manager of the United Feature Syndicate, went so far as to ask Eleanor's assistant, Tommy Thompson, to "jot down" anything interesting that Mrs. R. might say over the course of her day and send it along in case they needed extra material. At the time of its launch, only twenty-five papers bought the column, which was called My Day.

The early entries of My Day were exactly as advertised: chatty slices of the First Lady's daily life, both in her official capacity as a White House hostess and as a mother and grandmother. She offered a mix of news, advice, observations, and occasional preaching, any of which could veer dangerously close to inane: "What is it about going to a play or a concert, if you have a cough, which always brings on a tickling in your throat and makes you cough five times as badly as you have at anytime during the preceding hours?" she asked after reporting on a concert she'd attended the day before.[34] But what made My Day palatable, even enjoyable, was the context. Reading about her heroic battle to silence a ticklish throat was considerably more interesting once she mentioned that the wife of the Mexican ambassador started the whole coughing jag and the wife of the secretary of state was the one who quieted them both with a handy box of lozenges. Those kinds of mundane stories might sound unexceptional in the social-media era, but no one had ever pulled the curtain back like that before on a world so close to the president. Discovering that the First Lady of the United States had a lot in common with the average housewife was a revelation.

Eleanor didn't ignore politics, but she avoided obvious partisanship. When she noted that the Republicans had nominated Governor Alf Landon of Kansas to oppose her husband in 1936, she sounded like a small-town newsletter welcoming a new neighbor. "News has come of Governor Landon's nomination—not a great surprise to us . . . The platform which will be drafted by the Convention is of paramount interest. For once the Republican Party seems to be made up of as many varying elements as the Democratic has often been!"[35] She would salute her husband from time to time, but the results could sound calculating enough to validate Alice's cynicism. A column Eleanor wrote a week before the 1936 general election opened with this story: "'Please "Dod," let the President be fat,' so prayed a little three-year-old the other night. The next morning the friend who was taking care of her and her sister while mother and father had gone away for the night, inquired why she wanted the President to be fat. 'Because,' said she, 'then he won't never be hungry the way we were before he helped Daddy get a job.' Rather sweet and pathetic isn't it? She must be one of many thousands of children who had known real want in the course of the past few years."[36]

And so the ink-stained versions of Mrs. Democrat and Mrs. Republican were a lot like the cousins in life: polar opposites despite their common core. In one respect, their divergent outlooks were ideal. Their columns were supposed to compete with each other; My Day was actually rushed into print so it could debut a week before What Alice Thinks. That said, they never did speak the same language. Alice's lens was tightly focused on Washington, politics, and the dance of legislation; Eleanor's was a broader and softer report on the people and events that whirled through her active life. If Alice spent one day squawking about cabinet secretaries fighting for their share of WPA funds (as she did on May 8, 1936), on that same day Eleanor might recount her trip to the District of Columbia Training School for Delinquent Girls: "Never have I seen an institution called a 'school' which had so little claim to that name. Buildings are unfit for habitation—badly heated, rat infested, with inadequate sanitary facilities, without an educational program or a teacher, children walled in like prisoners in spite of ample grounds and beautiful views, no psychiatrist to examine and advise on the treatment of these unfortunate children who at such an early age have found the social conditions of the world too much to cope with—practically nothing but incarceration for a juvenile delinquent!"[37] Eight days after her column appeared, Eleanor invited sixty girls from the D.C. training school (fifty-two of them black) to the White House for a picnic. The First Lady roamed among them, chatting and smiling as they swallowed their ice cream and lemonade. Naturally, the girls' visit only brought more attention to the condition of their school, which soon received $100,000 from Congress to upgrade its facilities. Alice might have been the one dropping big names, but little by little Eleanor's column was establishing her own brand of squeaky-wheeled political power.

The columns did occasionally provide a clear contrast of the two cousins' worldviews, as events in the 1930s caused them to revisit their isolationism-versus-interventionism sparring of the early 1920s. The brutal Spanish Civil War, which began in earnest in the summer of 1936,[*] was one news story that both cousins wrote about frequently. Eleanor was

---

[*] Seen in retrospect as a dress rehearsal for World War II, the conflict pitted a right-wing coalition (backed by Germany and Italy) of the military, conservative Catholics, fascists, and monarchists against a loosely cobbled-together coalition of republicans, socialists, and communists (backed by the Soviet Union and attracting idealistic volunteers from western Europe and the United States). The war raged from 1936 to 1939, when the fascist general Francisco Franco triumphed and began a thirty-six-year reign as Spain's generalissimo.

careful not to openly contradict the U.S. government's studied neutrality,\* but she did bemoan the loss of life and the world's apparent indifference to the ongoing suffering. "It came over me again what a fearful waste it is that we have to go on killing each other before even a difference of opinion can be settled amongst people of the same nation," she said in the late summer of 1936.[38] Although she never called directly for intervention, her message was clear: it was morally indefensible to stand on the sidelines and watch innocents get slaughtered, especially when that slaughter was being abetted by outside forces. She returned to a similar message frequently in the next few years as the United States sat on the sidelines at the beginning of World War II.

On the other hand, Alice found herself in the unusual position of praising Franklin's foreign policy. She, too, lamented the suffering caused by the war, but she applauded the administration's refusal to get involved in what she believed would become a quagmire. "The neighbor who steps into a domestic brawl traditionally comes out through the window, much the worse for wear. This country cannot afford to take sides in the internal upheaval in Spain where issues are involved that Americans do not pretend to understand."[39] Alice was the cynic to Eleanor's idealist, the same roles they had played since they were teenagers.

But Alice's dogmatic aversion to foreign entanglements also led her to overlook fascist aggression—another foreshadowing of her World War II stands. In April 1937, when the Nazis assisted Franco's airborne assault on the Basque town of Guernica, Alice actually gave credence to dubious suggestions that the Reds were to blame:

> News coming out of Spain is so contradictory and apparently
> unreliable that American readers who wish to be impartial are
> learning to control their indignation against one side or the other
> in the civil conflict, or let it apply equally to both. After we are all
> ready to condemn the Fascists for destroying Guernica by airplane
> raids, a special dispatch from the New York "Times" tells us that the

---

\* Throughout the latter half of the 1930s, Congress passed a series of Neutrality Acts in the hopes of preventing U.S. involvement in a foreign war. The acts applied strict limitations on the government's—or U.S. citizens'—ability to aid a nation at war. By failing to differentiate between victim and aggressor, the laws had the practical effect of leaving nations such as China, Ethiopia, and Poland vulnerable to the militarized Axis powers.

correspondent, who has visited the town, saw no evidence of its destruction by air. The [Fascist] Rebels claim that anarchists within the town destroyed it by fire ... Now we hear that anarchists are rising in Barcelona, and that a destructive war within the red ranks is threatening that city. Doubtless there will be a contradiction tomorrow.

Although she redeemed herself somewhat at the end of the column when she wrote that "the one emotion that we are definitely justified in having is sympathy with the civil population of the strife-ridden land," the overwhelming evidence of fascist atrocities made Alice look to some observers like an apologist for Franco and his brutal cohorts.[40]

While What Alice Thinks was often a broadside fired at her cousins, there were notable exceptions. When Louis Howe died, Alice used her column to tip her hat to him. "He was not the sort of man to take any disagreement with his Chief to the public, or supply the gossip writers with hints of what went on behind the scenes," she said. "There is no doubt that his death is a great loss to the President, whose career owes so much to Mr. Howe's single-hearted devotion and political sense."[41] She made a similar gesture after FDR's longtime bodyguard Gus Gennerich died suddenly of a heart attack during an official visit to Latin America. She knew that Gennerich was in actuality much more than a bodyguard; he was the man who regularly lifted the handicapped president out of his wheelchair and into a car or a bathtub, and she knew that his loss would be felt keenly by Franklin. Likewise, in the twenty-seven years of My Day, Eleanor only mentioned Alice by name in the most amiable way, such as when they spent a day together in Cincinnati.

That didn't stop Washington insiders from looking for dirt. The closest the cousins seemed to come to hurling mud at each other was just before the election of 1936. In her column dated October 5, Eleanor did something almost unprecedented: she lost her temper (albeit in a thoroughly ladylike manner). Her fuse was lit by a newspaper op-ed piece with the headline "His 'Mollycoddle Philosophy' Is Called Typical of Roosevelt." A "mollycoddle" was a pampered, overprotected boy or man, a distant relative of the "Feather Duster" dig. It was also one of Theodore Roosevelt's favorite epithets for his political opponents, few of whom ever met his manly standards. Applied to the paralyzed president, of course, "mollycoddle" took on a new layer of meaning, and Eleanor wasn't going to let it pass quietly.

> I could not help smiling to myself over a headline in the paper, as we were driving up to church, my husband sitting beside me without a coat, while the rest of us pulled our coats closer around us. The headline: "His mollycoddle philosophy is called typical of Roosevelt." The Roosevelt, of course, is my husband and below his philosophy of security, and so-called popularization of dependency and an easy life, was contrasted with Theodore Roosevelt's philosophy of the "strenuous life." No one who really knew both men could have made that contrast. Theodore Roosevelt always preached the strenuous life to keep yourself fit physically, mentally and spiritually . . .
>
> No man who has brought himself back from what might have been an entire life of invalidism to strength, and activity, physical and mental and spiritual can ever be accused of preaching or exemplifying a mollycoddle philosophy.[42]

Eleanor's anger, not to mention her uttering the word "invalidism," was rare enough to startle her readers, then and now. The "mollycoddle" article to which Eleanor was reacting had Alice's stylistic signature all over it, and almost every biographer of either woman cites this column as an example of Alice's cruelty and Eleanor's unusual willingness to bite back. In fact, Alice had nothing to do with the "mollycoddle" story. It was actually written by a more distant Roosevelt cousin, Nicholas, in the *New York Herald Tribune*. Eleanor, who never mentioned the article's author in her riposte, clearly knew that. It's fair to assume that if Alice *had* been the person who wrote the article, Eleanor wouldn't have responded at all. She never—ever—chastised Alice publicly for the unkind things her cousin said about her and Franklin. It was as if Eleanor didn't take Alice's cruelty seriously, as if she said to herself, *Oh, that's just Alice trying to be contrary and conspicuous again. She doesn't really mean it.* Eleanor seemed to understand Alice, and because of that she forgave her.

But the fact that the rest of the world jumped to a different conclusion showed how deeply the Alice-Eleanor feud had penetrated the public's perceptions. Those preconceptions were totally understandable. Alice expressed her own "mollycoddle" theory often enough in private, such as in a letter she wrote to her father's friend and fellow Rough Rider Arthur Hamilton Lee: "He has the cripple's psychology ... he puts his disability out of his mind and makes the most of what is left to him. He treats the American people in the same way, distracting them with anything he thinks will keep them happy for the moment, but without any deep thought behind it."[43] Not surprisingly, Alice never disavowed the misattributed "mollycoddle" remark. By now, she considered what she called "detached malevolence" to be her stock-in-trade. "I am trying terribly hard to be impartial and malevolent at the same time," she told *Newsweek* when her column debuted, "but when I think of Frank and Eleanor in the White House I could grind my teeth to powder and blow them out my nose."[44]

———

Alice was perhaps the only woman on the planet who referred to the president as Frank. Naturally, she was more formal to his face. "I called him 'Franklin,'" she said. "He used to wince, as if he'd prefer me to call him 'Mr. President.' That would annoy him, you see. But we had a very good time together."[45] Which is to say, she had long enjoyed needling him, and he tolerated—and maybe even appreciated—her outrageous sense of humor. She certainly rarely pulled her punches. For instance, she attacked the administration relentlessly over its plan to take the United States off the gold standard. She saw it as yet another example of Franklin's power-mongering—in her columns she took to referring to him as an "economic royalist."[46] Alice lost that argument; President Roosevelt signed the Gold Reserve Act into law in January 1934. "Had the pleasure of sitting by Mrs. Alice Longworth in the Senate gallery when the gold bill was passed," Will Rogers wrote to a friend. "Alice, due to the Roosevelt tradition, took it right on the chin and smiled."[47] But she also had the last laugh once again. A few days later, on her next visit to a formal White House function, she showed up wearing a blue velvet gown along with an unusually large collection of accessories, all made of the same precious metal. "From her ears to her shoulders and below dangled gold Hindu earrings, shaped somewhat like horns of plenty. About her neck was a heavy chain of red gold, from which dangled a Chiriqui Indian frog in green gold. Her watch-bracelet was white gold. She even wore amber-golden sidecombs in her hair."[48]

Around this same time, Alice's gift for mimicry became the talk of the town with her imitations of her cousin Eleanor. Lampooning both the sound of her voice and what Alice saw as the trite and decorous things her cousin said, Alice's little act was soon infamous enough that Washington gossip columnists would report whenever she added new features to it. Marion Dickerman recalled being at a White House luncheon when Eleanor asked Alice an awkward question: "Alice, why don't you give one of your impersonations of me now?"[49] Dickerman recalled that the always self-assured Alice seemed, briefly, uneasy before performing the routine that had been generating guffaws at parties across the capital. Eleanor obligingly laughed along with the other guests that afternoon, but those who knew her well claimed to recognize the wounded look that appeared on Eleanor's face. If she was hurt, she didn't give Alice the satisfaction of responding in kind. "The most helpful criticism I ever received," Eleanor wrote in a Democratic Party newspaper, "was a takeoff of me on the radio done by my cousin, Alice Longworth. She did it for me one afternoon and I could not help being amused and realizing that it was a truthful picture, and that I had many things to correct."[50]

Always hungry for bitter fruit, the Washington chattering class started predicting Alice's exile from the White House once and for all. The story became such a hot topic that the reporters at one of Eleanor's weekly press conferences asked if it were true. They even questioned her about a note that the First Lady allegedly sent to her cousin suggesting Alice would no longer be invited to the White House. Eleanor denied it all categorically: "There is nothing to that. Long ago I told all those, including Alice, to whom invitations to all White House functions go regularly as a matter of routine, that I wanted them all to feel under no compulsion to accept all of them. But this alleged conversation with, or note to, Alice simply never happened."[51] Alice herself told a different story. Years later, she insisted that Eleanor dropped a series of hints to stay away:

> When Eleanor came to the White House, she said to me, "You are always welcome here but you must never feel that you have to come." So, [I went] with great alacrity and enthusiasm and had a lovely, malicious time. Then a little while later I had another communication from Eleanor. "I'm told that you are bored at coming to the White House, and I never want you to be that, so . . ." So I wrote her a very cheerful reply, saying, "How disagreeable people

are, trying to make more trouble than there already is between us, and of course I *love* coming to the White House. It couldn't be more fun and I have always enjoyed myself immensely, etc., etc." Needless to say, she never asked me there again.[52]

It was true that Alice could test the limits of her cousins' tolerance. When James Roosevelt proposed that his father appoint Alice to some unnamed government commission, FDR's reply, "which I shall censor somewhat," Eleanor told a friend, "was: 'I don't want anything to do with that woman!'"[53] But the invitations to the White House kept coming. Several newspapers reported that Franklin and Eleanor had Alice to the White House on February 12, 1934. That was Alice's fiftieth birthday, and Eleanor knew that her cousin would enjoy celebrating the landmark at her old home. The warm feelings could run in the other direction, too. On the day that they sat together in the Senate gallery to see the gold standard bill passed, Will Rogers noted a considerably more empathetic Alice. "She sincerely believes that no President ever carried the faith of as many people as this distant relative," Rogers said.[54] It was as if the cousins—and especially Alice—were playing the role of hissing cousins much more than they felt it. There was, after all, plenty of truly bad blood flowing through the extended family. When a friend suggested that Eleanor publicly acknowledge her aunt's tenacity and grit in light of a broken hip, Eleanor demurred. "I am afraid that Aunt Edith would not appreciate being mentioned in my column," she replied. "There is no love lost on that side of the family for this side of it."[55] In the fall of 1936, Eleanor Butler Roosevelt, Ted junior's wife, was scheduled to speak at the Fort Worth Town Hall on her experiences as the wife of the governor of the Philippines. Just days before her lecture, she learned that Franklin and Eleanor's son Elliott, who happened to be living in Fort Worth, had been asked to introduce her at the meeting. Ted's Eleanor was appalled. She quickly wrote him a letter, making it clear she wanted him to have no part in the event. Because her husband's politics "differed in every respect to those of your father, the President," Ted's Eleanor insisted that the family's conflicting political views "would make it embarrassing for all concerned for you to appear at the lecture."[56] She suggested that Elliott inform the organizers that he would be out of town and unable to perform the courtesy introduction he'd already agreed to make. Elliott agreed to bow out, but he made Eleanor Butler pay for his capitulation. He released her petulant letter to the press. When they asked her about the squabble during a pre-lecture interview, she replied tersely. "I have written no letter to the Roosevelt family," she said, "for publication."[57]

The First Lady only heard about the flap in the next day's newspapers. She once again found herself bemoaning her family's differences while appreciating those bonds that hadn't ruptured under the strain. "You are a grand political enemy to have," she wrote to her cousin Corinne Alsop, "because you do not carry it into your personal relationship, and as I don't either it is a great relief to find it in other members of the family! At the moment I happen to be a little distressed by a newspaper story about Eleanor, Ted's wife, refusing to be introduced by Elliott at a meeting in Fort Worth, Texas. It seems to me unfortunate to harbor that kind of political feeling in personal relationships."[58] It had always been Eleanor's nature to try to smooth over disagreements that might rattle family harmony. She'd been doing that since her parents' marriage started to crumble. But she could easily have abandoned her peacekeeper role and instead expected the family to fall in line behind her. After all, she was the one now sitting in the White House. She was the one whose column had become a success nationwide, appearing in sixty-two papers by 1938. On the other hand, by June 1937 Alice's career as a columnist was put to bed, eighteen months after it began. "The evening papers announced last night that this would be the final week for Mrs. Longworth's syndicated column," the general manager of Eleanor's syndicate wrote to the First Lady upon the cancellation of What Alice Thinks. "I make this report I hope without malice but I always knew what would happen to Alice."[59]

To be fair to Alice, Eleanor had enjoyed an advantage in the cousins' personal newspaper war. The First Lady received considerable mentoring from a top-notch journalist who had also become a very close friend. Lorena Hickok started covering Franklin for the Associated Press when he ran for governor of New York in 1928. She wasn't much interested in Mrs. Roosevelt at the time; Eleanor wasn't the story, and she fled Albany whenever she could anyway. "I don't remember anything Mrs. Roosevelt said at that first meeting. It must have been brief and formal. She was very plain—she would have used the word 'homely'—with prominent front teeth like her uncle Ted's. She wore her light brown hair tightly tucked under a hair net that even covered part of her forehead. Her clothes were unbecoming. I got the impression that she didn't care much how she looked, so long as she was tidy."[60]

But when Franklin began his campaign for the White House in 1932, Hickok was a savvy enough reporter to see that plain Mrs. Roosevelt could well blossom into a newsworthy person in her own right. Hickok badgered her bosses at the AP to let her cover Eleanor full-time, and one month before the general election they relented despite their doubts. "She's all yours now, Hickok. Have fun!" said her boss, Bill Chaplin.[61] Eleanor was equally skeptical about the idea when Hickok informed her. "Mrs. Roosevelt frowned a little, looked at me commiseratingly, sighed and shook her head. 'I'm afraid,' she said, 'that you won't have much to write about. I'll not be doing anything very interesting.'"[62] In the world of dead-wrong political predictions, Eleanor's was right up there with "Dewey Defeats Truman."

Yet Eleanor understood that Hickok had a job to do and respected how difficult it must have been for her to succeed in the macho newspaper world. Grudgingly, she allowed her personal reporter to put a toe inside her inner circle. When the mother of Missy LeHand, Franklin's indispensable personal secretary, died in far-upstate New York, Eleanor invited Lorena to go to the funeral with her. Over the next few days of long train trips and intensely personal time together, Eleanor let down her guard. She talked about her beloved yet doomed father, her mother's crazed and cruel siblings, her cold grandmother. "May I write some of that?" Lorena asked one night when they shared a sleeping cabin on a train, Eleanor in the top bunk, Lorena on the lower. "If you like," Eleanor replied. "I trust you."[63]

After that, their relationship—some strange hybrid of an intense new friendship and a mutual crush on a co-worker—deepened. When Hickok arrived at the twin Roosevelt town houses on election night, Eleanor kissed her sweetly and said, "It's good to have you around tonight, Hick."[64] On the night when news broke of FDR's being shot at in Miami, the two women had just left each other after dining at an Armenian restaurant in New York. Lorena jumped in a cab to Eleanor's house on Sixty-Fifth Street and made front-page news with her report on the First Lady elect's remarkable composure. Two and a half weeks later at the inauguration, Eleanor was wearing a sapphire ring that Hickok had given her. Eleanor still had the ring on her finger three days later, on March 7, which was Lorena's fortieth birthday. By then, Lorena had resigned from her job at the AP, realizing that she had become too close to her source to cover her objectively. Eleanor got her a job as an investigator for the Federal Emergency Relief Administration, which required Hickok to travel around the country to evaluate various New Deal poverty programs such as the one in Arthurdale, West Virginia. Though she would generally stay at the White House when she wasn't on the road, Hickok's distance from Eleanor quickly affected their relationship. "Hick darling, All day I've thought of you & another birthday I will be with you. Oh I want to put my arms around you. I ache to hold you close. Your ring is a great comfort. I look at it and think she does love me, or I wouldn't be wearing it."[65] In response, Lorena complained that she was crying herself to sleep because she missed Eleanor. Eleanor wrote back,

> I miss you greatly my dear. The nicest time of the day is when I write to you. You have a stormier time than I do but I miss you as much, I think. I couldn't bear to think of you crying yourself to sleep. Oh! How I wanted to put my arms around you in reality instead of in spirit. I went & kissed your photograph instead & the tears were in my eyes. Please keep most of your heart in Washington as long as I'm here for most of mine is with you. A world of love & good night my dear one.[66]

There are many, many letters like those—three thousand or more between the two of them. Lorena had suggested that Eleanor write to her daily, to form a sort of a diary that could later be transformed into a biography. As with every challenge she took on, Eleanor threw herself into the task, sometimes writing twice a day. That discipline and eye for detail helped make My Day an almost effortless success. (In fact, Hickok had strongly encouraged Eleanor to write a syndicated column.) Along the way, Hickok became the First Lady's sounding board, someone to unburden herself to about politics, her marriage, even her children. "I don't seem to be able to shake the feeling of responsibility for Elliott and Anna," Eleanor wrote to Lorena. "I guess I was a pretty unwise teacher as to how to go about living. Too late to do anything now, however, and I am rather disgusted with myself. I feel soiled, but you won't understand that."[67]

But the most revealing—yet confounding—topic of their letters was their feelings toward each other. It's unclear when Eleanor realized that Lorena was a lesbian, but she certainly knew early in their friendship. Lorena made no attempt to hide behind fictitious boyfriends or empty marriages. She had lived romantically with a woman for eight years in Minnesota before she began covering FDR. Eleanor wouldn't have cared much about Lorena's sexual orientation. Most of the First Lady's closest female friends were lesbians. The question is whether Lorena and Eleanor were themselves lovers. Divining the answer has become something of a homoerotic Rorschach test.

The evidence in favor is certainly powerful. Many of their letters are overripe with longing, physical as well as emotional. Eleanor wrote: "Gee! What wouldn't I give to talk to you & hear you now, oh, dear one, it is all the little things, tones in your voice, the feel of your hair, gestures, these are the things I think about & long for. I am trying not to think about your next trip. You will seem so far away."[68] If Eleanor was effusive, Hickok could be passionate. During an extended cross-country trip that kept them apart for two months, Lorena seemed to be almost counting the minutes until they would be reunited:

> Only eight more days. Twenty-four hours from now it will only
> be seven more—a week! I've been trying today to bring back your
> face—to remember just how you look. Funny how even the dear-
> est face will fade away in time. Most clearly I remember your eyes,
> with a kind of teasing smile in them, and the feeling of that soft
> spot northeast of the corner of your mouth against my lips. I won-
> der what we'll do when we meet—what we'll say . . . Good night,
> dear one. I want to put my arms around you and kiss you at the
> corner of your mouth. And in a little more than a week, I shall![69]

And that's just from the letters that still exist. Hickok burned hundreds more, chiefly those written by her, but also some of Eleanor's. "Your Mother wasn't always so very discreet in her letters to me," Hickok told Eleanor's daughter, Anna.[70] The implication was that those letters contained details too risqué to survive. But did they? Eleanor and Lorena never hid the intensity of their relationship. They would kiss each other hello in public. The first summer of Franklin's presidency, they took off—alone, without any Secret Service—on an extended road trip through the Northeast and parts of Canada. They had planned to travel anonymously, and they pulled it off until Eleanor got a little too chatty with a farmer in Maine. When they reached the next town, they found themselves greeted by a parade thrown in their honor. "I shall never forget how Miss Hickok looked; she was badly sunburned and had covered herself with sun-tan cream," Eleanor wrote. "I doubt if I looked much better, but there was no time to think of appearances. Miss Hickok said I used some unbecoming language as I tried to drive properly in the crowd and still wave with one hand."[71] Not surprisingly, Washington wags began to speculate about them. "And so you think they gossip about us," Eleanor wrote to Lorena in November 1933. "Well, they must at least think we stand separation rather well! I am always so much more optimistic than you are. I suppose because I care so little what 'they' say!"[72]

Eleanor's indifference to the gossip provides an important clue to her relationship with Lorena. She likely wouldn't have been so blasé if their relationship *had* contained a life-altering secret at its heart. Loyalty and self-control were the touchstones of her personality. Duplicity simply wasn't in her nature. She could never forgive Franklin's failings in that regard, and she was repeatedly disappointed when her children followed their father's weak example. Also, the fact remained that sodomy was illegal in the United States. The public was violently opposed to homosexuality. However accepting Eleanor might have been of Nancy Cook, Marion Dickerman, Esther Lape, Rose Schneiderman, and the others in her sapphic circle, if she and Hickok were lovers, the political fallout would have exploded Franklin's career and restored the Republicans to power. Her sense of duty to her country and to her family almost certainly wouldn't have allowed her to risk so much.

What's more, their emotionally charged correspondence isn't necessarily the smoldering gun it appears to be from our twenty-first-century viewpoint. "Remember, my mother was brought up in an era when children read the Brontes and read Jane Austen, and they adapted that effusive form of writing," Franklin junior said in 1979, when Hickok's collection of letters was opened to the public.[73] There's a sense of emotional hyperventilating in many of Eleanor's letters over the years. "My heart [is] full of love, and I hate my pen for being so inadequate—but you know without words I think what I feel always for you and yours," she wrote to her friend Isabella Greenway.[74] "I do so want to kiss you, and in a little over a month I will be able to," she wrote to her mother-in-law.[75] In 1947, Eleanor's bodyguard and friend from her days in Albany, Earl Miller, was sued for divorce by his third wife, Simone. Simone Miller threatened to name

Eleanor as a co-respondent in the divorce, claiming that she had been having an affair with Miller. The evidence: a cache of letters from Eleanor to Earl. The case was settled, and the letters, sealed by the court, have never been seen in public. When her son John asked if they would support Mrs. Miller's claims of adultery, Eleanor replied, "In the sense that you mean, there was nothing."*[76]

Eleanor's letters to Hickok sometimes showed the First Lady pushing back against a truly romantic relationship. "I know you often have a feeling for me which for one reason or another I may not return in kind but I feel I love you just the same & so often we entirely satisfy each other that I feel there is a fundamental basis on which our relationship stands," she wrote to Lorena in 1935.[77] Eleanor occasionally redirected their conversation, taking whatever same-sex impulses Hickok might have been experiencing and drowning them in heterosexual context. "Of course you should have had a husband & children & it would have made you happy if you loved him & in any case it would have satisfied certain cravings & given you someone on whom to lavish the love and devotion you have to keep down all of the time. Yours is a rich nature with so much to give that the outlets always seem meagre."[78] Even the fact that both women discuss "kissing at the corner of your mouth" suggests that Eleanor had drawn a line. That was the way society ladies greeted each other at tea or a mother kissed her adult son.

Whatever the truth about their relationship, one person who almost certainly wouldn't have minded if Eleanor had been a lesbian was Alice. Despite her quips about Eleanor's "female impersonators," Alice had always been remarkably open-minded about homosexuality. Years earlier, when Maggie Cassini tried to scandalize Alice by telling her that a mutual friend, Alice Barney, was in love with her, Alice's nonchalant reply was a disappointment: "I don't think that's nasty, why I think it's lovely, so nice. I'm so glad to hear she is."[79] Alice's innate iconoclasm gave her a natural affinity for gays and lesbians. With her sharp wit and sharper tongue,

---

* Eleanor's son John actually believed that his mother had an affair with Earl Miller. "There are two sides to every coin," he said. "As Victorian as mother may have been, she was a woman, too, who suffered from her self-imposed separation from father." If that were true, it implies that she either wasn't a lesbian or was actively bisexual. Could staid Eleanor Roosevelt, who once told her daughter that having sex was a "cross," secretly have had affairs with men and women? It doesn't seem likely.

she could have been a character in *The Boys in the Band*. In a town not exactly known for rebels, Alice was as close as anyone to being Washington's own gay icon. "I wonder what [my father] would have made of a letter I received from one of the Gay Liberation groups offering to make me their first Honorary Homosexual," she said when she was in her nineties. "I've always been a supporter of people's sexual rights 'as long as they don't do it in the street and frighten the horses,' as Mrs. Patrick Campbell* says. Who knows? Perhaps homosexuality is nature's way of keeping the population down. At least it is one of the best natural remedies we could possibly have, and if it keeps them happy and pleased, why not?"[80]

Unlike others in Washington's gossip-industrial complex, Alice apparently never even entertained the idea that Eleanor was a lesbian. She heard the rumor being bandied about in a fancy Washington restaurant one day, and her response was immediate—and loud. "I don't care what they say," she announced. "I simply *cannot* believe that Eleanor Roosevelt is a lesbian."[81] It's hard to know exactly what Alice meant by that. That she didn't think Eleanor would participate in anything taboo and illicit? That she didn't think Eleanor was interested in sex at all? That she couldn't accept having her cousin stake a claim to the title of Roosevelt family bad girl? Or maybe it was a little bit of them all.

---

* Beatrice Tanner, a.k.a. Mrs. Pat, was a British actress credited with coining this colorful phrase. Coincidentally, George Bernard Shaw, with whom she worked frequently, wrote the part of Eliza Doolittle in *Pygmalion* expressly for her.

# Chapter 9

# CLOUDS OF WAR

F ranklin collected stamps. Alice collected vices: smoking, gambling, gossiping, sleeping past noon; she was like a Girl Scout in reverse, gathering demerit badges. Among her most persistent temptations was her taste for a nice, ripe surprise. She pulled off plenty of them: jumping into a shipboard swimming pool wearing a dress, inviting Lucy Mercer to dinner without telling FDR, having a baby at forty-one—and with her lover, no less. Her latest shocker wasn't her juiciest, but it astonished Washington just the same. In April 1938, Alice announced she was going to launch a national speaking tour. She might have wielded a silver dagger of a tongue in her own dining room, but she was notoriously shy about talking in front of crowds. She almost never made a campaign speech, even in support of her father or brother. A microphone in a nearly empty room was enough to make her clam up. "After Nicholas Longworth died, Alice was somewhat straitened for funds," said Ruth McCormick's daughter Ruth Tankersley. "Dorothy Thompson and my mother arranged for her to go on a radio show with them, and even on a radio show in a studio she was absolutely struck dumb. She couldn't say a word."[1]

Money hadn't been powerful enough to unglue her lips, but blood apparently was. Alice titled her tour "The American People and Their Government," but the press knew that it could just as easily have been called "The Roosevelt Cousins and Their Rivalry." Eleanor had long been moonlighting as a lecturer, with various tours built around a theme—peace, social justice, international law, the changing role of women—and delivered in her high-pitched squeak to packed venues across the country. Even before Alice had spoken a word on her tour, the media was anticipating her tit-for-tat retorts to her cousin. "Verbal Political Exchanges with First Lady Seen as 'Princess Alice' Signs for Lecture Tour," wrote the *Washington Post*, which led its story with a nasty little jab cloaked in a high-minded literary allusion: "The late Rudyard Kipling told the world 'the female of the species is more deadly than the male,' but no one has ever authoritatively stated what may happen in a contest between two ladies. Especially when it is cousin against cousin."[2]

And so the battle of the dueling columnists (which Eleanor won handily) gave way to the dueling speakers. Once again, Alice found herself in an intra-family dogfight. Eleanor claimed, privately, to have outearned Franklin from the very first year of his presidency. She made as much as $1,400 per lecture (almost $25,000 in 2015 dollars), $1,000 a month for her My Day column, and thousands more for her books and assorted magazine articles. The president's salary in 1933 was $75,000. Some critics argued it was unseemly—even unethical—for the First Lady to profit from her position, and Eleanor ultimately donated most of her earnings to charity. But her paychecks kicked up far less controversy than the things she said and wrote to earn them. "There is no middle ground with regard to Eleanor Roosevelt," wrote the *New York Times*. "She is undeniably both an asset and a liability to the Democratic ranks. It is possible that no woman before her will have swung so many votes both for and against her candidate, though the sum total will necessarily remain conjectural."[3] Yet a little criticism was hardly enough to slow her down. The agency for Eleanor's speaking tour scheduled grueling itineraries, sometimes with multiple speeches per day to audiences of two thousand to three thousand people and little time in between. For Eleanor, the cold soup and restless nights in bad motels, the incessant jostling in Pullman sleeping cars and overnight flights, were worth it. Every time she stepped in front of an adoring, applauding crowd, she buried the shy, awkward, unlovable child of her past just a little bit deeper. By November 1936, she had gained so much confidence that she was able to write to Franklin, "It would be easy to be a lecturer or the wife of the President but both. Oh! My."[4]

Alice's tour was as different from Eleanor's as everything else about them. She was booked into just twelve cities, mostly in politically friendly venues such as the Greenwich, Connecticut, Women's Club and made even friendlier because the press was barred from attending. What's more, the audience had to write its questions on slips of paper and hand them up to her onstage, like Greeks making an offering to the Oracle of Delphi. The ticket buyers were also asked, improbably, to not blab to reporters about her comments.[5] The *Washington Times Herald* reported that she would receive $1,000 per lecture, regardless of ticket sales. That was 20 to 40 percent less than Eleanor.[6]

In Chicago, one member of the audience handed Alice the question she was waiting for: Would President Roosevelt seek a third term? It was a topic she addressed at every stop, along with the ballooning size of the federal government and the possibility that the United States would end up in another global war. Of course, a third term had been a bully idea three decades earlier when Alice's father wanted one; it even justified his splitting the Republican Party and launching his Progressive Bull Moose Party. Now that there was talk of FDR's wanting to extend his stay in the White House, Alice decided that a third term would be tantamount to installing a dictator—just the argument John Schrank made when he shot TR in Milwaukee in 1912. Her remedy for avoiding "the return to the kingship method of government in this country" was simple: amend the Constitution to limit the president to two terms. She got her wish, but not until 1951.

Less simple, however, was Alice's analysis. The question in Chicago had been whether FDR would "seek" another term. She replied, "I would say not 'seek' so it will be noticed too much."[7] What she meant was that it was obvious Franklin *wanted* a third term, but politically he couldn't appear to want it—to *seek* it. He needed to have it essentially bestowed upon him by a desperate nation grateful that he was willing to continue in office. In fact, that's exactly what happened. Less than two years later, despite FDR's protestations that he didn't want a third term, the Democrats drafted FDR on the first ballot. Yet however prescient Alice might have been, it was difficult to give her much credit, because the average listener wouldn't have been able to parse her explanation in the first place. She was simply unwilling, or incapable, of simplifying her style for the masses. The same thing happened when she was asked to explain why she'd taken so long to overcome her fear of public speaking. "I was afraid I would feel like Lady Godiva with a brushed up bob," she said.[8] In other words, she had been terrified of looking nakedly ridiculous. But the midwestern folks who paid to see the Rough Rider's daughter didn't all get that, nor did the reporters who managed to sneak into her lectures. They complained that Alice's legendary wit seemed to evaporate outside the rarefied air of her drawing room, much as her newspaper column had lain on the page like limp pasta. Without what the *New York Times* referred to as "the insouciance of the moment, the knowing flick of an eyelash and Mrs. Longworth's instinctive sense of timing . . . the rhythms of the born raconteur . . . and her aristocratic, often ironic, use of the language," Alice became the one thing she loathed most: a bore.[9] Even worse, she was more boring than Eleanor, at least according to one paper's side-by-side comparison: "Mrs. [Eleanor] Roosevelt is frank and gossipy, tells about herself, people in Washington, the human side of being a first lady. Mrs. Longworth, on the other hand, talks only about issues and does it in a very dreary manner . . . [She] talks with the spontaneity of a supreme court justice reading an opinion."[10]

Not surprisingly, Alice's interest in her career as a lecturer lasted about as long as an after-dinner cigarette. Toward the end of the tour, the audience was surprised to hear her discoursing not on politics but on entomology. "Mrs. Alice Roosevelt, lecturing in Cleveland, disclosed that she 'found it absorbingly interesting to consider the cockroach. How ancient is its history!' she exclaimed. 'In a straight line, we can see it runs back so far into the past that it fairly takes your breath away.'"[11] Reporters speculated that she was trying to get fired from her own lecture series.

Before that could happen, the cousins finally crossed paths, in Ohio. Less than two weeks after Alice warned that Franklin was an aspiring dictator, the aspiring dictator's wife dropped in at Rookwood, the old Longworth estate in Cincinnati. To the disappointment of the press gathered at the gates, Alice and Eleanor were all smiles. "The luncheon was strictly a family affair—we never allow politics to come between us," Alice told the reporters.[12] She even had thirteen-year-old Paulina show Eleanor her bedroom and her pets. "Paulina, who is apparently a born horsewoman and loves animals, showed us a Jerusalem donkey, her own horse and a fat little pony whose usefulness is long past. These animals wander around the grounds entirely free," Eleanor wrote.[13] Then the dueling lecturers parted, apparently as happy as five-year-olds romping together on the beach at Oyster Bay. Eleanor was typically sanguine about her relationship with her cousin when describing their meeting in her column the next day. "I always enjoy my cousin, for while we may laugh at each other and quarrel with each other's ideas or beliefs, I rather imagine if real trouble came that we might be good allies."[14]

———

Besides, Eleanor was far too busy to dwell on petty family arguments when she had bigger ones to pick—with her husband. Despite the Roosevelt administration's achievements in helping the poor and the elderly, Eleanor openly griped that FDR had brushed aside the needs of black Americans. Throughout the country, but especially in the South, mob violence and brutal vigilantism remained tools of terror wielded primarily against black Americans.[*] She lobbied behind the scenes for Franklin to give his backing to antilynching legislation, but he refused to take a stand. The president sympathized with his wife, but he felt that to preserve any hope of getting the rest of his ambitious domestic agenda through the legislature, he had to avoid antagonizing the Democratic Party's dominant southern wing. The southerners held strategic posts on most of the Senate and House committees, and they made clear they would block every bill FDR wanted Congress to pass if he moved too aggressively on the issue of race. In 1937, the Dixiecrats brought Congress to a standstill for six weeks, until an antilynching bill was withdrawn by its sponsor.[†]

Finally, in 1939, Eleanor had had enough of staying silent. At a conference concerning the "problems of the Negro and Negro youth" in Washington, Eleanor was asked if she would say what she thought about the antilynching bill that had been reintroduced but was again stuck in Congress. Her honesty won over the crowd and caused heartburn back at the White House. "Yes, I'll answer that on the clear understanding that I am speaking for myself, as an individual, and in no other sense," she said. "I doubt very much if that law would do away with lynching, but I would like to see it passed because it would put us on record against something we should all be against ... Even if it does not succeed at once in doing away with all the evils we would like to see done away with, I think it

———

[*] According to the Tuskegee Institute, 4,730 people—3,437 of them black—were lynched in the United States between 1882 and 1951.

[†] A determined opponent of federal antilynching legislation, because he believed it infringed on states' rights, was Alice's "friend" the Idaho senator William Borah.

would be a good thing."¹⁵ Four years later, with the nation still lacking an antilynching law, she picked up the challenge again in a public way. When the *Washington Post* wrote an editorial condemning lynching, Eleanor used her column to urge people to read it. Referring to "mass murder" and "mob violence," she argued that "we can not be trusted to deal justly with the rest of the world if we do not deal justly at home."¹⁶

Alice might have excelled in the gamesmanship of legislation—wooing the fence-sitters, building and toppling alliances, bartering for and counting votes—but Eleanor never enjoyed playing games. Yet like any good Roosevelt, she didn't like to lose either. So to get what she wanted on the race question, she resorted to her version of passive-aggressive political hardball. It started in November 1938, when she attended the inaugural meeting of the Southern Conference for Human Welfare in Birmingham, Alabama. The organizers had chosen Birmingham precisely because it sat in the belly of the segregation beast, the beast being the rabidly racist Commissioner of Public Safety Bull Connor. Eleanor, who was known to cut off any conversation in mid-sentence to avoid being late to her next appointment, intentionally arrived at the first session a few minutes after it was called to order. Without having to follow the crowd or the ushers, she was in a position to select her own seat—in the Negro section. It wasn't long before a Birmingham police officer tapped the First Lady on the shoulder. "I was told that I could not sit on the colored side," she wrote in her My Day column. "Rather than give in, I asked that chairs be placed for us with the speakers facing the whole group."¹⁷ Coverage in the local press was predictably scathing.

Yet Birmingham turned out to be just a warning shot. In January 1939, Howard University had applied to use Washington's Constitution Hall for a concert by the world-famous contralto Marian Anderson. Anderson would ultimately become the first black woman to perform with New York's Metropolitan Opera, and she was as renowned for her determination as she was for her voice. A few years earlier, she had been scheduled to make her Carnegie Hall debut; the day before her concert she fell and broke her ankle. She showed up at Carnegie as planned, singing her entire piece standing on her one good leg and braced against the piano for support.

She would need that steeliness for the Constitution Hall booking. The hall was owned by the Daughters of the American Revolution (DAR), a prestigious, social-patriotic organization made up of women who could trace their families to the Revolutionary War era.[18] The DAR also had a clause written into every contract to perform at Constitution Hall: "Concerts by white artists only."[19] That kind of door-slamming insult was hardly out of the ordinary in America's largely segregated capital. Washington had long acted like a southern city despite its lack of magnolia trees, decent cuisine, or enchanting accents. (As President Kennedy would later say, Washington was a city of southern efficiency and northern charm.) But Eleanor detested the idea that the past should dictate a person's destiny—or the destiny of an entire people. Because each First Lady was made an honorary member of the DAR, she was in a position to play the flamethrower, albeit in typically unassuming fashion. In her February 27 My Day column, which began with ruminations about the weather, friends' vacation plans, and a plea to save the redwoods in Yosemite, she slipped in a comment about ditching the DAR—without ever using the organization's name:

> I have been debating in my mind for some time, a question which
> I have had to debate with myself once or twice before in my life.
> Usually I have decided differently from the way in which I am
> deciding now. The question is, if you belong to an organization
> and disapprove of an action which is typical of a policy, should you
> resign or is it better to work for a changed point of view within
> the organization? In the past, when I was able to work actively in
> any organization to which I belonged, I have usually stayed in until
> I had at least made a fight and had been defeated. Even then, I have,
> as a rule, accepted my defeat and decided I was wrong or, perhaps,
> a little too far ahead of the thinking of the majority at that time. I
> have often found that the thing in which I was interested was done
> some years later. But, in this case, I belong to an organization in
> which I can do no active work. They have taken an action which
> has been widely talked of in the press. To remain as a member
> implies approval of that action, and therefore I am resigning.[20]

At a press conference the next day, the reporters demanded to know if the organization she referred to in her column was the DAR and if the action she disapproved of had anything to do with Marian Anderson. In true Washington fashion, Eleanor neither confirmed nor denied anything, insisting that it was the unnamed organization's prerogative to announce changes in its membership. Of course, her coyness led to even more press coverage; she wasn't Teddy Roosevelt's favorite niece for nothing. The letter she wrote to the DAR, however, was anything but coy: "I am in complete disagreement with the attitude taken in refusing Constitution Hall to a great artist. You have set an example which seems to me unfortunate, and I feel obliged to send in to you my resignation. You had an opportunity to lead in an enlightened way and it seems to me that your organization has failed."[21]

Eleanor knew that this wasn't just a battle. It was a war, and she kept right on fighting with gestures grand and subtle. She maneuvered behind the scenes with Secretary of the Interior Harold Ickes to facilitate another concert for Anderson, this one at the Lincoln Memorial on the Washington Mall. On Easter Sunday, April 9, 1939, it was Eleanor's friend, political ally, and singing teapot veteran Caroline O'Day who escorted Anderson to the microphones, where she performed to an integrated audience of more than seventy-five thousand people. The audience at home was even bigger, perhaps in the millions, thanks in part to the pressure Eleanor put on the radio networks that carried her popular talk show to broadcast the Anderson concert live.

Eleanor still wasn't finished. Less than two weeks later, on April 21, came the long-scheduled DAR reception at the White House, a tradition since the late 1890s. Even though the First Lady was no longer a member, the White House graciously opened its doors to the more than seventeen hundred DAR delegates who arrived for tea and finger sandwiches. At the head of the long reception line, the grandes dames were greeted cheerfully by Mrs. Garner, the wife of the vice president, and several of the wives of cabinet secretaries—but not by Eleanor. She had conveniently headed to Seattle for a few days to visit her daughter, Anna.

In June 1939, not long after the Easter Day concert on the mall, the First Lady invited Anderson to perform at another landmark occasion: a visit from the king and queen of the United Kingdom. King George VI and Queen Elizabeth were the first reigning British monarchs to visit their former colony. George hoped that his trip would humanize the royals and help encourage Americans to abandon their isolationism as Europe slipped closer to war. President Roosevelt and his Wilsonian wife were more than happy to join the charge; Eleanor was so eager to help recast the royals as just folks she picked a food fight of international proportions. Even more daunting, she took on her own mother-in-law.

It was an oppressively humid ninety-four degrees on the day King George and Queen Elizabeth arrived at Washington's Union Station, and it didn't help that the major public event of their stay was a fifteen-hundred-person garden party at the home of the British ambassador, Ronald Lindsay. A-list Washington hadn't pined for a social event this badly since Alice's wedding in 1906. Competition for an invitation to the Lindsay party was fierce, given that it was the politicians' wives who did most of the angling with the hostess, Lady Lindsay. "Ladies, my head is bloodied but unbowed," she said when asked about the danger of leaving some prominent people, such as the Republican leader of the Senate, off the list while including the likes of the labor leader John L. Lewis, an avowed FDR foe. Alice, however, had no problem making the cut. Lady Lindsay was born Elizabeth Hoyt of Oyster Bay, New York. The Hoyts' Long Island estate was just down the road from Sagamore Hill, and Elizabeth was a regular playmate and lifelong friend of both Alice's and Eleanor's. Naturally, Alice managed to repress her own indignant isolationism in order to be among the ne plus ultra to meet the royal couple. She even chatted alone for a few minutes with Queen Elizabeth. She did not, however, curtsy.

The biggest diplomatic kerfuffle of the royal visit unspooled a few days later, when the First Couple and the royal couple repaired for a few relatively quiet days to Hyde Park. As Eleanor herself noted repeatedly throughout her life, Springwood was never really her home. It belonged to Franklin—and to his mother. Sara, in fact, was the official "hostess" to the king and queen, and she had firm ideas about how they should be received. When the couples gathered before their first formal dinner at Hyde Park, the president pulled the king aside and gave him some bad news. "My mother does not approve of cocktails and thinks you should have a cup of tea," Franklin said. The king replied, "My mother would have said the same thing, but I would prefer a cocktail." At which point Franklin mixed the martinis.[22]

Franklin's mother didn't approve of the menu for the next day's lunch, either. When the White House announced that the First Lady was planning a good old American picnic for the royals complete with beer and hot dogs served on paper plates, the old guard was outraged. "Oh dear, oh dear, so many people are worried that 'the dignity of our country will be imperiled' by inviting royalty to a picnic, particularly a hot dog picnic," Eleanor wrote in her column about a week before the royal visit. She made a point of singling out one woman whose knickers had been especially twisted by the very idea: "My mother-in-law has sent me a letter she received, which begs that she control me in some way and, in order to spare my feelings, she has only written a little message on the back: 'Only one of many such.'"[23] It was a sign of Eleanor's growth that she not only felt confident enough to tweak Sara's pride in public; she also served the hot dogs—and to great success (though the queen still insisted on eating hers with a knife and fork). Alice, who was usually first in line to scramble the expectations of polite society, was still smarting years later at Eleanor's hot-dog-diplomacy triumph. In 1961, when the Kennedys threw their own outdoor shindig (for the Pakistani president), Jackie had the decor designed by Tiffany and served mint juleps, crab and chicken, and strawberries and cream. When Alice arrived and had surveyed the landscape, she walked up to the Republican senator Everett Dirksen and announced, "Humph! This certainly beats the hot dog parties that FDR used to give at Hyde Park!"[24]

———

Alice, being Alice, had her own battles to fight in the years leading up to the war. The most public feud—beyond the skirmishes with Franklin and Eleanor and their politics—was with Alexander Woollcott, the critic, commentator, and sometime actor. The Oyster Bay Roosevelts were an unusually literate family. They spent many an afternoon or evening reading and reciting poetry, much as families today gather around the television. TR would think nothing of dashing off a fan letter to Edna Ferber or chatting about his favorite Icelandic author with a random White House visitor. Writers ultimately filled a significant part of the family's social circle: Rudyard Kipling, Owen Wister, Will Rogers, and Booth Tarkington were all regular correspondents or dinner guests within the larger Roosevelt clan. It was Ted junior, while working as a vice president at Doubleday in the late 1930s, who befriended Woollcott. Aleck shared the family's quick and caustic humor, their obsession with politics, and of course their love of all things literary, right down to the revolving series of nicknames he used to address his letters to them: "Dear Mistress Quickly" he wrote to Ted's Eleanor, in a letter that he signed "Wackford Squeers."[25] (Quickly is an innkeeper who turns up in four Shakespeare plays; Squeers is the brutal headmaster in Dickens's *Nicholas Nickleby*.) Woollcott even talked Ted and Alice into editing an anthology of underappreciated poetry, *The Desk Drawer Anthology*, based on submissions from the listeners of his popular radio show, *Town Crier*. Ted junior sent a copy to cousin Eleanor for Christmas in 1937, and she gave it a nice plug in My Day. "No two people I know of are better fitted to do a book of this kind. They were brought up on poetry, for Uncle Ted and all his family loved to read and recite it. Colonel Theodore Roosevelt and his sister must have heard every variety, both classical and non-classical, from their earliest youth. I don't remember much about Ted's memory, but I have always regarded Alice's with awe, for she could recite a long poem after reading it over once."[26]

The fact that the Oyster Bay Roosevelts and Woollcott stood on opposite sides of the Democratic-Republican divide didn't seem to matter tremendously, especially when another Roosevelt cousin, the politically ambidextrous columnist Joe Alsop, joined their circle. Woollcott had great fun needling Alice on her political views, such as the time when he told his radio listeners about their $100 wager on the 1940 election: "The lovely Alice Longworth was so incautious as to make an election bet with me. Her check has just arrived with the suggestion that I give it to my favorite charity. I shall. It may console her to know that the entire sum will be devoted to providing food, clothing, shelter and medical attention for a poor broken-down old newspaperman named Alexander Woollcott."[27] Alice enjoyed a good sparring match as much as anyone, and Woollcott was perhaps the only person alive who could match her slashing wit. "I am a creature of shame for not having thanked you weeks ago for your check," she wrote to him on another occasion. "We owe a number of small vacation extravagances to you—and to Franklin—and of course to Czolgosz.* If I find myself within motoring distance of your island I might send you a wire and stop off for a meal, if it were convenient for you. Though possibly it were better for us not to meet until after the election."[28]

Woollcott could manage being away from Alice; he had an abundance

---

* Leon Frank Czolgosz (1873–1901), assassin of President William McKinley, without whom Alice's father might never have moved into the White House.

of Roosevelts at his disposal. About the same time that he, Alice, and Ted junior grew close, Aleck began cozying up to the Hyde Park side of the family. The attraction was largely toward FDR, but the president couldn't spare much time for Woollcott, so he turned his attention to Eleanor. He didn't have the same kind of intellectually symbiotic friendship with her that he shared with Alice. When Woollcott insisted that she see Thornton Wilder's landmark play *Our Town* right after it opened on Broadway in 1938, the First Lady admitted that she was unimpressed. "When you come right down to it," she wrote to him, "I missed the scenery."[29] But he doted on her, cultivated her, and ultimately came to adore her. "Mrs. Roosevelt is the greatest woman alive," Woollcott once told Booth Tarkington, "and if she came into this room, we all ought to get down on our knees before her."[30] Eleanor tolerated the manic brilliance that seemed to swirl around Aleck like a dust storm, and he seemed to know just how far he could push her. Early in their friendship, he invited Eleanor to tea at his suite in New York's Gotham Hotel. When Woollcott's buddies Harpo Marx and Charlie Lederer (who co-wrote the screenplays for *His Girl Friday* and *Gentlemen Prefer Blondes*) got wind of his esteemed guest, they asked if they could drop by to meet her. Aleck said no. Marx and Lederer weren't about to give up that easily, so they headed to a nearby sporting goods store, bought a croquet set, and assembled it in the hallway outside Woollcott's room, banging the ball into his door over and over again—all under the watchful eye of the First Lady's secret serviceman. Woollcott tried to ignore the commotion, but when Eleanor suggested he investigate, he had no choice. Woollcott opened the door and discovered his two pals standing there, mallets in hand amid the detritus of their makeshift game. "Is it someone for you, Aleck?" Eleanor bellowed. "There is no one here," he replied, barely swallowing his rage, "absolutely *no one.*" And with that he slammed the door in the men's faces.[31]

Woollcott could be plenty puckish with the First Lady, especially when he was bunking at the White House—"the best boarding house in Washington," he called it. She recalled one particularly challenging four-day visit when Woollcott was in Washington to play Sheridan Whiteside, the houseguest-from-hell character he himself had inspired in the Moss Hart and George S. Kaufman play *The Man Who Came to Dinner.* He liked to order food from the White House chefs when he returned after a show, sometime around midnight. Once he invited a houseguest to spend the night in a spare bedroom. When Eleanor appeared late one afternoon in his bedroom doorway, he looked up and graciously said to her, "Welcome, Mrs. Roosevelt, come right in. I am delighted to see you. Make yourself at home."[32]

Inevitably, Woollcott found himself caught in the middle of the hissing cousins. It was hard enough navigating the shifting winds of their relationship, especially as it turned into rich fodder for the Washington gossip mill. Woollcott became concerned when a nationally syndicated column called the Washington Merry-Go-Round reported on a skirmish between Eleanor and Alice. "At the annual stunt party of the National Women's Press Club every one of the 500 women present rose when Mrs. Roosevelt was presented, except her cousin and bitter administration hater Mrs. Alice Roosevelt Longworth," the story said. "Mrs. Longworth not only ostentatiously remained seated but talked to others near her during Mrs. Roosevelt's little speech."[33] Like so much else written about the family (and especially about Alice over the years), the story was apocryphal, at least according to one well-placed eyewitness. "You are quite right in not believing the particular item you read in the papers about Mrs. L. The Pearson-Allen story was, quite literally, made up out of whole cloth," Joe Alsop wrote to Woollcott. "The truth is that when Cousin Eleanor arrived at the dinner in question, Mrs. L not only rose; she also waved and smiled, and so did Cousin E."[34]

Whatever really happened, there's no question that Alice's tolerance for her Hyde Park relatives—and their supporters—was starting to wear thin. Alsop had to come to Aleck's defense after one particularly nettlesome radio broadcast. "I have taken the liberty of pacifying Mrs. A.L.R.L., by the way," he wrote to Woollcott. "I know you would have in the end, or far better than I could, but the longer she has a beamer on someone, the harder it is to eradicate. You really offended her in your speech, not in the speech itself, but by saying that President [Franklin] Roosevelt was 'the legal heir' of her father, which she took as an unkind slap at [her brother] Ted. You know she is very Tigerous about Ted, and I don't think you understand how religiously she takes politics."[35] He knew soon enough. In November 1940, just days before the election, Woollcott spent $3,500 ($59,000 in 2015 dollars) of his own money to buy fifteen minutes of national radio airtime to issue his endorsement for FDR's election to a third term. On November 4, the day before the election, he spoke at a "victory meeting" at Carnegie Hall, along with Dorothy Parker, Irving Berlin, Fiorello La Guardia, Bill "Bojangles" Robinson, and others, to cheer for the president.[36] By January 1941, Alice wanted nothing to do with him. "Alice Longworth has become such an isolationist that she no longer cares to meet me," Woollcott told a friend. Or as the columnist Leonard Lyons explained to his readers, "Alexander Woollcott and Alice Longworth have severed diplomatic relations because of fundamental differences." Woollcott remained close to the rest of the family, including Ted junior and his wife, Eleanor, but his friendship with Alice was finished.[37]

———

Eleanor was right about one thing: despite their various quarrels, the cousins sewed up their differences in times of serious stress, and the 1940s proved to be the most stressful decade of their lives. For Alice, the heartache began right with the new decade. On January 19, Borah died in his sleep of a cerebral hemorrhage. Although he was no longer considered a viable presidential prospect, the seventy-four-year-old Lion of Idaho was nonetheless a giant of the Senate, having pursued a unique path mixing conservative, progressive, and independent beliefs over his thirty-three years in office. In addition to being Alice's lover and the father of her only child (his only child, too), Borah had been her political soul mate through two decades of Capitol Hill battles and one of the rare intellects for whom Alice had unqualified respect.

Alice always affected a staunch indifference toward death, flicking it away like a crumb on her dining room table. When Nick died in 1931, she had allowed his current and former paramours semi-widow status throughout the rituals leading to his burial. With Borah, her situation was reversed. Officially, she was simply the senator's dear friend and ally. If Mary Borah ever knew the truth of her husband's relationship with Alice, she kept up a good front. Even when she was ninety, Mary still spoke of her "Billy" in the most glowing terms. "Billy was such a strong-minded man, people just didn't realize all his warmths and kindnesses," she said. "He was a sweet man and a fine husband."[38] What's more, she and Alice were good friends. They socialized frequently, often without their husbands. Mary would even telephone Alice in the morning when Borah planned to take the Senate floor on a particularly juicy topic.[39] Could she have stomached that arrangement if she even suspected the extent of her husband's entanglements with Alice and Paulina? Or maybe she was better at sharing Borah than anyone knew. She was so distraught at the passing of her allegedly devoted husband she hunkered down in a Senate antechamber throughout his official memorial service, to avoid going to pieces in public. And yet she knew that sitting in what would have been her seat in the front row of the Senate well was Alice, flanked on one side by her great friend Ruth McCormick Simms and on the other by the First Lady.

———

The funerals kept coming. Once again, Alice and Eleanor found themselves in remarkably similar situations: this time, mourning brothers who drank themselves to death. In Alice's case, the victim was her brother Kermit. When he was only nine, Edith called her second son "odd and independent."[40] By fourteen, he'd already developed a taste for tobacco and was trading cigarettes with his twenty-one-year-old big sister, Alice. Like so many of the Roosevelt men's addictions, Kermit's was fed in part by a lifetime of bad health, especially a case of malaria that recurred frequently after the expedition to the Amazon with his father in 1914. (A small consolation: along with the Rio Roosevelt, named in honor of his father, the Brazilians renamed one of its tributaries the Rio Kermit.) By the late 1930s, Kermit's shipping business, his marriage, and even his morning meals were on the rocks; according to one friend, "He was in the habit of having whiskey for breakfast."[41] Turning in desperation to the one thing Roosevelt men knew they could do well, Kermit volunteered with the British army in the early days of World War II (the United States hadn't yet entered the war). Despite his distinguished service in the failed Norway campaign against the German invaders, his epic drinking and the resulting enlarged liver got him mustered out of the British army in early 1941. Back home in New York that June, he returned to his habit of going on benders and disappearing for days or even weeks on end, often with a mistress—just as his uncle Elliott had done fifty years before.

Kermit had always been the Oyster Bay sibling closest to the Hyde Park side (Edith was apparently right when she called him "odd and independent"). He congratulated Franklin by telegram when he became governor and, much to the dismay of Edith and company, joined the president-elect on a pre-inauguration fishing trip to the Bahamas in 1933. So when Kermit went missing shortly after returning to New York that summer, his wife, Belle, called Eleanor, not Alice. After all, Kermit's big sister had frequently expressed little more than contempt for alcoholics. Alice had called her uncle Elliott "just a weakling" and a "drunkard" and surmised that Eleanor hated alcohol because "the riproaring example of Uncle Ellie would have been enough to turn anyone off drink for life."[42] Eleanor may have been wary of heavy drinking (Alice was only a moderate drinker herself), but Belle knew that she wasn't as judgmental as the Oyster Bay women could be on the topic. The First Lady promptly called in the FBI, who found Kermit on July 7 in a New York hospital where he had gone for treatment of cuts and bruises acquired in a fight with a taxi driver. The FBI file described him as syphilitic, fetid, and barely capable of walking. In a move reminiscent of Theodore's forcing his brother, Elliott, into rehab half a century earlier, Kermit's brother Archie had him tied to a stretcher and taken, screaming, to a sanitorium in Hartford. When he was released in the fall, he returned to his mistress and to the bottle, again just like Elliott. After Pearl Harbor, with his sons enlisted in the military and his mistress having finally deserted him, he returned to his wife. She pleaded again with her Hyde Park relatives, so FDR arranged for his entry into a U.S. Army unit based in Alaska, far enough from civilization to keep him out of trouble. Instead, Kermit sank into a deep depression. On the night of June 3, 1943, he asked a fellow soldier about his plans for the evening, and the soldier told him to get to sleep. "I wish I could sleep," Kermit said.[43] A few hours later he shot himself in the head. His cause of death was reported as heart failure, in large part to spare Edith, who, having lost Quentin in World War I, had now lost a second son on active duty.

Eleanor's brother Hall was two years younger than his cousin Kermit, but he seemed to have suffered far longer. Hall was only a one-year-old when his mother died, two when his brother died, and three when he lost his father. Orphaned, he was shipped off with Eleanor to his maternal grandmother's estate at Tivoli on the Hudson to share in his sister's dreary childhood. Eleanor did her best to honor her father's wishes and act as a surrogate parent. "I loved him deeply and longed to mean a great deal in his life," she wrote, and for a while Hall flourished, earning a Phi Beta Kappa key and a master's degree in electrical engineering at Harvard, launching a successful career at General Electric, and even serving briefly as the city comptroller of Detroit.

But like his father's, Hall's abundant charm was fortified with liquor, and it soon washed away most of what he achieved: his career, his marriages, even his home. After his second divorce, Eleanor found an apartment for him in the same building where she had an apartment in New York, but he was incapable of holding down a job for any length of time. He also almost killed his son, Daniel, in a drunk-driving accident after a party at Hyde Park. Eleanor suspected that her Val-Kill friends Nancy Cook and Marion Dickerman had irresponsibly allowed him to drive when he was obviously drunk, and her anger at the incident was one of the nails in the coffin of the Val-Kill partnership. But her fury was also directed at herself and her continued inability to protect Hall, just as she had not been able to save her father from himself. Those feelings of futility sometimes made her desperate. In 1938, Hall tried to circumvent the United States' weapons embargo on both sides in the Spanish Civil War with a convoluted and impractical scheme to get warplanes to the guerrillas fighting Franco. Eleanor couldn't resist the opportunity to help her brother, as well as the outgunned antifascists. She reached out to William Bullitt, the American ambassador to France, to help Hall and twenty-one-year-old Daniel in any way he could. Bullitt, a career diplomat, quickly contacted the president for guidance on how to respond to the First Lady's request that he help her and her brother break the law. FDR quickly scuttled the operation.

A year later, when Daniel died in an airplane accident, Hall's own descent accelerated. "By the time he realized that he could not stop drinking whenever he wanted to, he had been through so much that he no longer wanted to stop," Eleanor recalled.[44] She gave him a small cottage on the Hyde Park grounds, where he lived and drank in obscurity. In September 1941, he was taken to Washington in the final stages of cirrhosis. Eleanor visited him every day, a wrenching experience she nonetheless shared with her readers: "A good part of the past few days and nights has been spent in the Walter Reed Hospital with my brother ... I cannot say, however, that it is a very pleasant or easy way to spend one's time."[45] As candid as her confession was, especially for the times, Eleanor didn't divulge the full depth of her pain. On the night that her brilliant, long-suffering brother finally slipped away, she returned to the White House to tell Franklin. "Father struggled to her side and put his arm around her. 'Sit down,' he said to mother so tenderly I can still hear it," James remembered. "And he sank down beside her and hugged her and kissed her and held her head on his chest. I do not think she cried. I think mother had forgotten how to cry. But there were times when she needed to be held, and this was one."[46]

If Hall's death cut Eleanor deeply, the same couldn't be said of the woman who had died less than three weeks earlier: Sara. She was almost eighty-seven and had been in failing health since suffering a stroke in June 1941, though that hadn't stopped her from spending the summer in Campobello as always. By the time she returned to Hyde Park in early September, her voice, breathing, and even her skin had become as thin and fragile as a falling autumn leaf. When Eleanor came up to help settle her in at Springwood, she took one look at her mother-in-law and called Franklin at the White House. Come as soon as you can get away, she urged him. It just so happened that the president was unusually busy. The day before, on September 4, 1941, the USS *Greer*, an American destroyer, engaged in a brief gun battle with a German submarine off the coast of Iceland. Though neither ship was hit and details of the engagement were still murky, members of the administration were debating whether the *Greer* incident amounted to a German act of war. Only a few minutes before Eleanor called, FDR had been messaging Winston Churchill, informing the British prime minister that he was planning a "fireside" radio chat on Tuesday, September 9, to update the country on the tense situation. After Eleanor's urgent call, Franklin canceled the address, boarded his private railcar, and headed home to see his mother.

He arrived, after traveling all night, at 9:30 a.m. Sara was waiting in her room, lying on a chaise longue, propped up by pillows, and wearing her best silk housecoat and a blue ribbon in her hair. Like a drooping flower after a warm summer rain, she perked up immediately when he wheeled himself over to her. They spent the day, as they so often had in that big, rambling house, chatting about the latest news at home and in FDR's hectic world. Sara seemed markedly better when she started to nod off toward evening, and Franklin left her to have dinner. But sometime in her sleep, around 9:30 p.m., she slipped into a coma. Franklin returned to his mother's bedside and spent the night sitting next to her, listening to her shallow breathing. At around noon on September 7, she died.

Showing grief—or any emotion associated with weakness—is never easy for a head of state, and Franklin did his utmost to wall off his feelings. Sara's funeral, at the family's St. James' Church in Hyde Park, was open only to the immediate family, very close friends, and longtime Springwood employees. The police rerouted traffic to keep the two miles of road from the church north toward Springwood clear. "President Shuts Self from World" was the *New York Times* headline.[47] At the burial, the Associated Press reported that the president "blinked away tears," but the story also noted his determination to maintain his composure, even after one of the Springwood laborers fainted and had to be revived with smelling salts. "He never looked toward the grave as the casket, brightened with a single spray of assorted flowers, was lowered," the story said, "nor did he return an anxious glance cast his way by his wife."[48]

Franklin remained stoic; his one concession to grief was the black band he wore on his left arm for the next year as a silent tribute to Mama. He shared his raw feelings only with Eleanor. "Mother went to father and consoled him. She stayed with him and was by his side at the funeral and through the difficult days immediately afterward," James said. "She showed him more affection during those days than at any other time I can recall. She was the kind you could count on in a crisis, and father knew that."[49] Even the people who spent time in one of Eleanor and Franklin's inner sanctums—the White House, Springwood, Val-Kill, Warm Springs, the town house in Manhattan—could easily have concluded that their marriage had evolved into something like the Longworths'. They both featured a husband who was a leading politician, a wife who was a largely independent social and political force, and a relationship that was united in public but personally detached and emotionally indifferent. But Franklin and Eleanor had held on to something that the Longworths had lost: a deep and true affection. A clasped hand, a kiss on the cheek, an absent-minded caress—the signs were subtle but real. That said, Eleanor herself could not summon much feeling for Sara. "I couldn't feel any emotion or real grief or sense of loss, and that seems terrible after thirty-six years of fairly close association," Eleanor said.[50] Though they had mended many of the fissures in their often brittle relationship, they could never entirely overcome their own rivalries: for Franklin, for the children, and for control over their lives.

———

Loss didn't exactly unite Alice and Eleanor, at least not in any permanent way. They had both grown too much of a hard shell to let grief eat at them for very long. It was politics that lit their fires, and it was politics that connected them, albeit on their usual opposing sides of the battlefield. Alice spent much of the election of 1940 continuing to bray against the unspeakable doom that would follow a third term for her cousin. He was simply a power-monger—charismatic, of course, but when the public allows itself to be fooled by a smooth-talking wannabe dictator, "what you get in the end," Alice insisted, "is your Fuehrer, your Duce, your Rex."[51] (Note the initials of those three leaders' titles.) Alice even argued that it was Eleanor who deserved much of the credit for FDR's achievements. "It is very generally admitted by everyone who is capable of an ounce of detachment that Mrs. Franklin Roosevelt's journalistic and speaking activities are one of her husband's greatest assets," she said.[52]

Perhaps it was easier for the FDR camp to wave away Alice's attacks given her own chosen candidate in 1940: the Ohio senator Robert Taft, son of her father's successor and 1912 rival, President William Howard Taft. Alice herself sounded somewhat indifferent about the younger Taft in a lengthy article she wrote for the *Saturday Evening Post* that spring. She obviously thought she was endorsing Taft, but urging voters to support your candidate *despite* his ample weaknesses isn't a great strategy:

> He may make some poor speeches, but at least they are his own ideas or words . . . Take that Gridiron speech of his—concededly a flop. A good many people have been at a loss to explain why, on such a brilliant occasion, Bob should have made so feeble an effort. I have my own theory about that. It is this: Unfortunately, perhaps, for him, Bob was not properly impressed with the importance of the occasion. He did not grasp the fact that this was the most critical audience in the country; that, in addition to all the high-ranking politicians, there were present all the big-shot journalists and editors of the land, and that here, if anywhere, was the moment for a candidate to do his best . . . It was a mistake, but the fact that he underestimated the importance of his audience, rather than overestimated it, is, it seems to me, rather endearing than otherwise . . . The recovery of Bob from this debacle—because that was what it was—is just about as good an illustration of the man as you could want.[53]

Taft's team was so shocked by Alice's barrage of friendly fire they wondered if in fact "the estimable lady is a Trojan mare," secretly trying to avenge her father's 1912 Bull Moose goring.[54] Taft lost the GOP nomination, to Wendell Willkie. When her cousin Joe Alsop suggested that Willkie had grassroots support, Alice replied with yet another of her career-piercing epithets: "Yes, the grass roots of 10,000 country clubs."[55] Franklin handily won an unprecedented third term. Once again, Alice's candor, her inability to resist playing the Capitol court jester, gave her cousin Franklin an unintended boost.

Naturally, Eleanor let bygones be bygones. "Neither Franklin nor I ever minded the disagreeable things my cousin Alice Longworth used to say during the various campaigns," she said. To prove it, she invited Alice to the White House again and again, and Alice didn't just accept the invitations; she hogged the spotlight. "She finished that evening," the Associated Press reported in March 1941, "by taking a half hour of the President's time. People were waiting to greet him. But there sat Alice with her 'fifth cousin,' as she has called him, whispering to him. He chuckled several times."[56] The cousins' ability to compartmentalize their relationship, to wall off their political differences, baffled many in Washington. When the 1941 social season kicked off just after the campaign, the Roosevelts invited her to the annual diplomatic reception as usual. There was no way she would show her face, said General "Pa" Watson,* Franklin's aide. Hadn't she just likened the president to Hitler and Mussolini? Franklin was so sure that Alice would waltz through the portico as always he and Watson made a bet on it. On the night of the reception, when Alice was announced, Franklin looked at Pa with a grin and said in a loud voice, "Pa, you lose!"[57]

———

The cousins did erect one Maginot Line, one area that was off-limits to sniping. They rarely criticized each other's children in public, and there was plenty to pick on. When the Franklin Roosevelts moved into the White House, their youngest son, John, was at Groton, Franklin junior was about to enter Harvard, and the older three—Elliott, James, and Anna—were just starting their adult lives. At first, their behavior was typical of spoiled kids with too much time and money and too little guidance from their

---

* Edwin Martin "Pa" Watson was a major general who was a close friend of Franklin's and served in a role somewhat like a White House chief of staff.

type A parents. John made headlines for a drunken assault on the mayor of Cannes in 1937, Franklin junior liked to pummel photographers out to catch a snap of the misbehaving Roosevelt boys, and they all seemed a little too fond of wild parties, fast cars, and even faster women (except for Anna, who married a twenty-nine-year-old stockbroker named Curtis Dall when she was twenty, chiefly, she admitted, to get away from her parents). The gossip columns and the scandal rags loved them.

Rather than outgrow their rambunctiousness, they traded up to more adult scandals, primarily romantic ones. At a time when divorce, not to mention garden-variety public infidelity, was still scandalous, the Roosevelt children jumped into—and out of—relationships with stunning frequency. It was a rare year in the long FDR presidency that at least one of his children was not getting either married or divorced. It took a world war—with all four sons serving abroad—to bring a temporary halt to the marital bedlam. The final tally would be seventeen marriages among the five children.

Over the years, the White House became a kind of way station between marriages. Anna arrived just after the first inauguration in March 1933, fleeing with her two children, Buzzie and Sistie, from her marriage to Dall. She had actually held off filing for divorce until after the election, for fear of costing FDR votes among conservatives.* Elliott did her one better, dumping his estranged wife, Elizabeth, and their new baby at the executive mansion just days after the inauguration, then disappearing for several months on a westward journey. Inspired by his great-uncle Theodore, Elliott had a romantic notion of the American West as a place where men could discover themselves through a connection with nature and the landscape. Instead, Elliott discovered the Texas socialite Ruth Googins. He was good enough to telephone his parents and wife about the new love in his life. He then proceeded to Reno to get a divorce in July and, just days later, to Iowa to get married to Googins. When Eleanor's oldest son, James, started working at the White House as his father's assistant in 1937, his wife, Betsey, also edged her way into FDR's inner circle, planning social occasions, playing hostess, and regularly whispering advice in her father-in-law's ear. The fact that Betsey's maneuverings usually put her at odds with her mother-in-law wasn't her worst problem; Franklin couldn't

---

* It would take Anna another year to secure her divorce. She would remarry less than six months later.

resist the flattering attentions of smart, pretty women. Her downfall came from a different kind of misstep: she had married one of the Roosevelt children. By 1938, they had separated, and Betsey found herself packing her bags. James had met the woman who would be wife No. 2, his nurse at the Mayo Clinic where he had gone for treatment of severe stomach problems. (Betsey departed with considerably less fanfare than James's third wife, Irene, who stabbed him in the back in 1969 after a quarrel. He survived, but the marriage didn't.)

If their love lives made great copy for the gossip pages, their business lives often pushed them onto the front pages. Both Roosevelt presidents were lousy businessmen, so the next generation came by its failures semi-honestly. That said, during the years when their father was in the White House, the list of the Roosevelt children's employers read like a rogues' gallery of early-twentieth-century predator capitalism: Joseph P. Kennedy and his distilleries, William Randolph Hearst and his anti–New Deal newspapers, Howard Hughes and his lucrative wartime aircraft company, Samuel Goldwyn and his Hollywood studios, along with a barrelful of Texas oilmen. The kids were certainly bright; all of them but Elliott went to Ivy League colleges, mostly Harvard. Still, they were remarkably naive about their primary qualification for most of these jobs: their connection to Dad. Many a dubious deal was clinched by one of the Roosevelt kids because it was implied that the president would look favorably upon it. FDR's intervention helped his children get jobs, cut through government bureaucracy on behalf of his or her employers, get loans—and get them forgiven. In one case, when a Mr. George Washington Hill and an associate were visiting Warm Springs, James requested that his father's secretary "take especially good care of both of them because it is important in a business way to me."[58] This was just months after he had sold Hill a $2.5 million insurance policy. When James was hired at the end of 1938 as a vice president of Samuel Goldwyn's Hollywood movie studio, he couldn't explain to the assembled press just what his job would entail. "I will do whatever Mr. Goldwyn says," he reasoned.[59] Like his Oyster Bay cousins' jobs in the oil industry just before Teapot Dome, the eldest Roosevelt son couldn't imagine that his employer wanted him on his payroll simply because of his last name.

Alice did fire an occasional shot at Eleanor and Franklin's boys, but only when she was desperate to draw political blood. In her notorious *Saturday Evening Post* quasi endorsement of Taft, she seemed to take aim at the boys' assorted scandals. "Whether it has become accepted procedure, as now sometimes seems to be the case, for children of public men to engage in enterprises which, like kissing, can only come by favor, I cannot conceive of the Taft boys ever cashing in on any further eminence their father may attain." (The irony of Bob Taft's profiting from his father's legendary political career seemed to be lost on Alice, but then again so did her brother Ted's riding on TR's coattails.) Her general reticence about the younger Roosevelts might have come from her sense of honor; like civilians in warfare, relatives were innocent bystanders and generally off-limits. Her greater concern, however, might have been even more personal. To turn her spotlight on Eleanor's children would undoubtedly have invited attention for Paulina, and it was becoming painfully obvious that she would have wilted under that kind of searing scrutiny.

Paulina's life had been nothing like her Hyde Park cousins'. Unlike Eleanor's children, who were born when their parents were relatively unknown, Paulina was the daughter of a world-famous power couple. The public couldn't get enough of "Baby Valentine." The newspapers were filled with pictures of little Paulina on display: at the zoo, bouncing on her father's knee, strolling on the streets of Washington, going to school in Cincinnati. What was harder to find was a picture of her with a smile. In virtually every photograph, Paulina seems serious to the point of misery. Perhaps she sensed that she had been something of a disappointment from the start. "The baby was born by half past ten," her grandmother Edith wrote to Aunt Bye. "Such a satisfactory baby—apart from its sex."[60]

After attending elementary school in Cincinnati and living at Nick's family home there, Paulina attended the prestigious Madeira School in Virginia and then Vassar in 1942. She left college after only one year—or, more precisely, Vassar asked her to leave. Not long after she was expelled, Alice invited her brother Kermit's son, also named Kermit, to dinner. His staccato description of the evening in his diary is a stark portrait of an unhappy young woman: "Dinner Auntie Sister. Paulina was there—now become less attractive. Expelled from Vassar for taking an overdose of sleeping pills—suspected suicide attempt. She told me so herself—wonder if she was."[61]

If Eleanor's children suffered from an absent mother, Paulina had the opposite problem: Alice suffocated her. Relatives and friends said Alice could be domineering, constantly bearing down upon her cowed, intimidated daughter. "She would never let Paulina be," said Kristie Miller, the granddaughter of Ruth Hanna McCormick, Alice's closest friend. "She just overwhelmed her."[62] Paulina developed a stutter, and Alice developed the habit of finishing her sentences for her. Having failed at college, Paulina would next look to marriage as an escape.

———

As adept as they were at breaking down gender barriers, Alice and Eleanor had precious few models for balancing career and motherhood, as their unhappy children proved with every failure. Their husbands, though both affectionate fathers, were too busy to be much help. That tension between traditional and modern women's roles only intensified with the ultimate call to duty: the war. Throughout their lives in and around politics, no issue had obsessed the cousins like the question of America's role on the world stage. It was the centrifugal force that connected and divided them, allowing them to circle each other without breaking apart altogether. With the approach of World War II, the push-pull of that schism only intensified.

For Alice, that meant doubling down on her growing commitment to isolationism. Theodore Roosevelt might have been a red-meat interventionist (with San Juan Hill and a Nobel Prize to prove it), but that was the one segment of her father's doctrine that Alice renounced. She believed that greed and stubborn continental hatreds were seeding Europe's war clouds. Why should the United States get pulled into that, especially because she was convinced that Franklin's own motivation was entirely selfish: he wanted war to distract the country from the failures of the New Deal. "I'm fascinated by Franklin's note to the Polish President and Hitler," she had written in 1939 to her brother Ted, who shared and encouraged his sister's mistrust of the president's motives. "To use the phraseology of the L. of N. [League of Nations] to Hitler! Clanking the ball and chain of the Versailles treaty, which is Hitler's red flag, bloody shirt—the reason with a big R for everything he does. It must have been deliberate. 'Needling' the Fuhrer. It's proof that Franklin's trite pieties mean nothing. That he wants war. That he realizes that war is the only way he can retrieve his power which has been slipping away so rapidly—that only war can divert attention from his sweeping failures."[63]

Whether she was blinded by her personal stake or just gravitated toward noisy and dramatic gestures, by September 1940 Alice had joined forces with the America First Committee (AFC) as the honorary chairman of the Cincinnati chapter. At the time, America First was essentially an umbrella antiwar organization that collected the likes of Gerald Ford, Joseph Kennedy, a young Gore Vidal, and even the actress Lillian Gish. But within the year, the group's overall tone grew increasingly shrill and partisan. "The real motive behind many of these new committees with high-sounding names is not to promote patriotism or preserve peace but to continue the barrage against Pres. Roosevelt," wrote the editors of the *Capital Times* in Madison, Wisconsin. "There are always a number of dupes who lend their names to such committees, but really running the show will be found the chronic Roosevelt haters who organize outfits like the 'America First Committee' in order to spread their anti-Roosevelt venom."[64] The paper then printed a list of its chief suspects, among them Alice, who the paper said "would join any organization that would snipe at Pres. Roosevelt."[65]

The sniping soon turned into something darker, for America First and for a certified American hero. Charles Lindbergh, the country's premier aviator, had become the organization's chief spokesman. Lindbergh had what might have been politely called an image problem with regard to Nazi Germany. Although most of his trips to Germany throughout the 1930s were officially sanctioned—he reported back to the U.S. government on several occasions regarding German industry and air capabilities—he had a lousy sense of timing and imagery. He sat within spitting distance of Hitler in the stands during the 1936 Summer Olympics in Berlin, but apparently the only thing that came from his mouth was a smile. Two years later, he accepted the Silver Cross of the German Eagle from the Luftwaffe head, Hermann Göring. The ceremony took place just days after the Nazi occupation of the German-speaking parts of Czechoslovakia and just four weeks before the anti-Semitic fury of *Kristallnacht*.

It was Lindbergh's extensive knowledge of Germany's military-industrial complex that cemented his isolationist tendencies. Hitler's war machine seemed invincible, and Lindbergh feared that it would destroy any potential opponent, including the United States. In his mind, Lindbergh was just being practical. The problem was his delivery. In Oklahoma on August 29, 1941, he made a curious claim: do not trust the British. "England may turn against us, as she has turned against France and Finland . . . If you question my words now, I ask only that you read a history of the relationships between the United States and England during the last hundred and fifty years."[66] Many Americans naturally started to turn against Lucky Lindy. A furious White House aide called him "Hitler's mouthpiece." But rather than explain or deny or even defend their leader, the America First movement merely trotted out the impeccably patriotic credentials of its members, including the daughter of a president and widow of a Speaker of the House. "Does any one believe General Robert E. Wood[*] or Hanford MacNider[†] or Alice Longworth ... capable of representing the interest of so unspeakable a system as that of the Nazis?" asked the AFC.[67]

Two weeks later, Lindbergh seemed to answer that question in the worst way possible. Egging on the faithful at an America First rally in Des Moines on September 11, 1941, he now accused three groups of pushing the country into war: the British, the Roosevelt administration, and the Jews. Lindbergh insisted he didn't hold the Jews' alleged pro-war stand against them. "The persecution they suffered in Germany would be sufficient to make bitter enemies of any race. No person with a sense of the dignity of mankind can condone the persecution of the Jewish race," he said. But then Lindbergh crossed the line from empathizing with the Jews to deploring their dangerous influence on American politics and culture: "It is not difficult to understand why Jewish people desire the overthrow of Nazi Germany. But no person of honesty and vision can look on their pro-war policy here today without seeing the dangers involved in such a policy both for us and for them ... Their greatest danger to this country lies in their large ownership and influence in our motion pictures, our press, our radio and our government. We cannot blame them for looking out for what they believe to be their interests, but we also must look out for ours."[68]

The reaction was swift and nearly universal. "The most articulate isolationist group in the U.S. last week faced a crisis," wrote Henry Luce's conservative *Time* magazine. "The America First Committee had touched the pitch of anti-Semitism, and its fingers were tarred."[69] Alice's brother Ted,

---

[*] Robert Elkington Wood (1879–1969) was a veteran of World War I, chairman of Sears, Roebuck and Company, and a conservative Republican.

[†] Hanford MacNider (1889–1968) was a veteran of World War I, former ambassador to Canada, and occasional Republican presidential aspirant.

a longtime friend of Lindbergh's who had joined in his sister's enthusiasm for America First, publicly resigned from the group, lest he be dragged under by Lindbergh's bigotry. "The fact is that we hurt ourselves—the United States—more by persecuting Jews than we hurt the Jews. If we persecute any racial or religious group we are committing a grave offense against our concept of government," Ted said.[70]

And Alice said—nothing. Instead, she joined a group of eleven AFC national committee members in a private meeting in Chicago to plot their group's reply. Once again, they decided to back their hero and blame their accusers: "Colonel Lindbergh and his fellow members of the America First Committee are not anti-Semitic. We deplore the injection of race issue into the discussion of war or peace. It is the interventionists who have done this."[71] Alice never spoke publicly about America First. Surrender just wasn't in her vocabulary. But Eleanor wasn't going to let the matter fade away: "There is no such thing as isolation. We desire peace for the protection of our people from the horrors of war, but we cannot cut ourselves off from the conditions which prevail in other nations. What they suffer, we must feel one way or the other."[72] In fact, when she took up the issue in her My Day column, she could have been speaking right to Alice. "I want to see all the nations of the world reduce their armaments. Mr. Chamberlain has suggested it, but I have seen no acquiescence on the part of Mr. Hitler. Have you? Who is taking a belligerent attitude in the world today? The American people cannot afford to consider this as a partisan question and use it as such, and the women, above all, must think clearly on this subject for the future of those whom they love may depend upon their influence."[73] Her fatalism proved to be both prescient and personal. When the Japanese attacked Pearl Harbor on December 7, 1941, all of Eleanor and Franklin's boys and Alice's three surviving brothers (and a bunch of their sons) enlisted and were soon headed to the far-flung battlefronts of Europe, Africa, and Asia.

———

"War does not determine who is right," said Bertrand Russell, "only who is left." Yet Russell was the most pragmatic of philosophers, and when the Battle of Britain brought Hitler to his own backyard in 1940, the famous pacifist had a sudden change of heart. It's safe to say that Americans of every political stripe experienced a similar conversion when photographs of flaming battleships arrived on their doorsteps with the morning papers in December 1941. Four days after the attack on Pearl Harbor, the America First Committee voted to disband, the folly of its head-in-the-sand philosophy having been blown to pieces by the Japanese. Ted junior had already reported for duty with his old unit from World War I. His wife, Eleanor, "the other Eleanor Roosevelt," also immediately volunteered, returning to her work with the Red Cross she had begun during World War I. She was now a fifty-three-year-old grandmother.

By October 1942, the First Lady herself ventured overseas, accepting Queen Elizabeth's invitation to see the British women mobilized for war and at work in hospitals, soup kitchens, factories, and beyond. Not since Dolley Madison fled the White House moments before the British arrived to burn it in 1814 had a First Lady found herself so close to a war front. Eleanor spent three weeks in Britain, where she also toured army barracks and air bases and had a chance to spend time with her son Elliott, now in uniform. She visited wounded and bereaved civilians, chatted with American soldiers who were on the verge of their first battle, and offered encouragement to the pilots of the Royal Air Force. This being Eleanor, she naturally slipped a political statement into her itinerary where she could, such as when she made a point to visit with—and write about—units of segregated "colored" troops. Once again Eleanor had become Franklin's personal reporter—"his greatest asset," as Alice had conceded. Only now she was also reporting back to the entire country. Her My Day column became a sort of travelogue, "disaster tourism" before it became fashionable, bringing the grim yet noble reality of war to Americans who hadn't all been sure they wanted to go there:

> I was in no way prepared for such great areas of destruction. When buildings such as the fine old Guildhall, and many beautiful old churches are destroyed, they are a loss to the whole world, I think. So much skill and artistic ability, not to speak of historic interest have simply been swept away and the whole world is poorer. But even more poignant is the destruction that we viewed a little bit later in Stepney. Here a crowded population lived over small shops and in rows of two-story houses. Today there is only one-third of the old population left and each empty building speaks of a personal tragedy . . . It seemed to me as I walked through the brick

compartments of that shelter that I learned something about fear, and the resistance to total destruction which exists in all human beings. How could people be herded together like this, night after night without some epidemic being the result and yet it was done and the spirits of kindness and cheerfulness pervaded, and those who had lost so much still managed to smile.[74]

Eleanor's trip also offered an opportunity for a mini–Roosevelt reunion. On her way to visit Queen Mary at Badminton House in Gloucestershire one afternoon, the First Lady—"burning many gallons of gasoline on her jaunts around the British countryside," snorted one paper—dropped in on Ted's wife, Eleanor. She had been in England for a few months, living and working for the Red Cross in a derelict, hundred-room, eighteenth-century mansion she'd procured and converted into a recreation center for American soldiers in the town of Tidworth, about eighty miles west of London.[75] Ted's Eleanor, dressed primly in her blue-gray Red Cross ensemble, met the First Lady at the front door and took her on a tour. She asked about the family back home, especially Edith, who had developed a series of cardiac-related ailments. Then the two Eleanor Roosevelts listened to a group of soldiers perform "Home on the Range," which Franklin's Eleanor said was her husband's favorite song. Finally, the First Lady let the soldiers go back to relaxing with their donuts and magazines and moved on to dinner with the queen. The First Lady praised her cousin's "magnificent work" and her "incredible energy and persistence."[76] In her My Day column, Eleanor gave a brief shout-out to her cousin: "There is no other place for the boys to go near by, so the movies and dances and 'eats' offered by the Red Cross are very much appreciated."[77] The papers reported that the gathering of the Eleanors was a grand success, even though several reporters along for the visit asked if the two kinswomen had discussed politics. "It was their first meeting since six months ago in New York," said the *Chicago Tribune*, "and each said she was delighted to see the other."[78]

One of the Eleanors might have begged to differ. Though it had been almost two decades since the singing teapot helped take the steam out of her husband's campaign for governor, Ted's wife never stopped resenting the First Lady's self-proclaimed "rough stunt." In *Day Before Yesterday*, her 1959 memoir, Eleanor Butler Roosevelt was still complaining about the teapot. In fact, her telling of the teapot story includes the only reference to her cousin in the entire book. There is no mention of her years as the most famous First Lady in history, nor of their well-publicized afternoon together at Tidworth. Curiously, Ted's Eleanor does go into great detail about a visit to the Red Cross canteen only days earlier from Secretary of the Treasury Henry Morgenthau Jr. She describes him as reacting with an almost comic, Gilbert and Sullivan–worthy arrogance when the soldiers barely looked up from their magazines to greet him. "Mr. Morgenthau finished the story by saying incredulously, 'None of them had ever heard of me.'"[79] Was it a coincidence that the person who paid for the teapot stunt was none other than Elinor Morgenthau, the wife of the officious secretary? Eleanor Butler also complained about an official government edict ordering the press to omit Theodore Roosevelt Jr.'s name from any battlefield reporting. The directive, which also prohibited mentioning Vice President Wallace's son as well as Ted's nephew Quentin, was likely intended to prevent the enemy from targeting a trophy soldier. Though she never pointed her finger at anyone in particular, Ted's Eleanor clearly believed that someone very high in the chain of command—perhaps someone who shared her last name—was conspiring to cheat her husband out of his share of glory. Even Alice didn't go that far. "They all said that Franklin wanted it, thought Ted would gain prestige from the war and might come in [to elective office] again. I don't believe it," she said. "I think it was someone who wanted to curry favor with Franklin."[80]

So while the war managed to unite most Americans under the same patriotic cloak, the extended First Family carried on its own uncivil skirmishes. Even Franklin, who always seemed to laugh off Alice's disloyal opposition, joined the Roosevelt scrum. In later years, Alice would claim that she suddenly found herself disinvited from the White House in the run-up to the war. "They dropped me like a well-known hot potato on any occasions that were historic," she said. "They didn't like it because I laughed and I was doing a thing in the paper at that time and saying mean things about them. And when he was elected the second time, I said he'll be up for a third term next time. I could see that was in the cards."[81] She exaggerates a bit—FDR won that bet that she would show up in 1941—but the president did seem to target his cousin-tormentor during one particular press conference in January 1942. At the time, Washington was being overrun by the influx of defense workers arriving to crank up the war machine. The president was lamenting the lack of housing in the capital to the press corps when he hit upon an idea: Why not write stories suggesting that the less-essential residents leave town? He even offered a headline: "Are You a Parasite?" Parasites, FDR explained, were "people who had no real duties in the nation's capital but came here because they enjoyed the social life or liked to have their children educated in local schools ... and those who had twenty-room houses on Massachusetts Avenue."[82] Several publications noted that one of the few large mansions still in private hands was at 2009 Massachusetts Avenue. It was the home of Alice Longworth. Needless to say, she didn't leave town.

———

As dirty deeds go, Franklin had already dealt Alice a doozy. After the Germans invaded France in May 1940 and Paris fell six weeks later, the president received an urgent visit from René de Chambrun, the son-in-law of the former French premier Pierre Laval. The de Chambruns were a prominent noble family and direct descendants of the Marquis de Lafayette, the French general who fought under George Washington in the Revolutionary War. René had dined with Franklin, Eleanor, and Alice in 1934 during the centenary commemorations of Lafayette's death and was actually both a French and American citizen.* He had himself fought bravely on the front lines against the Germans in the brief period before the French army collapsed, so when his government was desperate to persuade FDR to end American neutrality in the months before Pearl Harbor, Laval's son-in-law, René, seemed as strong an emissary as anyone—even if he went by the nickname Bunny.

However willing the president might have been to help France in 1940, he knew that de Chambrun's real task was to win over hard-core isolationist politicians on the Republican side such as Senator Taft. Taft wasn't likely to open his door to de Chambrun on FDR's request, especially on this topic; the two men were jockeying to run against each other in that year's presidential election, and the war was the main issue. But Franklin knew someone who might help de Chambrun: Alice. She was Taft's confidante and greatest booster. Even better in this remarkably inbred world of power, she was Bunny's aunt.

---

* In appreciation for Lafayette's heroic service during the American Revolution, all of his male descendants were entitled to U.S. citizenship.

De Chambrun's mother was Nick Longworth's sister Clara, who had moved to France after marrying Count Adelbert de Chambrun in 1901. Though Clara and Alice never got along—like all the Longworth women, Clara didn't much like sharing Nick with the president's glamorous daughter*—René and Alice were very close. "She has always been, and would remain until her death ... my favorite aunt on both sides of the Atlantic," René said.[83] The first lawyer admitted to the bar in both New York and France and a friend of both Henry Luce and General John J. Pershing, he had grown up to become just the kind of dashing, well-connected man Alice enjoyed. She and Paulina had traveled to Paris in 1935 to attend his wedding to Josée Laval, whose father had just become premier for the second time.

What made steering René to Alice so devious was that FDR realized it would put her in a bind. The president knew that the old Irreconcilable would sooner quit smoking, gambling, *and* sleeping late than lend a hand to a Frenchman looking for American support in the war. On the other hand, FDR understood that Alice's "tribal feelings" would make it impossible for her to resist at least chatting with de Chambrun. Political conviction versus family loyalty—which would she choose? De Chambrun wasn't sure it would be him. "Neither Taft nor Alice had any liking for Britain, and I was going to plead her cause, as a kind of spokesman for Franklin Roosevelt for whom neither had particularly fond feelings," he said.[84] Alice did agree to have a private lunch with her nephew, and after he made his case, she arranged one of her famous dinners, with Taft as the guest of honor. When René gave FDR an interim progress report, the president was delighted, but he warned, "Those two will be hard nuts for you to crack!"[85]

At an intimate dinner at Alice's house a few nights later, René got to make his pitch. He also got a ringside seat to the Roosevelt family circus. Only Bob and Martha Taft were there, along with fifteen-year-old Paulina: "The hors d'oeuvre of the meal was a stunt that I remember to this day," de Chambrun said. "Paulina was training a very young fox terrier and had taught it to do its business on a newspaper ... As a curtain raiser to the evening, young Paulina put down in the middle of the drawing room floor a magazine with the picture on the front page of the President of

---

* Clara's 1933 hagiography of her brother, *The Making of Nicholas Longworth: Annals of an American Family*, barely mentions his wife.

the United States, all smiles and slightly prominent teeth. The little dog immediately performed as expected and disappeared into the kitchen."[86]

Still, naughty Aunt Alice helped to arrange more meetings for René with key members of Congress. She made the rounds with him at the Republican National Convention in Philadelphia and even tutored him on what to say to whom for maximum effect. Later that summer, he went on a lecture tour in the Midwest in an attempt to boost public opinion for a U.S. role in Europe. Though it was too late for France, René's efforts did help get additional war supplies shipped to the U.K., for which the British ambassador expressed his gratitude to him directly: "Almost alone, you have been able to change official public opinion in favor of my country. Your amazingly energetic action during the dark days of June was a godsend and an inspiration for everyone. You were able to find at exactly the right moment those arguments and those words which convince the highest authorities of the United States of America and American Senate's Foreign Relations Committee."[87] Alice's tutoring had paid off. To the Allies, de Chambrun was starting to resemble his famous ancestor, General Lafayette.

And then he made a stunning political about-face. A few months after the Germans had installed a puppet government run out of the southern city of Vichy, de Chambrun published a best-selling book titled *I Saw France Fall.* Rather than mourn the loss of his country's sovereignty, he celebrated it, arguing that France had been morally bankrupt before the war, but the new Vichy leaders were "capable and far-sighted" stewards.[88] Perhaps he was swayed by the fact that the new Vichy leaders were none other than Marshal Pétain, René's eighty-four-year-old godfather, and Pierre Laval, his father-in-law.

With Laval now in regular consultations with Hitler and his henchmen, de Chambrun had begun to stake out the morally ambiguous swamp of collaboration. On November 10, 1940, René announced his plans to leave the United States and return to German-occupied Paris "to reopen his law practice."[89] Although he studiously avoided any official appointments or posts, he became a key intermediary between and counselor to Laval and Pétain. By August 1942, René's friend Henry Luce included him on a "Blacklist" of collaborators in *Life* magazine. "Since Count de Chambrun's return to the office of his father-in-law he has played an important part. It is said in Vichy, 'If you want anything from Pierre [Laval], see Rene first,'" said the *New York Times*.[90] Under the Vichy government's watch, the Germans were allowed to round up and deport tens of thousands of foreign-born Jewish men, women, and children. They also took an active part in the brutal battle against the French Resistance. A year earlier, René de Chambrun had received personal advice from the president of the United States on how to save his country. Now he had become counselor to two of the most loathed men on the planet.

Neither history nor the Allies were kind to de Chambrun's circle. His parents had stayed in Paris until the end: Clara, a renowned Shakespeare scholar, took over the leadership of the American Library there; Adelbert managed Paris's other big American institution, the American Hospital. After V-day, they were both arrested and their house was looted by Resistance fighters, but their connections on both sides of the Atlantic won them a grudging clemency from Charles de Gaulle. Pétain and Laval weren't as lucky. Both were sentenced to death. Pétain's sentence was commuted, on account of his age and his having been a hero of World War I. Laval was granted a short and chaotic trial, attempted suicide, and was ultimately shot as a traitor just south of Paris at Fort Châtillon in October 1945.

However, René himself was barely bruised by his brush with the Nazis. The liberation forces detained him and Josée briefly—their arrest was widely seen as a successful maneuver to induce Laval to return from Spain, where he had sought refuge with his fellow fascist Francisco Franco—but de Chambrun quickly turned his work under the Vichy regime into something of a second career. He devoted the rest of his long life to the Sisyphean task of redeeming Laval: creating archives, writing books, and even appearing in the documentary *The Sorrow and the Pity*, arguing that his father-in-law was a misunderstood patriot who consorted with Germans merely to save France. His reputation as France's premier advocate for collaborators brought him clients such as Coco Chanel, who had several of her own ugly Vichy skeletons to bury. The de Chambruns' Nazi fingerprints weren't entirely forgotten or forgiven. In 1974, Alexandre Rosenberg, son of a prominent French Jewish art collector, showed up with the police at a Paris art auction to claim Braque's *Table with Tobacco Pouch*, one of the many Rosenberg paintings looted by the Nazis. The woman selling the Braque was Josée de Chambrun. She surrendered it on the spot. If Alice was bothered by her kinsmen's compromised past, she didn't show it. She never cared much about public opinion, and by frequently inviting Adelbert and René to her house for dinners with the Washington establishment, she might well have helped wipe their slates clean. In fact, the year after Josée handed over her ill-gotten Braque, Capitol Hill gossip columnists noted that René was in town for work, and he was staying at Aunt Alice's place.

––––––

In April 1943, Eleanor undertook another battlefield tour, this one a twenty-five-thousand-mile journey of the Pacific theater, from Australia and New Zealand all the way to newly conquered Guadalcanal. Despite her exhaustion and the logistical difficulties of filing her column from halfway around the world every day, she continued to file stories, and she continued to lace them with her own political views whenever possible, such as in this report from a cemetery in Guadalcanal:

> A flag waves over the cemetery. Someday grass will grow, palms will wave in the breeze and cast their shade over the white crosses and it will be peaceful here. I think, however, the real memorial to show the love we bore for those who lie here, must be built where we live by the way in which we make our lives count. We must build up the kind of world for which these men died. They may never have put it into words, but I think they wanted a world where no one is hungry or in want for the necessities of life as they saw them. I am sure they wanted freedom and opportunity, but I question whether for many of them the results of opportunity would have been measured only by the success in acquiring this world's goods. Too many soldiers have discovered that the things which bring them happiness cannot always be bought with money.[91]

If her writing had found a new lyricism, perhaps that's because no woman—and certainly no other fifty-eight-year-old grandmother writing on a deadline—had paused at more freshly dug graves, comforted more wounded soldiers, or toured more military depots filled with eager and nervous soldiers, sailors, and pilots.

Just as the war was reaching its peak, it became all the more personal for her, and for the rest of the family. Although Ted junior had been in lockstep with Alice in opposition to FDR's foreign policy, when war came, he was ready to serve. He was in his mid-fifties and hobbled by arthritis, a bad heart, and his wounds from the previous war. But that didn't stop him from making his way to the front lines in the African and Italian campaigns, just as his father would have expected. And when the Americans trudged through the water and onto the beaches of Normandy on June 6, 1944, the highest-ranking officer to make land that day was Theodore Roosevelt Jr. A month later, while sleeping in a truck that had recently been captured from the Germans, he died of a heart attack. He was buried in the American Cemetery in Normandy and received a posthumous Medal of Honor for his extraordinary courage on the beaches of France. But even before that, he received a heartfelt send-off from his cousin and occasional rival:

> We were all saddened this morning to hear of the death of Brigadier-General Theodore Roosevelt. When he was young and went into the last war, his father told me that of all his sons, Ted was the one to whom soldiering seemed to be the real fulfillment of an inner desire . . .
>
> It is a loss to our fighting forces for him to be taken at this time, and to his mother, his wife, and his children, it is a sad blow. And yet even they, I am sure, feel grateful that he was able to render this service to his country. I think he would prefer to leave this world in just such sudden fashion, having done a hard day's work, and knowing that the tide of victory was turning for the Allies.[92]

Typically, Alice said nothing publicly about the death of her favorite brother and closest companion. She, too, was a sort of soldier in her father's mold, someone who merely nods at grief and quickly moves on to the next battlefield. In the summer of 1944, just three weeks after D-day, the Republican National Convention opened in Chicago. Alice, naturally, was there, though unlike the previous two conventions, she was not a delegate. That didn't mean she was any less in the public eye. The press was eager to get her thoughts on her cousin Franklin's decision to run for an unprecedented fourth term, and she was eager to tell them. "The Republican Party is here to elect a President," she said, "and not retain a dictator."[93]

They were also interested in Alice's latest political companion: nineteen-year-old Paulina. It was her first national convention, and her mother had gotten her work as a page, perhaps hoping to sprinkle a little political fairy dust on her. It didn't seem to work. In a brief interview during the convention, Paulina protested her joy a bit too much: "It's the greatest thrill of my life. I never dreamed it would be this much fun; something exciting happening every minute . . . This is something I will never forget." Yet when the reporter asked Paulina the standard convention question—who was her pick for president?—the allegedly budding political junkie had nothing to say. "Mother's judgment is worth a lot more than mine there," she said. "Ask her."[94]

To be fair, Paulina had more important things on her mind. Only days after she and her mother returned from the convention in Chicago came word that Paulina was engaged. Alexander Sturm was a polo-playing Yale graduate from a wealthy Connecticut family. Tall, handsome, and talented, he published his first children's book—*The Problem Fox*, which he also illustrated—when he was seventeen. After Yale, he worked briefly for the OSS, a precursor to the CIA. He went on to co-found (with $50,000 of Paulina's money) Sturm, Ruger, and Company, which would become a celebrated manufacturer of high-end firearms. On paper, he was perfect son-in-law material. In fact, Alice didn't like him. Whether that was because Sturm was eccentric (he often put on a beret and an affected British accent) or a drinker or simply because he challenged Alice's control over her troubled daughter was never entirely clear.

In any event, the wedding had been scheduled for late August, which turned out to be only six weeks after Ted junior's death. Alice was unusually subdued as she watched Paulina walk down the aisle on the arm of Ted's son Cornelius. Paulina's gown featured the spoils of her mother's long-ago trips of plunder, including lace from the Russian imperial family and pearls from Cuba. It was a small affair, taking place in an Episcopal church in Massachusetts with a reception at one of Alice's relatives from the Lee side of the family. Edith, having just lost her third son to war, managed to attend, accompanied by Ted's and Kermit's widows. The papers reported that on account of Ted junior's death Alice hadn't mailed out invitations. Instead, she phoned and wired the families on both sides. Franklin and Eleanor did not receive a call.

TOP: Theodore and family in the spring of 1895, when Alice (standing dead center, naturally) was eleven. *(Roosevelt R500.P69a-017, Houghton Library, Harvard University)*

BOTTOM: Elliott with (from left) Gracie Hall, Eleanor, and Elliott Jr. in 1892, on one of the rare occasions when he was permitted to see his children. It is the last known picture taken of them together. *(Franklin D. Roosevelt Presidential Library)*

TOP, LEFT: Franklin and Eleanor at Hyde Park in 1906, the year after they were married. *(Franklin D. Roosevelt Presidential Library)*

TOP, RIGHT: Eleanor in her wedding dress. "I saw a picture of Eleanor at her wedding the other day and thought it was a picture of me at mine," Alice later recalled. "We looked so much alike." *(Franklin D. Roosevelt Presidential Library)*

LEFT: Eleanor at Campobello in 1920 with (from left) Elliott, John, Franklin Jr., Chief the dog, and Anna. "For ten years," she said, "I was always just getting over having a baby or about to have one." *(Franklin D. Roosevelt Presidential Library)*

TOP: Alice and Taft in Yokohama during their 1905 Asian tour. Their Japanese hosts were awed by Alice's glamour—and Taft's girth. Alice collected the headlines—and some exquisite souvenir loot—while Taft's quiet diplomacy laid the groundwork for President Roosevelt's Nobel Prize. *(Library of Congress)*

MIDDLE: Alice was determined not to let her father steal the spotlight at her 1906 wedding, as the president did when he gave away his niece, Eleanor, the year before. When it came time to cut the cake, Alice grabbed the sword from a White House military aide and, like a Samurai, started slicing away. *(Library of Congress)*

BOTTOM: After Alice had christened the *Meteor*, Germany's Prince Henry gave her an expensive token of his country's appreciation: a gold bracelet embossed with Kaiser Wilhelm's portrait—made from diamonds. *(Library of Congress)*

TOP: Alice and Eleanor were both bridesmaids when Franklin's half niece, Helen Roosevelt, married Aunt Corinne's son, Teddy Robinson, in 1904. Alice is standing next to the bride; Eleanor is the third woman from the groom. She and Franklin, who is behind her on the left, were themselves secretly engaged at the time. *(Franklin D. Roosevelt Presidential Library)*

BOTTOM: One of the few photos of Eleanor (seated) and Alice together. It was taken in 1898 at Aunt Corinne's estate in Orange, New Jersey. *(Franklin D. Roosevelt Presidential Library)*

LEFT: TR and FDR (flanking Teddy's lawyer) at the 1915 Barnes libel trial in Syracuse, New York. In defending the former president on the stand, Franklin identified himself as Uncle Ted's "fifth cousin by blood, nephew by law." (*Franklin D. Roosevelt Presidential Library*)

BELOW: There aren't many families that produced two women worthy of the cover of *Time* magazine. Alice made it in 1927; Eleanor in 1933 (and again in 1939 *and* 1952). *(TIME Covers © 1927 and 1933 Time Inc. TIME and the Red Border Design are trademarks of Time Inc, registered in the U.S. and other countries. Used with permission.)*

RIGHT: Using an ordinary Buick touring car as the base, Eleanor designed the "singing teapot" to help take the steam out of her cousin Ted Roosevelt Jr.'s 1924 campaign for governor of New York. She later regretted masterminding the "rough stunt" that effectively ended Ted Jr.'s political career. *(The Queens Borough Public Library, Archives, New York Herald-Tribune Photograph Morgue Collection)*

TOP: Ted Jr. (left), Alice, and Will Rogers, one of the many celebrated writers and commentators who were befriended by the extended Roosevelt clan (1922). *(Library of Congress)*

LEFT: Thanks to her parents' fame, Paulina was in the spotlight from the day she was born in 1925, though she was frequently overshadowed by them. On February 12, 1927, Capitol Hill photographers came to the Longworth house in large part because it was Alice's forty-third birthday. (Paulina's birthday was two days later—Valentine's Day.) *(Library of Congress)*

RIGHT: Thumbing her nose yet again at the expectations of "respectable society," Alice hawked Lucky Strike cigarettes to her fellow Americans in 1937.

TOP: Eleanor never cared that people gossiped about her friendship with Lorena Hickok (wearing the long scarf). The First Lady arranged a government job for the former journalist, often vacationed with her, and took her along on official trips, such as this fact-finding mission to Puerto Rico in 1934. *(Franklin D. Roosevelt Presidential Library)*

MIDDLE: Sara, Eleanor, and FDR arriving to cast their votes at the Hyde Park Town Hall in November 1940. Eleanor spent decades steeling herself to overcome the domineering influence of her mother-in-law, who died less than a year after the 1940 election. "I couldn't feel any emotion or real grief or sense of loss," Eleanor said about Sara's death, "and that seems terrible after thirty-six years of fairly close association." *(CSU Archives/Everett Collection)*

BOTTOM: Eleanor attending a hearing before the United Nations Special Committee on Palestine, July 1, 1947. While her male colleagues initially scoffed when President Truman appointed her as a UN delegate, Eleanor's diplomatic triumphs earned her the nickname "First Lady of the World." *(UN Photo/KB)*

LEFT: When Eleanor was laid to rest on November 10, 1962, Presidents Kennedy, Truman, and Eisenhower traveled to Hyde Park, making this the first time that three presidents attended the funeral of an American woman. Just over a year later, Vice President Johnson, standing behind and to the right of JFK, would move into the White House as well. *(CSU Archives/Everett Collection)*

RIGHT: Alice was a close friend and confidante of Nixon's throughout his career in Washington. Despite the building Watergate scandal, he still dropped by her Massachusetts Avenue town house in 1973 to wish her a happy eighty-ninth birthday. *(Richard Nixon Presidential Library and Museum)*

BOTTOM: In 1976, ninety-two-year-old Alice paid her last visit to the White House to dine with the visiting Queen Elizabeth II, carrying the purse that the Queen's great-grandfather Edward VII had given her exactly seventy years earlier. "Someone once calculated that I'd been to an average of 2.7 dinners a year at the White House over a sixty-year period," Alice once said. "That's an awful lot of dinner." *(Gerald R. Ford Presidential Library)*

Chapter 10

# COLD PEACE

very family has its troublemaker, its eccentric, its black sheep. In Franklin's extended family, the outlier was Laura Delano, Franklin's first cousin on his mother's side. The family called her Aunt Polly because when she was young she insisted on drinking only Apollinaris springwater, and those esoteric tastes flowed through the decades. She dyed her graying hair purple and painted on a pronounced widow's peak every morning with an eyeliner pencil. She wore gobs of jewelry, too. "Rope upon rope of pearls, a silk blouse open to the waist, gold bracelets clattering up and down each arm—until we all wondered how she could lift it," said one relative.[1] Like Alice, Polly specialized in caustic candor. After Winston Churchill's first visit to the White House in December 1941, her most burning question to Eleanor was, "Now, was Churchill sexy when he was wearing his jump suit?"[2] Despite having a fair number of suitors, she never married. Instead, she devoted herself to dogs—she used to judge at Kennel Club shows, still bedecked in her jewels—and to her cousin Franklin, who was three years older than she. In fact, Franklin was her middle name.

It was Aunt Polly who insisted that Alice's antagonism toward Eleanor sprouted from jealousy over losing Franklin. "Alice was crazy as a coot," Polly said. "She was angry because she didn't catch him."[3] Polly specialized in—delighted in—bad tidings. Once, when she was visiting at Campobello, FDR told her that there would be a solar eclipse the next day but not to be scared by the darkness. Polly arrived at breakfast dressed to the nines and with her jewelry box at the ready. "Despite what you have said, Franklin, this clearly is the end of the world," she explained. "I have dressed for the occasion. I have my jewels and I am ready to go to heaven."[4]

So it's not surprising that when FDR collapsed in the living room at Warm Springs on April 12, 1945, it was Aunt Polly who scurried off to telephone Eleanor. The president had gone south to rest and catch his breath after Yalta; the Russia trip had left him so exhausted that when he addressed Congress on March 1, 1945, he spoke, for the first time, sitting down. He had been recuperating in Georgia for a week, with the help of his Hyde Park neighbor Daisy Suckley, his secretary Grace Tully, and Polly. It was about 3:00 p.m. when she called Eleanor in Washington with the news. The doctor didn't think the situation seemed dire, Polly reported. His blood pressure was stabilizing—though FDR had been unconscious for almost an hour at that point—and Eleanor should go ahead with her day's appointments.[5] The First Lady had been meeting at the White House with Charles Taussig, one of the members of FDR's "brain trust," when Polly called, and she soon took a car to the exclusive Sulgrave Club for a 4:00 p.m. fund-raiser for the Thrift Shop, one of Eleanor's favorite charities. The First Lady delivered a short opening speech—Louis Howe would have been so proud—then sat down next to President Wilson's widow, Edith, at the head table to listen to the performers on the program. At about 4:50 p.m., during a piano concerto, one of the ladies tiptoed up to Eleanor and whispered that she had a phone call. Eleanor waited patiently until the pianist finished, excused herself, and took the call. It was from FDR's press secretary, Steve Early, who said only that she should go home as soon as possible. "I got into the car and sat with clenched hands all the way to the White House," she remembered. "In my heart I knew what had happened, but one does not actually formulate these terrible thoughts until they are spoken."[6]

Early and Tommy Thompson were waiting for the First Lady in her sitting room. They told her what she already knew in her gut: the president was dead. The first thing Eleanor did was write a telegram note to her four boys, who were all out of the country serving in the military. "Father slept away. He would expect you to carry on and finish your jobs. Bless you. All our love. Mother."[7] (Only Elliott would make it home in time for FDR's funeral.) Then she waited for Vice President Truman, who was meeting with Speaker of the House Sam Rayburn when Early called him and summoned him to the White House without explanation. Anna and her husband, John Boettiger, had arrived and were comforting Eleanor when Truman walked into her sitting room at about 5:25 p.m. ER stepped over to him and placed a gentle, almost motherly hand on his shoulder. "Harry," she said as quietly as if she were in church, "the President is dead." Truman was stunned, silent. When he regained his composure, he looked at the First Lady and said, "Is there anything I can do for you?" Eleanor's reply, so typically selfless and filled with an almost aching devotion to duty, was soon quoted in newspapers around the world. "Is there anything we can do for *you*? For you are the one in trouble now."[8]

It was one of an astonishing series of humble gestures from a woman who had just lost her husband of forty years. The next was to ask Truman if it would be appropriate for her to take a government plane to Georgia to collect Franklin. He assured her it was, and she arrived in Warm Springs just before midnight, greeted by Polly, Daisy, and Grace. Eleanor hugged each of them, then sat down on the living room sofa and asked the women to tell her everything that had happened that day. Daisy and Grace explained how Franklin was sitting in his chair reading the newspapers and smoking a cigarette when he began rubbing his temple before awkwardly letting his left arm fall. "Did you drop something?" said Daisy, looking up from her crocheting. "I have a terrific pain in the back of my head," FDR said.[9] And then he slumped in his chair. He never regained consciousness.

But that was not the entire story. Naturally, it was bad-news Polly who wanted to make that perfectly clear, despite what had obviously been a conspiracy to do the opposite. There were two other women with Franklin when he died, she told Eleanor. One of them was Elizabeth Shoumatoff, who had come to paint the president's portrait. She had been accompanied by—in fact, hired by—Lucy Mercer Rutherfurd. They had been staying at the Little White House for three days at the time of Franklin's attack and had left immediately when it was clear what had happened. Now it was Eleanor's turn to be stunned into silence. She had scarcely heard Lucy's name in thirty years. Had she been lurking in the shadows all that time? Eleanor slowly stood up, walked into the room where Franklin's body lay, and closed the door behind her. Five minutes later, she emerged looking as if someone had opened a wound and drained her of all feeling. There was no anger. No sadness. She was, in this moment, more like Alice than she would have ever wanted to admit. She was utterly emotionless in the face of death. She also had to live with the realization that it was her husband's lover who was with him at the end, just as Nick Longworth died in the arms not of Alice but of his mistress, Laura Curtis.

For the last twenty-five years of FDR's life, the resentment from Oyster Bay had sprouted like weeds around his ever-blossoming career. When he died, the anger withered almost instantly. Eleanor Butler and Aunt Edith, the two women who accused Franklin most bitterly of usurping their husbands' legacies, wrote Eleanor touching condolence notes, which she responded to with equal grace. "Many thanks for your kind wire," she wrote to Edith. "It was a shock, but I am glad he died working without pain or long illness."[10] Alice wrote Eleanor a note as well, though the contents have never been made public.[11] She didn't comment publicly on FDR's death either, at least not until years later. By then, she seemed to blame her side of the family for the feud at least as much as Franklin and Eleanor. "I knew how silly we were," she said in 1967, five years after Eleanor had died. "Suddenly we see this creature called Roosevelt come in, like a big cookoo, into our nest. That would have been the way I felt about it."[12]

And yet despite the moment of détente that accompanied FDR's death, Alice and Eleanor didn't manage to repair their relationship. If anything, they seemed to grow further apart. Some of that was geographic: Eleanor moved back to New York, while Alice continued to reign as the queen bee of Washington. But living in separate spheres also magnified their rivalry, like two boxers who had retreated to their opposing corners. For the first time since they were teenagers, the cousins were social and political equals. They were both popular widows of powerful men—at least as beloved, in their circles, as any of the male Roosevelts. If they weren't the two most famous women in the country, they were among a handful known simply by their first names and in an even more exclusive circle of females to make the cover of *Time* magazine.

Of course by now Alice had been flying solo for years with great success. With Franklin's royal reign (as she would call it) at an end, she made the most of her prime perch. A month after FDR's death, Bess Truman attended her first social event as First Lady, a luncheon with the American Newspaper Women's Club, and naturally Alice was there. Two months later, she had a front-row seat next to Senator Robert Taft's wife when the

Senate began to debate whether to adopt the United Nations charter.[13] She was even gossiped about as someone who could negotiate an end to the United Mine Workers' strike of 1946, by virtue of her influence with her latest powerful lover, the president of the United Mine Workers, John L. Lewis. The idea of Alice as peacemaker was dismissed just as quickly as it surfaced, once a columnist pointed out that she wasn't likely to come to the rescue of FDR's vice president and successor. "One thing on which both Mrs. Longworth's and Lewis's friends agree is that hatred of Roosevelt brought them together," wrote Drew Pearson in his syndicated Washington Merry-Go-Round column. "Both disliked him passionately, both continue to hate almost everything connected with him. That seems to be the chief bond between them."[14]

Capitol Hill was Alice's main stage, but it wasn't the only place she received the superstar treatment. In 1945, the brilliant but rabidly anti-Semitic poet Ezra Pound was sentenced to St. Elizabeths mental hospital near Washington after a judge ruled that a series of anti-American radio broadcasts he made in Italy during the war amounted to treason. Not long after Pound began his internment, Robert Lowell, one of many eminent American writers who lobbied for Pound's release, asked him what, if anything, might help his case. "Well, I'd like to meet Alice Longworth," said Pound. "She is a good friend of Senator Robert Taft, who will win the presidential nomination at the Republican Convention this summer. Taft will be elected in November, and I have something that I want him to read. If he reads it, America will be saved."[15]

Pound was wrong about Taft—needless to say, his political instincts were consistently rotten—and the reading material that would "save" America turned out to be his translation of a Confucius essay called "Unwobbling Pivot." Still, after her first visit, Alice became a regular at St. Elizabeths, alongside author Huntington Cairns, the librarian of Congress Archibald MacLeish, and a string of eminent writers from T. S. Eliot to E. E. Cummings. "In the winter it was really unpleasant. You had to go through one locked door after another, and there he was in an alcove off the general ward . . . occasionally a fellow inmate slouching in, staring at him," Alice remembered. "He used to wear three hats piled on top of each other. At the time it seemed quite natural, but now as I look back it does seem rather odd."[16] Pound held special appeal for Alice, a woman who had memorized far more poetry than most people read in a lifetime. He had also been an unabashed fan of TR. More recently, he had emerged as something of the in-house bad boy among conservatives who had opposed the war and, especially, FDR. Certainly the Democrats weren't looking to help the foul poet. At one point, Pound did try to take his case to Eleanor, writing to her sporadically and flattering her as "Madame President" and "Her Excellency Mrs. Roosevelt" in hopes that she would convey his isolationist views to the president.[17] Many years later, after the war and after his letters to Eleanor had all gone unanswered, Pound changed his tune. "[She] has carried vulgarity to the point of obscenity," he wrote to a friend, "and has the mind of a lavatory attendant."[18]

———

Alice was called many names over the years, but no one ever accused her of being simpleminded. After all, there weren't many people—not to mention people who had never attended high school—who could chat about Confucianism with Ezra Pound one day and champion an obscure book of short stories set in Polynesia the next. In fact, if it weren't for Alice, the world might never have heard of James Michener or his *Tales of the South Pacific*. Omnivorous, nocturnal reader that she was, Alice had come upon Michener's volume of stories and began talking about them to her friends, one of whom happened to be Arthur Krock, an eminent *New York Times* writer who for many years was also the chairman of the Pulitzer Prize committee for fiction. When Alice heard through the grapevine that *Tales of the South Pacific* finished fifth in the Pulitzer voting in 1948, she was incensed, and she called Krock to tell him off. "That's a nothing work. No vitality!" she announced about the book that had been selected (and remains unnamed, and unheralded, to this day). "Do you know something better?" Krock replied. "I certainly do," she said, at which point she insisted that the committee reconsider *Tales of the South Pacific*. "When they finished, they agreed with me," Alice crowed. She only met Michener years later at a party, but she was still thrilled with having single-handedly changed the course of his career. "You received the prize most deservedly, I must say," she told him, before grasping him warmly by his hands and adding, "I'm proud of the fact, Michener, that you didn't let us down."[19] By "us," she meant the Pulitzer committee—and its not-so-silent partner.

Alice's footprint had been so big for so long it's hard to appreciate the uniqueness of her cultural longevity. Unlike during her salad days as the daughter of the president, the wife of the Speaker of the House, and the lover of a revered senator, she no longer had a personal connection to power. As a full-time resident of Washington, she couldn't even vote in a presidential election until 1964. Her continued claim on the country's attention was based on two things: her wit and her bloodline. She hated being called princess, but for Americans fascinated with dynasties Alice was as close to royalty as you'd find. She was the foremother to all those women named Kennedy and Clinton who parlayed their family names and their powerful personalities into their own kinds of relevance. It's telling that in July 1948, when a group called the Women's Club for America conducted a poll asking what woman would be best qualified to become vice president, Alice finished in the No. 2 spot. No. 1, of course, was her cousin Eleanor.[20]

No one was more surprised by ER's enduring prominence than Eleanor herself. Unlike Alice, who was so despondent about having to vacate the White House in 1909 that she planted voodoo dolls on the grounds, Eleanor was eager to slip out of the spotlight following FDR's death. After she loaded his body on a train in Warm Springs and performed her grieving-widow duties at his Hyde Park funeral, the Trumans insisted she take as much time as she needed to find a new address. She packed up everything—twelve-plus years of belongings, enough to fill twenty army trucks—and retreated to New York within a week. "The Trumans have just been to lunch & nearly all that I can do is done," she wrote to Hickok from the White House for the final time. "The upstairs looks desolate & I will be glad to leave tomorrow. It is empty & without purpose to be here now."[21] About a year earlier, she and Franklin had taken an apartment in New York's Washington Square, and when she arrived there at about 10:00 p.m. on April 20, Lorena was already inside arranging the boxes of flowers and condolence cards and Tommy was at her side ready to help unpack. A few days later, a reporter buttonholed her as she was leaving her building. She had very little to say. "The story," she told the reporter, "is over."[22]

Perhaps she really did expect to settle back into a quiet life of teaching and writing. Success, no matter how substantial, never did convince Eleanor that she was much more than a hardworking but modestly gifted woman. She had learned to take a backseat to Franklin whenever his career demanded it, and she expected to follow a similar path now that he was gone. "I had to tell several people quite forcibly that nothing would induce me to run for public office or to accept an appointment to any office at the present time," she wrote in My Day on April 19, a week after the president's death. Of course, she was probably the only person on the planet who believed that, as the high-profile job offers soon proved. Harold Ickes, FDR's secretary of the interior, wanted her to run for senator. She said no. Her old friends Harry Hooker and John Golden arrived at her apartment one day and announced they were going to help manage her career. She showed them the door. The United Feature Syndicate asked her to travel to the Soviet Union to meet and write about Stalin. Realizing that the Soviets would consider her a quasi-government dignitary by dint of their affection for FDR, she declined.[23]

But Eleanor Roosevelt could never *not* stay busy, and before long her restless mind got the best of her stubborn humility. That was clear from a column she wrote a mere twelve days after Franklin's death. "Someday," she wrote, "we will actually find ourselves sitting down to read a book without that guilty feeling which weighs upon one when the job you should be doing is ignored."[24] For a while, that job was tending the flame of her husband's memory. She entertained a constant stream of dignitaries at Hyde Park, including Madame Chiang Kai-shek, General Eisenhower, President de Gaulle, and Churchill, who laid a wreath of white flowers on FDR's grave and looked surpassingly glum, even by his usual standards. At the same time, she and the children prepared to make good on Franklin's request that his lifelong home be turned over to the Department of the Interior and transformed into the FDR Presidential Library and Museum, the first presidential center of its kind. FDR's will stipulated that Eleanor and the children could stay until their deaths, but she had no great love for Springwood. She was only too happy to retreat across the road to Val-Kill. But the finality of the move took its emotional toll, especially after Eleanor unearthed a small watercolor of Franklin by Madame Shoumatoff, the painter who, along with Lucy Mercer, was with him when he died. Eleanor had only recently discovered that Lucy had, on at least one occasion, visited the White House when she was away. And to twist the knife further, their daughter, Anna, had been the hostess there that evening. Anna never told her mother, until ER confronted her after finding out about Lucy's being with FDR at the end. Anna still didn't back down.

"All that mattered was relieving a greatly overburdened man, to make his life as pleasant as possible when a few moments opened up for relaxation," she explained later.[25] Anna also failed to mention that she called Lucy to commiserate in the days after FDR's death and that Lucy had written her a lovely and personal condolence note in reply. "This blow must be crushing to you—to all of you—but I know that you meant more to your father than anyone and that makes it closer & harder to bear," Lucy wrote.[26]

Fortunately, Harry Truman made it impossible for Eleanor to dwell on the past. Almost immediately after he became president in 1945, he struck up an extraordinary working friendship with her, turning the former First Lady into his personal sounding board via dozens and dozens of letters, phone calls, and visits. They discussed how to handle the Russians, Churchill, domestic employment, Japanese internment camps, and more, a head-spinning collection of policies to debate with someone outside the administration, not to mention a woman who had never held elective office. Truman corresponded with ER so often—he remembered her birthday and commented on her My Day columns, too—that she urged him to start having his letters typed. It was taking her too long to decipher his handwriting.

———

Truman finally persuaded Eleanor to get back to work, though it took some doing. In early December 1945, he called her at home in New York to ask if she would join the first American delegation of the United Nations, meeting in London in January. "But Mr. President, I have no experience in foreign affairs. I don't know parliamentary procedure. I couldn't possibly do it," she told him as Franklin junior sat beside her, listening in as Truman pressed his case. "All right, Mr. President. I will think it over." She wasn't the only one who had doubts. Although she relented and was ultimately confirmed by the Senate, the four other members of the UN delegation, all-male, weren't exactly thrilled to have the former First Lady on their team. While they were all crossing the Atlantic en route to England on the *Queen Elizabeth*, she ran into Senator Arthur Vandenberg, a Republican heavyweight who would soon become chairman of the Foreign Relations Committee. "Mrs. Roosevelt," he bellowed importantly, "we would like to know if you would serve on Committee Three."

Eleanor remembered having two "rather contradictory reactions" to Vandenberg's invitation. "First, I wondered who 'we' might be. Was a Republican senator deciding who would serve where? And why, since I was a delegate, had I not been consulted about committee assignments?"[27] For someone who claimed to lack the proper experience to serve, she certainly possessed a sharp enough grasp of negotiations and power politics. Of course, she proceeded to hide her light under a bushel of insecurity. "My next reaction crowded these thoughts out of my mind. I realized that I had no more idea than the man in the moon what Committee Three might be."[28]

As it turned out, neither did Vandenberg. The men knew, on paper at least, that Committee Three was the committee on social, cultural, and humanitarian issues, seemingly a perfect, and perfectly harmless, parking spot for Mrs. Roosevelt and her bleeding heart. What Vandenberg didn't realize was that Committee Three was going to rule on one of the most contentious issues facing this first United Nations session: the fate of Europe's one million war refugees. The British, the Americans, and other countries in Western Europe believed that the refugees—or "displaced persons," as they were called—should be allowed to settle wherever they wished. The Soviets thought they should be forced back home. They disliked the possibility, and the implication, of comrades from Poland, the Balkans, the Baltics, and other Iron Curtain countries refusing to return from Germany and elsewhere. After all, many of them didn't deserve asylum, according to the Soviet Union's Andrei Vyshinsky. "These criminals, these traitors, are not refugees," Vyshinsky said. "Those who still pass themselves off as refugees should be sent back forthwith to their respective countries for trial and for the just appeasement of the public conscience, which has been deeply stirred by the fascist aggression perpetrated with the participation of these criminals."[29]

The Americans didn't buy that argument, but they were also intimidated by Vyshinsky. He was the fiercest litigator and diplomat in the Soviet Union, having served as the chief prosecutor during Stalin's show trials in the late 1930s that purged the supreme leader's Bolshevik enemies and sent them to the firing squads. When it came time for a member of the American delegation to face off with him on the floor of the United Nations, the men decided they knew just the right woman for the job. "'Mrs. Roosevelt,' he [John Foster Dulles, later secretary of state] began lamely, 'the United States must speak in the debate. Since you are the one who has carried on the controversy in the committee, do you think you could say a few words in the Assembly?'" Eleanor wrote.[30] Perhaps Dulles and the others thought that Vyshinsky wouldn't attack a woman as he would a man. Perhaps they finally realized that Mrs. Roosevelt—after her private lunches with the royal family and the Churchills, her almost daily interviews on the BBC, and her keynote speech at Albert Hall welcoming the UN delegates—could handle herself after all. She certainly had her fellow American delegates figured out. Just a few days earlier, she had written a none-too-flattering assessment of them to her friend Elinor Morgenthau. "J. Foster Dulles I like not at all," she said. "Vandenberg is smart & hard to get along with and does not say what he feels."[31]

But when duty called, Eleanor Roosevelt always answered. She prepared meticulously for her showdown with Vyshinsky and addressed the assembly without notes, speaking until nearly 1:00 a.m. after the Soviet finally finished his long diatribe. "I was badly frightened. I trembled at the thought of speaking against the famous Mr. Vishinsky," she said. "The hour was late and we knew the Russians would delay a vote as long as possible on the theory that some of our allies would get tired and leave. I knew we must hold our South American colleagues until the vote was taken because their votes would be decisive. So I talked about Simón Bolívar and his stand for the freedom of the people of Latin America. The South American representatives stayed with us to the end, and when the vote was taken, we won."[32] When she had finished, the members of the assembly applauded for a full two minutes.[33]

It was a small victory for the United States but a huge one for Delegate Roosevelt, over both the Soviets and her own comrades. "You will be amused," she wrote to Joe Lash on the morning after the vote, "that when Mr. Dulles said goodbye to me this morning he said, 'I feel I must tell you that when you were appointed I thought it terrible and now I think your work here has been fine'!"[34] Vandenberg was a convert as well, telling many a dinner-party acquaintance, "I want to say that I take back everything I ever said about her, and believe me it's been plenty."[35] Mrs. Roosevelt had gone to London as a celebrity. She returned to New York as a diplomatic superstar. "Mrs. F.D. Passes UNO Test," wrote the *Boston Daily Globe*, one of the virtually unanimous slate of favorable press accounts.[36] Within days, there was talk of nominating her for the Nobel

Peace Prize.[37] Within months, President Truman asked her to serve on the United Nations Commission on Human Rights. This time she accepted readily, and this time her fellow delegates more than appreciated her abilities: they elected her chair by acclamation.

She spent the next two years globe-trotting as the driving force behind the Universal Declaration of Human Rights, a document based on the Magna Carta and the Bill of Rights giving countries a framework for fair treatment of their citizens. Overall, the Human Rights Commission proved similar to her work on Committee Three, including lengthy and maddening philosophical fights with the Soviets over how to ensure individual liberties in both democracy and communism. (The touchiest, and perhaps most ingenious, Soviet argument was to question what right the United States had to determine the notion of individual freedom given the plight of American blacks living under Jim Crow laws. Unfortunately for the Soviets, Eleanor Roosevelt was the last person to pick that fight with.) As with her first battle against Vyshinsky, the Soviets dragged their feet at every opportunity. The final vote on the Declaration of the Rights of Man, on December 10, 1948, wasn't tallied until 3:00 a.m. Once again, Eleanor triumphed. And once again, the General Assembly erupted into applause for her, only this time they gave Madame Chairman an almost unheard-of standing ovation. She would later call her Human Rights Commission work the "most important task" of her life.[38]

———

Alice Longworth had spent the last twenty-five years using her cousin for target practice, with her mocking dinner-party imitations and her withering quips about her politics, her appearance, and her husband as ammunition. Without Franklin, Eleanor had perhaps an even bigger bull's-eye painted on her back. Alice's "irreconcilable" objections to international peacekeeping organizations coupled with Eleanor's prominence at the United Nations set them on another potential collision course. Yet Alice largely held her fire-breathing tongue regarding Eleanor's work at the UN. One of her few punches was to publicly endorse a group that wanted to abolish United Nations Day in October in favor of something to be called United States Day. But for someone who helped trounce the League of Nations, that was small potatoes. (Only the governor of Utah signed on to the plan.)

Alice didn't entirely leave Eleanor in peace. One of the more sensational Capitol Hill hearings of 1947 happened to feature Franklin and
Eleanor's second son, Elliott. A former air force colonel, he was accused of
having accepted numerous gifts from Hughes Aircraft to lobby his father
for a $70 million order of experimental spy planes. Elliott admitted to
the Senate War Investigating Committee that Hughes had paid exactly
$576.83 (about $6,000 in 2015 dollars) for his sixteen-day honeymoon stay
at the Beverly Hills Hotel and that John W. Meyer, a publicity manager for
Hughes, had actually given Elliott's (third) wife away at the 1944 wedding
ceremony. But he called the graft charges "complete nonsense," adding
that he'd never even spoken to his father about Hughes and, besides, the
president had "more important matters" on his mind in 1944.[39]

If these hearings set off an echo of the nepotism charges leveled against
Ted junior and Archie Roosevelt during the 1924 Teapot Dome hearings,
it wasn't lost on Alice. She turned up regularly at the Senate War Committee room, beaming for the cameras in her trademark broad-brimmed
hats. As usual, she landed herself a prime seat, right next to Myrtle Ferguson, whose husband, Homer, was the Republican chairman of the Senate
War Investigation Subcommittee. Alice kept up a running commentary
with Mrs. Ferguson, primarily complaining that her husband wasn't being
tough enough on the witnesses. At one point, Alice became so agitated
that her stage whispers threatened to drown out the testimony. "Senator
Walsh or Burt Wheeler would never have allowed a witness to get away
with that," Alice was overheard declaring to Mrs. Ferguson. "Your husband
isn't being firm enough." At which point Mrs. Ferguson stood up from her
seat, walked over to her husband, and scolded him: "Homer, can't you be
firmer?" Apparently, he could. "The Senator reacted a short time later by
laying down the law to Howard Hughes," reported one newspaper. "He
was so firm that Claude Pepper, the Florida Democrat, protested he was
too tough."[40] Eleanor didn't attend the hearings, but she was clearly aware
of them, and she could not have been happy about Alice's antics. "I saw
Mrs. Roosevelt angry only once and that was over one of her children,"
said Eleanor's friend Representative Helen Gahagan Douglas. "It was at
breakfast, early as usual. She started to read the newspaper. On the front
page, there was a story about one of her boys. An incident greatly exagger-
ated and but for the fact that he was the son of the President of the United
States, it would have received no attention at all. I can hear Mrs. Roose-

velt say, 'Someday I will write the story of what is done to the children of those in public life.'"[41]

———

Still, even icebergs thaw around the edges, and Alice could occasionally let go of her old fighting spirit. She had said as much in 1944, at the Republican National Convention, which she deemed unconscionably tepid compared with the bad old days of, say, 1912. "Then—then, one really felt violent," said Alice, with nineteen-year-old Paulina at her side in Chicago. "It was a bath of hate and fury. There hasn't been anything like it since. Oh, it was wonderful."[42]

Feeding her own torpor was a case of the Alice blues. She had long expected that once FDR was deposed, the Republicans would rise again. Instead, Truman narrowly held on to the White House in 1948, and Alice herself deserved at least part of the blame for sinking his opponent, Thomas Dewey. Dewey had also run for president in 1944 against FDR, and she was unimpressed. With the kind of life-threatening paper cut that only Alice could administer, she dismissed the stiff, short, mustached Dewey as looking like "the bridegroom on a wedding cake." When Dewey returned to face Truman in 1948, Alice's epithet stuck to him like heavy butter-cream frosting. Many voters looked at him and saw a charisma-challenged man devoid of stature in almost every way—the little man on the cake. The candidate saw it too. "Dewey has quit wincing at these jabs, but he is still cautious about anything that might bring criticism," said the columnist Drew Pearson.[43] While much of the political world, and an embarrassed newspaper or two, were proclaiming, "Dewey Defeats Truman," Alice was one of the few who knew better and predicted the worst.

If her political world looked bleak, the 1940s turned into an especially dark personal time for Alice. In 1943, her brother Kermit committed suicide after years of depression and alcoholism. In 1944, Ted junior died on the battlefield in France. Shortly after that, her closest friend and partner in political high jinks, Ruth Hanna McCormick, died of pancreatitis on New Year's Eve. Their fathers had been Republican sparring partners, and the two women had known each other for decades; it had been to Ruth that Alice turned when she found herself pregnant with Borah's child in 1924. In 1948, her eighty-seven-year-old stepmother, Edith, died at Sagamore Hill. They were never close, at least from Alice's point of view. Alice couldn't get over feeling like a second-class member of the family, and the fact that Edith's will divided her estate equally among her biological children while leaving Alice a token $1,000 couldn't have helped. Edith's reasoning was that Alice still had an income from the Lee side of her family. Besides, she threw in the sketch of the White House drawn for Alice by John Singer Sargent. But the loss of the only mother she had ever known was real, even for a woman who believed that mourning was about as useful as voting for a Democrat.

And in the 1940s, Alice's daughter, Paulina, continued on her roller-coaster ride through life. Paulina seemed to be on the upswing on July 9, 1946, when she gave birth to Joanna Sturm, in New York City. Grandma's stature was such that news of Joanna's birth and a smattering of baby pictures made their way into the newspapers, and Alice rushed to New York to meet the child. But her relationship with Paulina and her husband, Alex, was strained at best. Alice saw her daughter infrequently, either at the Sturms' home in Connecticut or on those occasions when the mother could press her daughter into political service, such as attending the 1948 GOP convention in Philadelphia, where Paulina worked for a group called Twenties-for-Taft.[44] Their relationship became even more fraught in November 1951. Alex Sturm, who long had a drinking problem, died in a Connecticut hospital of hepatitis-related illness. He was twenty-eight. His daughter was five.

Unhappy and occasionally unstable, Paulina became a widow and a single mother at twenty-six. She reacted badly. Within months, a maid at her Manhattan hotel-apartment found her lying unconscious on the floor. The police report blamed a "sudden illness," but given her suicide attempt in college and Alice's own explanation that her daughter was going through "a difficult period of readjustment" since Alex's death, it seemed more likely that a bottle of pills or liquor was to blame.[45] Paulina and Joanna then moved back to Washington, to a house in Georgetown about a mile from Alice. It was something of a mixed blessing. Alice knew her daughter needed help, but she also knew she didn't really know how to provide it. "She said to me once that she was so glad that Paulina was coming to live in Washington, but of course she couldn't live with *her*," said Hermann Hagedorn, a Roosevelt family biographer and friend.[46]

Instead, Paulina gravitated toward Roman Catholicism to soothe her grief. The solitude of prayer appealed to her, as did the opportunity to lose herself in the good work done at Catholic hospitals and with the progressive Catholic Worker movement. "There was always something child-like and shy about Paulina, but she was valiant too," said Dorothy Day, the founder of the movement. When Day was arrested for civil disobedience in 1956, it was Paulina who put up the $1,000 bail.[47] It's hard not to wonder whether Paulina's Christian activism wasn't its own sort of disobedience against her mother. After all, Alice had long equated being "frightfully good" with being "frightfully boring," at least as far as Eleanor was concerned. For Paulina, using rectitude as her weapon against her notoriously rebellious mother would have been a delicious irony (as would the fact that she spent time working on New York's seedy Lower East Side, where Eleanor's own community-service work began).

But religion proved to be a Band-Aid that covered only Paulina's most superficial wounds. She continued to suffer from debilitating headaches and had difficulty sleeping. The *Washington Post* contacted Alice in February 1953, a little more than a year after Alex's death, to see how she and her daughter would be celebrating their birthdays. Alice was born on February 12; Paulina, born on February 14, lived in her mother's shadow yet again—and again every February. The *Post* story was called "2 Birthdays but Not 1 Celebration," and in it Alice explained that no one in the Longworth family felt much like celebrating yet. "If we all survive," she said, "a year from now I shall be 70 and that WILL be something to celebrate."[48]

They all did survive that year, but Alice's morbid premonition played itself out soon enough. Just before dinnertime on January 27, 1957, ten-year-old Joanna walked into the living room of the Sturms' small house in Georgetown and found her mother lying unconscious on the couch, barely breathing but alive, with an empty bottle of pills nearby. She called a neighbor who called an ambulance, but Paulina died on the way to the hospital. Some newspapers hinted that she had finally succeeded in killing herself, a serious enough charge to prompt the Washington coroner to perform an autopsy. For some reason, he took more than a month to deliver his verdict: heart failure, caused by a combination of prescription drugs and alcohol. Even more curious: the coroner ruled her death to be an accident, despite noting that Paulina had bought a bottle of twelve barbiturates and a bottle of forty-eight tranquilizers the day before, and both were now empty. Could Alice have exerted her significant influence to avoid the stigma of a suicide? On the other hand, would a newly devout Roman Catholic such as Paulina have ever considered such a thing? Washington whispered about various possibilities, but Paulina was laid to rest with dignity. In fact, one of her pallbearers was Vice President Richard Nixon.

———

At the time of Paulina's death, Alice and Eleanor were rarely in contact. Eisenhower was in the White House, and Eleanor had no official duties in Washington. The days of dinner and birthday invitations were long over, though they did bump into each other at the occasional society party or in some other unexpected location. Several years before, it was a chance meeting on a train. "Came up in the train this morning," Eleanor wrote to her friend Joe Lash in 1943, "and [Alice] had to sit with us as the train was full & I enjoyed her. She is a vivid & amusing creature no matter how unkind at times! She remarked that no matter 'how much we differed politically there was always a tribal feeling between us'!"[49] Now that tragedy had visited the family, that tribal feeling pulled the distant cousins toward each other again. Eleanor immediately wrote Alice a short, earnest letter, dated the day after Paulina's death:

*My dear Alice:*

*Though we do not often meet, I was happy to see you at Agnes'* *party. I am shocked that this great grief has come to you, and I am glad you have the small grandchild. If there is anything I can ever do for you, please let me know.*

*With my deepest sympathy.*
*Affectionately,*
*Eleanor*[50]

It's perhaps not surprising that the sensitive, ever-thoughtful Eleanor reached out to Alice. She was always at her best when someone was in need, and in this case there was an extra tug on her heart. Even though she barely knew Paulina and had never met Joanna, the pain of burying a child was all too real, forty-eight years after the death of the first Franklin junior.

More surprising—even shocking—was Alice's response. If the con-

---

* Agnes Meyer, whose family owned the *Washington Post*.

ventional wisdom had been correct, cruel Alice would have snubbed her cousin's heartfelt overture as if it were an invitation to a second-rate party. Even some of the people closest to the Roosevelts bought that story line. "Mrs. R. made a lovely gesture of friendship toward Mrs. Longworth when her daughter committed suicide," said Maureen Corr, who took over from Tommy Thompson as Eleanor's personal secretary. "Mrs. R. told me of Alice's malice (but said) 'even so, I must write her.' Even said we must see each other some time. Alice L never answered."[51]

But she did answer. It took Alice five months to reply to Eleanor, but the reasons for the delay had nothing to do with callousness, as the letter itself makes painfully clear:

*Dear Eleanor*

*For months after Paulina died whenever I tried to write I simply crumpled. I do hope you understand, because I want you to know how touched I was by your thoughts, your telegram, the spring blossoms on your letter. Joanna is with me now. We leave in a few days for a couple of months on a ranch in Wyoming. Perhaps some time when you are in town you would let me know and we could have a "family" moment together. I should so much like to have Joanna know you, and for me it would be a pleasure, as it was to have a glimpse of you at the Meyers' party.*

*Affectionately,*
*Alice*[52]

*Crumpled.* It's hard to imagine the redoubtable Alice Roosevelt Longworth crumpling under any circumstances. And yet it's hard to think of a time when she seemed more vulnerable than in this letter. Even her use of "affectionately" seems uncharacteristically soft and warm. She was, by all accounts, destroyed by Paulina's death. "It nearly killed her. It really did," said Marian Christie, one of Alice's friends.[53] If she didn't exactly blame herself for her daughter's years of unhappiness, she was more aware than ever that her own conspicuous persona—the "bride at every wedding, corpse at every funeral" temperament she inherited from her father—had not served shy, sweet Paulina well.

Yet Alice was determined to atone for her maternal missteps. Naturally, she opted for the most dramatic gesture imaginable. She insisted on retaining custody of ten-year-old Joanna. "I remember everyone was very upset, very shocked and flabbergasted at a sister who had decided to take over raising of this very young child," said Kermit Roosevelt, the grandson of Alice's brother Kermit. "All sorts of people predicted a very short attention span given to it, she'll never be able to relate to the child, et cetera."[54] Alice still had difficulty relating to children. She tended to forget that what was interesting to a grande dame might not amuse a teenage girl. "She had the strangest idea about children," said Ruth Tankersley, the daughter of Alice's best friend, Ruth McCormick. "I remember one birthday, when Joanna was about thirteen, the other guests were Vice President Nixon and J. Edgar Hoover. Not exactly people that would interrelate with a thirteen-year-old child."[55] But Alice knew enough about her shortcomings to make allowances for them. Joanna spent most days after school playing at her friend Kristie Tankersley's house, doing her homework and riding horses before being picked up in Alice's chauffeur-driven car. The ranch trip to Wyoming that Alice mentioned to Eleanor became a regular grandmother-granddaughter bonding ritual, even though one year, when Alice was seventy-six, she was thrown from her horse and broke a foot (and kept right on going with the vacation).[56] By the same token, she didn't try to force-feed Joanna the same all-politics diet she inflicted on Paulina. "Quite to the surprise of a lot of people, she turned out to be an extraordinarily good mother to Joanna, far better than she had been to her own daughter," said Kermit.[57] Alice ultimately came to the same conclusion. "I should have been a grandmother, not a mother," Gore Vidal remembered her saying.[58]

———

Eleanor's battles weren't of the same magnitude, but as was the case with Alice, her failings as a mother dominated her personal life. Having been absent or overwhelmed or marginalized by her mother-in-law for most of the children's youth and early adulthood, she became determined to make it up to them however she could. Money was often their chief concern, whether it was to start a new business, finance another campaign, or pay for a vacation. Eleanor was hardly destitute, what with the family money and a steady stream of income from her lectures, articles, and books; she wrote six in her lifetime, including a Christmas book and an advice book for teenagers, and that doesn't include the collections of her essays and letters. But the children always seemed to have their hands out, ready for a deposit from Mother R. When they came to New York, they stayed at her apartment and left her with the bills. Even the phone cost her a small fortune. "Her bill for this month was $205 [$2,180 in 2015 dollars]," her assistant Dorothy Dow wrote. "Mostly unnecessary, too. Elliott just sits here and calls Los Angeles, San Diego, St. Louis, Washington, time after time, and it's senseless. None of it is pressing business. I think it makes him feel like a big shot."[59]

Mother didn't only hold the purse strings. The siblings all knew that her most valuable asset—and theirs—was the Roosevelt family name. They each wanted, at some point, to leverage it for their own gain, and as the matriarch and Franklin's widow she had the power to decide which child could manage which piece of the family heritage. More often than not, she was forced to choose among the children in ways that would have made Solomon dizzy. Elliott, a high school graduate in a family of Ivy Leaguers, was by far the neediest, forever wandering off in search of a new venture that invariably failed. But because he was the least likely to succeed—it seemed like fate that Elliott was named for Eleanor's own fragile father—she supported most everything he tried. There were some doozies: Christmas tree and dairy farms at Hyde Park, wholesale pharmaceuticals in Batista's Cuba, boat rentals in Miami (or as he billed them "A Roosevelt Yacht"). In 1952, he sold Top Cottage, Franklin's getaway in Hyde Park and the setting for the famous barbecue with the king and queen of England, apparently without informing his mother. She read about the sale in the *New York Times*.

Perhaps his most controversial deal, as far as his brothers and sister were concerned, came in 1947, when ER agreed to let Elliott edit a collection of Franklin's private papers. The other siblings hated that one brother would have the power of the pen to introduce and characterize their father's personal letters without their approval. And they didn't appreciate that Elliott would get 50 percent of the royalties while the other four and ER would split their 50 percent—minus Elliott's advance. Anna wrote to Elliott and demanded to know just how much his expenses would be and why he was receiving so much more of the money than the rest. He went running to his mother. "Elliott gave me your letter to him to read & I hardly think you realize what a critical & almost hostile letter it sounded like," Eleanor wrote to Anna.[60] Elliott himself insisted that he had already spent $12,000 researching and preparing the book but his advance was only for $10,000. "So you can readily see that I am not riding a free gravy train as your letter implies," he told Anna.[61]

There were similarly heated discussions when Columbia Pictures and the director Stanley Kramer approached the family wanting to make a film about FDR's life, and less heated ones when Eleanor agreed to host a radio program with Anna in 1948 and another with Elliott in 1950. On those rare instances when she pushed back, it was when the children wanted to go into the family business—politics. As a protective mother, she was leery of her sons being compared with their legendary father. As a proud wife, she guarded FDR's legacy, and the boys didn't always embrace their father's ideals. (John, the only one of the four Roosevelt boys who never ran for office, actually became a Republican after his father's death and actively supported Eisenhower for president in 1952, even though his mother was the primary force behind his opponent, the Democrat Adlai Stevenson.) It didn't help that James and Franklin junior were unremarkable politicians, as they were the first to admit—about each other. "He had a dreadful record in Congress," James said about Franklin junior. "He was smart, but not smart enough ... He coasted instead of working at his job, considering it beneath him, while he aimed for higher positions."[62] They were both elected to Congress for a few terms (James from California, Franklin junior from New York) on the strength of the family's golden coattails, but they lost more contests than they won over time. Eleanor would warn them against jumping into a potentially losing race. She was convinced that James's front-page marital troubles in 1954 would kill his congressional career. (He ran anyway and won.) She told Franklin junior he would never defeat the Democratic machine if he went after the nomination for governor of New York in 1954. (He did anyway and failed.) But she played the good soldier and stumped for them when they asked, such as James's ill-fated campaign for California governor in 1950. "[He] insists that I come out to speak for him and for Helen* which seems a mistake to me but I have agreed to go," she wrote to Anna in 1950.[63] Jimmy's way

---

* Helen Gahagan Douglas, who was running for Senate with James on the Democratic ticket.

of expressing his gratitude, along with his independence, was to act as if his mother had been no help at all. "She never told me to run, not to run, what to emphasize, what issues to talk about. I can never remember her really giving me any overall advice," said James. "I felt I had to be my own person and that I shouldn't rely on running on her reputation or father's reputation or anything. So I made a conscious effort to be there on my own."[64]

# Chapter 11

# MONUMENTS

❧❀❧

For all her acclaim as a human-rights champion, Eleanor had almost as much success advocating for a completely different kind of person in need—Democratic politicians. In 1934, she became the first First Lady to actively campaign for a congressional candidate: Caroline O'Day, one of the merry pranksters on the singing teapot a decade earlier, who went on to serve four terms as an at-large congressman from New York. Women in Connecticut, Maryland, and Oregon all owed their congressional careers, in part, to Eleanor's campaigning. She supported men too, most famously Adlai Stevenson, the vacillating, Hamlet-like governor of Illinois who ran for president twice, in 1952 and 1956. ER advised him on his stump speeches, helped plan strategy, and, most crucial of all, jetted around the country to drum up supporters, especially among the African-American and female voters with whom she was hugely popular. "I have been running around so madly speaking for Adlai that I had forgotten that I was a grandmother, and a great-grandmother at that!" she wrote back to her friend (and future New York congressman) Allard Lowenstein, after he had wished her Happy Mother's Day in 1956.[1]

Though Stevenson lost both times, there's little question that without Mrs. Roosevelt (as he always referred to her) his candidacies would have been fiascoes rather than merely noble defeats. He might not have even stayed in the race in 1956. Just before the Democratic convention, former President Truman finally announced that he would endorse Averell Harriman, not Stevenson. Adlai and Eleanor had flown to Chicago together for the convention, and as they sat in the backseat of a cab on their way into town, his attitude took a turn toward the desperate. "There are many people who could wage this campaign just as well as myself," Stevenson said. "I don't know that I'd be the right candidate. I don't think I should carry on as the standard bearer." Eleanor replied like the mother she was: "You are the only one who can possibly do it, and you will do it." Stevenson's childlike response: "But I'm not sure I want to." Eleanor: "Oh yes you *do*!"[2]

As the longest-serving and most influential First Lady in history, it's not surprising that Eleanor reigned as a kind of Washington king- (and queen-) maker. She not only had her own passionate following; she stood guard at the door to FDR's substantial legacy, allowing access only to an ideologically select few. But the Republicans had an equal and opposite female force—Alice. She might not have incited the same grassroots loyalty as Eleanor, but she had been her party's éminence grise for far longer than her cousin. Vetting candidates, advising politicians, plotting strategy, even telling her side to man up had been Alice's obsessions for decades. "I can hardly recollect a time when I was not aware of the existence of politics and politicians," she wrote decades before as the first line of *Crowded Hours*.[3] She, too, held the keys to her half of the vaunted Roosevelt kingdom.

So the cousins' duels continued into their sixties, only now they clashed largely via politicians to whom neither was related. They didn't back a candidate merely to foil the other, but their natural differences tugged them toward rival camps. Stevenson was a persistent thorn for Alice, who again backed Taft in 1952 before casting a wan glance toward "probably the dullest man I've ever known"—Dwight Eisenhower.[4] Alice didn't know Stevenson well, but she managed to dispose of him with an observation that, classically, was both laughably shallow and crushingly on target. "A ridiculous name—Adlai. How silly," she said. "Can you imagine someone with a name like Adlai as president?"[5] Beyond his name, the epithet that came to symbolize the essence of Adlai's effete snobbery was "egghead." It was coined by the Washington columnist Stewart Alsop (Alice and Eleanor's first cousin, once removed), who wondered, in the wake of Nixon's defiant Checkers speech, if Stevenson's cerebral coolness would stand up to the brawny general Eisenhower and the GOP's warriors. "Sure, all the egg-heads love Stevenson," Alsop wrote, "but how many egg-heads do you think there are?"[6]

Of all the politicians backed or bucked by the cousins in their last decade of sparring, the biggest, and baddest, was Richard Nixon. Alice had been an admirer since 1948, when he made his mark as the freshman congressman who brought down Alger Hiss in front of the House Un-American Activities Committee. While Nixon's brand of jugular slashing clearly appealed to her, in most ways he didn't seem to be her type. She favored politicians either with towering intellects (such as Borah) or with larger-than-life personalities (Longworth). Her father had them both. Nixon had neither. "He's a level-headed fellow, and I think he does know more about what goes on in the world," she explained about Nixon in 1970. "I think he's a very able man."[7] His one superior trait—the ability to survive—seemed merely tactical, worthy of respect rather than devotion. Not to Alice. She gravitated to him precisely because he was an outsider fighting to get in. Despite her seat near the head of the Republican table, there was a part of Alice that viewed herself as the cast-off Roosevelt daughter who never fit the mold of her family. If establishment Washington disdained scrappy Dick Nixon, that made him all the more appealing to her. "There was always a stubborn, persistent quality about him which some people admired and others couldn't stand. They *minded* him so, even long before Watergate," she said.[8]

The less obvious aspect of Nixon's appeal to Alice was that he needed her more—and cultivated her favor more—than other politicians. In that sense, Nixon was Alice's own Adlai Stevenson. He relied on her access and advice, and he made sure the rest of Washington knew it. It was Alice, Nixon said in his memoir, who persuaded him to consider the vice presidential slot in 1952 if Eisenhower offered it to him. "If you're thinking of your own good and your own career you are probably better off to stay in the Senate and not go down in history as another nonentity who served as Vice President," she told him over dinner one night a few weeks before the Republican National Convention. "However, if Eisenhower gets the nomination, someone will have to go on that ticket who can reassure the party regulars and particularly the conservatives that he won't take everyone to hell in a handcart, and you are the best man to do it."[9] When her advice paid off, he kept coming back for more. They became regular lunch and dinner partners, often with his wife, Pat, in tow, and he usually dropped by her house on her birthday and on election nights. In late September 1955, Eisenhower had a heart attack while on vacation in Denver, and on the morning of October 2, Vice President Nixon received his first presidential intelligence briefing. But he was out of the office for four hours later that day, because he and Pat were having lunch at Alice's. In 1956, Nixon named Alice one of the sixteen official American delegates to the inauguration of the Brazilian president Juscelino Kubitschek, in part as a nod to TR and Kermit's Amazonian jungle adventures of four decades earlier.

Not surprisingly, ER was hard-pressed to find much about Nixon to admire. Politically, he was as far to the right as she was to the left, though she sometimes accused him of borrowing liberally from the liberals, such as when he began to embrace the idea of a nuclear-test-ban treaty during the 1960 campaign. "He will forget that he ever opposed it or that Adlai Stevenson advocated it in the campaign four years ago," she wrote in her My Day column.* "Mr. Nixon never has anything but hindsight."[10]

But she had crossed Nixon's path long before he became a perennial opponent of her man Stevenson, and he, a rotten egg in the making, left a putrid aftertaste. The case involved Nixon's political mauling of her good friend Helen Gahagan Douglas. In the 1930s, Melvyn and Helen Douglas were becoming one of Hollywood's golden couples. They had met while acting in a Broadway play called *Tonight or Never*, then moved to Los Angeles. Tall and dashing with a pencil mustache, Melvyn worked opposite Claudette Colbert, Greta Garbo, and Joan Crawford and ultimately won two Oscars (*Hud* and *Being There*). Helen had an earthy, square-faced beauty, like a poor man's Myrna Loy, and she debuted in a 1935 sci-fi movie called *She* with Randolph Scott. But she hated the glacial pace of filmmaking. She did a smattering of theater, got pregnant, appeared in a Smiles of Lady Lux soap ad, and more or less retired. She never made another film.

Yet Helen, like Eleanor, wasn't good at sitting still. Shocked by the poverty she'd seen driving west from New York, she helped found the John Steinbeck Committee to Aid Agricultural Organization in 1938 and joined the California branch of the National Youth Administration (NYA). Melvyn helped establish the Hollywood Anti-Nazi League and became involved in the state Democratic Party. Before long, their work for liberal causes caught the eye of Aubrey Williams, the national director of the NYA, who invited the Douglases to meet Mrs. Roosevelt in Washington.

---

* Although My Day maintained its chatty, diary-like feel, once she was no longer First Lady, Eleanor was more comfortable in being overtly political in her column.

The Roosevelts and the Douglases quickly became close friends and allies. When Eleanor would travel to California, she often stayed at the Douglases' seventeen-room mansion on the edge of the Wilshire Country Club, an outrageously lavish base for Helen and ER's daytrips to Southern California's migrant-worker camps, one of Helen's favorite causes. The Douglases were likewise frequent guests at the White House, though they never did get used to the stodgy custom of having married couples sleep in separate rooms. (One night Melvyn snuck into the Lincoln Bedroom to be with his wife, then in the morning went back and mussed up his own bed so it looked as if he'd slept in it.)[11] In 1940, Melvyn became the first A-list actor to serve as a delegate to a national political convention. Helen was an alternate and sang "The Star-Spangled Banner" at the opening session.[12] Four years later, when the Democrat Tom Ford retired from the House, the president turned to Helen. By then she was knee-deep in Democratic Party politics as a vice-chairwoman of the California State Democrat Committee. But she didn't know if she was ready for Congress. Eleanor, with her usual dose of tough love, made sure she was. "You mustn't let Franklin influence you, Helen," she said. "He thinks it would be nice to have you in Washington. Don't you run for Congress unless you're very sure you'll be elected."[13] She was sure, and she won.

In 1950, after she had served three terms in Congress, Helen decided to run for the Senate. Her opponent: Congressman Nixon. That was the same year that Eleanor's son James chose to run for governor of California (against his mother's advice), so she had a front-row seat to what is still considered one of the nastiest campaigns in history. Because Nixon's great success had been his evisceration of Alger Hiss, he made fighting communism the center of his Senate campaign. Douglas was hardly a communist, but in the hands of a master manipulator her liberal voting record could easily be twisted into a more sinister shape. First, Nixon began to call her the "Pink Lady." Lest anyone think "lady" was too polite to scare anyone, he added that she was "pink right down to her underwear."[14] Then his campaign printed a flyer highlighting her most liberal votes and describing them as "Against Loyalty and Security Legislation" and "Communist-Line Foreign Policy Votes." Most damning of all, Nixon's hatchet men printed the flyer on pink paper—the "Pink Sheet," as it came to be known. Douglas was forced to spend much of her time rebutting Nixon's accusations (along with innuendo about Melvyn's Jewish background and the fitness of female politicians).[15] Her campaign faltered. In desperation, she began to fling her own mud, and she hit upon what has become Douglas's most enduring contribution to American politics. She was the first person to call Nixon "Tricky Dick."

Yet the trick that hit closest to home for Eleanor didn't involve Red-baiting. Nixon and Douglas didn't campaign face-to-face very often—she knew he'd skin her alive at a debate—but in May 1950 they shared the stage for a pair of speeches at San Francisco's Commonwealth Club. Nixon spoke first, and as he stood up at the podium he pulled a telegram from his pocket. It was, he said, an endorsement letter from none other than Eleanor Roosevelt. The Republicans in the audience roared. "Of course I was shocked," Douglas recalled. "Eleanor Roosevelt had endorsed me and we were friends." Helen was so bewildered, she couldn't think straight for the rest of the evening, which was evidently part of Nixon's scheme. Her mind racing, she could only come up with one possible explanation. "I [was] not sure whether Mrs. Longworth, Teddy Roosevelt's daughter, was ever called anything but Alice Longworth . . . because the telegram was sent from Long Island—Oyster Bay or Oyster someplace else."[16] In fact, the telegrammed endorsement was legitimate, and it did come from Eleanor Roosevelt—Ted's widow, Eleanor. Very tricky indeed.

———

Alice would have been delighted to be implicated in one of Nixon's schemes. She proudly claimed that he was one of the two "trickiest politicians I've known—and I like tricks." Her other favorite rascal was Robert F. Kennedy. For a die-hard Republican, Alice had a curiously close relationship with the Kennedy family. Politically, they weren't all that far apart, especially their fervently anticommunist views on foreign policy. It's worth noting that both Alice and JFK were invited to, and attended, Senator Joseph McCarthy's big church wedding to one of his staff members in 1953, when McCarthyism was at its brutal height and Robert Kennedy worked alongside McCarthy on the House Un-American Activities Committee. Alice insisted she had no real use for the Red-baiting senator. To prove it, she liked to tell a story about a party they both attended in 1950, where he walked up to her and planted his arm around her like an overeager teenager with his girl. "With a kind of yokel jocularity, he brayed, 'Ah, here is my blind date. I'm going to call you Alice,'" she recalled. She turned her blue-eyed death stare on him full force. "No,

Senator McCarthy, you are not going to call me Alice," she said. "The truckman, the trashman, and the policeman on my block may call me Alice but you may not."[17]

Yet the Kennedys' main attraction for Alice wasn't political. She liked their style, their energy, their sprawl. They resembled her own ample and rambunctious family. "The Kennedys were a fascinating, incredible outfit. There hasn't been anything like them since the Bonapartes," she said.[*][18] Alice was a regular visitor to the Kennedy White House; she was especially delighted to be there when eighty-four-year-old Pablo Casals performed in 1961, having met the legendary Spanish cellist during his first White House visit in 1904, when she was nineteen and her father was president. She spent a lot of time with Bobby, too, both at his Hickory Hill estate and at her own dinner parties. "You are a temptress—our Eve of the New Frontier," Ethel Kennedy wrote to her. "It's always jolly eating meat on Friday."[19] Alice enjoyed both brothers but in different ways. "I see Jack like a nice little rosy-faced old Irishman. Bobby was brooding. Bobby could have been a revolutionary, very Sinn Fein," she said.[20] Their affection for the grande dame of the Republican Party was a tonic for Alice in her sunset years. "The Kennedy administration added a new high point to her career. She was by then eighty, but the young president and his still younger wife and brother Bobby all adored 'Mrs. L,' as they, too, called her," wrote Joseph Alsop. "She was better company than ever, and it always used to entertain me, watching all the young beauties grow green with envy because this woman of eighty managed to be surrounded by all the most admired men in the city."[21] In 1962, the president gave Mrs. L. the perfect token of his friendship: he invited her to attend the ceremony renaming the "new" House Office Building. Thanks to JFK's signature on Public Law 87-453, it was now called the Longworth House Office Building.

Somehow, Alice managed to keep her relationship with the Kennedys from interfering with her alliance with Nixon. In fact, it gave her an unusual sort of objectivity on the 1960 election. Joseph Alsop, who was a rabid JFK supporter, had been in the studio audience in Chicago for the

---

[*] As usual, Alice was unbelievably well sourced to make such a comparison. She actually knew some of the Bonapartes. Her father's attorney general had been Charles Joseph Bonaparte, grandnephew of the French emperor.

fateful first Nixon-Kennedy televised debate. He was certain that Nixon had done well—until he called his cousin Alice. It was 3:30 a.m., but she was awake and as sharp as ever. "Well, Joe, your man's in, my man's finished," she told him. "I don't see why they bother to go on with the election. Dick has finished himself off."[22] Over time, that became the conventional wisdom, but it was Alsop's first inkling that image would decide the election in ways it never had before. It also reminded him about the Roosevelt women's special skill, honed over a lifetime of watching, listening, and studying elections like some fans obsess over baseball. "I considered then, as I still consider, that the three best political handicappers of their era were the three first cousins Alice Longworth, Eleanor Roosevelt, and my mother [Corinne Robinson Alsop]," he said.[23] Alice could act like a politician, too, as when she deftly conceded the defeat of her "man" while ingratiating herself with his vanquisher. "Dear Jack," she wrote to the president-elect a few weeks after the 1960 election, "I hardly need say that I hoped Dick would win! But more I want to send you my congratulations on your election, and best wishes to you and Jackie—and to that engaging Caroline—for happy years in the White House. Yours sincerely, Alice Roosevelt Longworth."[24]

In theory, Alice's unprecedented support for and friendship with a Democrat in the White House should have aligned her with Eleanor for the first time since the days of the first president Roosevelt. But the cousins stood so far apart now—on opposite poles in almost every way—that even Alice's willingness to consort with the enemy didn't bring them together. In fact, Eleanor didn't like, or trust, Kennedy very much. Alice would later say that was because Eleanor was a bigot, or at least a snob. "She didn't like the Catholics. Partly Catholics, but also because she was old-fashioned," Alice said. "In those times, the Irish were cops. They were of a certain class. It was a class thing, despite all she did."[25] It may sound like just another one of Alice's inflammatory cracks, but she wasn't the only one who felt that way. "She was worried about the influence of Cardinal Cushing in Boston and of the Roman Catholic Church in general," said Eleanor's grandson Curtis Roosevelt. "She was very plain about the fact that history showed that for politicians of avowed Roman Catholic persuasion this was a problem."[26]

Whether that was true—and Eleanor's support for Al Smith in 1924 would seem to undermine that theory—Kennedy had other strikes against him in Eleanor's mind. She thought he was inexperienced (especially in foreign affairs), arrogant, and too conservative. She especially disliked that he still refused to denounce McCarthy, even after she had called him out on it years earlier. In an excerpt from her autobiography *On My Own* published in the *Saturday Evening Post* in 1958, she said explicitly that she hadn't supported Kennedy as a 1956 vice presidential candidate because he'd never condemned McCarthy.[*] Here was another blunt contrast between practical Alice and principled Eleanor. Alice might have said she hated McCarthy, but that didn't stop her from holding her nose and following the crowd of insiders who attended his wedding. Eleanor not only couldn't let go of her convictions; she used them to beat Kennedy into a corner. He was eager to get Eleanor's blessing, but McCarthy had been the well-liked boss of his brother Robert and a friend of his father, Joe senior, who invited McCarthy to stay at the Kennedy houses in both Hyannisport and Palm Beach. Denouncing McCarthy now, even a year after his death, wouldn't be easy for JFK. "I would not, by the way, underestimate the importance of the kind of misgiving expressed by Mrs. R.," Arthur Schlesinger, Kennedy's chief adviser, warned in a letter in 1958. "You really have to meet it effectively before 1960."[27]

What Kennedy really needed, if he wanted to win the election, was to meet with Mrs. R. and plead his case. At seventy-five, and fifteen years removed from the White House, she still held sway over many of Franklin's supporters, especially the legions of black voters who adored her. In what was destined to become one of the closest presidential races in history, Kennedy couldn't afford to have any Roosevelt Democrats sit out the election. She finally agreed to meet with him, reluctantly, and only after her beloved Adlai Stevenson refused to run for a third time. "I remember saying to her, in her sitting room in Val-Kill, 'I don't think you can avoid seeing him. I think you've got to give him time. You'll be really criticized if you try to stay neutral but obviously not neutral by the very fact that you won't even see him, will not receive him,'" said Curtis. "She looked at me, long and hard, and said, 'All right, you can tell him to telephone.'"[28]

---

[*] On the day the Senate voted 67–22 to censure McCarthy, then-senator Kennedy was in a New York hospital undergoing an operation on his spine. When he went back to work and reporters asked how he would have voted, Kennedy begged off by saying, "Oh, that was a long time ago."

They scheduled a meeting for a Sunday morning in August. Kennedy was nervous enough to insist that his New York campaign coordinator make the pilgrimage to Hyde Park with him. "I want an ally with me," he said.[29] Then, to make matters worse, Eleanor's thirteen-year-old granddaughter Sally, one of John's daughters, was thrown from a horse while away at summer camp and died the day before Kennedy was due to arrive. *Grandmère* spent the night at her granddaughter's deathbed, and when word reached Kennedy of the tragedy, he offered to postpone their appointment. True to her family's death-be-not-proud ethos, the First Lady insisted that Kennedy come anyway, even though she had only an hour or two of sleep before he arrived. They talked for about an hour over folding tables and snacks. If she had thought him an untested, cocky politician who owed his success largely to his father's checkbook, he was determined to grovel and flatter his way into her good graces. "A visit to Hyde Park is both a pilgrimage and a challenge," he told the press corps waiting afterward to see if they had worked out a peace treaty. "For I come to Hyde Park not to instruct but to learn. And I think that we can all agree that Eleanor Roosevelt is a true teacher. Her very life teaches a love of truth and duty and courage."[30] That was apparently just what Eleanor needed to hear. "I liked him better than I ever had before because he seemed so little cocksure, and I think he has a mind open to new ideas," she wrote to a friend.[31] She signed on as honorary co-chair of the New York Committee for Kennedy and campaigned for him in several other states, including California, Illinois, and Indiana. She even felt comfortable enough to give the youngster a few pointers. Like Alice's conversation with Alsop, Eleanor had a few observations about the Nixon-Kennedy debate, and she dutifully wrote JFK a letter the next day, reporting the reaction among the people who watched on TV with her. "One person said to me that he felt you spoke a little too fast and had not yet mastered the habit of including your audience at every point," she said. "Someone else said they thought you appeared a little too confident. I did not agree with this, but I thought I should tell you."[32]

———

Once Kennedy settled into the Oval Office, Eleanor continued to treat him like a child in need of guidance, and he played the good son (and savvy politician). When she marched herself into the White House to complain about the paltry number of highly placed women in his administration, he created the President's Commission on the Status of Women—and made her co-chair.* He appointed her a delegate to a special session at the UN and the advisory board of the Peace Corps. He fielded her assorted job-candidate recommendations and even thanked her for yet another "most thoughtful and helpful" critique of one of his speeches, in which she admonished, "I still feel there is too much strain on your throat which should be completely free. Please try to take some lessons in breathing and projection because in the long run it will be useful in saving you time and effort."[33]

What neither Kennedy nor the rest of the world realized was that Eleanor Roosevelt was starting to die. Just before the election, she had been diagnosed with a bone marrow disease that slowly sapped her strength and energy. She was, of course, the last person who would accept that. "I suppose I should slow down," she said on October 11, 1961, her seventy-seventh birthday. "I think I have a good deal of my Uncle Theodore in me, because I could not, at any age, be content to take my place in a corner by the fireside and simply look on. Life was meant to be lived."[34] At seventy-five, she had accepted a job as a guest lecturer at Brandeis University, which meant hauling herself to Massachusetts for classes. She traveled as far as Europe to host her ongoing PBS public affairs show, *Prospects of Mankind*, and continued to write her My Day column until less than two months before she died.† And she was still lining up new projects. "I would like to invite you to appear with me on the first program of my new series of one-hour discussions," she wrote, in a letter dated September 21, 1962, to Martin Luther King Jr., with whom she had corresponded for many years.[35] The show, scheduled to be recorded on October 23, never happened. She died at her New York City apartment, surrounded by her children, on November 7, 1962. King sent the family a telegram

---

* The commission's most significant recommendation was that women deserved equal economic and civil rights, still a radical notion in the early 1960s. One relatively immediate result was that each of the fifty states established its own committee to study the question of gender equality. Unfortunately, Eleanor never got to see those seeds take root. She died before the commission's final report was presented to President Kennedy on October 11, 1963, a date chosen because it would have been her seventy-ninth birthday.

† Her final piece, dated September 26, 1962, starts by discussing a prominent New York City murder case before segueing into a call for school desegregation.

the next week. "Eleanor Roosevelt, as does Lincoln, belongs to the ages," he wrote.[36]

Though King never got a final meeting with Eleanor, she became a magnet to friends and family eager to spend time with her as she grew weaker. "Once Eleanor invited Helen [Mrs. Douglas Robinson, her first cousin] and myself over to Val-Kill for lunch," said Mary Morgan, another cousin and a Hudson valley neighbor. "We thought it would be a nice, small, intimate party and give us a chance to talk with Eleanor. Before we knew it, a delegation of 200 ladies arrived—colored. That was the way it was in the last years."[37]

She cherished these gatherings more than ever. "To me, all goodbyes are more poignant now," she wrote to Joe Lash.[38] For her final New Year's Eve, Eleanor invited a crowd to Val-Kill, almost like an open house. New Year's had always been an event at the Roosevelts'. When the family lived in the White House, they would frequently follow dinner with a movie or a live dramatic performance in the run-up to midnight. (There could be so many young people among the invitees that in 1939 two Washington teenagers were able to pass themselves off as guests, sneak up to the third floor of the White House, and ask the president for his autograph. He gave it to them.)[39] Typically, as the hour approached, the crowd would gather in the Oval Office, switch on the radio to check the exact time, and raise their cups of eggnog. FDR would issue his toast, "To the United States of America!" and the rest would echo him. After the president's death, Eleanor continued the tradition, whether she was in New York City or Hyde Park. In 1961, the family gathered at a serenely snowy Val-Kill. Eleanor gave FDR's traditionally patriotic tribute. The others in the room responded by raising their glasses to her.

Needless to say, Alice was not with Eleanor that night, though she could have been. "She invited everybody in the family, including Alice," said Nina Gibson, one of Eleanor's granddaughters who lived on the grounds of Val-Kill for the last decade of Eleanor's life. "She invited Alice all the time. She never showed." Given their history, it would be easy to chalk up Alice's absences to cruelty or indifference. But that wouldn't be fair. Alice had always been allergic to sentiment and especially to the conventions surrounding death. More than five years later, on June 7, 1968, she received a phone call from a woman named Marcella Comès Winslow, a well-known Washington portraitist who had been painting Alice. "Mrs.

Longworth, I'm sure you don't want to sit today, do you?" Winslow said. "Why not? What's wrong with you?" Alice replied. "Robert Kennedy has been shot," Winslow said. "Well, yes, what's wrong with you?" The sitting went on as scheduled.[40] (To top that off, Alice was equally incensed that Bobby was honored by being buried at Arlington National Cemetery, and at taxpayer expense. "It's beyond anything," she said. "Something so *forced* about it.")[41]

So the fact that Alice didn't say good-bye while Eleanor was alive, or at her star-studded funeral in Hyde Park (to which she was also invited), or at the memorial service in Washington's National Cathedral two miles from her Massachusetts Avenue town house, doesn't mean Alice didn't care. On the contrary, she might have cared too much. "It might have been that she felt so strongly that she didn't want to be seen in public, wrestling with her emotions," said Kristie Tankersley Miller, close friend of Alice's granddaughter, Joanna. "By then there was this very strong narrative about their being rivals. It would have been impossible to go to anything like that without having everybody scrutinize you. That's a no-win situation."[42]

Which isn't to say that Eleanor's death didn't affect Alice. Up to this point, she had limited her candor largely to politics. She had never agreed to interviews of any length. When she wrote about herself or her family in magazines, newspaper columns, or even her own autobiography, the results were defanged to the point of mush. After Eleanor died, she glee-fully started spilling her guts, opening the door and her mouth to almost anyone with a notebook. As one of the few Roosevelts from her genera-tion still alive, she took the opportunity to give her take on the past with-out fear of rebuttal. One reporter, Michael Teague, got enough from her to turn his chats into a book, *Mrs. L: Conversations with Alice Roosevelt Long-worth*, in which Alice calls Eleanor's insecurity about Franklin "pathetic" while she praises Lucy Mercer as "beautiful, charming, and an absolutely delightful creature."[43] When she turned eighty-five, the television news-magazine *60 Minutes* profiled Alice for the first time (it came back again when she turned ninety), and she again trotted out her Franklin-and-Lucy stories. This time she added that cruel explanation for having encouraged their affair: "He deserved a good time because he was married to Elea-nor."[44] With the cameras rolling and only a momentary stab at diffidence ("Oh, I don't think I ought to!"), she proceeded to share her infamous imitation of the First Lady with America. With her lips pulled tight and wide over her teeth, her chin pitched down toward her chest, and her eyes squinting and wild, she looked a bit like one of those toy monkeys that clap cymbals, only dressed in a conservative brown tweed suit.

But Alice and Eleanor's eight-decade relationship was nothing if not complicated, and Eleanor's death shook some surprising responses from her cousin. For one thing she became uncharacteristically complimentary. "Dame Rebecca West was rather funny once about Eleanor's tendency to treat this country as a giant slum area, and it is true that she could be both a prig and a bore," Alice told an interviewer. "But that does not detract from some of her really remarkable achievements. She had an extraordinary career. Of all the Presidents' wives, none used her position in quite the same effective way that Eleanor did."[45] It's tempting to say that Alice was mellowing with age, and that might have been part of it. In 1964, she even voted for Lyndon Johnson, the first time she'd ever pulled the lever for a Democrat. (She thought that Goldwater was "too mean.") But it's also true that without Eleanor—or her parents, her aunts, her brother Ted, Borah, and most of the family to whom she felt closest—she was free. She had spent much of her life creating her bad-girl persona. It was a sort of shield against the expectations and reputations of her uniquely accomplished family. "I'm the old fire-horse. I just perform. I give a good show—just one of the Roosevelt show-offs," she said in 1969.[46] Now that they were gone, she could afford to drop the mask on occasion and give Eleanor and Franklin their due. Her first public overture came in the spring of 1965, on the twentieth anniversary of FDR's death. A seven-ton block of Vermont marble was placed in front of the National Archives building that day, inscribed simply, "In Memory of Franklin Delano Roosevelt, 1882–1945." Among the smattering of relatives, friends, and politicians who attended (including President Johnson) was Alice. She paid her respects again in 1967, when the Johnsons invited her to the White House for the unveiling of a portrait of FDR—by Madame Shoumatoff, the artist who was painting FDR at the behest of Lucy Mercer when he died.

Alice didn't play nice for all that long. The next time she came to the Johnson White House, in 1968, she gleefully performed her Eleanor imitation, along with an equally biting version of Nellie Taft. "I like her tremendously," Lady Bird wrote in her diary that day, "although I always have the feeling that I must gird my armor, not so much as to do battle but to be ready, alert, at least."[47] Lady Bird was right: you can't teach an old dowager many new tricks, and for a long time now malice had been Alice's calling card. It's what kept her relevant, socially more than politically, well into her eighties. She was eighty-two when she slapped on a thirty-five-cent checkerboard mask and walked through the doors of New York's Plaza hotel for Truman Capote's "black and white" ball. By ninety, she was still in high demand. Her annual birthday party attracted enough fanfare to be featured on the national news. President Nixon was drowning in Watergate and would resign only six months later, but he still showed up at Alice's place, along with Pat, a music box with the presidential seal, and two tins of caviar, direct from the shah of Iran. Alice, in turn, was good enough to hide the Watergate banner she'd hung up in her house in the name of "good, unclean fun." "After he left, she took it out with great glee and delight," said her nephew Kermit.[48]

There were, however, two mainstays at the Longworth town house. In the summer, there was always poison ivy growing along the walkway leading to her front door. "Please, Mrs. L., couldn't I hire a yard man to clean out that ivy?" Stewart Alsop once asked her. "You cannot," she replied. "I like it."[49] The other fixture was a pillow embroidered with the saying "If you can't say something good about someone sit right here by me."

If Alice's game of spite and malice could be truly ugly at times, it was mitigated somewhat by her willingness to turn on herself. In 1970, when she was eighty-six, she had her second mastectomy. People didn't talk about cancer in polite company then, and they certainly didn't discuss female anatomy. But Alice Longworth did. She proudly proclaimed herself "Washington's Only Topless Octogenarian." She didn't include "Washington" in that description by accident. No town was (and still is) more full of itself than Washington, and no one punctured pomposity better than Alice. She knew more presidents—attended parties with them, played cards with them, exchanged advice and gossip with them—than anyone in history, yet she was determined to shrug it off as something just this side of mundane. "Somebody once calculated that I had been to an average of 2.7 dinners a year at the White House over a 60-year period," she once said. "That's an awful lot of dinner."[50]

Alice wasn't there for the most infamous White House meal in history—the day Richard Nixon ate crow. She was watching her old friend on TV on August 9, 1974, when he addressed the White House staff just after resigning from office. Ironically, Nixon's televised remarks that day did more to feed Alice's soul than any state dinner she ever attended. Ever the survivor, the now ex-president wanted his staff—and the world—to know that even this moment of abject humiliation and failure wouldn't defeat him. To make his point, he read an extended excerpt from the diary of another president who had faced the darkest of times and yet managed to come through them. "This quote is about a young man," Nixon explained by way of introduction.

> He was a young lawyer in New York. He'd married a beautiful girl. And they had a lovely daughter. And then suddenly, she died. And this was what he wrote. This was in his diary. He said, "She was beautiful in face and form and lovelier still in spirit. As a flower she grew and as a fair young flower she died. Her life had been always in the sunshine. There had never come to her a single great sorrow. None ever knew her who did not love and revere her for her bright and sunny temper and her saintly unselfishness. Fair, pure, and joyous as a maiden, loving tender and happy as a young wife. When she had just become a mother, when her life seemed to be just begun, and when the years seemed so bright before her, then by strange and terrible fate death came to her. And when my heart's dearest died, the light went from my life forever."

Sitting at home, Alice realized that the man Nixon was quoting was her own father, lamenting the loss of her mother. She had never heard any of this before. "Father never mentioned my mother's name to me, not once in my life. Just put her out of his mind, I thought," Alice said. Suddenly a light went on in the darkness—Alice's darkness. She could finally accept that her father had loved her mother. That, in turn, helped fill a gaping hole in her relationship with TR. "Listening to that part of the diary," Alice told the *New York Times* columnist William Safire when he came to her house for tea, "was like revealing a mystery."[51]

Alice had one other source of fulfillment in her sunset years: Joanna, the only child of her only child, the orphan Alice took in for her second chance at motherhood. Like Eleanor, who ultimately became a doting and beloved grandmother of twenty-four, Alice proved to be far more successful in her relationship with Joanna than she ever had been with Paulina. Alice and Joanna remained a tight-knit and intensely private family unit. As Alice aged into her tenth decade, Joanna subtly morphed from ward to caregiver. "Joanna, when did I start losing my memory?" Alice asked her when Safire was visiting. "You only began to get soft in the head about a year ago, Grandmother," she replied. "Wonderful child—irreverent, like me," the delighted Alice said.[52] When Safire remarked on how well Alice looked, she said, "I'm getting thin, but it's better to shrivel than to swell."[53]

Alice made her last visit to the White House as a guest of Nixon's successor, Gerald Ford, in the summer of 1976. Queen Elizabeth II was visiting the United States for the bicentennial, and Alice, who had met just about every British royal of the twentieth century, was a natural addition to the guest list. While Alice chatted with the queen about her memories of dining with Elizabeth's great-grandfather, Edward VII, she was carrying a diamond-rimmed purse that he had given her as a wedding present seventy years before. Alice also spotted Lady Bird Johnson across the room. "Shall I ask her how Lyndon is?" she inquired of her escort. "You can't do that, because he's dead," he replied. Even with her fading, ninety-two-year-old memory, Alice was still as quick as most folks can ever hope to be. "Oh, then," she said. "I shall ask her how Lyndon *was*."[54]

———

The month of February loomed large in Alice Longworth's life. It was the month of her birth, and, of course, of her mother's and grandmother's deaths. It was the month in which she was married and the month when Paulina was born. Fittingly, it was also when Alice Lee Roosevelt Longworth died, on February 20, 1980, eight days after her ninety-sixth birthday. There were numerous places she might have been buried: next to her husband in Cincinnati, her mother and grandmother in Brooklyn, or her father and stepmother in Oyster Bay. She chose a plot next to Paulina, in the heart of the city she adopted and adored. Washington's Rock Creek Church Yard sits less than five miles from the U.S. Capitol, which made it an ideal spot for the city's powerful men and women to pay their respects to "Washington's Other Monument." Except, perhaps for the first time, Alice didn't want their company. At the end of her life, she finally got the one thing that would have made her cousin Eleanor truly jealous: a burial service so private the date wasn't even publicized. There was no memorial, no visit from the president (which was just as well, given that the Democrat Jimmy Carter was hardly her type and was the first president in nine decades that Alice hadn't met). She didn't even have any last words. Her granddaughter, Joanna, who was at Alice's bedside when she died in her Massachusetts Avenue home, said that instead her grandmother issued a final gesture: she stuck out her tongue. Alice Roosevelt Longworth was defiant to the very end.

———

They were born in the same year and neighborhood, shared the same friends, lived in the same houses (including the White one), married the same types of men. They were arguably the most famous women in the country, if not the world, for extended periods of their lives, important enough to command audiences with presidents and kings. They were writers and lecturers, terrible mothers but beloved grandmothers. Above all, they were politicians. Even though they never ran for office, few women waded as deeply into the issues of the day. One of them whispered behind the scenes and one of them spoke to audiences around the world, but they both made their voices heard—and count. Even for a family knit into an extraordinarily tight cloth, Alice and Eleanor stopped at a remarkable number of the same milestones in their long and eventful lives.

It's tempting, because they shared so much yet ended up as political rivals, to choose sides between the sugar-and-spice cousins. Pitting Alice and Eleanor against each other was a favorite Washington parlor game for most of their later lives, a sort of Capitol Hill version of "Roosevelt Family Feud." To both women's credit, the partisans didn't always line up behind the expected choice. Arthur Schlesinger, JFK's close adviser, once remarked in his journal how he was surprised by "my reluctant recognition that I would rather spend an evening with Alice Longworth than with Eleanor Roosevelt. Politics, I came to conclude, is not everything."[55]

There's no question that Eleanor was more empathetic or that Alice was probably more fierce (even if Eleanor intimidated the hell out of JFK). Eleanor certainly accomplished more, both as the First Lady and as a United Nations delegate. But Alice changed history in her own ways, breaking social taboos and converting her celebrity into political access more effectively than any twenty-first-century PR genius could. Then again, meek Eleanor learned to love the limelight, too. She was even the first—and perhaps still the only—wife of a president to turn up on a TV game show: *What's My Line* in 1953. She tried to fool the blindfolded panelists about her identity. She failed.

There is certainly one way in which Eleanor triumphed over her cousin. She is still beloved, almost deified in some quarters, more than fifty years after her death. Alice outlived her by almost two decades, yet when she's remembered at all, it's for a cutting quip that she denied coining in the first place. Eleanor is historic. Alice is receding into a footnote. Why? In large part because Alice couldn't be bothered with the kind of "important" work required to earn a place in history. She didn't care much for work at all. It was, after "bore," second on her list of four-letter words, something to be avoided at all costs, like a quiet dinner followed by knitting. Alice lived in the moment and for her own amusement, an understandable attitude for a girl whose mother and grandmother died two days after she was born. Life is short. Enjoy it while you can. "The key to eternal youth," she liked to say, "is arrested development." The only problem with that carpe diem philosophy, as far as posterity is concerned, is that it's not all that concerned with posterity. The most blunt evidence of that is written right on Alice's death certificate. In the space asking for her occupation, the word that's been filled in is "gadfly."[56]

Some people would consider that line of work a disappointment, if not an outright failure. Eleanor certainly did. "Her life gave me a feeling of dreariness & waste," she'd said about her cousin. The feeling was mutual. While Alice ultimately gave Eleanor credit for her significant achievements, she never really thought that the First Lady was fulfilled. How could she be? Eleanor once said in a My Day column that there were three "fundamentals for human happiness": work, love, and faith—in that order. None of those would have made Alice's three-item short list. Like so many quotes attributed to her, there's no proof that she actually said, "I have a simple philosophy: Fill what's empty. Empty what's full. Scratch where it itches," but it's an apt (and fittingly ribald) distillation of her do-it-if-it-feels-good credo. In a way, the cousins were reverse role models for each other, examples of how *not* to live. They spent a good deal of their lives looking over their shoulders at each other and running as fast as they could in the opposite direction. It's hard to blame them. Princess Alice was Washington royalty for almost eighty years. Eleanor became the First Lady of the World. Who would want to compete with either of them?

———

But focusing on the differences between Mrs. Republican and Mrs. Democrat shouldn't distract from their unique bond. For a country that has so thoroughly embraced a republican form of government, America has produced a surprising number of political dynasties. The Adamses, Harrisons, and Bushes each produced two presidents, and the Kennedys filled a remarkable number of elective offices at all levels. By some measures, the Roosevelts were the most successful of them all. In the first half of the twentieth century, either Theodore or Franklin was on a national ticket for eight of the twelve presidential elections between 1900 and 1944. What's more, no other political family dominated two political parties—three, if you include TR's short-lived Progressives. And no other family produced two women who dominated the national conversation as thoroughly as Alice Longworth and Eleanor Roosevelt. Collectively, their names appeared on the front page of the *New York Times* more than four hundred times, on matters trivial to international. Between them, they lived in the White House for more than twenty years. They met countless heads of state, over a span of eight decades and representing countries on every continent save Antarctica. "Intellectually, spiritually, the city is dominated by the last good thing said by Alice Longworth," said the British author Rebecca West after touring the United States in 1935, just as Eleanor was reaching the height of her influence during the FDR administration.

For all their prominence, it's hard not to wonder how much more these two fearless and determined female Roosevelts would have accomplished if they hadn't been pushing against gender barriers at almost every turn. Despite their refusal to abide by many of society's taboos, Alice and Eleanor couldn't help but be conscious of, and to some extent restrained by, them. Certainly, few men would have so consistently underplayed their accomplishments, their experience, and the clout that accrues from rubbing elbows with the most powerful people in the country. Yet Eleanor spent most of her life denying she had any real influence, over either her husband or the world at large.* Alice would argue the same about her ability to sway her father, her husband, her lover, or any of the politicians who went out of their way to seek her counsel for the better part of fifty years. "I knew what was going on, and I enjoyed talking to people, but I never

---

* "I was often supposed to be a great influence on my husband politically," Eleanor wrote in *The Autobiography*. "Frances Perkins's appointment to the Cabinet is a case in point. As a matter of fact, I never even suggested her. She had worked with Franklin in New York State and was his choice" (132). What she conveniently forgets to mention was that she lobbied hard to get Franklin to appoint Perkins the labor commissioner in New York State and kept close tabs on Perkins's progress throughout her years working with FDR. Lash, *Eleanor and Franklin*, 323.

exerted influence intentionally," Alice said in 1967. "Women may have influence but not political influence."[57] Maybe she believed that, or maybe she thought ladies shouldn't brag. In either case, she was clearly selling herself short. Alice had enough "influence" to generate regular bursts of enthusiasm to draft her as a senatorial or vice presidential candidate. A similar Eleanor-for-VP bubble formed in 1948. Even Truman didn't have the nerve to shoot down the idea. Eleanor took care of that herself.

And yet despite their social, political, and personal handicaps, their passions have proven to be both resilient and timeless. The issues they fought over so fiercely—the role of government in helping the poor or righting the economy, the role of America on the world stage—have reclaimed the debate with a force not seen since Franklin's administration. Many of Alice's rants against the New Deal would sound utterly current in twenty-first-century America; so would Eleanor's laments about social and economic inequality. In fact, their feuding itself seems of the moment, right down to the multimedia mudslinging that is a bitter hallmark of America's deeply divided, red-blue political landscape. Bickering politicians often seem like a big dysfunctional family. Given that the Roosevelts *were* a big dysfunctional family, the hissing cousins may offer valuable lessons for today.

It's easy to forget that Alice's and Eleanor's larger ideas flowed from the same political headwater: Theodore Roosevelt. A brilliant man, a canny politician, and a larger-than-life personality, he sat astride the American consciousness as surely as he and his neighbors, Washington, Lincoln, and Jefferson, gaze out from Mount Rushmore.* Roosevelt's views on war and peace, regulating corporate America, protecting the environment, social justice, government spending, and more were complex and at times confounding enough that both his daughter and his niece could legitimately claim to be carrying on his legacy, even as they followed it along vastly different paths. Maybe that's why Alice and Eleanor fought like kids on the school yard yet never forgot they were playing for the same American team. They could still occasionally eat dinner together or attend a wedding—or a funeral. In times of crisis—whether it was Pearl Harbor

---

* It said much about his stature and impact that the decision to include Theodore Roosevelt with the nation's three most revered presidents on Mount Rushmore attracted little controversy, even though he had been dead less than ten years.

or the death of Paulina—they managed to call a truce, at least for a time. "Fundamental Roosevelt characteristics gravitate toward each other in times of stress,"[58] Eleanor wrote optimistically in My Day. And when the crisis had passed or the dinner was done, in the true spirit of TR, the battle was joined anew.

# ACKNOWLEDGMENTS

..........................................

When people ask us where we got the idea for a book on the esteemed Roosevelt family, we get a kick out of replying with the honest-to-goodness truth: from a children's book called *What to Do About Alice?* Written by Barbara Kerley and illustrated by Edwin Fotheringham, it was a gift to our young daughters—and a revelation to us. We had read about and studied the Roosevelts over the years, but we knew almost nothing about the high-spirited "guttersnipe" who drove her presidential father to distraction. She was so naughty, so funny—and so unlike that *other* Roosevelt woman we knew. Or was she? The more we delved into Alice's story with our own girls, the more we discovered remarkable parallels between her and Eleanor, starting with their common birth year (1884) and including their heartbreaking childhoods, philandering husbands, and, of course, a shared address: 1600 Pennsylvania Avenue. With all the books written about the Roosevelts, surely someone had explored the overlapping lives of these extraordinary first cousins. When we found that no one had, we decided to take the plunge. And here we are, five years later.

We owe an enormous debt to the countless dedicated professionals working in libraries and research institutions who assisted us. The Theodore Roosevelt Collection at Harvard, the Franklin Delano Roosevelt Library at Hyde Park, the Library of Congress, the New York Public Library, the Columbia University Library, and the Courtauld Institute of Art were all welcoming and invaluable sources of information.

In a moment of true serendipity, Liz Perelstein gave us our first introduction to the Oyster Bay Roosevelts, which allowed us to begin researching the various branches of the family tree. Several Roosevelt family members and friends shared their invaluable recollections with us. In particular, Stacy Cordery, Kermit Roosevelt, Nina Roosevelt Gibson, Curtis Roosevelt, Eleanor McMillan, Ruth Tankersley, and Kristie Miller helped us to see past the myths and get closer to the women at the heart of our story.

Beatrice Stein first alerted us to Alice's connection to her remarkable and largely unknown French nephew, René de Chambrun. Paul Bailey and Linda Lees both toiled countless hours in far-flung research institutions helping us track down some hard-to-find letters and photos. Hal Freedman and Margy Popper not only volunteered to read our first complete draft; they devoured and dissected it with the kind of care and comprehension any writer would cherish.

We are grateful to Nan Talese for taking a chance on us, and we are enormously indebted to our brilliant, patient, and wise editor, Ronit Wagman. And when this whole project was still just a half-baked idea, Richard Pine at Inkwell Management listened to it, painstakingly shaped it, and found just the right place to publish it.

Last, we have to thank our families and friends, who suffered through years of Roosevelt-laden dinner conversations and did their best to at least *seem* interested. Through our years in the greater *Newsweek* family, we were lucky to befriend a few successful authors, and to a person they made us believe that our project would someday join theirs on the bookshelf. In our determination to tell this story as accurately and completely as possible, we were always guided by the spirit of Thomas J. Dwyer, whose love of history informs every page of this book.

# NOTES

........................................

*Abbreviations*

CUOHP Columbia University Oral History Project.
FDRL Franklin Delano Roosevelt Library, Hyde Park, N.Y.
LOC Library of Congress.
TRB Theodore Roosevelt Birthplace.
TRC Theodore Roosevelt Collection, Houghton Library, Harvard University.


CHAPTER I: ORPHANS

1.  Levy and Russett, *Extraordinary Mrs. R*, 245.
2.  Patricia Peabody Roosevelt, *I Love a Roosevelt*, 218.
3.  "Hearing Set for 2 Men Accused of Having Signs at Mrs. Roosevelt's Rites," *Poughkeepsie Journal*, Nov. 14, 1962.
4.  The Reverend Gordon Kidd, oral history interview, June 7, 1978, FDRL.
5.  Lash, *Eleanor: The Years Alone*, 271.
6.  Corinne Roosevelt to Anna Roosevelt, Aug. 1, 1888, TRC.
7.  ARL, interview by Henry Brandon, May 25, 1967, LOC.
8.  Edmund Morris, *Rise of Theodore Roosevelt*, 240.
9.  Anna Bullock to Corinne Roosevelt, Feb. 1884, TRC.
10. TR diary, Feb. 14, 1884, TRC.
11. Sewall, *Bill Sewall's Story of T.R.*, 47.
12. Teague, *Mrs. L*, 22.
13. Ibid., 13.
14. Ibid., 5.
15. Ibid.
16. Ibid., 18.
17. Ibid., 10.
18. Joseph Alsop, *I've Seen the Best of It*, 30.

19. "The Week in Society," *New York Daily Tribune*, Nov. 25, 1883.
20. "Chimes at Calvary," *New York Evening Telegram*, Dec. 1, 1883.
21. Cook, *Eleanor Roosevelt*, 1:62.
22. Eleanor Roosevelt, *Autobiography*, 9.
23. Eleanor Roosevelt, *This Is My Story*, 5.
24. Anna Gracie to Corinne Roosevelt, (n.d.), TRC.
25. Anna Gracie to Anna Roosevelt, June 6 (no year), TRC.
26. Lash, *Eleanor and Franklin*, 31.
27. Anna Gracie to Corinne Roosevelt, June 6 (no year).
28. TR to Anna Roosevelt, Sept. 20, 1886, TRC.
29. Teague, *Mrs. L*, 5.
30. Anna Roosevelt Cowles, unpublished memoir, 3, TRB.
31. "Elliott Roosevelt Mad," *New York Herald*, Aug. 18, 1891.
32. Cook, *Eleanor Roosevelt*, 1:68.
33. Lash, *Eleanor and Franklin*, 41.
34. Eleanor Roosevelt, *This Is My Story*, 17–18.
35. Anna Roosevelt to Anna Roosevelt Cowles, TRC.
36. Eleanor Roosevelt, *This Is My Story*, 13.
37. ER, interview by Mary Hagedorn, CUOHP, Jan. 18, 1955.
38. Teague, *Mrs. L*, 154.
39. Eleanor Roosevelt, *This Is My Story*, 35.
40. Steinberg, *Mrs. R*, 65.
41. Ibid., 11.
42. Teague, *Mrs. L*, 42.
43. Eleanor Roosevelt, *Autobiography*, 19.
44. Teague, *Mrs. L*, 109.
45. Ibid., 51.
46. Teague, *Mrs. L*, 18.
47. Helen Roosevelt Robinson, oral history, interview conducted by William Savacool, Dec. 8, 1955, CUOHP.
48. Hagedorn, *Roosevelt Family of Sagamore Hill*, 38.
49. Edith Roosevelt to Emily Carow, n.d., TRC.
50. Teague, *Mrs. L*, 30.
51. Cook, *Eleanor Roosevelt*, 1:75.
52. Elliott Roosevelt to ER, Oct. 9, 1892, FDRL.
53. Eleanor Roosevelt, *This Is My Story*, 29.
54. Ibid., 15–16.
55. Lash, *Eleanor and Franklin*, 44.
56. Eleanor Roosevelt, *This Is My Story*, 59.
57. Steinberg, *Mrs. R*, 27.
58. ER to Elliott Roosevelt, n.d., FDRL.
59. TR to Anna Roosevelt, Aug. 18, 1894, TRC.
60. Cook, *Eleanor Roosevelt*, 1:87
61. Ibid., 88.
62. Eleanor Roosevelt, *This Is My Story*, 13.
63. Ibid., 35.
64. Corinne Robinson Cole, interview by Joseph Lash, April 17, 1967, FDRL.
65. Persico, *Franklin and Lucy*, 26.

66. Longworth, *Crowded Hours*, 12.
67. Teague, *Mrs. L*, 13.
68. Edith Roosevelt to Gertrude Carow, Nov. 4, 1893, TRC.
69. Edith Roosevelt to Anna Roosevelt Cowles, May 18, 1895, TRC.
70. Rixey, *Bamie*, 76.
71. ER to Aunt Bye, Nov. 15, 1895, TRC.
72. Corinne Alsop diary, 3, TRB.
73. Mrs. Sheldon Tilney, oral history, April 24, 1955.
74. Eleanor Roosevelt, *Autobiography*, p. 18.
75. Teague, *Mrs. L*, 155.
76. Collier, *Roosevelts*, 106.
77. Helen Roosevelt to FDR, Nov. 9, 1897, FDRL.
78. Teague, *Mrs. L*, 52–53.
79. Ibid., 18.
80. Cordery, *Alice*, 36.
81. TR to Anna Roosevelt Cowles, Feb. 23, 1898, TRC.
82. Teague, *Mrs. L*, 57.
83. Ibid., 108–9.
84. Longworth, *Crowded Hours*, 26.
85. Ibid.
86. Mr. and Mrs. Sheffield Cowles, oral history interview with Hermann Hagedorn, Dec. 28, 1954, CUOHP.
87. Steinberg, *Mrs. R*, 35.

CHAPTER 2: HOME ABROAD

1. Edmund Morris, *Rise of Theodore Roosevelt*, 169.
2. Theodore Roosevelt, *Autobiography*, 76.
3. Edmund Morris, *Rise of Theodore Roosevelt*, 171.
4. Longworth, *Crowded Hours*, 34.
5. www.nps.gov/thri/theodoreRooseveltbio.htm.
6. Longworth, *Crowded Hours*, 34.
7. Edmund Morris, *Rise of Theodore Roosevelt*, 729.
8. Teague, *Mrs. L*, 62.
9. ER to ARL, dated only "Tuesday," FDRL.
10. Eleanor Roosevelt, *This Is My Story*, 55.
11. Ibid., 58.
12. Ibid., 59.
13. Lash, *Eleanor and Franklin*, 81.
14. Eleanor Roosevelt, *This Is My Story*, 29.
15. Cook, *Eleanor Roosevelt*, 1:115.
16. Teague, *Mrs. L*, 151.
17. "Few Girls So Prominent," *Baltimore Sun*, Feb. 26, 1902.
18. "Fair Debutante of the White House," *Los Angeles Times*, Jan. 4, 1902.
19. "White House Ball," *Baltimore Sun*, Jan. 4, 1902.
20. Longworth, *Crowded Hours*, 47.
21. Teague, *Mrs. L*, 76.

22. Franklin Delano Roosevelt, *Personal Letters*, 1:467.
23. "A Brilliant Gathering Greets Miss Alice Roosevelt," *Washington Post*, Jan. 4, 1902.
24. "Miss Roosevelt as She Really Looks—from Photographs Taken a Few Days Ago," *Chicago Tribune*, Jan. 27, 1902.
25. "Miss Roosevelt Much in the Public Eye," *Los Angeles Times*, Jan. 10, 1902.
26. "Miss Roosevelt Names Kaiser Wilhelm's Yacht," *New York Times*, Feb. 26, 1902.
27. Cook, *Eleanor Roosevelt*, 1:115.
28. Corinne Roosevelt Cole, interview by Lash, April 17, 1967, FDRL.
29. "Society at Home and Abroad," *New York Times*, Dec. 14, 1902.
30. Eleanor Roosevelt, *Your Teens and Mine*, 48.
31. ARL diary, Dec. 17, 1902, LOC.
32. Steinberg, *Mrs. R*, 44.
33. Cook, *Eleanor Roosevelt*, 2:132.
34. Steinberg, *Mrs. R*, 44.
35. Ward, *Before the Trumpet*, 307.
36. Rowley, *Franklin and Eleanor*, 29.
37. Kleeman, *Gracious Lady*, 197.
38. Jean Edward Smith, *FDR*, 32.
39. Sara Delano Roosevelt, *My Boy Franklin*, 55–56.
40. Ward, *Before the Trumpet*, 307.
41. Ibid., 308.
42. SDR diary, Nov. 26, 1903, FDRL.
43. Ibid., Dec. 1, 1903.
44. ER to SDR, Dec. 2, 1903, FDRL.
45. *Town Topics*, July 2, 1903.
46. ARL diary, Jan. 27, 1902.
47. TR to ARL, Nov. 19, 1903, TRC.
48. Teague, *Mrs. L*, 71–72.
49. "Miss Roosevelt Betrothed?," *Baltimore African-American*, Feb. 28, 1903.
50. "Alice Roosevelt's Suitors," *Baltimore Sun*, May 4, 1902.
51. ARL diary, May 8, 1902.
52. Hagedorn, *Roosevelt Family of Sagamore Hill*, 188.
53. "Miss Alice Roosevelt Not Yet Caught by Cupid," *Atlanta Journal-Constitution*, July 19, 1902.
54. Felicia Warburg Roosevelt, *Doers and Dowagers*, 221.
55. *Washington Mirror*, June 3, 1905.
56. "Alice Roosevelt and Her Cane," *Baltimore Sun*, May 11, 1902.
57. "Public Likes Miss Roosevelt," *Washington Bee*, May 28, 1904.
58. "Miss Roosevelt Loses Her Way," *New York Herald*, Aug. 19, 1902.
59. "Miss Alice Weeps," *Los Angeles Times*, June 14, 1903.
60. TR to Corinne Roosevelt Robinson, Sept. 23, 1903, TRC.
61. "An 83-Year-Old Enfant Terrible," *New York Times*, Aug. 6, 1967.
62. "President's Daughter an Enthusiast," *Motor Age*, Oct. 6, 1904, 21.
63. Beard, *After the Ball*, 134.
64. Cassini, *Never a Dull Moment*, 188.
65. Beard, *After the Ball*, 172.
66. ER to FDR, Jan. 6, 1904, FDRL.
67. ER to FDR, Jan. 30, 1904, FDRL.

68. Eleanor Roosevelt, *This Is My Story*, 108.

69. Teague, *Mrs. L*, 151, 160.

70. Ibid., 36.

71. Lash, *Eleanor and Franklin*, 123.

72. Corinne Alsop diary, 37, TRB.

73. Ibid., 36–37.

74. "President Sees His Cousin Wed," *New York Times*, June 19, 1904.

75. ARL to ER, n.d., FDRL.

76. Lash, *Eleanor and Franklin*, 138.

77. ARL to ER, n.d., FDRL.

78. Eleanor Roosevelt, *Your Teens and Mine*, 184–85.

79. Longworth, *Crowded Hours*, 67.

80. Teague, *Mrs. L*, 72.

81. Pottker, *Sara and Eleanor*, 112.

82. Teague, *Mrs. L*, 156.

83. Lash, *Eleanor and Franklin*, 140.

84. Pottker, *Sara and Eleanor*, 113.

85. Eleanor Roosevelt, *This Is My Story*, 50.

86. Teague, *Mrs. L*, 156.

87. Cordery, *Alice*, 101.

88. http://www.ohiohistorycentral.org/w/Nicholas_Longworth.

89. Teague, *Mrs. L*, 76.

90. *Town Topics*, Feb. 11, 1904.

91. Cordery, *Alice*, 100.

92. Martin, *Cissy*, 93.

93. Cassini, *Never a Dull Moment*, 190.

94. Ibid., 199.

95. Cordery, *Alice*, 107.

96. ARL diary, May 1, 1904.

97. Cassini, *Never a Dull Moment*, 200.

98. ARL diary, May 1, 1904.

99. Cassini, *Never a Dull Moment*, 188.

100. TR to George von Lengerke Meyer, Feb. 6, 1905, in *Letters of Theodore Roosevelt*, 4:1115.

101. TR to John Hay, April 2, 1905, in *Letters of Theodore Roosevelt*, 4:1156.

102. TR to ARL, May 27, 1903.

103. Bradley, *Imperial Cruise*, 244.

104. Ibid., 260.

105. Teague, *Mrs. L*, 98.

106. Ibid.

107. Ibid.

108. Longworth, *Crowded Hours*, 71.

109. Ibid., 78.

110. Bradley, *Imperial Cruise*, 254.

111. Cordery, *Alice*, 130.

112. Bradley, *Imperial Cruise*, 245.

113. Cordery, *Alice*, 133.

114. Ibid., 135.

115. FDR and ER to SDR, June 22, 1905, FDRL.
116. Pottker, *Sara and Eleanor*, 137.
117. ARL to ER, Dec. 5, 1905, FDRL.
118. "Miss Alice Roosevelt's Engagement Announced," *New York Times*, Dec. 14, 1905.


CHAPTER 3: DOMESTIC AFFAIRS

1. "The President a Guest at Longworth Dinner," *New York Times*, Feb. 16, 1906; "Mr. Longworth a Busy Man Two Days Before Wedding," *Washington Post*, Feb. 16, 1906.
2. "Miss Roosevelt Goes Back to Washington," *New York Times*, Feb. 1, 1906.
3. "10,000 Wedding Invitations," *Baltimore Sun*, Jan. 19, 1906.
4. "Miss Roosevelt Climbs Rope Ladder to Liner," *New York Times*, Jan. 31, 1906.
5. Longworth, *Crowded Hours*, 111.
6. Ibid., 110.
7. "Ohio Senate Divided," *New York Times*, Feb. 16, 1906.
8. "Rehearse Wedding," *Boston Daily Globe*, Feb. 16, 1906.
9. "Longworth Gets Wedding License," *Chicago Daily Tribune*, Feb. 16, 1906.
10. Cordery, *Alice*, 144.
11. "Wit and Oratory Flow from Fingers of Mutes," *New York Times*, Feb. 9, 1906.
12. "Girls Cheer Wedding," *New York Times*, Feb. 18, 1906.
13. Gould, *Edith Kermit Roosevelt*, 69.
14. Wister, *Roosevelt*, 87.
15. Teague, *Mrs. L*, 84.
16. "Roosevelt Coat of Arms on the Wedding Dress," *New York Times*, Feb. 4, 1906.
17. Ibid.
18. Lash, *Eleanor and Franklin*, 154.
19. Teague, *Mrs. L*, 128.
20. David Roosevelt, *Grandmère*, 98.
21. Eleanor Roosevelt, *This Is My Story*, 151.
22. Ibid., 163.
23. Ibid., 165.
24. James Roosevelt, *My Parents*, 25.
25. Eleanor Roosevelt, *This Is My Story*, 162.
26. Pottker, *Sara and Eleanor*, 162.
27. Longworth, *Crowded Hours*, 134.
28. Clara Longworth de Chambrun, *Making of Nicholas Longworth*, 184.
29. Ibid., 193.
30. Teague, *Mrs. L*, 138.
31. "Where Alice Roosevelt Will Live After Her Marriage," *Chicago Daily Tribune*, Jan. 28, 1906.
32. Teague, *Mrs. L*, 137.
33. Longworth, *Crowded Hours*, 134.
34. Teague, *Mrs. L*, 139.
35. Teichmann, *Alice*, 70.
36. Longworth, *Crowded Hours*, 137.
37. Cordery, *Alice*, 188.
38. "Princess Alice Is Vote-Getter," *Weekly Sentinel* (Ft. Wayne, Ind.), Nov. 7, 1906.

39. "Helping Her Husband," *Washington Post*, Nov. 5, 1906.
40. Cordery, *Alice*, 180.
41. "Helping Her Husband," *Washington Post*, Nov. 5, 1906.
42. Longworth, *Crowded Hours*, 148.
43. Ibid.
44. Ibid., 149.
45. "Women in the Picture," *Washington Post*, June 18, 1908.
46. "Alice Compelled to Remove Merry Widow," *San Francisco Chronicle*, June 17, 1908.
47. Butt, *Letters*, 327.
48. Teague, *Mrs. L*, 140.
49. Ibid.
50. ER to Isabella Ferguson, Jan. 8, 1909, FDRL.
51. ARL to ER, Dec. 23, 1907, FDRL.
52. Grenville Clark, Roosevelt Memorial Issue, *Harvard Alumni Review*, April 28, 1945.
53. Persico, *Franklin and Lucy*, 73.
54. Davis, *FDR*, 246.
55. Eleanor Roosevelt, *This Is My Story*, 174.
56. Ibid., 171.
57. Steinberg, *Mrs. R*, 80.
58. Lash, *Eleanor and Franklin*, 178.
59. Howe to FDR, July 1912, FDRL.
60. Alter, *Defining Moment*, 38; Freidel, *Franklin D. Roosevelt*, 150.
61. Steinberg, *Mrs. R*, 82.
62. Rollins, *Roosevelt and Howe*, 59.
63. Butt, *Taft and Roosevelt*, 840.
64. "Roosevelt to Make a Statement To-day," *New York Times*, Feb. 25, 1912.
65. "My Hat's in the Ring," Associated Press, Feb. 22, 1912.
66. ARL diary, Feb. 16, 1912, LOC.
67. Longworth, *Crowded Hours*, 186.
68. ARL diary, Feb. 15, 1912, LOC.
69. Ibid., Feb. 16, 1912.
70. Longworth, *Crowded Hours*, 192.
71. ARL diary, Feb. 21, 1912, LOC.
72. Ibid., Feb. 16, 1912.
73. Edmund Morris, *Colonel Roosevelt*, 215.
74. "Longworth in Trouble," *New York Times*, June 24, 1912.
75. "Delegates Begin to Arrive," *New York Times*, June 24, 1912.
76. Ibid.
77. Teague, *Mrs. L*, 158.
78. ER to Isabella Ferguson, July 8, 1912, in *A Volume of Friendship*, 47.
79. "Delegates Begin to Arrive," *New York Times*, June 24, 1912.
80. Eleanor Roosevelt, *This Is My Story*, 189.
81. Longworth, *Crowded Hours*, 206.
82. Eleanor Roosevelt, *This Is My Story*, 189.
83. Cook, *Eleanor Roosevelt*, 1:197.
84. Gilbert King, "Theodore Roosevelt's Life-Saving Speech," *Smithsonian Magazine* blog, April 25, 2012.
85. Cordery, *Alice*, 233.

86. Lewis, *Life of Theodore Roosevelt*, 381.

87. "Mrs. Roosevelt Left Theatre in Tears," *New York Times*, Oct. 15, 1912.

88. "Would-Be Assassin Is John Schrank, Once Saloonkeeper Here," *New York Times*, Oct. 15, 1912.

89. ARL diary, Oct. 4, 1912.

90. "Johnson Quits Indiana," *New-York Tribune*, Sept. 21, 1912.

91. Longworth, *Crowded Hours*, 218.

92. ARL diary, Nov. 3, 1912.

CHAPTER 4: OTHER WOMEN

1. Eleanor Roosevelt, *This Is My Story*, 207.

2. Gunther, *Roosevelt in Retrospect*, 209, 89.

3. Stirling, *Sea Duty*, 142.

4. Eleanor Roosevelt, *This Is My Story*, 195–96.

5. "The History of the Calling Card," americanstationery.com, posted Dec. 3, 2012.

6. Eleanor Roosevelt, *This Is My Story*, 206.

7. Ibid.

8. Longworth, *Crowded Hours*, 225.

9. Ibid.

10. "The Boudoir Mirrors of Washington," *Baltimore Sun*, Feb. 24, 1924.

11. Eleanor Roosevelt, *This Is My Story*, 206.

12. Ibid., 206–7.

13. Longworth, *Crowded Hours*, 234.

14. Ibid., 238.

15. Cordery, *Alice*, 243.

16. Felsenthal, *Princess Alice*, 96.

17. "Longworths Back in Capital," *Washington Post*, Feb. 26, 1915.

18. ER to Isabella Ferguson, Dec. 21, 1915, in *A Volume of Friendship*, 130.

19. Teague, *Mrs. L*, 156.

20. Ibid., 156–57.

21. TR to ER, March 15, 1915, FDRL.

22. "Franklin Aids T.R.," *Baltimore Sun*, May 5, 1915.

23. TR to FDR, May 29, 1915, FDRL.

24. Kay, *Roosevelt's Navy*, 171–72.

25. Ibid., 87.

26. Ward, *Before the Trumpet*, 335.

27. Teague, *Mrs. L*, 156.

28. June Bingham, "Before the Colors Fade: Alice Roosevelt Longworth," *American Heritage*, Feb. 1969, 42–43, 73–77.

29. Teague, *Mrs. L*, 157.

30. Asbell, *FDR Memoirs*, 229.

31. SDR to ER, March 24, 1915, FDRL.

32. FDR to ER, July 7, 1916, FDRL.

33. Persico, *Franklin and Lucy*, 98.

34. FDR to ER, July 16, 1917, FDRL.

35. FDR to ER, July 25, 1917, FDRL.

36. Persico, *Franklin and Lucy*, 100.
37. Bingham, "Before the Colors Fade."
38. Woollcott to Joseph Alsop, Dec. 26, 1936, Houghton Library, Harvard University.
39. Lash, *Love, Eleanor*, 69.
40. Lash, *Eleanor and Franklin*, 226.
41. ARL, interview by Lash, April 5, 1966, FDRL.
42. Persico, *Franklin and Lucy*, 84.
43. ARL, interview by Lash, April 5, 1966.
44. ARL, interview by Jonathan Aitken on "The Reporters," aired April 22, 1969.
45. Nina Roosevelt Gibson, author interview, March 5, 2013.
46. Teague, *Mrs. L*, 157.
47. ARL, interview by Lash, Feb. 2, 1967, FDRL.
48. Stewart Alsop, *Center*, 80.
49. Joseph Alsop, *I've Seen the Best of It*, 92.
50. Cordery, *Alice*, 250.
51. Persico, *Franklin and Lucy*, 108.
52. Joseph Alsop, *FDR*, 67.
53. Ferguson to ER, n.d., *A Volume of Friendship*, 137.
54. ER to Ferguson, June 21, 1916, *A Volume of Friendship*, 139.
55. Eleanor Roosevelt, *This Is My Story*, 251.
56. TR to Archibald Roosevelt, Sept. 8, 1917.
57. Edmund Morris, *Colonel Roosevelt*, 486.
58. Tumulty, *Woodrow Wilson as I Knew Him*, 288.
59. Eleanor Roosevelt, *This Is My Story*, 251.
60. Teague, *Mrs. L*, 162.
61. Longworth, *Crowded Hours*, 258.
62. Teichmann, *Alice,* 100.
63. Teichmann, *Alice*, 102.
64. Cordery, *Alice*, 269.
65. ER to Ferguson, April 2, 1918, FDRL.
66. Lash, *Eleanor and Franklin*, 215.
67. Felsenthal, *Princess Alice*, 138.
68. Eleanor Roosevelt, *This Is My Story*, 255.
69. Felsenthal, *Princess Alice*, 138.
70. "How to Save in Big Homes," *New York Times*, July 17, 1917.
71. Cook, *Eleanor Roosevelt*, 1:211.
72. Sally Quinn, "Alice Roosevelt Longworth at 90," *Washington Post*, Feb. 12, 1974.
73. Teague, *Mrs. L*, 162.
74. Ibid., 162–63.
75. Collier, *Roosevelts*, 232.
76. Hagedorn, *Roosevelt Family of Sagamore Hill*, 413–14.
77. F. Trubee Davison, interview by Mary Hagedorn, March 30, 1955.
78. ER to Isabella Ferguson, July 28, 1918, in *A Volume of Friendship,* 157.
79. FDR to ER, July 27, 1917, FDRL.
80. FDR to ER, Aug. 15, 1917, FDRL.
81. Persico, *Franklin and Lucy*, 102.
82. Roosevelt and Brough, *Untold Story*, 89.
83. ER to FDR, n.d., FDRL.

84.  Margaret Cutting, interview by Lash, Aug. 13, 1966, FDRL.

85.  Teague, *Mrs. L*, 160–61.

86.  Franklin Delano Roosevelt, "European Inspection Tour, July 30, 1918," in *F.D.R.: His Personal Letters, 1905–1928*, 391.

87.  Eleanor Roosevelt, *This Is My Story*, 267.

88.  ER to SDR, July 17, 1918, FDRL.

89.  Cook, *Eleanor Roosevelt*, 1:227.

90.  Eleanor Roosevelt, *This Is My Story*, 268.

91.  Kay, *Roosevelt's Navy*, 238.

92.  Lash, *Love, Eleanor*, 66.

CHAPTER 5: THE BREAK BEGINS

1.   Sylvia Jukes Morris, *Edith Kermit Roosevelt*, 431; Edmund Morris, *Colonel Roosevelt*, 541.

2.   "Roosevelt Bitter in Beginning War on the President," *New York Times*, Oct. 29, 1918.

3.   Robinson, *My Brother Theodore Roosevelt*, 365.

4.   "Bury Roosevelt with Simple Rites as Nation Grieves," *New York Times*, Jan. 9, 1919.

5.   Renehan, *Lion's Pride*, 222.

6.   ER to SDR, Jan. 9, 1919, FDRL.

7.   Lash, *Eleanor and Franklin*, 226.

8.   ER to SDR, Jan. 22, 1918, FDRL.

9.   Persico, *Franklin and Lucy*, 125.

10.  Morgan, *FDR*, 208.

11.  Daniels, *Washington Quadrille*, 145.

12.  Anna Halsted, interview by Lash, 4, FDRL.

13.  Cook, *Eleanor Roosevelt*, 1:179.

14.  James Roosevelt, *My Parents*, 101.

15.  Ibid., 102.

16.  Lash, *Eleanor and Franklin*, 230.

17.  Eleanor Roosevelt, *This Is My Story*, 274.

18.  Cook, *Eleanor Roosevelt*, 1:234.

19.  Roosevelt, *This Is My Story*, 293.

20.  ER to SDR, Oct. 10, 1919, FDRL.

21.  Longworth, *Crowded Hours*, 283.

22.  James Roosevelt, *My Parents*, 44.

23.  Longworth, *Crowded Hours*, 285.

24.  "Capital Greets Wilson Warmly," *New York Times*, July 9, 1919.

25.  Longworth, *Crowded Hours*, 285.

26.  Mr. and Mrs. Sheffield Cowles, oral history interview by Hermann Hagedorn, Dec. 28, 1954, CUOHP.

27.  Frederick W. Haberman, *Nobel Lectures, Peace, 1901–1925*.

28.  Barrymore, *Memories*, 234.

29.  Byrd, *Senate, 1789–1989*.

30.  Longworth, *Crowded Hours*, 288.

31. ARL, interview by Brandon, May 25, 1967.
32. "Rise of Senator Borah from Obscure Lawyer to Eminence in Nation and Party," *New York Times*, Jan. 20, 1940.
33. "Clarence Darrow Is Dead in Chicago," *New York Times*, March 14, 1938.
34. Longworth, *Crowded Hours*, 300.
35. Martin, *Cissy*, 189.
36. Amanda Smith, *Newspaper Titan*, 234.
37. Longworth, *Crowded Hours*, 292.
38. Borah, *Closing Speech of Hon. William E. Borah*, 16.
39. Longworth, *Crowded Hours*, 292.
40. "Cheers for Wilson Continue 21 Minutes, but They Lack Heart," *New-York Tribune*, June 29, 1920.
41. Pietrusza, *1920*, 245.
42. Ward, *First-Class Temperament*, 511.
43. "Roosevelt Career Like That of Cousin," *New York Times*, July 7, 1920.
44. Ernest Harvier, "Sees Roosevelt as Second Arthur," *New York Times*, July 25, 1920.
45. "Franklin D. Roosevelt: A Snapshot," in *The Outlook* 125, May–August 1920, 494.
46. Eleanor Roosevelt, *This Is My Story*, 311.
47. ER to Ferguson, July 11, 1919, in *A Volume of Friendship*, 160.
48. Lash, *Eleanor and Franklin*, 250.
49. Ibid.
50. Eleanor Roosevelt, *This Is My Story*, 316.
51. Steinberg, *Mrs. R*, 120.
52. Eleanor Roosevelt, *This Is My Story*, 318.
53. Ibid., 319.
54. Cook, *Eleanor Roosevelt*, 1:278.
55. "The Democrats and Theodore Roosevelt," *Chicago Daily Tribune*, Oct. 21, 1920.
56. Roosevelt, *An Untold Story*, 211.
57. Collier, *Roosevelts*, 259.
58. Longworth, *Crowded Hours*, 203.
59. Corinne Roosevelt Robinson speech, 1920.
60. TR to William Sheffield Cowles, in *The Letters of Theodore Roosevelt*, 2:803, March 29, 1898.
61. Eleanor B. Roosevelt, *Day Before Yesterday*, 52.
62. "Groom Roosevelt for a City Office," *New York Times*, March 23, 1919.
63. "Democratic Filibusters Delay Vote on Expulsion of Socialists in Stormy Debate in Assembly," *New York Times*, April 1, 1920.
64. Eleanor B. Roosevelt, *Day Before Yesterday*, 126.
65. "To Follow Roosevelt," *New York Times*, August 14, 1920.
66. "Raps Franklin Roosevelt," *New York Times*, September 18, 1920.
67. Longworth, *Crowded Hours*, 291.
68. Helen Bullitt Loury, "Washington's Social Lobby," *New York Times*, April 2, 1922.
69. Anthony, *Florence Harding*, 288–89.
70. Longworth, *Crowded Hours*, 323–24.
71. Ibid., 323.
72. Pottker, *Sara and Eleanor*, 190.
73. Ibid., 191.
74. Eleanor Roosevelt, *This Is My Story*, 323.

75. Ibid., 325.
76. Ibid., 324.
77. Lash, *Eleanor and Franklin*, 264.


CHAPTER 6: THE SINGING TEAPOT

1. Lash, *Eleanor and Franklin*, 108–9.
2. "F. D. Roosevelt Is Better," *New York Times*, Sept. 15, 1921.
3. "F. D. Roosevelt Ill of Poliomyelitis," *New York Times*, Sept. 16, 1921.
4. Ibid.
5. Ward, *First-Class Temperament*, 603.
6. TR Jr. to ER, n.d., FDRL.
7. "Alice Longworth Looms as Power Behind Congress," *Atlanta Constitution*, Dec. 9, 1923.
8. Theodore Roosevelt Jr. diary, Sept. 27, 1923, LOC.
9. Hannah Mitchell, "Mrs. Alice Longworth a Silent Influence in Capitol Politics," *New-York Tribune*, March 21, 1920.
10. "What Congressmen Know," *New York Times*, Feb. 9, 1922.
11. "Alice Longworth Looms as Power Behind Congress."
12. ARL, interview by Ted Weintal, Sept. 28, 1967, LOC.
13. "Charles G. Dawes, 30th Vice President," *United States Senate History* (Washington, D.C.: Senate Historical Office), 1997.
14. Anna Halsted, interviewed by James E. Sargent, May 11, 1973, CUOHP.
15. Eleanor Roosevelt, *This Is My Story*, 337.
16. Roosevelt and Brough, *Untold Story*, 142.
17. Faber, *Life of Lorena Hickok*, 281.
18. Marion Dickerman, oral history interview, conducted by M. B. Starr, Jan. 10, 1972, CUOHP.
19. Eleanor Roosevelt, *This Is My Story*, 124.
20. Ibid., 342–43.
21. Teague, *Mrs. L*, 160.
22. Anna Halsted, interview by Lash, May 22, 1967, FDRL.
23. Bok, *Americanization of Edward Bok*, 267.
24. Krabbendam, *Model Man*, 187.
25. "Misleading the People," *Washington Post*, Jan. 13, 1924.
26. Charles de Benedetti, "The $100,000 American Peace Award of 1924," *Pennsylvania Magazine of History and Biography*, April 1974, 226–27.
27. Constance Drexel, "Attending Hearings Becomes Pastime for Capital Women," *Washington Post*, Feb. 3, 1924.
28. Esther Lape, interview by Lash, March 3, 1970, FDRL.
29. "Miss Lape Proves Match for Hecklers at Bok Hearing," *New York Tribune*, Jan. 24, 1924.
30. ER to FDR, Feb. 6, 1924, FDRL.
31. "The Chronology of the Roosevelt Teapot Dome Affair," *Auburn Citizen* (NY), Oct. 28, 1924.
32. Collier, *The Roosevelts*, 288.
33. Frank R. Kent, "Archie Roosevelt's Teapot Story Proves Bombshell," *Baltimore Sun*, Jan. 23, 1924.

34. Ibid.
35. Eleanor B. Roosevelt, *Day Before Yesterday*, 157.
36. Ward, *First-Class Temperament*, 684.
37. "Smith and All Ticket Renamed," *Schenectady Gazette*, Sept. 27, 1924.
38. "Roosevelt Sees Smith as a Czar," *New York Times*, Oct. 28, 1924.
39. "Some of My Best Friends Are Negro," *Ebony*, Feb. 1953.
40. "Democrats Issue a Campaign Book," *New York Times*, Oct. 12, 1924.
41. "Local News," *Fulton Patriot*, Oct. 29, 1924.
42. "Teapot to Sing Across North Land—Davis and Smith Women Campaigners Not Coming Here," *Ogdensburg Republican-Journal*, Oct. 23, 1924.
43. Emily Smith Warner, interview conducted by William Keylor, June 25, 1967, CUOHP.
44. Anna Roosevelt Cowles to Corinne Roosevelt Robinson, Oct. n.d., 1924, TRC.
45. "3 Women Debate Campaign Issues," *New York Times*, Nov. 2, 1924.
46. Teichmann, *Alice*, 127.
47. Roosevelt, *This I Remember*, 31.

CHAPTER 7: NEW ROLES

1. "Mrs. Longworth Has Mumps," *Washington Herald*, Jan. 11, 1915.
2. William Allen White, *Puritan in Babylon*, x.
3. Ibid.
4. Cordery, *Alice*, 315.
5. Edith Roosevelt to Anna Cowles, Nov. 22, 1924, TRC.
6. Kermit Roosevelt to Belle, Nov. 14, 1924, in Cordery, *Alice*, 314.
7. Davis, *Invincible Summer*, 35.
8. Ibid.
9. Lash, *Eleanor and Franklin*, 298.
10. Eleanor Roosevelt, *Autobiography*, 145.
11. Pottker, *Sara and Eleanor*, 237–38.
12. "Princess Alice," *New Yorker*, Feb. 28, 1925.
13. Felsenthal, *Princess Alice*, 157.
14. "Princess Alice," *New Yorker*.
15. John K. Winkler, "The Playboy of Politics," *New Yorker*, April 10, 1926, 15.
16. "Teddy's Daughter Is Power in Politics," *Evening Republican*, Nov. 17, 1924.
17. "National Committee G.O.P. Post Refused by Mrs. Longworth," *Chicago Daily Tribune*, Oct. 2, 1926.
18. "Alice Rules 'Nick' Out," *Los Angeles Times*, Oct. 25, 1927.
19. Helen Roosevelt Robinson to Corinne Roosevelt Robinson, n.d., TRC.
20. "A Woman Speaks Her Political Mind," *New York Times*, April 8, 1928.
21. Cook, *Eleanor Roosevelt*, 1:379.
22. ER to Jane Hoey, April 9, 1930, FDRL.
23. "Capital in Hostile Camps," *Los Angeles Times*, May 8, 1929.
24. Will Rogers, "Will Rogers Remarks," *Los Angeles Times*, May 14, 1929.
25. "Capital Society Girds for Warfare," *New York Times*, May 7, 1929.
26. Pearson and Allen, *Washington Merry-Go-Round*, 15.
27. Ibid., 332.
28. "'Alice' Greets 'Dolly' at White House Fete," *New York Times*, Dec. 9, 1930.

29. "Princess Alice," *New Yorker*.
30. Longworth, *Crowded Hours*, 335.
31. Robert Barry, "Alice Rules 'Nick' Out," *Los Angeles Times*, October 25, 1927.
32. "Alice Longworth as Governor Choice of Filipino Newspaper," *New York Times*, Dec. 15, 1931.
33. "Roosevelt Invokes an 'Olympic Peace,'" *New York Times*, Feb. 5, 1932.
34. Frances Perkins, oral history conducted by Dean Albertson, 1951–1955 (various dates), CUOHP.
35. Gore Vidal, "Theodore Roosevelt: American Sissy," *New York Review of Books*, Aug. 13, 1981.
36. "Governor and Wife Mourn Longworth," *New York Times*, April 9, 1931.
37. Kermit Roosevelt to Elizabeth Willard Herbert, April 25, 1931, LOC.
38. Eleanor Roosevelt, My Day, Jan. 13, 1941.
39. TR Jr. to Edith Kermit Roosevelt, Nov. 9, 1930, LOC.
40. Teague, *Mrs. L*, 159.
41. "Notification Made a Social Occasion," *New York Times*, Aug. 11, 1932.
42. Edith Kermit Roosevelt to TR Jr., Aug. 18, 1933, LOC.
43. "Mrs. Hoover Hailed by Mid-west Crowds," *New York Times*, Oct. 29, 1932.
44. "Makes 31-Word Speech," *New York Times*, Nov. 2, 1932.
45. Ibid.
46. ARL, interview by Weintal, Sept. 28, 1967, LOC.
47. ER to Corinne Roosevelt Robinson, Sept. 23, 1932, TRC.
48. "Mrs. Robinson Keeps Silent on National Race," *New York Times*, Nov. 3, 1932.
49. ER to Corinne Alsop, Nov. 18, 1932, TRC.
50. Hickok, *Reluctant First Lady*, 42.
51. Edith Kermit Roosevelt to Eleanor Butler Roosevelt, Feb. 13, 1933, LOC.
52. Eleanor B. Roosevelt, *Day Before Yesterday*, 302.
53. "Mrs. Roosevelt Takes News Calmly," *New York Times*, Feb. 16, 1933.
54. Longworth, *Crowded Hours*, 31.

CHAPTER 8: IN THE ARENA

1. Hickok, *Reluctant First Lady*, 103.
2. "Mrs. Roosevelt Shatters Traditions in a Single Day," Associated Press, March 5, 1933.
3. Roosevelt and Brough, *Rendezvous with Destiny*, 28.
4. Ibid.
5. ARL, interview by Norman St. John-Stevas, Jan. 31, 1970, LOC.
6. Collier, *Roosevelts*, 388.
7. "Rallying Support by Staying on Point," *Silver City Sun-News*, Feb. 26, 2009.
8. Eleanor Roosevelt, *This I Remember*, 69.
9. "The Eleanor Roosevelt Press Conferences," Washington Press Club Foundation, group interview by Ruth Montgomery, May 22, 1989.
10. "Curb on Women Hit by Mrs. Roosevelt," *New York Times*, April 11, 1933.
11. Eleanor Roosevelt, My Day, July 24, 1937.
12. Hickok, *Reluctant First Lady*, 136.
13. Eleanor Roosevelt, *Autobiography*, 179–80.
14. Longworth, "What Alice Thinks," Oct. 9, 1936.

15. Alice Roosevelt Longworth, "The Ideal Qualifications for a President's Wife," *Ladies' Home Journal*, Feb. 1936.

16. Ibid.

17. Kathleen McLaughlin, "Mrs. Roosevelt Goes Her Way," *New York Times*, July 5, 1936.

18. "Mrs. Roosevelt Approves a Day Coach for Her Journey," *New York Times*, March 23, 1937.

19. "Mrs. Roosevelt Bans Police Guard," *New York Times*, March 16, 1933.

20. "Eleanor Everywhere," *Time*, Nov. 20, 1933.

21. Rollins, *Roosevelt and Howe*, 442.

22. Ibid., 443.

23. Stiles, *Man Behind Roosevelt*, 279.

24. Ibid., 287.

25. ER to Hickok, in "Empty Without You," 183, April 19, 1936.

26. Longworth, *Crowded Hours*, 313.

27. Ibid., 325.

28. Ibid., 340.

29. "The Best Sellers," *New York Times*, Nov. 13, 1933.

30. Bingham, "Before the Colors Fade."

31. "Two Roosevelt Women Try to Fill Will Rogers's Shoes," *Newsweek*, Jan. 4, 1936.

32. Letter from M. V. Atwood to V. V. McNitt, Feb. 19, 1936.

33. Longworth, What Alice Thinks, Jan. 28, 1936.

34. Eleanor Roosevelt, My Day, Jan. 16, 1936.

35. Eleanor Roosevelt, My Day, June 11, 1936.

36. Eleanor Roosevelt, My Day, Oct. 30, 1936.

37. Eleanor Roosevelt, My Day, May 8, 1936.

38. Eleanor Roosevelt, My Day, Sept. 3, 1936.

39. Longworth, What Alice Thinks, Aug. 22, 1936.

40. Longworth, What Alice Thinks, May 7, 1937.

41. Longworth, What Alice Thinks, April 22, 1936.

42. Eleanor Roosevelt, My Day, Oct. 5, 1936.

43. Sylvia Jukes Morris, *Edith Kermit Roosevelt*, 482.

44. "Two Roosevelt Women Try to Fill Will Rogers's Shoes."

45. Henry Brandon, "A Talk with an 83-Year-Old Enfant Terrible," *New York Times*, Aug. 6, 1967.

46. Longworth, What Alice Thinks, Oct. 20, 1936.

47. Will Rogers, Daily Telegram, Jan. 28, 1934.

48. "Mrs. Longworth Takes Gold into White House," *Washington Post*, Feb. 1, 1934.

49. Marion Dickerman, oral history, CUOHP.

50. "One Roosevelt Aids Another," *Christian Science Monitor*, July 31, 1937.

51. "First Lady Tells of Joining Guild," *New York Times*, Jan. 5, 1937.

52. Teague, *Mrs. L*, 161.

53. Lash, *Eleanor and Franklin*, 510.

54. Will Rogers, *Daily Telegram*, Jan. 28, 1934.

55. Lash, *Eleanor and Franklin*, 509.

56. "Roosevelt Clans Clash in Texas," *New York Times*, Nov. 11, 1936.

57. Ibid.

58. ER to Corinne Roosevelt Alsop, Nov. 11, 1936, TRC.

59. George A. Carlin to ER, June 15, 1937, FDRL.

60. Hickok, *Reluctant First Lady*, 10.
61. Ibid., 43.
62. Ibid., 44.
63. Ibid., 49.
64. Ibid.
65. ER to Hickok, March 7, 1933, FDRL.
66. ER to Hickok, March 11, 1933, FDRL.
67. Doris Faber, *The Life of Lorena Hickok*, 139.
68. ER to Hickok, Jan. 27, 1934, FDRL.
69. Hickok to ER, Dec. 1933, FDRL.
70. Streitmatter, *Empty Without You*, xxii.
71. Eleanor Roosevelt, *This I Remember*, 124.
72. ER to Hickok, Nov. 27, 1933, FDRL.
73. "Eleanor Roosevelt's Intimate Letters to Woman Writer Bared," *Miami News*, Oct. 22, 1979.
74. ER to Greenway, Oct. 4, 1922, FDRL.
75. Pottker, *Sara and Eleanor*, 122.
76. Lash, *Eleanor: The Years Alone*, 174.
77. ER to Hickok, May 13, 1935, FDRL.
78. ER to Hickok, Feb. 1, 1935, FDRL.
79. Sally Quinn, "Alice Roosevelt Longworth at 90," *Washington Post*, Feb. 12, 1974.
80. Teague, *Mrs. L*, 81–82.
81. Martin, *Cissy*, 360.

## CHAPTER 9: CLOUDS OF WAR

1. Ruth Tankersley, interview by author.
2. "Verbal Political Exchanges with First Lady Seen as 'Princess Alice' Signs for Lecture Tour," *Washington Post*, March 24, 1938.
3. Kathleen McLaughlin, "Mrs. Roosevelt Goes Her Way," *New York Times*, July 5, 1936.
4. ER to FDR, Nov. 11, 1936, FDRL.
5. "Roosevelt Lecturers," *St. Petersburg Times*, Dec. 1, 1938.
6. "Speaker Alice Longworth," *Washington Times Herald*, April 3, 1938.
7. "Mrs. Longworth Urges a Limit on the Presidency," *Chicago Daily Tribune*, Nov. 3, 1938.
8. June Provines, "Wisecracks from the Lecture Platform," *Chicago Daily Tribune*, Nov. 4, 1938.
9. "The Doyenne of the Drawing Room," *New York Times*, Aug. 23, 1981.
10. "Roosevelt Lecturers."
11. Josephine Robertson, "Mrs. Longworth's Discovery," *New York Herald Tribune*, Nov. 1, 1938.
12. "Mrs. Roosevelt Pleads for Racial Justice," *New York Herald Tribune*, Nov. 15, 1938.
13. Eleanor Roosevelt, My Day, Nov. 15, 1938.
14. Ibid.
15. "Lynch Bill Urged by Mrs. Roosevelt," *New York Times*, Jan. 13, 1939.
16. Eleanor Roosevelt, My Day, Jan. 4, 1943.
17. Eleanor Roosevelt, *This I Remember*, 175.

18. http://www.pbs.org/wgbh/americanexperience/features/biography/
    eleanor-anderson/.
19. Swift, *The Roosevelts and the Royals*, 121.
20. Eleanor Roosevelt, My Day, Feb. 27, 1939.
21. National Archives, http://www.archives.gov/exhibits/american_originals/eleanor
    .html.
22. Eleanor Roosevelt, *This I Remember*, 196.
23. Eleanor Roosevelt, My Day, May 27, 1939.
24. George Dixon, "Tenting Tonight," *Washington Post*, July 14, 1961.
25. Woollcott to Eleanor Butler Roosevelt, June 30, 1938, TRC.
26. Eleanor Roosevelt, My Day, Dec. 30, 1937.
27. Teichmann, *Smart Aleck*, 283.
28. ARL to Woollcott, n.d., Northeast Harbor, Maine, TRC.
29. ER to Woollcott, March 23, 1938, TRC.
30. Steinberg, *Mrs. R*, 248.
31. Teichmann, *Smart Aleck*, 278.
32. Eleanor Roosevelt, *This I Remember*, 250.
33. The Washington Merry-Go-Round, United Feature Syndicate, March 20, 1940.
34. Joe Alsop to Woollcott, March 20, 1940, Harvard University.
35. Joe Alsop to Woollcott, n.d., Harvard University.
36. "Roosevelt Forces in 'Victory Rally,'" *New York Times*, Nov. 5, 1940.
37. Leonard Lyons, "The New Yorker," *Washington Post*, Jan. 12, 1941.
38. "Mary Borah Alert, Lively 90," *Pittsburgh Press*, Aug. 17, 1965.
39. Mayme Ober Peak, "That Pickle Joke Was Mrs. Borah's: Perfect Washington Wife
    Gave Alice Longworth Coolidge Quip," *Boston Daily Globe*, Feb. 9, 1940.
40. Cordery, *Alice*, 45.
41. Renehan, *Lion's Pride*, 229.
42. Teague, *Mrs. L*, 157.
43. Collier, *Roosevelts*, 413.
44. Eleanor Roosevelt, *This I Remember*, 229.
45. Eleanor Roosevelt, My Day, Sept. 24, 1941.
46. James Roosevelt, *My Parents: A Differing View*, 113.
47. Kathleen McLaughlin, "President Shuts Self from World," *New York Times*, Sept. 9, 1941.
48. "Tears Fill President's Eyes at Burial of His Mother," *Washington Post*, Sept. 10, 1941.
49. James Roosevelt, *My Parents*, 113.
50. ER to Anna Roosevelt Boettiger, Sept. 10, 1941, FDRL.
51. Alice Roosevelt Longworth, "What's the Matter with Bob Taft?," *Saturday Evening
    Post*, May 4, 1940.
52. Ibid.
53. Ibid.
54. "GOP Foreign Policy Plank Is Jigsawed," *Hartford Courant*, June 28, 1940.
55. Joseph Alsop, *I've Seen the Best of It*, 93.
56. "'Princess Alice' Longworth Finds Her Minority Role Exciting at Capital," AP, March
    26, 1941.
57. Eleanor Roosevelt, *This I Remember*, 219.
58. "James Roosevelt Admits Asking Aid," *New York Times*, Aug. 19, 1938.
59. "James Roosevelt on Job," *New York Times*, Dec. 5, 1938.
60. Edith Kermit Roosevelt to Anna Roosevelt Cowles, Feb. 1925, TRC.

61. Kermit Roosevelt diary entry, March 24, 1943.
62. Kristie Miller, interview by author, April 22, 2013.
63. ARL to TR Jr., Aug. 26, 1939, LOC.
64. "The 'Hate Roosevelt' Committees," *Madison Capital Times*, Feb. 4, 1941.
65. Ibid.
66. "Lindbergh Says Air Isolates Us," *New York Times*, Aug. 30, 1941.
67. "Lindbergh Views Hotly Assailed," *New York Times*, Aug. 31, 1941.
68. "Lindbergh Sees a 'Plot' for War," *New York Times*, Sept. 12, 1941.
69. "War & Peace: Follow What Leader?," *Time*, Oct. 6, 1941.
70. Eleanor B. Roosevelt, *Day Before Yesterday*, 417.
71. Ibid.
72. Eleanor Roosevelt, My Day, July 18, 1940.
73. Eleanor Roosevelt, My Day, Feb. 3, 1939.
74. Eleanor Roosevelt, My Day, Oct. 27, 1942.
75. Seymour Korman, "Eleanors Meet; One in Red Cross; Other on a Tour," *Chicago Tribune*, Nov. 2, 1942.
76. Eleanor Roosevelt, *This I Remember*, 261.
77. Eleanor Roosevelt, My Day, Nov. 4, 1942.
78. Seymour Korman, "Eleanors Meet: One in Red Cross, Other on Tour," *Chicago Daily Tribune*, November 2, 1942.
79. Eleanor B. Roosevelt, *Day Before Yesterday*, 432.
80. ARL, interview by Weintal, Sept. 28, 1967, LOC.
81. Ibid.
82. "President Asks 'Parasites' to Quit National Capital," *New York Times*, Jan. 31, 1942.
83. René de Chambrun, *Mission and Betrayal*, 72.
84. Ibid., 81.
85. Ibid., 80.
86. Ibid., 81.
87. René de Chambrun, *France During the German Occupation*, 1,378.
88. Joseph Barnes, "A Frenchman Speaks for Vichy," *New-York Tribune*, Oct. 20, 1940.
89. "De Chambrun to Leave; Son-in-Law of Laval Intends to Reopen Paris Law Office," *New York Times*, Nov. 10, 1940.
90. "3 Paris Journalists Punished by Laval," *New York Times*, Feb. 18, 1943.
91. Eleanor Roosevelt, My Day, Sept. 23, 1943.
92. Eleanor Roosevelt, My Day, July 15, 1944.
93. Cordery, *Alice*, 424.
94. Hope Ridings Miller, "Paulina Longworth Runs," *Washington Post*, June 24, 1944.


CHAPTER 10: COLD PEACE

1. Ward, *Closest Companion*, 21–22.
2. Eleanor Wotkyns, interview by Emily Williams, June 19, 1978, FDRL.
3. Laura Delano, interview by Joseph Lash, June 25, (no year), FDRL.
4. James Roosevelt, *My Parents*, 9.
5. Asbell, *When F.D.R. Died*, 49.
6. Eleanor Roosevelt, *Autobiography*, 276.
7. Eleanor Roosevelt, *This I Remember*, 344; James Roosevelt, *My Parents*, 285.

8. Truman, *Year of Decisions*, 5.
9. Ward, *Closest Companion*, 418.
10. Sylvia Jukes Morris, *Edith Kermit Roosevelt*, 511.
11. Cordery, *Alice*, 426.
12. ARL, interview by Weintal, Sept. 28, 1967, LOC.
13. Marie McNair, Town Topics, *Washington Post*, July 27, 1945.
14. Drew Pearson, Washington Merry-Go-Round, May 17, 1946.
15. "Lowell Off the Page," *Kenyon Review* 22.1 (Winter 2000), 255–74.
16. Jean vanden Heuvel, "The Sharpest Wit in Washington," *Saturday Evening Post*, Dec. 4, 1965.
17. Wilhelm, *Ezra Pound*, 82.
18. Ibid., 305.
19. Michener, *World Is My Home*, 287.
20. Grace Grether, "Mrs. Vice President?," *Salt Lake City Tribune*, July 2, 1948.
21. Lash, *World of Love*, 189.
22. Lash, *Eleanor: The Years Alone*, 15.
23. Ibid., 33.
24. Eleanor Roosevelt, My Day, April 24, 1945.
25. Daniels, *Washington Quadrille*, 298.
26. Lucy Rutherfurd to Anna Boettiger, May 9, 1945, FDRL.
27. Eleanor Roosevelt, *Autobiography*, 302.
28. Ibid., 303.
29. Eleanor Roosevelt, *Human Rights Years*, 244.
30. Eleanor Roosevelt, *Autobiography*, 308.
31. ER to Elinor Morgenthau, Jan. 20, 1946, FDRL.
32. Eleanor Roosevelt, *Autobiography*, 308.
33. Russell Barnes, "Mrs. F.D. Passes UNO Test," *Boston Daily Globe*, Feb. 15, 1946.
34. ER to Lash, Feb. 13, 1946, FDRL.
35. Lash, *Eleanor: The Years Alone*, 56.
36. Barnes, "Mrs. F.D. Passes UNO Test."
37. "For the Nobel Prize," *Boston Daily Globe*, Feb. 19, 1946.
38. "Mrs. Roosevelt at a Remarkable 75," *New York Times*, Oct. 4, 1959.
39. Howard M. Norton, "Elliott Clashes with Meyer on 'Procuring' Girls," *Baltimore Sun*, Aug. 6, 1947; Mary Spargo, "Hughes Hospitality Had No Influence on Plane Contracts. Senators Informed: Elliott Roosevelt Challenges Items in Meyer's Accounts," *Washington Post*, Aug. 5, 1947.
40. "When Women Are Firm," *Hagerstown (Md.) Daily Mail*, Aug. 14, 1947.
41. Douglas, *Eleanor Roosevelt We Remember*, 35.
42. *Chicago Tribune*, July 23, 1944.
43. Drew Pearson, "Dewey Called Best of GOP Lot," *Washington Post*, June 19, 1948.
44. "Granddaughters of Mark Hanna and Theodore Roosevelt Aid Taft," *New York Herald Tribune*, April 23, 1948.
45. "Mrs. Longworth's Daughter Suffers 'Sudden Illness,'" *Washington Post*, May 8, 1952.
46. Mr. and Mrs. Sheffield Cowles, oral history interview by Hermann Hagedorn, Dec. 28, 1954, CUOHP.
47. Dorothy Day, "On Pilgrimage," *Catholic Worker*, Feb. 1957.
48. Marie McNair, "2 Birthdays but Not 1 Celebration," *Washington Post*, Feb. 8, 1953.
49. ER to Lash, Oct. 23, 1943, FDRL.

50. ER to ARL, Jan. 28, 1957, FDRL.
51. Corr to Lash, April 20, 1966, FDRL.
52. ARL to ER, June 30, 1957, LOC.
53. Felsenthal, *Princess Alice*, 236.
54. Kermit Roosevelt, interview by author.
55. Ruth Tankersley, interview by author.
56. Dorothy McCardle, "She's Putting Best Foot Forward," *Washington Post*, Aug. 19, 1958.
57. Kermit Roosevelt, interview by author.
58. Vidal, "Theodore Roosevelt."
59. Dow, *Eleanor Roosevelt, an Eager Spirit*, 226.
60. ER to Anna, July 28, 1947, FDRL.
61. Elliott Roosevelt to Anna, July 29, 1947, FDRL.
62. James Roosevelt, *My Parents*, 314.
63. ER to Anna, Aug. 21, 1950, FDRL.
64. James Roosevelt, oral history, FDRL.

## CHAPTER II: MONUMENTS

1. Lash, *Eleanor: The Years Alone*, 245.
2. Henry, *Eleanor Roosevelt and Adlai Stevenson*, 119.
3. Longworth, *Crowded Hours*, 1.
4. ARL, interview by St. John-Stevas, Jan. 31, 1970, LOC.
5. Ibid.
6. Stewart Alsop, "How Many Egg-Heads Are There?," *Washington Post*, Sept. 26, 1952.
7. ARL, interview by St. John-Stevas, Jan. 31, 1970.
8. Teague, *Mrs. L*, 197.
9. Nixon, *Memoirs*, 85.
10. Eleanor Roosevelt, My Day, Feb. 1, 1960.
11. Mitchell, *Tricky Dick and the Pink Lady*, 20.
12. Denton, *Pink Lady*, 62.
13. Helen Gahagan Douglas, *The Eleanor Roosevelt We Remember*, 36.
14. http://www.nixonlibrary.gov/thelife/apolitician/thesenator.php.
15. Mitchell, *Tricky Dick and the Pink Lady*, 140.
16. Helen Gahagan Douglas interviews by Amelia Fry, April 4, 1973, to Sept. 14, 1976, 201, CUOHP.
17. Teague, *Mrs. L*, 199.
18. Ibid., 194.
19. Cordery, *Alice*, 454.
20. ARL, interview by Jean vanden Heuvel, Sept. 26, 1969, LOC.
21. Joseph Alsop, *I've Seen the Best of It*, 92.
22. Ibid., 430.
23. Ibid.
24. ARL to JFK, Nov. 28, 1960, JFK Library, Boston.
25. ARL, interview by Norman St. John-Stevas, Jan. 31, 1971.
26. Curtis Roosevelt, interview by author.
27. Schlesinger to JFK, March 11, 1958, in *The Letters of Arthur Schlesinger*, 156.
28. Curtis Roosevelt, interview by author.

29. Lash, *Eleanor: The Years Alone*, 297.

30. Schlesinger, *Letters*, 212.

31. Ibid., 213.

32. ER to JFK, Sept. 27, 1960, JFK Library, Boston.

33. ER to JFK, July 28, 1961, JFK Library, Boston.

34. *New York Herald*, Oct. 11, 1961.

35. ER to Martin Luther King Jr., Sept. 21, 1962, FDRL.

36. Martin Luther King Jr., telegram, "Epitaph of a First Lady," FDRL.

37. Lash, *Eleanor: The Years Alone*, 310.

38. Lash, *World of Love*, 547.

39. http://www.whitehousehistory.org/whha_shows/eleanor_Roosevelt/theme_my
   -day-christmas.html.

40. *Washington Post*, July 9, 1989.

41. ARL, interview by vanden Heuvel.

42. Kristie Miller, interview by author.

43. Teague, *Mrs. L*, 157.

44. *60 Minutes,* April 4, 1969.

45. Teague, *Mrs. L*, 160.

46. Bingham, "Before the Colors Fade."

47. Lady Bird Johnson, Jan. 17, 1968, *A White House Diary*, 615.

48. Kermit Roosevelt, interview by author.

49. Bingham, "Before the Colors Fade."

50. Teague, *Mrs. L*, 197.

51. William Safire, "Weaned on a Pickle," *New York Times*, Feb. 25, 1980.

52. Ibid.

53. Ibid.

54. Cordery, *Alice*, 474.

55. Schlesinger, *Journals*, 436.

56. Teague, *Mrs. L*, xvii.

57. Brandon, "Talk with An 83-Year-Old Enfant Terrible," 8.

58. Eleanor Roosevelt, My Day, Nov. 15, 1938.

# BIBLIOGRAPHY

................................................

Alsop, Joseph. *FDR: A Centenary Remembrance*. New York: Viking, 1982.

————. *I've Seen the Best of It*. With Adam Platt. New York: W. W. Norton, 1992.

Alsop, Stewart. *The Center*. London: Hodder and Stoughton, 1968.

Alter, Jonathan. *The Defining Moment: FDR's Hundred Days and the Triumph of Hope*. New York: Simon & Schuster, 2006.

Anthony, Carl Sferrazza. *Florence Harding*. New York: William Morrow, 1998.

Asbell, Bernard. *The FDR Memoirs*. Garden City, N.Y.: Doubleday, 1973.

————. *When F.D.R. Died*. New York: Holt, Rinehart and Winston, 1961.

Barrymore, Ethel. *Memories*. New York: Harper, 1955.

Beard, Patricia. *After the Ball*. New York: HarperCollins, 2003.

Beasley, Maurine H. *Eleanor Roosevelt and the Media*. Urbana: University of Illinois Press, 1987.

Bok, Edward William. *The Americanization of Edward Bok*. New York: Charles Scribner & Sons, 1921.

Borah, William Edgar. *Closing Speech of Hon. William E. Borah*. Washington, D.C.: Government Printing Office, 1919.

Bradley, James. *The Imperial Cruise*. New York: Little, Brown, 2009.

Brough, James. *Princess Alice*. Boston: Little, Brown, 1975.

Butt, Archibald Willingham. *The Letters of Archie Butt*. Garden City, N.Y.: Doubleday, 1924.

————. *Taft and Roosevelt: The Intimate Letters of Archie Butt*. Garden City, N.Y.: Doubleday, 1930.

Byrd, Robert C. *The Senate, 1789–1989*. Washington, D.C.: Government Printing Office, 1988.

Caroli, Betty Boyd. *The Roosevelt Women*. New York: Basic Books, 1998.

Cassini, Marguerite. *Never a Dull Moment*. New York: Harper, 1956.

Chambrun, Clara Longworth de. *The Making of Nicholas Longworth*. New York: R. Long and R. R. Smith, 1933.

Chambrun, René de. *France During the German Occupation, 1940–1944*. Stanford, Calif.: Hoover Institution Press, Stanford University, 1986.

————. *Mission and Betrayal, 1940–1945: Working with Franklin Roosevelt to Help Save Britain and Europe*. Stanford, Calif.: Hoover Institution Press, Stanford University, 1993.

Collier, Peter. *The Roosevelts: An American Saga*. New York: Touchstone, 1994.

Cook, Blanche Wiesen. *Eleanor Roosevelt*. Vol. 1. New York: Viking, 1992.

———. *Eleanor Roosevelt*. Vol. 2. New York: Viking, 1999.

Cordery, Stacy. *Alice: Alice Roosevelt Longworth, from White House Princess to Washington Power Broker*. New York: Viking, 2007.

Daniels, Jonathan. *Washington Quadrille: The Dance Beside the Documents*. Garden City, N.Y.: Doubleday, 1968.

Davis, Kenneth S. *FDR: The Beckoning of Destiny, 1882–1928: A History*. New York: G. P. Putnam's Sons, 1972.

———. *Invincible Summer: An Intimate Portrait of the Roosevelts*. New York: Atheneum, 1974.

Denton, Sally. *The Pink Lady*. New York: Bloomsbury Press, 2009.

Dorn, Linda. *The Roosevelt Cousins*. New York: Knopf, 2001.

Douglas, Helen Gahagan. *The Eleanor Roosevelt We Remember*. New York: Hill and Wang, 1963.

Dow, Dorothy. *Eleanor Roosevelt, an Eager Spirit: The Letters of Dorothy Dow, 1933–1945*. New York: Norton, 1984.

Faber, Doris. *The Life of Lorena Hickok*. New York: Morrow, 1980.

Felsenthal, Carol. *Princess Alice*. New York: St. Martin's Press, 1988.

Flynn, John T. *The Roosevelt Myth*. New York: Devin-Adair, 1948.

Freidel, Frank. *Franklin D. Roosevelt: The Apprenticeship*. Boston: Little, Brown, 1952.

Goodwin, Doris Kearns. *No Ordinary Time*. New York: Simon & Schuster, 1995.

Gould, Lewis L. *Edith Kermit Roosevelt: Creating the Modern First Lady*. Lawrence: University Press of Kansas, 2013.

Gunther, John. *Roosevelt in Retrospect*. New York: Harper & Row, 1950.

Haberman, Frederick W. *Nobel Lectures, Peace, 1901–1925*. Amsterdam: Elsevier Publishing Co., 1972.

Hagedorn, Hermann. *The Roosevelt Family of Sagamore Hill*. New York: Macmillan, 1954.

Henry, Richard. *Eleanor Roosevelt and Adlai Stevenson*. New York: Palgrave Macmillan, 2010.

Hickok, Lorena. *Reluctant First Lady*. New York: Dodd, Mead, 1962.

Johnson, Lady Bird. *A White House Diary*. New York: Holt, Rinehart, 1970.

Kay, James Tertius de. *Roosevelt's Navy*. New York: Pegasus, 2012.

Klara, Robert. *FDR's Funeral Train*. New York: Palgrave Macmillan, 2010.

Kleeman, Rita. *Gracious Lady*. New York: D. Appleton–Century, 1935.

Krabbendam, Hans. *The Model Man: A Life of Edward Bok, 1863–1930*. Amsterdam: Rodopi, 2001.

Lash, Joseph P. *Eleanor and Franklin*. New York: W. W. Norton, 1971.

———. *Eleanor: The Years Alone*. New York: W. W. Norton, 1972.

———. *Love, Eleanor*. Garden City, N.Y.: Doubleday, 1982.

———. *A World of Love: Eleanor Roosevelt and Her Friends, 1943–1962*. Garden City, N.Y.: Doubleday, 1984.

Levy, William Turner, and Cynthia Eagle Russett. *The Extraordinary Mrs. R*. New York: John Wiley & Sons, 1999.

Lewis, William Draper. *The Life of Theodore Roosevelt*. Philadelphia: John C. Winston, 1919.

Longworth, Alice Roosevelt. *Crowded Hours*. New York: Charles Scribner's Sons, 1933.

Martin, Ralph. *Cissy*. New York: Simon & Schuster, 1979.

McCullough, David. *Mornings on Horseback*. New York: Simon & Schuster, 1981.

McKeever, Porter. *Adlai Stevenson: His Life and Legacy*. New York: William Morrow, 1989.

McKenna, Marian C. *Borah*. Ann Arbor: University of Michigan Press, 1961.

Michener, James A. *The World Is My Home*. New York: Random House, 1992.

Miller, Kristie, and Robert H. McGinnis. *A Volume of Friendship*. Tucson: Arizona Historical Society, 2009.

Mitchell, Greg. *Tricky Dick and the Pink Lady*. New York: Random House, 1998.

Morgan, Ted. *FDR: A Biography*. New York: Simon & Schuster, 1985.

Morris, Edmund. *Colonel Roosevelt*. New York: Random House, 2010.

———. *The Rise of Theodore Roosevelt*. New York: Random House, 2010.

Morris, Sylvia Jukes. *Edith Kermit Roosevelt: Portrait of a First Lady*. New York: Coward, McCann & Geoghegan, 1980.

Naylor, Natalie A., Douglas Brinkley, and John Allen Gable, eds. *Theodore Roosevelt: Many-Sided American*. Interlaken, N.Y.: Heart of the Lakes, 1992.

Nesbitt, Henrietta. *White House Diary: FDR's Housekeeper*. Garden City, N.Y.: Doubleday, 1948.

Nixon, Richard M. *The Memoirs of Richard Nixon*. New York: Grosset & Dunlap, 1978.

Pearson, Drew, and Robert S. Allen. *Washington Merry-Go-Round*. New York: Horace Liveright, 1931.

Persico, Joseph. *Franklin and Lucy*. New York: Random House, 2008.

Pietrusza, David. *1920: The Year of the Six Presidents*. New York: Carroll & Graf, 2007.

Pottker, Janice. *Sara and Eleanor: The Story of Sara Delano Roosevelt and Her Daughter-in-Law, Eleanor Roosevelt*. New York: St. Martin's Press, 2004.

Renehan, Edward J., Jr. *The Lion's Pride*. New York: Oxford University Press, 1998.

Rixey, Lilian. *Bamie: Theodore Roosevelt's Remarkable Sister*. New York: David McKay, 1963.

Robinson, Corinne Roosevelt. *My Brother Theodore Roosevelt*. New York: Scribner's, 1921.

Rollins, Alfred B., Jr. *Roosevelt and Howe*. New York: Knopf, 1962.

Roosevelt, David B. *Grandmère*. New York: Warner Books, 2002.

Roosevelt, Eleanor. *The Autobiography of Eleanor Roosevelt*. New York: Harper & Row, 1961.

———. *The Eleanor Roosevelt Papers: The Human Rights Years, 1945–1948*. Detroit: Thomas Gale, 2007.

———. *This I Remember*. New York: Harper, 1949.

———. *This Is My Story*. New York: Harper & Brothers, 1937.

———. *Your Teens and Mine*. Garden City, N.Y.: Doubleday, 1961.

Roosevelt, Eleanor, and Anna Roosevelt. *Mother and Daughter: The Letters of Eleanor and Anna Roosevelt*. Edited by Bernard Asbell. New York: Coward, McCann & Geoghegan, 1982.

Roosevelt, Eleanor B. *Day Before Yesterday: Reminiscences of Mrs. Theodore Roosevelt Jr.* Garden City, N.Y.: Doubleday, 1959.

Roosevelt, Elliott, and James Brough. *Mother R.: Eleanor Roosevelt's Untold Story*. New York: G. P. Putnam's Sons, 1977.

———. *A Rendezvous with Destiny: The Roosevelts of the White House*. New York: G. P. Putnam's Sons, 1975.

———. *An Untold Story: The Roosevelts of Hyde Park*. New York: G. P. Putnam's Sons, 1973.

Roosevelt, Felicia Warburg. *Doers and Dowagers*. Garden City, N.Y.: Doubleday, 1975.

Roosevelt, Franklin Delano. *F.D.R.: His Personal Letters*. New York: Duell, Sloan and Pearce, 1950.

Roosevelt, James. *My Parents: A Differing View*. With Bill Libby. Chicago: Playboy Press Book, 1976.

Roosevelt, Patricia Peabody. *I Love a Roosevelt*. Garden City, N.Y.: Doubleday, 1967.

Roosevelt, Sara Delano. *My Boy Franklin*. New York: R. R. Smith, 1933.

Roosevelt, Theodore. *The Autobiography of Theodore Roosevelt*. New York: Macmillan, 1913.

———. *The Letters of Theodore Roosevelt*. Cambridge, Mass.: Harvard University Press, 1951.

Rowley, Hazel. *Franklin and Eleanor*. New York: Farrar, Straus and Giroux, 2010.

Schlesinger, Arthur. *Journals, 1952–2000*. New York: Penguin, 2007.

———. *The Letters of Arthur Schlesinger*. New York: Random House, 2013.

Sewall, William Wingate. *Bill Sewall's Story of T.R.* New York: Harper and Brothers, 1919.

Smith, Amanda. *Newspaper Titan*. New York: Knopf, 2011.

Smith, Jean Edward. *FDR*. New York: Random House, 2007.

Steinberg, Alfred. *Mrs. R: The Life of Eleanor Roosevelt*. New York: G. P. Putnam's Sons, 1956.

Stiles, Lela. *The Man Behind Roosevelt*. Cleveland: World, 1954.

Stirling, Yates. *Sea Duty: The Memoirs of a Fighting Admiral*. New York: G. P. Putnam's Sons, 1939.

Stratton, David Hodges. *Tempest over a Teapot*. Norman: University of Oklahoma Press, 1996.

Streitmatter, Roger, ed. *Empty Without You: The Intimate Letters of Eleanor Roosevelt and Lorena Hickok*. New York: Free Press, 1998.

Swift, Will. *The Roosevelts and the Royals*. Hoboken, N.J.: Wiley & Sons, 2004.

Teague, Michael. *Mrs. L: Conversations with Alice Roosevelt Longworth*. London: Gerald Duckworth, 1981.

Teichmann, Howard. *Alice: The Life and Times of Alice Roosevelt Longworth*. Englewood Cliffs, N.J.: Prentice-Hall, 1979.

———. *Smart Aleck*. New York: Morrow, 1976.

Truman, Harry S. *Memoirs of Harry S. Truman: Year of Decisions*. Garden City, N.Y.: Doubleday, 1956.

Tumulty, James. *Woodrow Wilson as I Knew Him*. Garden City, N.Y.: Doubleday, Page, 1921.

Wagenknecht, Edward. *The Seven Worlds of Theodore Roosevelt*. New York: Longmans, Green, 1958.

Ward, Geoffrey C. *Before the Trumpet*. New York: Harper & Row, 1985.

———. *Closest Companion*. New York: Houghton Mifflin Harcourt, 1995.

———. *A First-Class Temperament*. New York: Harper & Row, 1989.

White, Annie R. *Polite Society at Home and Abroad*. Chicago: Monarch, 1891.

White, William Allen. *A Puritan in Babylon*. New York: Capricorn, 1965.

Wilhelm, J. J. *Ezra Pound: The Tragic Years*. University Park: Pennsylvania State University Press, 1994.

Wister, Owen. *Roosevelt: The Story of a Friendship*. New York: Macmillan, 1930.

# INDEX